HOW TO RULE

THE WORLD

HOW TO RULE
THE WORLD

The Coming Battle
over the Global Economy

Mark Engler

NATION
BOOKS

New York

Published by Nation Books, a Member of the Perseus Books Group

116 East 16th Street, 8th Floor
New York, NY 10003

Nation Books is a copublishing venture of the Nation Institute and the Perseus Books Group

Library of Congress Cataloging-in-Publication Data
   How to rule the world : the coming battle over the global economy / by Mark Engler.
      p. cm.
   Includes bibliographical references.
   ISBN 978-1-56858-365-5 (alk. paper)
   1. International economic relations. 2. International trade. 3. International relations.
4. Globalization—Economic aspects. I. Title.

HF1359.E6176 2007
337—dc22
                                                                                2007045504

10 9 8 7 6 5 4 3 2 1

Contents

INTRODUCTION

Amid all the dull news stories from the January 2003 World Economic Forum in Davos, Switzerland, one vivid account stood out. The World Economic Forum is an annual retreat that allows high-level political officials from across the globe to mingle with Fortune 500 CEOs at a picturesque resort high in the snow-topped Alps. Some journalists are allowed to join the world leaders, but many of the discussions are off the record. For this reason, Laurie Garrett's personal description of attending the exclusive gathering not only provided a well-observed glimpse into the rarified space occupied by some of the most powerful people on the planet—it told a story that was not being widely reported to the public.

Garrett, a reporter for New York's *Newsday*, took in the event with the help of an exclusive all-access pass, a privilege that surprised even her. Although she is a veteran science writer and winner of many of her profession's highest honors, including the Pulitzer Prize, Garrett exudes the sensibility of a down-to-earth, no-nonsense reporter. After her week in the secluded Swiss ski town, she wrote a conversational, twenty-one-hundred-word e-mail about her experiences, originally intended only for a small list of friends. Her e-mail, however, leaked onto the Internet, giving a much wider audience a window into happenings at the forum.

Davos, Garrett reported, "is a breathtakingly beautiful spot, unlike anything I'd ever experienced . . . . The EXTREMELY powerful arrive by helicopter. The moderately powerful take the first class train. The NGOs and we mere mortals reach heaven via coach train or a conference bus. Once in Europe's bit of heaven conferees are scattered in hotels that range from B&B to ultra luxury 5-stars, all of which are located along one of only three streets that bisect the idyllic village of some 13,000 permanent residents."[1]

For the World Economic Forum, Davos had been transformed into a virtual military compound, in part to keep out any protesters who tried to near the mountaintop chalets. "Antiglobalization folks didn't stand a chance. Nor did Al Qaeda. After all, if someone managed to take out Davos during [the forum] week the world would basically lose a fair chunk of its ruling and governing class POOF, just like that. So security was the name of the game," Garrett wrote. To guard the conference's 3,000 participants, Switzerland dispatched 1,000 police officers, plus another 400 soldiers, some of whom oversaw a deployment of tanks, armored troop transports, and missile launchers. Delegates were admitted to the conference only after stopping at a security checkpoint to scan their specially designed badges, which gave authorities behind a computer instant access to a photo of the participant, plus readouts detailing their height, weight, and identity.

After passing through security and reaching the inside of the forum, Garrett made thorough use of her access to influential figures. "It was full-on, unfettered, class A hobnobbing," she wrote. She had dinners with the chief of Saudi secret police and Afghanistan's foreign minister. She lounged in the hotel room of the President of Mozambique, who gave her a play-by-play reaction to a simulcast of Bill Clinton's off-the-record speech to the forum. She tailed Bill Gates and George Soros.

Garrett concluded with a reflection on the powerful figures she met:

Finally, who are these guys? I actually enjoyed a lot of my conversations, and found many of the leaders and rich quite charming and remarkably candid. Some dressed elegantly, no matter how bitter cold and snowy it was, but most seemed quite happy in ski clothes or casual attire. Women wearing pants was perfectly acceptable, and the elite is sufficiently multicultural that even the suit and tie lacks a sense of dominance . . . .

The world isn't run by a clever cabal. It's run by about 5,000 bickering, sometimes charming, usually arrogant, mostly male people who are accustomed to living in either phenomenal wealth, or great personal power. A few have both. . . . They are comfortable working across languages, cultures and gender, though white Caucasian males still outnumber all other categories. They adore hi-tech gadgets and are glued to their cell phones.

Welcome to Earth: meet the leaders.

After Garrett's e-mail started circulating online, discussion focused on whether the note was authentic (Garrett, although not terribly pleased about the unexpectedly broad distribution, confirmed that it was) and on the limits of privacy in an Internet age. Something that received less comment, but that was ultimately very significant, was the discord within the global elite that Garrett documented.

In January 2003, the invasion of Iraq loomed on the horizon. Unsurprisingly, it was a main topic of conversation at Davos. At the forum, U.S. military representatives advocated for war, arguing, according to Garrett, "We need to attack Iraq not to punish it for what it might have, but preemptively, as part of a global war. Iraq is just one piece of a campaign that will last years, taking out states, cleansing the planet."

Among corporate leaders, the reaction was almost uniformly negative. These participants were not salivating over possible profits in Iraq. Rather, they saw bad times for capitalism ahead. Garrett wrote, "the business community was in no mood to hear about a war in Iraq. Except for diehard American Republicans, a few Brit Tories and some Middle East folks the [forum] was in a foul, angry anti-American mood." CEOs deplored arrogant White House unilateralism and its potentially harmful consequences for the global economy. In Garrett's words, "the rich—whether they are French or Chinese or just about anybody—are livid about the Iraq crisis primarily because they believe it will sink their financial fortunes."

The most dramatic confrontation came after the U.S. secretary of state made an unreserved push to persuade the conference to support Washington's invasion. "When Colin Powell gave the speech of his life, trying to win over the non-American delegates," Garrett reported, "the sharpest attack on his comments came not from Amnesty International or some Islamic representative—it came from the head of the largest bank in the Netherlands!"

This image—the irate banker sniping at the secretary of state—stayed in my head long after I first read Garrett's e-mail. It is striking because it is so unlike the scenes we more commonly picture of CEOs and powerful politicians clinking martini glasses, drinking to one another's prosperity. The confrontation that occurred at Davos illustrated a divide that has been become increasingly significant over the past decade, though we rarely consider it. It embodied a debate, now raging, about how to rule the world.

What World Order?

Currently there is an argument taking place among international elites over two competing visions for the global order. One vision, which I call "corporate globalization," advocates an expanding, transnational, corporate-controlled world economy. Another vision, which I call "imperial globalization," is based on solidifying a U.S. empire. These visions are not entirely distinct. This book explains how they overlap and also how, at critical points, they conflict with one another. The book is written, however, in the hopes that neither vision will prevail. My hope is that they will be supplanted by a third vision, a "democratic globalization," or globalization from below.

When experts talk about the global economy, the discussion can quickly become mired in obscure aspects of trade and development policy. Yet, the debate about globalization is not fundamentally a technical matter; it is an argument over what values should define the international order in which we live. This book is for those who think the Washington militarists and Wall Street CEOs should not rule at all, those who believe the world should be governed according to principles of democratic participation and self-determination. It is for those who oppose a never-ending war to reshape the world and those who believe that the United States should have a role in international affairs other than global policeman or overlord. It is for those who are offended by the growing chasm between the rich and the poor, by sweatshop labor abroad, and by jobs in the domestic economy that fail to provide families with enough money to escape poverty. It is for those who demand government that is more accountable to the public it claims to represent.

I contend that since the turn of the millennium a major change has occurred in the politics guiding the global economy: There has been a shift from the corporate model of globalization to an imperial model of globalization—a shift that has often been overlooked or misconstrued. To understand what has happened to the global justice movement since it first seized the media spotlight in Seattle at the end of 1999, to combat U.S. militarism and the expansion of corporate power after George W. Bush, and to create a truly democratic world order, I believe that we urgently need a new understanding of globalization politics.

In the summer of 1999, I returned to the United States after having spent a year working as an assistant to and speechwriter for Oscar Arias, the former president of Costa Rica and winner of the 1987 Nobel Peace Prize. Although I enjoyed living in Costa Rica, I was eager to come home. The political climate in the United States felt ripe. Among those of us who had worked on antisweatshop campaigns as student activists or on living wage drives in our communities, who had been concerned about the increasing penetration of multinational corporations into our daily lives, who had joined in international solidarity with Latin American communities struggling for social and economic justice in the wake of disastrous U.S. interventions, who had supported pro-democracy movements in countries such as South Africa, Burma, and Indonesia, who had protested the massive expansion and privatization of prisons in our own country, and who had engaged in local battles against environmental destruction, there was a sense that many of the issues we cared about were coming together in an exciting way. I don't think anyone could have predicted that Seattle would explode in the manner that it did just a few months later, during the WTO conference in late November of 1999. Yet, the pressure for a citizens' revolt against corporate globalization had been building for a long time. When it could no longer be contained, the moment was exhilarating.

I protested in Seattle and joined several of the major mobilizations that followed, and I have remained intimately concerned with the issues that motivated these demonstrations. Over the past eight years, I have worked as a freelance journalist and as an analyst with Foreign Policy In Focus, reporting on and scrutinizing new developments in the politics of the international economy, as well as in the global justice movement. During this time, I have seen many changes.

When the global justice protests of the late 1990s erupted, social movements criticized the Clinton administration's model of corporate globalization, challenging multilateral institutions like the World Trade Organization (WTO), the International Monetary Fund (IMF), and the World Bank. When George W. Bush assumed the presidency, most progressives expected that the new administration, with its close ties to big business and its fervent championing of "free trade" capitalism, would continue to push the same agenda for the global economy, and they focused on highlighting the continuity between the new White House and the old.

Although this perspective remains widely accepted, I have come to believe that it is seriously flawed. After the Bush administration used the attacks of 9/11 to launch the neoconservatives' long-desired war in Iraq, many outraged Americans, including myself, turned their attention to protesting the White House's catastrophic foreign policy. In general, global justice activists argued that this foreign policy was an extension of the same model for corporate domination that had prevailed before. I, too, made these arguments. But, increasingly, I felt that the critique we were making—about corporate profiteering, about the connections between war and globalization, about how the global economy was being managed—missed something. I started to feel that we were overlooking an important divide between ruling interests. As I investigated the issue further over the next several years, I became convinced that this divide has critical implications for our politics, especially as we move into the post-Bush era.

I now contend that the Bush administration has reshaped the politics of globalization in ways that are little understood but that will affect us for years to come. Changes in U.S. foreign policy have helped to create a setting that few of us who demonstrated in Seattle, Prague, Quebec City, or Buenos Aires could have ever foreseen. Global trade talks are collapsing, and the once-unstoppable goliath of the World Trade Organization has fallen into disarray. Other institutions that drew protests, such as the IMF and the World Bank, have dwindled in power and now face uncertain futures. Moreover, U.S. unilateralism and intervention in the Middle East have created international schisms that endanger the future progress of the type of multilateral globalization that thrived throughout the 1990s. These unforeseen developments have not only thrown the global justice movement off-balance but have also created a situation that is bewildering for many leading advocates of "free trade." Together with other geopolitical pressures, these changes are dethroning the strain of market fundamentalism that has dominated trade and development politics at least since the Reagan era.

I believe that we have entered a period when the very nature of the world economy is up for grabs. The opening years of the post-Bush era will be critical in determining whether international relations will be structured around a new form of U.S. empire, around the expanding power of multinational corporations, or around a democratic alternative. To realize the democratic alternative will require the concerted action of concerned citizens across the globe.

DEFINING THE BATTLE: GLOBALIZATION OR NEOLIBERALISM?

This book explores the shift from the corporate model of globalization to the imperial model of globalization and describes how it has set the stage for a coming battle over the global economy. It examines how the shift took place, how it affects our understanding of key events like the

Iraq War, and how it helped to dramatically alter the roles of the international financial institutions. It then describes how both models might be replaced by a democratic globalization that is more just, more equitable, and more inclusive. But first, it is necessary to define some terms of debate.

One of the key reasons U.S. observers have consistently overlooked major changes in international politics is that we have failed to effectively challenge the misleading vocabulary that pundits and politicians use to talk about trade and development issues. Often, it can be difficult to understand what this global struggle is even about—and that's not an accident. The vague and politicized use of the word *globalization* has long created confusion about the world economy. This confusion works to the advantage of those who are benefiting most from the status quo. Efforts to create a fairer and more democratic international order must begin by challenging dominant ideas about what globalization is, and then they must assert a new vision of what it can be.

Globalization is a word that suggests many things but has little concrete meaning. Certainly, globalization in some form has existed at least since the time of Christopher Columbus; its history can be traced through the legacies of exploration, trade, colonialism, and Cold War intervention. But the term itself is relatively new. Rarely heard before 1995, it exploded as a media buzzword in the late 1990s. In some contexts, it refers to increased cultural exchange, to advances in telecommunications and computer technology, and to patterns of human migration. In other contexts, it is an economic idea, related to expanding international capital flows, trade, and the reach of multinational corporations. As an academic term, globalization stands alongside "postmodernism" as an idea that is dissected and debated incessantly, with little satisfying result.

Yet debates about globalization are not merely academic; they have real political consequences. The vagueness of the term has two effects. First, if globalization is a sweeping and inevitable condition of modern life, it cannot be opposed or changed. Protesters who take issue with globalization seem nostalgic and impractical; those in power can easily dismiss them as Luddites unwilling to accept the Internet age. Second, the term suggests a consensus about the global economy that does not exist. As politicians and pundits across the political spectrum line up in support of globalization in one form or another, the word obscures important disagreements among different elites. Especially in recent years, as a vital shift in U.S. policy concerning the global economy has taken place, the idea of globalization as a broad, evolutionary process, for which no one in particular is responsible, has helped critical changes slip by unnoticed.

The shortcomings of the word globalization become even clearer when we compare the terminology used in the United States with the vocabulary used elsewhere in the world. More precise and useful terms for talking about the global economy exist—and are even household words in other countries. One term that is long overdue for popular introduction in the United States is "neoliberalism."

I began to reflect on the absence of this term in the United States after the death of Pope John Paul II. In the wake of John Paul's passing, I was invited to participate in a radio forum about the economic ethics of the departed pontiff, a topic that was generally ignored in the discussion of his legacy. Obituaries tended to focus on the John Paul's unwaveringly conservative stances on issues such as abortion, birth control, gay rights, and the ordination of women. Few noted that his vision of globalization stood in sharp contrast to the pro-corporate triumphalism advocated by "free trade" boosters. Although the pope was an ardent critic of Stalinist communism, he was hardly an intellectual sidekick to Ronald Reagan, as many conservatives tried to suggest.

During his 1998 visit to Cuba, a place and time when he could have easily lashed out in Reaganite fashion, John Paul instead reflected more generally on the process of globalization. He contended that the world was "witnessing the resurgence of a certain capitalist neoliberalism which subordinates the human person to blind market forces." He claimed that "[f]rom its centers of power, such neoliberalism often places unbearable burdens upon less favored countries." Continuing his reflections, he remarked with concern that "at times, unsustainable economic programs are imposed on nations as a condition for further assistance." Because of these programs, he said, we "see a small number of countries growing exceedingly rich at the cost of the increasing impoverishment of a great number of other countries; as a result the wealthy grow ever wealthier, while the poor grow ever poorer."[2]

For most U.S. listeners, Pope John Paul II's use of the word *neoliberalism* would be a source of confusion, but his selection of this term rather than globalization was highly significant. While globalization has the connotation of being a largely benign, inescapable transition to a high-tech age, neoliberalism is something quite different. It is a precise term referring to a specific set of policies that John Paul was criticizing for bringing hardship and suffering to the world's poor. Neoliberalism has a defined history, clear ideological roots, identifiable advocates, and concrete implications for countries that implement its economic prescriptions. It has created a small pool of winners who benefit from its policies, as well as a much larger group of people who are harmed by them. It is also far from inevitable. Right now neoliberalism is being opposed—often successfully—throughout much of the world.

The Roots of Market Fundamentalism

Neoliberalism is an ideology that policymakers long considered too radical to actually implement, and it took a series of dramatic events to put the extremist "free market" doctrine into practice. Throughout the 1950s and '60s, the school of thought was incubated exclusively in universities, by professors such as Milton Friedman in the United States and Friedrich von Hayek in Europe. What we now know as neoliberalism is drawn from theories associated with the Austrian and Chicago schools of economics, which, in the postwar decades, shared a common disdain for then-dominant Keynesian economics. Contrary to the connotation of the term liberal in U.S. politics, neoliberals expound a zealous ideology of the market that strongly opposes the welfare state and, in principle, rejects virtually all government involvement in the economy, harkening back to earlier visions of laissez-faire capitalism—the "classical liberalism" of economic theory.

Of course, a select group of socioeconomic elites stood to profit handsomely from the implementation of Milton Friedman's ideas, and they were naturally eager to see them put into practice. The event that provided the neoliberals a real-world opportunity to test their ideas was one of the most famously ignoble moments in Latin American history: the 1973 assassination of Chile's democratically elected president, Salvador Allende, and the installation of dictator Augusto Pinochet. This Chilean "regime change" was undertaken with U.S. support, and North American influence continued as the new junta took power. Milton Friedman was among the American advisors who consulted with members of the Pinochet government. Two years after the coup, a group of conservative Chileans—University of Chicago alumni who had become freshly minted economic advisors for the new government—invited their old professor to visit the country and advise the regime on combating inflation. As historian Greg Grandin related in his chronicle of the event, Friedman's colleagues, who became known as the "Chicago Boys," "recommended application of what Friedman had already taken to calling 'shock treatment.'"[3]

The Chicago Boys convinced the military junta to follow a recipe that subsequently became familiar throughout the developing world. It called for massive layoffs of government workers, privatization of public services, an end to wage floors and price ceilings, and major cuts to government social spending. Other ingredients were the removal of many trade barriers, deregulation of finance, and the lifting of government controls on capital investment, with new measures that allowed foreign companies to send 100 percent of their Chilean-made profits to their home countries.

As they would elsewhere, these policies had traumatic consequences for Chile, especially for working people there. The country's economy experienced wild fluctuations between 1975 and 1982, moving from spiraling unemployment and economic recession, to a rebound period of quick economic expansion based on speculative investment and borrowing, and finally to a severe economic crisis. When the economy finally unraveled in 1982, one-third of the workforce was unemployed, bankruptcies soared, the nation's private banking system imploded, and the Central Bank hemorrhaged nearly half of its reserves. The Pinochet regime scrambled to recover, reversing many neoliberal reforms and relying on a bailout from the IMF to stabilize the economy.[4]

Despite these difficulties, a strange thing happened. Chicago School defenders focused on the Chilean economy's periods of quick growth and championed Chile as a model for other nations; Milton Friedman dubbed it an "economic miracle" in an early 1982 interview with *Newsweek*.[5] The devastating recession of the following year should have put this appraisal to shame. Yet, even today, conservatives point to Chile as a success story because of its subsequent recovery and strong growth in the 1990s. In doing so, they ignore the growing chasm between rich and poor that formed in Chile over the past two decades, as well as the fact that the growth that later occurred was largely due to subsequent government controls on capital and to export promotion initiatives. As economist James Cypher noted, what successes the Chilean economy has enjoyed since the neoliberal collapse "owe more to state intervention than to the invisible hand of the free market."[6]

Unfortunately, such lessons have been trumped by conservative ideology. As a generation of neoliberal economists gained power over time in both universities and government, their ideas became a new orthodoxy in international affairs. Throughout the 1980s and '90s, the World Bank, the IMF, and the U.S. Treasury—three bodies whose common views became known as the "Washington Consensus" because of their headquarters' locations within the District of Columbia—knit together a collection of neoliberal policies into a one-size-fits-all uniform for development. This is the real-world neoliberalism we now know.

In country after country, they recommended privatizing public industries, creating scenes in which public electricity, water, and telephone assets were sold away, often at fire-sale prices, to rising billionaires like Mexico's telecom mogul Carlos Slim. They pushed the opening of markets to foreign investment and competition, reshaping economies that were traditionally based on small-scale agriculture. They demanded fiscal austerity programs to curtail government spending, which cut away at safety nets for the displaced. They promoted reforming taxes, often shifting the burden away from the wealthy. They advocated tight monetary policy, which limited governments' ability to stimulate their economies and reduce unemployment. And they favored removing controls on capital flows, changing investment from a long-term, "bricks-and-mortar" endeavor to a speculative game in which billions of dollars could cross borders in an instant. Although some recommendations could be justified in specific situations—high interest rates, for example, used at critical points to control runaway inflation—the international financial institutions promoted them as universal prescriptions, paying little attention to either local contexts or the social impact of the policies.

To establish neoliberalism as the dominant ideology in international economics, the Washington Consensus institutions relied on the help of local elites in the developing world. What happened with Milton Friedman's Chilean protégés is not unusual. Scions of the jet-setting upper classes in Latin America, Asia, and Africa often train in U.S. universities and are tutored in market fundamentalism. When they return to take positions of power in their countries, they remain in the privileged minorities most likely to profit from "trickle-down" economics. Their circles are often made up of people positioned to reap windfalls from buying up newly privatized public assets, for example. Therefore, they usually need little convincing to help make the neoliberal program into official government policy.

But even those national leaders in the global South who are not politically inclined toward neoliberalism often find few other options available to them. In reality, they face a form of blackmail. Needing capital and foreign investment for development, poorer nations must turn to the gatekeepers of international finance—the IMF and World Bank—for help. In the past two decades, the favorite response of these bodies has been the "structural adjustment" loan, which requires countries to submit to IMF oversight and to implement a series of neoliberal reforms in exchange for needed infusions of capital. Since wealthy nations, the United States first among them, hold decisive shares of voting power in the international financial institutions, the U.S. Treasury Department has a dominant role in determining what economic policies are considered acceptable for poorer nations. Quietly over the past few decades, with little attention from the American public, the mechanisms of neoliberalism have allowed the United States to assume the position of economic overseer in a new international order.

Who Benefits?

This is not the role in world politics that most Americans, who generally support the idea of promoting international democracy, want for the United States. And this is why the language used to define the debate is critical. If opposing globalization is one thing, opposing neoliberalism is something very different. Pope John Paul II's decision to denounce neoliberalism by name drew attention to the ugly history of this economic dogma. When examined closely, many of the developments cited as the hallmarks of globalization—unrestricted capital flows, privatized industries, and liberalized markets, for example—are clearly not the inevitable result of technological progress. Rather, they are the products of ideology and of political power shrewdly applied.

This is not the end of the story, however. Although neoliberalism has become dominant in the world system, there is considerable disagreement among elites about how neoliberal policies should be enforced and managed—even among those who are most benefiting from the current state of affairs. There is also debate about how central U.S. power should be in this system. In the Bush era, disagreements about these issues have resulted in a tumultuous political climate; they have produced the political shift that is at the core of this book's argument. But before discussing these changes, it is important to look quickly at the track record of neoliberal economics. This record of failure has sparked protests throughout the world.

Conservatives are desperate to spin Chile into a success story partly because there are few places where neoliberalism has been anything other than an abject failure. The evidence shows this "free market" ideology has not fared well in practice—at least in terms of promoting sustainable development and lifting people from poverty. A few facts are central. The first is that neoliberal policies have performed poorly even in the terms that bankers most easily understand: economic growth. The Center for Economic and Policy Research reported that from 1960 to

1980, the two decades preceding the widespread implementation of neoliberal policies, gross domestic product (GDP) in Latin America grew
by 75 percent per person—a sizable increase. Between 1980 and 2000,
twenty years in which neoliberal principles held sway, GDP grew only a
paltry 7 percent.[7] This represents a dramatic downturn in development
as it is traditionally defined. Each twenty-year period featured the typical
ups and downs of the business cycle; the difference was that neoliberalism proved to be a wretched development strategy in the end.

A second relevant fact is that there were winners as well as losers in
neoliberal globalization. Much of the growth that has occurred in recent
decades has benefited only the wealthy. In the years since Milton Friedman first flew to Chile, the gap between rich and poor has widened dramatically throughout the world. As the United Nations Development
Program's *Human Development Report 2003* noted, the top 1 percent of
the world's population now receives as much income as the poorest 57
percent.[8]

The report also noted a third key fact: Some of the countries that implemented the most orthodox neoliberal programs have encountered
the most serious economic problems. Discussing the report, UNDP Administrator Mark Malloch-Brown explained that fifty-four already poor
countries grew even poorer during the "free trade" 1990s and that the
"poster children of [that decade were] among those who didn't do terribly well."[9] Early in the new millennium, the neoliberal poster child most
frequently in the news was Argentina. Throughout the 1990s, the IMF
cited Argentina as a model of economic reform. Yet in late 2001, the
country, which had been in recession since 1998, plunged into a down-
ward economic spiral. This related directly to its leaders' neoliberal policy choices: Argentina's globalized economy had been hit hard by
international crises that drove up interest rates and made its debts un-
payable. A privatized social security system deprived the government of
needed revenue. And newly liberalized capital rushed to flee the country.
It was a potent recipe for crisis. Very swiftly, the country's GDP declined
by more than 20 percent from its pre-recession peak, more than 5 million people fell below the poverty line, and millions took to the streets in
protests, ousting a succession of governments.[10] Argentina's experience

became a cautionary tale about the dangers of unreservedly linking an economy to turbulent international markets.

As we will see, the failure of neoliberalism to deliver on promises of prosperity has contributed to a backlash against Washington Consensus economic policies—fueling massive demonstrations and electoral upheavals in Latin America and beyond. This failure is one of the factors that have created a uniquely volatile setting for international politics as we enter the post-Bush era. Another is the shift of U.S. policy away from the business-minded, multilateral globalization of Clinton's 1990s to a new vision for how to rule the world—a vision so aggressive and unilateralist that it has inflamed a world full of tensions.

THE END OF MULTILATERALISM

Those who oppose U.S. hegemony and corporate power are often skilled at spotting divisions within social movements. We know that citizen activists continually struggle for unity but rarely achieve it. In contrast, it can be tempting to imagine that those in power work in a tightly coordinated cabal—to presume that proponents of neoliberal globalization maintain a unified front in pursuit of world domination. This is a mistake. Elites in business and government also harbor their own divided loyalties and conflicting interests. Understanding these divisions can be critical to advancing an alternative.

In recent years, a divide has emerged between defenders of Clinton's corporate vision of globalization and partisans of Bush's imperial version. During the Clinton years, when globalization first emerged as a media buzzword, enthusiasm about the "New Economy" was rising. The White House linked America's expanding affluence with a cooperative international system of trade and development; this is the multilateral order that critics call "corporate globalization." For the Clinton administration, strengthening corporate globalization meant pursuing a "free trade" agenda. In the first years of his presidency, Clinton brokered the North American Free Trade Agreement (NAFTA), a pact to liberalize trade with Mexico and Canada. On a broader scale, he watched over the formation of the WTO in 1995 and the start of talks for the Free Trade Area of the Americas (FTAA).

At the 1999 WTO Ministerial Conference in Seattle, President Clinton stressed that these agreements would facilitate "an expanded system of rule-based trade that keeps pace with the changing global economy and the changing global society." Not only would this benefit the United States, but the multilateral system of corporate globalization would also give other countries "mechanisms by which they could work toward a shared prosperity."[11]

No doubt, the administration's multilateral rhetoric always deserved some skepticism. President Clinton showed that he was willing to exercise unilateral power when he deemed it necessary, and nationalistic calculations always figured large in international negotiations. Still, talk of a cooperative approach to globalization reflected a distinctive strategy for how America engaged with the world. The WTO, IMF, and World Bank became crucial mechanisms in U.S. foreign policy under the strategy of corporate globalization. Although these bodies included international input and made heavy use of the language of "shared prosperity," they were fundamentally controlled by Washington. In practice they operated as mechanisms of U.S. soft power, which could compel, without resort to military coercion, developing countries to accept economic policies favored by American and international elites. Defending these institutions against detractors, Lawrence Summers, an economist who became Treasury Secretary during Clinton's second term, described their function very straightforwardly: The IMF and World Bank promoted "vital U.S. interests" with their "capacity to . . . promote market-oriented development in the world."[12]

When George W. Bush took office in 2000 as the first president to hold an MBA, many predicted that he would continue on Clinton's established path for corporate globalization. Instead, Bush took a different path. He began crafting a more aggressive, unilateralist vision for international affairs—a strategy I call "imperial globalization." Imperial globalization combines U.S. nationalism, go-it-alone arrogance, political partisanship, interventionist militarism, and an allegiance to certain sectors of the economy—notably Big Oil and Big Arms—over others. With this new approach, the United States has overtly antagonized many of its traditional capitalist allies in pursuit of nationalistic gains. And it has pursued policies that would have been hard for many of corporate globalization's protesters to foresee.

Both corporate and imperial visions of globalization envision a global, capitalist market economy, but they differ significantly in their management of international politics. The difference between the two visions has presented a new set of challenges to those resisting U.S. hegemony and corporate power. The administration's assertive militarism and disregard for U.S. soft power are part of the shift. Another part has been an effort to sidestep or even undermine the multilateral structures of corporate globalization, which did so much to promote the rise of neoliberalism in past decades. While the United States largely dominates these bodies, they nevertheless require compromise. At times, these institutions can obstruct White House designs—something anathema to the unilateralists in power in the Bush administration. In a remarkable twist, some of the main institutions constituting the Washington Consensus are now in danger, in part due to resistance from social movements and dissident governments, but also as a consequence of Washington's growing indifference and, at times, hostility from the Bush administration.

It is important to understand how the new paradigm became established. Imperial globalization reflected the deep ideological biases of certain branches of American conservatives. Although 9/11 would ultimately provide cover for the shift, the move toward an imperial strategy started during Bush's first year in office, and it was not impossible to predict in advance. As far back as the 2000 presidential election, Walden Bello, a leading globalization analyst and director of the Bangkok-based advocacy group Focus on the Global South, foresaw that the IMF and World Bank, which served as dominant mechanisms for exercising American power through the 1990s, would face inhospitable years under Bush. "The Bretton Woods institutions," Bello wrote, "will lose their liberal internationalist protectors like Treasury Secretary Larry Summers who believe in using the Fund and Bank as central instruments to achieve U.S. foreign economic policy objectives."[13]

Signs of a new nationalist edge started to emerge shortly after President Bush took office. One notable incident that occurred early in his first term involved China. Although the Clinton administration had focused on bettering economic ties with the country, the Bush administration quickly began to quarrel with the Asian superpower. In April 2001, a Chinese fighter jet collided with a U.S. spy plane, forcing the American aircraft to make an emergency landing in China and prompting a heated diplomatic standoff between the two countries. Tensions between the two nations worsened later that month, when the United States sold submarines and naval ships to Taiwan. Economists and international business groups worried that strained relations might jeopardize China's entry into the WTO. Indeed, tensions had not entirely abated when the Asian giant eventually became a member of the trade organization in September 2001.

The display of more robust nationalism was a hint of changes to come—many of which came quickly in the wake of terrorist attacks on American soil. The events of September 11, 2001, moved the Bush administration's new imperial vision for the global order from the background of international politics to the fore. Commencing a "war on terror," the White House chose to base American foreign policy on the country's status as the world's sole military superpower rather than on its past successful role in building international alliances and fostering a profitable, cooperative global economy.

From the start, many business leaders were wary of the shift. Increasingly contentious relations with Europe were a troubling marker of the changes taking place. In the lead up to the invasion of Iraq, the Bush administration denigrated historical NATO allies as inhabitants of "Old Europe" because of their objections to the U.S. military aggression. Traditionally, European nations had played a critical role as junior partners in corporate globalization; they cooperated with the United States in crafting policy at the IMF and World Bank, and their corporations also profited in the neoliberal 1990s. Yet the embittered Bush administration cared little about these alliances and insisted on cutting off its critics. After the invasion, the United States announced what the Associated Press described as a "policy banning opponents of the war in Iraq from receiving billions of dollars in reconstruction contracts." The policy "effectively exclude[d] companies from countries such as Russia, France, Germany and Canada" from taking advantage of the economic opportunities that would come from Iraq's reconstruction.[14]

All of this was cause for serious concern among advocates of multilateral corporate globalization. Many began sounding the alarm. The *Washington Post* reported on March 23, 2003, "Discord over the Iraq War is putting uncomfortable strains on economic links between the United States and Europe, a relationship that many view as a cornerstone of global prosperity. Guardians of transatlantic harmony are scrambling to keep the diplomatic rift from poisoning economic ties." The article continued, "The animosity that has flared of late appears almost certain to seep into transatlantic trade and investment issues," provoking concerns "that lingering acrimony among top policymakers will spark tit-for-tat trade wars, and wreck the U.S.-European cooperation needed to strike a worldwide trade accord that could help spur global growth."[15]

The fear was well founded. Trade wars had already started breaking out during Bush's tenure. The White House provoked a crisis in March 2002 when President Bush imposed protective tariffs for the American steel industry. This move blatantly disregarded international trade rules and prompted the filing of a formal complaint at the WTO—accompanied by harsh rebukes from the European Union, Brazil, China, Japan, Korea, New Zealand, Norway, and Switzerland. By the time the WTO ruled against the tariffs in November 2003, a climate of hostility pervaded trade talks. Celebrations of "shared prosperity" seemed like a distant memory. America's international partners from the corporate globalization days were struggling to adjust to more adversarial U.S. counterparts. From their vantage point, it was clear that something significant had changed: a new set of policymakers had taken charge, bringing with them a troubling new vision of U.S. power.

ENTER THE NEOCONSERVATIVES

It has been noted countless times in recent years that the Bush administration acted on a radical vision of consolidating presidential power and exercising U.S. military might. Far less often, however, do we hear that the Bush administration also brought with it a distinctive orientation toward the global economy. A main project of this book is to consider how its economic approach challenged many common assumptions about the politics of globalization and created a new terrain for battle over international economic issues.

Because many of us involved in the globalization debate invested considerable time scrutinizing the IMF, World Bank, and WTO, it can feel jarring to encounter a world in which these institutions' roles are quickly shifting. For me, a lesson about the changing political landscape we face came during the previously mentioned radio show on the legacy of John Paul II. When I pointed out during the discussion John Paul's criticisms of the IMF and World Bank, a conservative guest came back with an interesting response. In essence he replied, "Those of us on the right don't like those institutions either." Of course, he didn't mention that, unlike the pope, conservatives who distrust the institutions do so because the bodies are *not forceful enough* for their tastes in promoting a U.S. imperial agenda. Nevertheless, his reply highlighted a real problem for the IMF, World Bank, and WTO today: Under imperial globalization, these institutions have fewer defenders than ever.

Critics on the right come in different ideological shades, but one of the most distinctive and important is "neoconservative." The neocons, as a group, became widely known owing to their influence in shaping the Bush administration's "war on terror" and in pushing the invasion of Iraq. Those who actively identified with the philosophy of neoconservatism— frequently associated with German-born philosopher Leo Strauss—made up only a minority of White House officials during the Bush years. Yet the administration's foreign policy has more closely matched their outlook than it has the past realism that often characterized Republican foreign policy. After 9/11, when President Bush fashioned U.S. foreign relations around a vision of America as a moral agent in the world and a preference for bold action over calculating restraint, neocon ideology provided the intellectual framework for his policies.

In the new millennium, liberal internationalists like Al Gore, Larry Summers, and past World Bank president James Wolfensohn were out. The Bush administration replaced them with characters such as Elliott Abrams (who became Deputy National Security Adviser for Global Democracy Strategy), Douglas Feith (Defense Department Undersecretary for Policy during Bush's first term), Lewis "Scooter" Libby (Dick Cheney confidante and long-time Chief of Staff), and Paul Wolfowitz (who was Deputy Secretary of Defense before his rocky stint as World Bank President). Many of these figures were collaborators in the neoconservative think tank called the Project for a New American Century. They have been leaders in promoting a new vision for foreign affairs in the post-9/11 era and championing the policies of imperial globalization. Dick Cheney, one of the most influential vice presidents in American history, was himself a signer of the Project for a New American Century's founding document, and he helped bring an uncompromising, militarist emphasis to U.S. foreign policy.

Like their predecessors in the Clinton administration, the neoconservatives are ardent capitalists. But while they support the economics of the Washington Consensus in principle, the neocons have a very different outlook on foreign affairs, one centered on bolstering U.S. supremacy. In order to promote national dominance, they are willing to risk destabilizing an international system that has allowed multinational corporations to flourish. Dismissive of multilateral institutions, the neocons stress the need, in the words of the Project for a New American Century's 1997 statement of principles, "to accept responsibility for America's unique role in preserving and extending an international order friendly to our security, our prosperity, and our principles." Most centrally, America's unique role is a military one. Embracing it means making significant increases in Pentagon spending and adopting a more assertive posture toward "regimes hostile to our interests and values."[16] Of course, the use of force has a long history in U.S. foreign policy, and American military supremacy was never questioned under the Clinton program. But under imperial globalization, a focus on hard power would become much more overt.

The influence of the neocons and other conservative unilateralists has affected not only America's military posture but also its economic stance. After 9/11, a new nationalism entered into U.S. negotiations around trade and development issues—and not just with Europe. True to form, the Bush administration took a bare-knuckles approach to promoting U.S. interests. Along with the global economic downturn that followed the dot-com crash, this approach made trade talks combative, tense, and often unproductive. It also put the multilateral institutions of corporate globalization at risk. By the WTO's September 2003 Ministerial Conference in Cancún, Mexico, the *New York Times* reported that the United States had "compiled a long record of violating trade rules" and noted that "[t]op officials at the World Trade Organization say they are worried that the Bush administration's go-it-alone policy is threatening international trade."[17]

Ironically, while social movement protesters deride the WTO as an instrument of U.S. power, imperial globalists dislike the institution. Bush administration officials who bristled at ever having to submit to an international "litmus test" eyed the WTO (which, in principle, operates on a one-country-one-vote basis) with suspicion; they viewed it as a potential multilateral check on U.S. prerogatives. This suspicion resulted in greater stubbornness at the bargaining table. Even as protesters rallied outside the Cancún WTO Ministerial Conference, negotiations there failed largely because the United States was unwilling to make the type of compromises around agricultural markets necessary to keep the talks afloat. With negotiators from poorer nations demanding that the United States lower its own trade barriers before they agreed to further open their markets, the WTO talks stalled in a deadlock. Although trade boosters attempted to resurrect the negotiations, talks again ground to a halt in July 2006. Observers officially declared the "collapse" of WTO negotiations. Today the organization cannot be written off altogether. Agreements made at the WTO in earlier years are still in effect, and the organization still has power to arbitrate many trade disputes. But the drive to expand the institution's agenda and strengthen the multilateral framework for trade has faltered. After the summer 2006 collapse, India's trade minister, Kamal Nath, quipped that the trade talks were somewhere "between intensive care and the crematorium."[18]

Other institutions of corporate globalization have been similarly damaged in the Bush years, leaving protesters in unfamiliar waters. The same type of U.S. intransigence that disabled forward progress of the WTO also contributed to the failure of talks for a Free Trade Area of the Americas (FTAA), which was all but dead by early 2005. Or consider the World Bank and the IMF. While Clintonites had been eager to channel foreign assistance through these bodies, the Bush White House has preferred using direct bilateral aid to further its political aims. Often, as when the administration tried to assemble a "coalition of the willing" for the Iraq War, it explicitly tied bilateral aid packages to recipient countries' support for U.S. military policy.

To some extent, the difference between the corporate approach to globalization and the imperial one is a difference of tactics—the two are distinct approaches to advancing the same goals. But it is more than that as well. Both visions are broadly supportive of neoliberalism. Yet, as we will see, imperial globalists often prioritize narrow U.S. nationalism over a wider concern for global capital, making moves transnational businesspeople regard as reckless. They propose an expansion of American power that might not be economically sustainable. And they create conflicts between the elites of different nations and industries, many of whom feel they have something to lose in a neocon dream world.

Although the WTO, IMF, World Bank, and FTAA each attracted major demonstrations in the Clinton era, these protest targets have increasingly been pushed from center stage. Mainstream boosters of neoliberal multilateralism have started taking note of the altered ground of the globalization debate. Sebastian Mallaby of the *Washington Post* lamented the change in an April 24, 2006 column:

Fifteen years ago, there were hopes that the end of Cold War splits would allow international institutions to acquire a new cohesion. But the great powers of today are simply not interested in creating a resilient multilateral system. . . . The United States remains the only plausible quarterback for the multilateral system. But the Bush administration has alienated too many players to lead the team effectively. Its strident foreign policy started out as an understandable response to the fecklessness of other powers. But unilateralism has tragically backfired, destroying whatever slim chance there might have been of a workable multilateral alternative.[19]

While figures like Mallaby might wish for a retreat from an imperial path for globalization and a return to a corporate one, the real challenge in the post-Bush era is more profound. It is to highlight the failure of both approaches and to build something new from their ruins.

TOWARD A DEMOCRATIC ALTERNATIVE

A favorite ploy of pro–"free trade" pundits is to condemn their opponents as spoiled hypocrites who pout about living in the Internet age even as they enjoy its benefits. Jonah Goldberg of the conservative *National Review* captured this tone of haughty disgust perfectly when writing about an April 2000 demonstration against the IMF and World Bank. "This is the real irony of these protests," he asserted. "These Very Serious Young People, who espouse a hatred of all that is modern, themselves reap the fruits of the very system they despise . . . . They spoke on cell phones by Nokia and drank coffee made from beans grown in Colombia. They organized over an Internet that is the central nervous system of the new global economy they oppose."[20]

Such a line of reasoning is possible if we regard globalization as a sweeping, undefined process. But when we understand the policies of neoliberalism as a specific set of choices, with specific consequences, Goldberg's argument falls apart. Those who have protested the privatization of health care in El Salvador, organized to protect free access to clean water in South Africa, or interrupted the once-staid meetings of World Bank bureaucrats in Washington, D.C., are no more against internationalism or modernity than was John Paul II—who traveled extensively, used advanced telecommunications to spread his message, and was lauded as the pope of globalization at the same time as he attacked the greed and destructiveness of neoliberal ideology. He saw no contradiction because there was none.

Just as corporate globalization and imperial globalization are based on defined policies, there is an alternative agenda that is emerging in favor of a globalization from below, a democratic globalization. This agenda is based on a core set of principles: allowing local citizens to have a voice in shaping the economic policies that affect their communities; removing the straitjacket of the Washington Consensus and allowing diverse approaches to development to flourish; restructuring or replacing international financial institutions with bodies that have truly democratic representation; and crafting laws to protect the rights of people and the environment rather than merely the rights of capital.

While these ideas stand in stark contrast to both of the elite visions that have guided the politics of the global economy, they are not new. Concerned citizens have pushed for alternative globalization policies for as long as there has been a public discussion. What is new is the context in which these ideas are being debated. We face a setting in which many of the political assumptions that guided social movements as recently as the 1999 protests in Seattle now need to be reconsidered.

We are entering a period when the future of globalization is in question—when a battle over the global economy is set to commence. As the Bush era comes to a close, it is likely that a new administration, of whatever party, will continue to voice support for "free trade" policies. But it is unclear whether new leaders will continue with the hard-edged imperial model for globalization or attempt to return to something closer to the softer policies of corporate globalization—the model still favored by many Democrats. It is also unclear whether a new administration will be able to resurrect the Clintonian approach, even if it wanted to.

U.S. unilateralism has wounded many international institutions, perhaps fatally. Combined with other pressures on the global economy—coming from boisterous social movements, from the failure of neoliberalism in the developing world, and from economic downturns affecting much of the planet—it has helped to create a crisis of confidence in the Washington Consensus. As a result, the next ten years will make up a decade of uncertainty and change, of new threats and new opportunities.

Those wishing to promote more equitable systems of trade and development must not only reject the brutish policies of imperial globalization but also ward off any attempts to revive Clinton's corporate model for how to rule. This will be especially critical when the polarizing figure of George W. Bush is no longer the focus of progressive ire and a new set of leaders will need to be held accountable. The distinctions between corporate, imperial, and democratic globalization are not matters of semantic quibbling or academic classification. Instead, as the global order is reshaped once again in the coming years, understanding the shifts between these models allows for fresh thinking about how to resist corporate power and U.S. militarism.

The purpose of this book is to chart the new politics of globalization—to shed light on recent events that seem incongruous with our past assumptions about the global economy and to point a way toward the future. In looking at today's changing landscape, I aim to answer two guiding questions that are on the minds of many people concerned with global justice: What has happened to the vibrant international movement that seized the media spotlight following the 1999 Seattle protests? And, what impact has this movement made on the unfolding globalization debate? The answers to these questions will shed light on the challenges relevant to the next phase of citizen action and will illuminate how social movements can influence the creation of a different world order.

The first part of this book examines the project of imperial globalization. It considers how the war in Iraq represents a serious break from previous strategies of corporate globalization, and it describes the costs of the war for many transnational corporations. Looking forward, the section explores ways in which neoconservative policy has helped to create a turbulent and conflict-ridden global economy. And it explains how the 1998 Asian financial crisis and the 2001 meltdown in Argentina, coupled with global protests, have hastened the end of the neoliberal era.

The second part of the book looks at how the debates about trade and development policy are taking sharp turns from the courses they followed through the 1980s and '90s. These shifts are evident in the rapidly changing roles of the World Bank, the IMF, and the WTO. Looking at these institutions' uncertain futures provides insights into the new international order that might arise from the old. Alongside the international financial institutions, I also consider the work of leading globalization commentators Thomas Friedman and Joseph Stiglitz, discussing what these pundits tell us about the altered state of global politics.

The third and final part of this book shows how the democratic model for globalization is already being brought to life. From victories on issues like debt relief to upheavals throughout Latin America and beyond, communities are standing in support of vibrant alternatives to both neoliberalism and U.S. empire. Those who assemble at Davos should take notice. Even as they carry on their own debate, the arrived-by-helicopter billionaires and "cleanse the planet" militarists may be forced to face an uncomfortable reality: Citizens movements across the globe are rising to tell them that the world is not theirs to rule.

PART ONE

The Imperial Moment

1

War Without Profit

When President Bush took office in January 2001, *USA Today* noted, "Twenty-six of 42 presidents, including Bill Clinton, were lawyers. Seven were generals. George W. Bush becomes the first with an MBA."[1]

By that time, discussion of Bush's business training had become a familiar trope. Commentators regularly posited that the new president and his cabinet, with close ties to the corporate world, were bringing a new sensibility to the executive branch. *USA Today* predicted that the "MBAs might reshape the White House," that their degrees would make the administration "all about business."[2]

Other corporate leaders were quick to laud the rise of fellow businessmen George W. Bush and Dick Cheney in government. David Wilson, president and CEO of the Graduate Management Admission Council asserted that Bush's business training was an excellent asset. "President Bush will find his MBA skills invaluable," he said, "as he implements the power of teamwork, fiscal responsibility and understanding his new customer base of approximately 250 million people."[3]

Dick Cheney's corporate success was noted as a sign of even greater promise. "He's as top-notch a businessman as he is a statesman," said

Roger Enrico, CEO of PepsiCo, who sat with Cheney on the board of Electronic Data Systems. John Pepper, chairman of Procter & Gamble, where Cheney was also a board member, declared, "I have developed a deep appreciation for his business wisdom."[4]

As Bush's term in office commenced, progressives were likely to agree that the administration was "all about business." They responded to celebrations of the "nation's first MBA president" by arguing that Bush and Cheney's business ties made for a White House unfailingly biased toward corporate America. Put the vice president's secretive Energy Task Force and massive tax cuts for the wealthy together with corporate lobbyists writing regulations for their own industries, and the idea makes a lot of sense. The administration, the argument went, was diligently doing the bidding of Wall Street.

Although versions of this notion are still prevalent, it is worth considering a contrary notion: Maybe George Bush and Dick Cheney aren't very good capitalists after all.

George W. Bush's history as a failed businessman is well known. As Princeton economist and *New York Times* columnist Paul Krugman pointed out, by 1986 Bush "had run through millions of dollars of other people's money" in two failed business ventures, "with nothing to show for it but a company losing money and heavily burdened with debt. But he was rescued from failure when Harken Energy bought his company at an astonishingly high price," thanks to Bush family connections.[5]

Dick Cheney, who was portrayed by conservatives as a brilliant ex-CEO and by progressives as a Halliburton shill, also has a suspect past. Although he certainly increased Halliburton's profile in his nearly five-year tenure as its chief, his foremost accomplishment was the $7.7 billion acquisition in 1998 of Dresser Industries, a rival that turned out to be plagued with staggering asbestos-related liabilities. In the wake of Cheney's reign, multiple Halliburton divisions sought bankruptcy protection, and the company's stock price plunged. For several years, the company was a losing investment, although it would later rebound with Cheney out of the corporate driver's seat (and in a more helpful position in government).

Many analysts held Cheney accountable for the company's distressing downturn. Those detractors argued that Dresser's asbestos problems, which cost Halliburton billions, were predictable.[6] Even the less harsh critics have questioned Cheney's success as a business leader. For instance, Jason E. Putman, an energy analyst at Victory Capital Management, stated that, as a Halliburton executive, "overall, Cheney did maybe at best an average job."[7] *Newsweek*'s Wall Street editor, Allan Sloan, was less complimentary, maintaining that Cheney was a "CEO who messed up big-time."[8]

In retrospect, the past business failings of White House leaders might have been an omen—especially with regard to their foreign policy. When it comes to Iraq, we hear a lot about the government largesse flowing toward Halliburton, Bechtel, and a handful of other favored firms. Less often do we consider the possibility that the administration's "war on terror" has been a major business blunder.

When we consider the war's impact on business, the blatant profiteering of military contractors like Halliburton is only part of the story. That must be weighed against the fearful warnings of business executives who opposed the invasion of Iraq from the start, as well as the discontent of companies that have been negatively affected by the war as it has played out. Not all of corporate America is happy. And the anger of sizable portions of the business community raises some important questions: Does the war in Iraq really represent a new stage in the advancement of corporate globalization? Or is it more accurate to understand it as a sharp—and potentially costly—break from the pro-corporate agenda that had been smoothly unfolding at least since the end of the Cold War?

As the occupation of Iraq drags on, the business press has started suggesting that many business leaders, who once hoped the Bush administration would push the corporate globalization of the Clinton years to new heights, are now anxious about the international order the Bush administration has created. Tax cuts and deregulation on the domestic front have been obvious bonuses, but otherwise many U.S. multinationals face a troubling scene. The White House's failed CEOs pursued an imperial globalization agenda that directly benefited only a narrow slice of the American business community and left the rest exposed to a world of popular resentment and economic uncertainty. When it comes to the interventions of Bush, Cheney, Rice, and the neocons in the global economy, "at best an average job" might be a charitable judgment, and "messed up big-time" could be closer to reality.

A Constructive Challenge

The first section of this book is devoted to understanding the project of imperial globalization, especially with regard to the invasion of Iraq. Putting globalization politics in the context of a debate among elites about how to rule the world can change one's perspective on key international events. I believe the Iraq War is one of these. Although progressive commentators often treat the war as a part of a coherent, unified plan for global dominance, I argue that we should see it as a conflict that fostered divisions among ruling interests and set the stage for a contentious debate about the management of the global economy. Ultimately, it may be less accurate to say that the neoconservative hawks in power during the Bush era outdid the corporate globalists of earlier years than to suggest that neocons betrayed their predecessors.

To be radical, in the oldest sense of the word, is to go to the root. A strength of radical political analysis is that it strives to place what appear to be isolated events in a larger context. It seeks to make connections between seemingly disparate political issues by revealing underlying ideological frameworks. And so it has been a central task, in the post-9/11 era, for activists to demonstrate how the "war on terror" and the drive for corporate globalization are one and the same—how peace and global justice movements share vital common ground. That these issues are connected, in a fundamental way, has become an article of faith on the left, reinforced by the fact that many of us who participated in the globalization protests of past years have mobilized more recently against the Bush administration's militarism.

The drive to connect is a valuable impulse. Yet it is not infallible. Like many ideas that have hardened into articles of faith, the link between war and globalization deserves some constructive skepticism. Many of the arguments linking the war in Iraq with a strategy for neoliberal expansion are not very convincing. They often interpret tangential relationships as causality, and in their efforts to connect, they sometimes overlook important disjunctures between the Bush administration's foreign policy and the type of international relations preferred by many business elites.

ARGUING FOR A LINK

There are three popular arguments linking the "war on terror" and the drive for corporate globalization. The first involves profiteering. The White House was eager to make big business a partner in the execution of the Iraq War and the subsequent occupation. This was most prominently evidenced by the high-priced, no-bid reconstruction contracts snatched up by well connected companies such as Halliburton and Bechtel. Profiteering is something consistently and rightly condemned by peace and justice activists. The idea that this type of corporate greed is at the core of the war effort surfaces regularly in speeches at antiwar demonstrations and has been promoted by many progressive public figures, most notably filmmaker Michael Moore.

A second argument connecting the war and corporate globalization highlights the fact that the president used the war to advance a neoliberal agenda on the domestic front. This thesis is advanced most comprehensively by the prominent sociologist Frances Fox Piven in her 2004 book, *The War at Home*. Progressives like Piven point out that the Bush administration employed the rhetoric of the "war on terror" to attack unions—as in the summer of 2002, when it threatened to intervene for "national security" purposes in a strike by West Coast dockworkers. Moreover, the White House pushed neoliberal measures like tax cuts for the wealthy and the further erosion of the social safety net, using the war as political leverage to enact these policies. In March 2003, as the administration promoted a new round of tax cuts and reductions in social service programs, the *New York Times* reported, "Republicans are discovering that the conflict [in the Middle East] can provide a new tool of persuasion." It described how "House leaders pounded home the idea that it was not time to embarrass the president by defeating his budget plan."[9] Many of these same leaders used the war abroad to suppress public dissent. The $87 billion bill passed by Congress in October 2003 to partially pay for the occupation of Iraq also included $8.5 million for policing the November 2003 Miami ministerial conference, where activists were expected to protest the Free Trade Area of the Americas.[10] Conservatives both inside and outside the administration painted antiwar and globalization protesters as not only unpatriotic but even helpful to terrorists.

The third key argument connecting the war and corporate globalization highlights the privatization of Iraq's economy and asserts that this economic restructuring will ultimately allow U.S. companies to seize control of the country's massive oil reserves. Political commentators Naomi Klein[11] and Antonia Juhasz,[12] among others, have done important work detailing how the occupation of Iraq allowed the United States to restructure the country's economy based on strict neoliberal principles. Taking advantage of its role as occupying power, the United States, through the Coalition Provisional Authority, implemented a radical series of economic reforms. Following what the *Economist* magazine called a "wishlist that foreign investors and donor agencies dream of for developing markets,"[13] Washington instituted measures providing for the privatization of two hundred Iraqi state firms, for 100 percent foreign ownership in Iraqi companies outside the oil production and refinement sectors, for full repatriation of profits, and for a 15 percent cap on corporate taxes.

First implemented by executive fiat in 2003 under Coalition Provisional Authority administrator Paul Bremer, the economic reforms remain largely in effect, even after the creation of a new Iraqi constitution.[14] Pressure from the White House, as well as the post-invasion entry of the IMF into Iraq, helped to ensure that this was the case. In short, thanks to America's guiding hand, Iraq now has one of the most neoliberal economies in the world.

How Deep a Connection?

Although these three arguments linking neoconservative militarism and corporate globalization have merit, each of them has important weaknesses. Because it is the most straightforward, let's consider the second argument first—the "war at home" thesis. There is no question that the Bush administration has used the specter of terrorism to push a regressive domestic agenda. However, this can be considered opportunistic behavior rather than evidence of a systematic relationship between war and corporate globalization. Although the war in Iraq provided politically convenient cover for many actions, it was hardly a necessary condition for advancing Bush's domestic neoliberalism. After all, the president succeeded in passing his first, landmark round of tax cuts in the first half of 2001, several months before 9/11 and the start of the "war on terror." Many of the realist Republicans who worked to pass this legislation would later become critics of the invasion of Iraq.

Frances Fox Piven convincingly shows that the Republicans milked 9/11 and the looming war in Iraq for maximum political advantage in the midterm elections of 2002 (and they certainly did so again in the presidential elections of 2004). But as Piven pushes the argument further, it lands on shaky ground. Taking a stance reminiscent of the "wag the dog" charge against Bill Clinton—the accusation that he sought to intervene abroad to draw attention away from the Monica Lewinsky scandal—she suggests that the Bush administration launched the invasion to dispel lingering memories of the disputed elections of 2000 and to increase its political capital. The Republicans' desire to pursue neoliberalism at home was, she says, "another reason for war" that should be placed alongside America's imperial impulses.[15] According to Piven, the invasion of Iraq was not simply a foreign policy matter: "the war is also a domestic strategy, rooted . . . in calculations geared to shoring up the Bush regime's domestic power and its ability to pursue its domestic policy agenda."[16]

"To suggest a domestic dimension of foreign policy is actually not particularly novel," Piven maintains. "That the Cold War was useful because it justified the domestic Red Scare of the 1950s and the resultant taming of American labor is a common enough observation, for example."[17] That may be true. But to propose that the Cold War was pursued *because* it provided cover for domestic union-busting would be a considerably more controversial idea. Just because a conflict is "useful" does not mean this utility was a motive for war.

⸙Consider a related situation: Without a doubt, the Bush administration benefited enormously from the swell of patriotic support created by the attacks of 9/11. Yet Piven would certainly object to conspiracy theorists who contend that the White House secretly plotted the destruction of the World Trade Center to secure this political windfall. Nevertheless, much of the "war at home" argument uses a similar logic. For all the vivid examples Piven is able to provide of the Republicans shamelessly invoking the "war on terror" to promote tax cuts for the rich and diminished social services for the poor, there is little to support her contention that the White House entered into war with an explicit aim of gaining leverage for its domestic agenda.

To the extent that the war *was* designed to help advance domestic neoliberalism, it may well have backfired. Piven herself noted in 2004 that the political benefit from the war would be temporary. This proved to be a wise prediction. Since then, the political fallout for the administration has been dramatic. By the 2006 elections, the war had become a significant liability for the Republicans, contributed greatly to their losing control of Congress, and crippled their domestic agenda. As bad news continued to stream from the war front, President Bush's approval ratings plummeted, hastening his lame duck status. The Republicans' 2005 drive to privatize Social Security failed, and no comparable policy initiative has any chance of passing Congress in the waning days of the Bush administration. In the end, while the administration wrought tremendous damage, the Iraq War may well have helped to halt, rather than aid, the advance of its "war at home."

THE PROFITEERS

Another of the three central arguments is that the invasion of Iraq was a war for corporations such as Halliburton. This contention also runs into problems. Although corporations have exhibited shameless opportunism in seizing business opportunities created by U.S. military action, this does not connect war and globalization in a deep way. Filmmaker Michael Moore is a prominent advocate of the "war for profit" thesis. But as progressive commentator Robert Jensen argued in his critique of *Fahrenheit 9/11*, Moore's overreliance on this idea results in a weak explanation of the causes of the war and leads him to overlook Democratic Party patronage of the military-industrial complex.

In *Fahrenheit 9/11*, as described by Jensen, "A family member of a soldier who died asks, 'for what?' and Moore cuts directly to the subject of war profiteering." Jensen takes issue with this juxtaposition: "[D]oes Moore really want us to believe that a major war was launched so that Halliburton and other companies could increase its profits for a few years?" Jensen contends: "Yes, war profiteering happens, but it is not the reason nations go to war. This kind of distorted analysis helps keep viewers' attention focused on the Bush administration . . . not the routine way in which corporate America makes money off the misnamed Department of Defense, no matter who is in the White House."[10]

The criticism is well put. And this is only one of several problems with the "war for profit" idea. A focus on short-term profiteering risks ignoring the stated neoconservative goal of reshaping the Middle East, which has much more serious consequences than quick kickbacks to corporate sponsors, as we will see. It also assumes that the objectives of specific businesses like Halliburton and Bechtel accurately reflect the interests of multinational corporations as a whole.

As it turns out, for every Halliburton eager to hitch onto the government war machine, there are dozens of other companies affected in negative ways by the Iraq War. Although corporations from a select few slices of the economy may have lobbied for war, a much larger segment of the business elite preferred Clinton's multilateralist globalization to Bush's imperial version. The complaints of these corporate malcontents constitute one of the fascinating untold stories of the war. It is worth examining them in some detail, and not only because they cast new light on many common assumptions about corporate attitudes. They also highlight divisions that are influencing the direction of the global economy as George W. Bush leaves office.

A Bungled Brand America

In recent years, KFC has had some trying moments in the Muslim world. In September 2005, a bomb exploded inside one of the company's fried-chicken outlets in Karachi, Pakistan.[19] It was not the first time the chain had been targeted. In May of the same year, a Shia mob, angered by U.S. backing for President Pervez Musharraf and by reported abuses at Guantánamo, had turned on another KFC outlet. Spotting a fast-food storefront decked out with large images of Colonel Sanders set atop fields of stars and stripes, they burned it down.[20] Two other branches had been destroyed shortly after the U.S. attack on Afghanistan in 2001.

The woes troubling KFC go well beyond one fast-food chain— McDonald's, too, has been attacked in Pakistan and Indonesia—and the torching of fast-food outlets is only one sign of the new business climate fostered by Bush's changes to American foreign policy. If President Clinton's diplomatic affairs could be described as a sustained effort to make the world safe for Mickey Mouse, Microsoft, and popcorn chicken, the Bush-Cheney agenda was something altogether more dangerous for business. If Bush was an oil president, he was not a Disney president, nor a Coca-Cola one. Cheney may have worked diligently to help Halliburton rebound, but the war he promoted has not worked out nearly so well for Starbucks.

Prior to the war, many corporate leaders feared that the invasion of Iraq would be bad for business. The contentious climate that Laurie Garrett documented at the 2003 World Economic Forum in Davos was in many ways quite remarkable. In the high-flying Clinton years, a feeling of exuberance pervaded the forum—despite protests outside the meetings. By January 2003, however, the mood in Davos had soured. Corporate leaders showed little more enthusiasm for Washington's impending invasion than did the protesters outside. As Garrett reported, "U.S. unilateralism is seen as arrogant, bullyish. If the U.S. cannot behave in partnership with its allies—especially the Europeans—it risks not only political alliance but BUSINESS, as well." Of the internationalists and CEOs who had assembled, she said, "These WEF folks are freaked out. They see very bad economics ahead, war, and more terrorism."[21] Such widespread business unease in advance of the war belies the idea that the invasion was the result of Wall Street lobbying—that it was a war originally launched to benefit corporate America, even if it has since gone awry and become unprofitable. In fact, White House militarists went to war despite a chorus of corporate objections.

Business displeasure about the war has continued to simmer in the years since the invasion. We have already seen that the Bush administration's shift to imperial globalization represented a break from earlier approaches to managing the international economy. Although it is possible that the administration's bold gamble for U.S. global dominance will prove lucrative in the long run, the short-term business costs of its foreign policy have become evident.

For starters, there is the new wave of anti-Americanism sweeping the planet. This goes far beyond KFC bombings in South Asia and widespread hostility in the Middle East. In Asia, the *South China Morning Post* noted that a "strong, growing hostility" toward the United States complicated Disney's expansion plans in the area.[22] Bush's imperial foreign policy sparked consumer backlash even among traditional allies. In December 2004, Jim Lobe of Inter Press Service reported on a survey of 8,000 international consumers released by Seattle-based Global Market Insite (GMI), Inc. The survey noted, "one-third of all consumers in Canada, China, France, Germany, Japan, Russia, and the United Kingdom said that U.S. foreign policy, particularly the 'war on terror' and the occupation of Iraq, constituted their strongest impression of the United States." Dr. Mitchell Eggers, GMI's chief operating officer and head pollster, remarked, "Unfortunately, current American foreign policy is viewed by international consumers as a significant negative, when it used to be a positive."[23]

Brands the survey identified as particularly at risk included Marlboro cigarettes, America Online (AOL), McDonald's, American Airlines, Exxon-Mobil, Chevron Texaco, United Airlines, Budweiser, Chrysler, Barbie (a division of Mattel), Starbucks, and General Motors.

In the years following the GMI survey, business publications running stories about war-related corporate malaise ranged from *Forbes* ("Is Brand America in Trouble?")[24] to the British *Financial Times* ("World

Turning Its Back on Brand America")[25]. A 2005 *U.S. Banker* magazine article relayed the results of an Edelman Trust Barometer survey of high-end global consumers. The study found that "41 percent of Canadian elites were less likely to purchase American products because of Bush Administration policies, compared to 56 percent in the UK, 61 percent in France, 49 percent in Germany and 42 percent in Brazil."[26]

It was not just snooty foreigners who were negative, either. American business leaders themselves linked economic woes to imperial policy. As *U.S. Banker* warned, "the majority of American CEOs, whose firms employ eight million overseas, are now acknowledging that anti-American sentiment is a problem." A 2004 *Boston Herald* story, titled "Mass. Execs: Iraqi War Hurting; U.S. Competitiveness Becoming a Casualty," further pointed out that "sixty-two percent of executives surveyed by Opinion Dynamics Corp. said the war is hurting America's global competitiveness."[27]

Regularly featured in stories about America's image problems is a group of corporate executives who have organized as Business for Diplomatic Action (BDA) to bring attention to the problem. While avoiding an explicit stance on the Iraq War, the BDA argues: "The costs associated with rising anti-American sentiment are exponential. From security and economic costs to an erosion in our ability to engender trust around the world and recruit the best and brightest, the U.S. stands to lose its competitive edge if steps are not made toward reversing the negativity associated with America."[28]

Compared to the adverse impacts of Bush's imperial globalization, the administration's efforts at brand rehabilitation—anyone remember White House public relations liaison Karen Hughes's 2005 listening tour in the Middle East?—are laughable. The BDA knows it. Taking diplomatic matters into its own hands, the organization flatly states, "Right now the U.S. government is not a credible messenger."[29]

A Quagmire for Corporations

Further reports have maintained that the problem is not just one of America's image, but rather that the wages of war actually cut into business profits. In June 2004, *USA Today* reporter James Cox described how financially ailing companies were pointing to the war as the culprit. "Hundreds of companies blame the Iraq War for poor financial results in 2003, many warning that continued U.S. military involvement there could harm this year's performance," he reported. "In recent regulatory filings at the Securities and Exchange Commission (SEC), airlines, home builders, broadcasters, mortgage providers, mutual funds and others directly blame the war for lower revenues and profits last year."[30]

Among those who complained, Hewlett-Packard claimed that the occupation of Iraq created uncertainty and hurt its stock price; meanwhile, media companies Hearst-Argyle Television, Sinclair Broadcast Group, and Journal Communications bemoaned the number of TV and radio ads preempted by war news. While blaming the war might just have been a convenient excuse for some underperforming executives, the level of grumbling was noteworthy, as were the comments of outspoken fund managers profiled by Cox:

> "The war in Iraq created a quagmire for corporations," David J. Galvan, a portfolio manager for Wayne Hummer Income Fund, says in his letter to shareholders.
>
> Vintage Mutual Funds concludes that "the price of these commitments (in Iraq and Afghanistan) may be more than the American public had expected or is willing to tolerate. . . ."
>
> In an SEC filing, Domenic Colasacco, manager of the Boston Balanced Fund, calls the ongoing U.S. occupation "sad and increasingly risky."[31]

Of course, we know that companies involved in Iraqi reconstruction posted profits, and sales of war-related equipment, such as gas masks and armored Humvees, went up after the war started. But those companies constitute a small segment of the corporate spectrum. If you look through the economy sector by sector, it is surprising how few firms really stood to benefit from the war.

Industries that are sensitive to public relations like tourism and hospitality have taken a huge blow during the "war on terror." Delta Air Lines, JetBlue, Orbitz, Priceline.com, Morton's steakhouses, Fairmont

Hotels & Resorts, and Host Marriott, to name just a few, have blamed disappointing returns in recent years on Bush administration policy. Travel industry leaders have warned:

> The U.S. is losing billions of dollars as international tourists are deterred from visiting the U.S. because of a tarnished image overseas and more bureaucratic visa policies. . . . "It's an economic imperative to address these problems," said Roger Dow, chief executive of the Travel Industry Association of America, tourism's main trade body. . . . Mr. Dow stressed that tourism contributed to a positive perception of the U.S. . . . "If we don't address these issues in tourism, the long-term impact for American brands Coca-Cola, General Motors, McDonald's could be very damaging."[32]

By early 2007, travel industry lobbyists declared a "travel crisis, one that hurts our economy, national security and global standing."[33] Yet for business people concerned with America's tarnished foreign image, the prognosis was grim. The Associated Press reported in March 2007 that in a poll conducted by the BBC World Service, "the United States was found to have a mostly negative influence in 20 of 26 countries surveyed." Worse still, "views of U.S. influence are consistently negative in Canada, Latin America and the Middle East." Speaking before Congress about these findings, Steven Kull of the University of Maryland, who helped conduct the poll, explained that criticism singled out the U.S. war in Iraq and, in the words of the Associated Press, "centered on the United States playing the role of world policeman." Kull warned, "The numbers we are seeing today are the lowest numbers that have ever been recorded."[34]

The effects of the war on some sectors of the economy can be counterintuitive. Although there are influential firms, like Halliburton, that no doubt helped to propel the war, divisions can be spotted even in industries that are closely aligned with the imperial globalization agenda. For example, most people would assume that big arms manufacturers would be among those profiting handsomely from the Iraq War. But this is not the case. Undoubtedly, defense contractors have benefited greatly in the post-9/11 environment. Prolonged, decades-long conflicts like the

Cold War or the "war on terror" help to justify bloated Pentagon budgets year after year, producing lucrative contracts. But a large troop deployment, such as the one in Iraq, is a very different matter.

"Where the contractors really make their money is from big ticket weapons systems," according to Frida Berrigan of the Arms Trade Resource Center. "They make a lot of money in research and development. They want Defense money going toward building new things. Wars on the ground, war actually taking place, use the old systems."[35]

Defense contractors may have hoped that the Iraq invasion would provide free advertising for their wares, as did the first Persian Gulf War, which they could then profitably export throughout the world. But the unpopular, ongoing occupation of Iraq does them little good. Berrigan's colleague, William Hartung, explained: "Contrary to popular wisdom, not all wars are good for weapons contractors. Wars of counterinsurgency are far more likely to require basic equipment than the multibillion programs for fighter planes, submarines, missile defense and nuclear weapons that are the bread-and-butter of the Lockheed Martins and Northrop Grummans of the world."[36] Profits from the sale of basic equipment does not pay the bills for the major defense contractors. Furthermore, these firms have generally not been leading suppliers of services to the troops in Iraq.

Instead, the war has threatened to deplete their normally reliable funding streams. To the extent that Congress directs money away from long-term weapons development and toward equipment for soldiers deployed in the Middle East, the big defense contractors lose out. Worried about potential budget cuts for their programs, executives of arms corporations held a dinner meeting in December 2005 with Deputy Defense Secretary Gordon England, who had written an internal memo calling for tightening the budget of the Pentagon.[37] England reassured the contractors that any cuts would likely come from reductions in Air Force personnel, rather than weapons systems. The *Wall Street Journal* reported, "The shift is good news for the nation's major defense contractors, which appear to have dodged major cutbacks in big-ticket weapons purchases."[38] As the war has stretched on, however, defense companies have been forced to continue defending their turf.

ECONOMIC NIGHTMARES FORETOLD

Even before the war started, there were those who predicted that it could become an economically burdensome disaster. In a policy report titled *The Economic Costs of a War in Iraq*, progressive economists Dean Baker and Mark Weisbrot documented worrisome prospects for business.[39] Beyond the costs of anti-Americanism abroad, they focused on three additional areas of concern: a war-related oil shock that could cost the American economy hundreds of thousands of jobs over a seven-year period; a heightened risk of terrorist attacks in the United States, which could result in increased security costs, slowing the growth of the gross domestic product (GDP); and a likelihood that increased oil prices could drag the developing world into a deep recession.

When asked in late 2005 how relevant the report's concerns proved to be, Baker emphasized that the worst has not come to pass. However, he noted some troubling signs. Oil prices indeed skyrocketed, owing largely to increased worldwide demand, but exacerbated by Iraq's slowed oil production.[40] There have been other effects as well. Each new intelligence estimate predicts that we are less, not more, secure as a result of the Iraqi occupation; because of the war, the risk of new economy-crippling terrorist attacks has grown. Already, Baker pointed out, the hours we spend waiting in security lines at the airport or delayed in city subways represent costly economic losses.

Then, of course, there is the as yet unrealized possibility that spreading guerrilla warfare and terrorism could lead to escalating sabotage against vast and largely indefensible stretches of oil pipeline in the Middle East. It is this scenario, among others, that led professor of Middle Eastern history and *Informed Comment* blogger Juan Cole to liken Bush's Iraq debacle to "throwing grenades around in the cockpit of the world economy."[41] Continued military aggression, particularly a U.S. attack on Iran, might still provoke serious havoc.

Such real and potential costs suggest that the prewar pessimism in Davos was well justified. And the above list hardly exhausts the possible economic "downsides" to Bush administration policies in Iraq and beyond. The direct cost of the war for U.S. taxpayers is already stratospherically beyond the initial estimate of $50–60 billion used by the White House to sell its war to the public.[42] That number was meant to conjure memories of the previous Gulf War—Operation Desert Storm—an engagement Americans recall as swift and relatively painless, in part because an array of allies helped to pay for it. The United States ponied up only $7 billion for that conflict. When White House economic advisor Larry Lindsey publicly suggested in late 2002 that a military return to Iraq would cost closer to $100 billion to $200 billion, he was quickly ousted from the administration.[43]

It turns out that Lindsey greatly underestimated the cost. In the years since Baghdad fell, several analysts have sought accurate estimates for the war's true cost. In August 2005, Phyllis Bennis and Erik Leaver at the Institute for Policy Studies issued a paper predicting that the total cost could reach $700 billion at the then-current spending level of $5.6 billion per month.[44] This figure included only direct congressional appropriations.

In early 2006, Nobel Prize–winning economist Joseph Stiglitz and Harvard's Linda Bilmes released a report that took a wider view. Hinting at the human cost of the occupation—which, of course, requires its own ghastly page in the ledger of wartime accounting—the report factored in the government-assigned "value of statistical life" for U.S. troops killed in combat. (It did not include the loss of Iraqi lives.) It also tallied items such as the costs of health care for wounded veterans, increased recruitment spending for a Pentagon desperate for new enlistees, and the opportunity costs of more productive public investments that might have been made had funds not been diverted overseas. Following Congressional Budget Office predictions for troop deployment, the report considered the possibilities of full U.S. withdrawal by 2010 to 2015. All told, the two economists put the cost at between $1 trillion (their most "conservative" estimate) and $2.2 trillion (their "moderate" one).[45] Members of the business community, and certainly U.S. taxpayers, are right to worry about the war's economic costs. In the long run, it seems unlikely that Colonel Sanders will be the only one to feel the pain.

CHOOSING WAR

The last of the three central arguments linking war and globalization focuses on the forced privatization of Iraq's economy. The extreme Bremer Orders provide perhaps the most vivid link between war and neoliberalism. There is no question that the U.S. occupying authority opportunistically used its power to impose radical "free market" reforms on Iraq's economy. That much is not controversial. The question is whether the restructuring in Iraq was part of a wider plan for reshaping the global economy, whether it signals a new phase of corporate globalization in which the "freeing" of markets will be more militaristically enforced. The lack of business savvy exhibited by the imperial globalists and the unsustainability of their aggressive foreign policy suggest that this is not the case.

An undercurrent of militarism has always accompanied globalization. *New York Times* columnist Thomas Friedman famously described this condition in his 1999 book *The Lexus and the Olive Tree*: "The hidden hand of the market will never work without a hidden fist. McDonald's cannot flourish without McDonnell Douglas, the designer of the U.S. Air Force F-15. And the hidden fist that keeps the world safe for Silicon Valley's technologies to flourish is called the U.S. Army, Air Force, Navy and Marine Corps."[46]

Friedman's point is well taken. Yet it is important to note that the columnist was writing about the Clinton years, an era in which a multilateral consensus around a post–Cold War U.S. military dominance was being carefully cultivated. The Bush administration's post-9/11 decision to take the fist out of hiding and wield it in a widely unpopular war significantly shook the international order that for years had provided a climate of economic stability. As revealed in the complaints of groups like Business for Diplomatic Action, President Bush ended up illustrating how the interests of McDonald's and the interests of McDonnell Douglas can collide. Privileging specific sectors of the U.S. economy, such as energy companies and engineering firms, the White House rattled the global marketplace in which U.S. consumer-based industries and financial capital must operate.

Some on the left have suggested that the Bush administration's hand was forced, that militarism was a response to challenges holding back corporate globalization. The International Forum on Globalization, a group of leading progressive scholars and analysts, have proposed this type of motivation for the invasion of Iraq: "[F]ailing systems become desperate, trying somehow to save their far-flung, overextended lines of supply and control. . . . If economic controls start failing, then war is an option."[47] Likewise, in a January 2003 address to the World Social Forum in Porto Alegre, Brazil, writer and activist Arundhati Roy argued that international grassroots pressure against the advance of corporate globalization compelled those in power to adopt a more militaristic posture. "We may not have stopped [empire] in its tracks—yet," she argued, "but we have stripped it down. We have made it drop its mask. We have forced it into the open. It now stands before us on the world's stage in all its brutish, iniquitous nakedness."[48]

The problem with these arguments is that they overlook the ways in which the war in Iraq was indeed a war of choice. The pressures on global neoliberalism are real, as we will see. But corporate globalization was not sidestepped because it was exhausted. It was pushed aside in favor of a different vision of the world order, one that puts U.S. nationalism ahead of the interests of a wide swath of multinational corporations.

Ultimately, business discontent with the Iraq War raises a vital set of questions: If a substantial portion of the corporate elite feared the war would hurt the global economy, who would choose to go forward with such an endeavor? If the war was not launched for the benefit of Wall Street, why *was* it waged? In the end, the answers point to a political worldview that may be far more frightening than simple crony capitalism.

2

VISIONS OF DOMINANCE

By 1999, the United States had reached an unparalleled level of power and prosperity. A decade earlier it had emerged from the Cold War triumphant. Then, in the 1990s, it embarked on the longest sustained economic expansion in its history. Its military and economic supremacy were matched only by its cultural influence. People throughout the world clamored to watch Hollywood movies and drink Coca-Cola. For the champions of American-led corporate globalization, it was the best of times.

Yet, despite this affluence and acclaim, many conservatives were unhappy. Notwithstanding the economy's success and CEOs' skyrocketing pay, they were dismayed by what they viewed as a critical missed opportunity: America's hard power was only sparingly deployed. The nation's all-powerful military, they lamented, was going to waste.

Corey Robin, the author of *Fear: The History of a Political Idea*, encountered this peculiar phenomenon in the summer of 2000. When Robin was conducting interviews with conservative luminaries such as Irving Kristol, considered a godfather of neoconservatism, he found them deeply unsatisfied with the role of the United States in the post–Cold War world. "What's the point of being the greatest, most powerful nation in the world and not having an imperial role?" Kristol complained. "It's unheard of in human history. The most powerful nation always had an imperial role."[1]

President Clinton helped to advance corporate globalization, but, curiously, in Kristol's view, this was part of the problem. The standing of the United States among "capitalist democracies with a strong emphasis on economic growth and economic prosperity" interfered with its ability to act like other empires. Its preoccupation with commerce inhibited its willingness to make use of the country's unrivaled military. "It's too bad," Kristol said. "I think it would be natural for the United States . . . to play a far more dominant role in world affairs. Not what we're doing now but to command and to give orders as to what is to be done."[2]

Just a few years later, with George W. Bush in office and the "war on terror" launched, commanding and giving orders would become much more overt features of U.S. foreign policy. Kristol's feelings proved to be widely shared by the conservatives who came to staff the new Bush administration. What was distinctive about this group of policymakers was not their professed belief in "free markets." Virtually everyone on the American right, and indeed the great majority of Democrats, held the triumphalist view that global capitalism was the natural and rightful guiding force for the post–Cold War world. Instead, the neoconservatives' distinctive traits were their faith in hard power, their sense of moral certainty, and the ardor of their imperial ideology. What set apart the Bush administration militarists was a willingness to pursue their vision of U.S. power at all costs—even at cost to business.

By now, the story of the neocons' rise to prominence in the White House and their leading role in promoting war in Iraq has been recounted many times. When told by progressives, the tale often presents the Bush administration's ascendant imperial impulses as logical extensions of corporate globalization—the next step down the road of big-business dominance. But there is a problem with this narrative. It fails to take into account the new Republican militarists' ambivalent attitudes toward the booming 1990s and the "free trade" diplomacy of the Clinton era. The neocons are clearly capitalists. Yet the noneconomic aspects of their thinking—their ideological fervor and attraction to good-versus-evil showdowns—have surprising implications. At key moments when nationalism and commerce have conflicted, the Bush administration militarists have chosen nationalism. They have pursued an America-first vision of national interest that values U.S. strength over the more general well-being of global capital. They have confounded Wall Street analysts and international trading partners with their imperial fantasies. And they have presented a vision of globalization brimming with frightening hubris.

The Iraq War is a prime example of the tension between corporate and imperial worldviews. Far more than by crony capitalism or the desire to expand corporate power, the war was driven by a neoconservative vision of how to rule the world. Understanding the central reasons for war requires us to appreciate this distinctive mind-set, to examine a philosophy of geopolitics imbued with grandiose ambitions and reckless recommendations for action. Neoconservative ideology has aimed to secure a new century of global dominance for America, not simply engage in a short-term war for profit. Its extremist tenets have shocked the international community and violated core principles of democracy—and if pursued further, they may well lead the country to economic ruin.

One's Own Petty Affairs

Many conservatives experienced the 1990s as a decade of dissatisfaction. That President Clinton was the head of state was a source of seemingly unlimited consternation. But there was also a more novel feature of their unease. On a cultural level, neocons took issue with the decadence that accompanied the high-flying U.S. economy. And on a political level, they rejected the idea of corporate globalization as a self-sustaining ideology. Corey Robin brilliantly dissected this malaise: "While neocons are not opposed to capitalism, they do not believe it is the highest achievement of civilization."[3] Rather, they are part of a conservative tradition, stretching back at least to Edmund Burke, that lauded the decisive role of great men in history and valued the "mystery and vitality" of political engagement, especially in times of war.

During the Cold War, the battle against communism was an all-consuming preoccupation, a noble crusade that required sacrifice and perseverance. After this defining conflict ended, the neocons watched uneasily as trade and globalization became the watchwords of the Clinton era. These conservatives supported "free markets," sure. But faith in market forces was no substitute for the type of grand political struggle they were accustomed to waging. They felt that the praise bestowed upon corporate globalization encouraged too much self-centered thinking and not enough nationalism. Conservative pundits thus spoke out against the self-indulgence of the roaring dot-com era. Corey Robin noted that *Weekly Standard* scribe (and now *New York Times* columnist) David Brooks wrote dismissively of the 1990s as a time when we "renovated our kitchens, refurbished our home entertainment systems, invested in patio furniture, Jacuzzis and gas grills." The well-known conservative political theorist Francis Fukuyama denounced the business-minded decade as promoting a "preoccupation with one's own petty affairs."[4]

These conservatives worried that those who focused on commerce overlooked the importance of building America's military and maintaining its superpower status. Just when the United States had won the right to exercise imperial influence, they saw Clinton's "free trade" multilateralists squandering the opportunity, naively acting as if friendly business ties would somehow create a stable international order. The neocons held that the corporate globalists misunderstood the very nature of American dominance. In neocon thinking, America's "soft" power—its cultural influence and ability to lead by engendering respect among allies—was a chimera. All of the 1990s hoopla about globalization's cooperative ethos amounted to little in their view. What mattered was military might. In the words of Michael Steinberger, senior correspondent at the *American Prospect*, the neocons believe that "the world is in a Hobbesian state, power resides mainly in the belly of a B-52, and the only reliable way to keep the barbarians at the gate is to step outside the gate and kill them."[5]

Giving voice to this attitude, some of the key documents of the neoconservative movement in the 1990s contain fascinating critiques of market-oriented thinking. In 1997, the neocons' flagship organization, the Project for a New American Century (PNAC), opened its "Statement of Principles" by blasting "the incoherent policies of the Clinton Administration." The partisan attack was hardly unexpected. More surprising was the organization's declaration that Wall Street's greed was also part of the problem. Why? Because capitalists' desire for quick profits blinded them to the need to invest in long-term U.S. hegemony. "We are living off the capital—both the military investments and the foreign policy achievements—built up by past administrations," the statement contends, going on to note, "the promise of short-term commercial benefits threatens to override strategic considerations."[6]

This assertion was not an anomaly. In their book *Present Dangers*, PNAC founders Robert Kagan and William Kristol (son of Irving Kristol and carrier of the neocons' ideological torch) go so far as to declare the 1990s a "squandered decade."[7] From a business perspective, this is an extraordinary claim. The neocons write off one of the country's greatest economic booms as wasted time, and they dismiss out of hand the Clinton administration's efforts to promote corporate expansion. More remarkable still, this sentiment made it out of right-wing editorials and into major presidential statements. George W. Bush echoed the idea in his postreelection inaugural address of 2005, utterly dismissing the period between the Cold War and the "war on terror." He stated: "For half a century America defended our own freedom by standing watch on distant borders. After the shipwreck of Communism came years of relative quiet, years of repose, years of sabbatical—and then there came a day of fire."[8]

This assertion left many commentators in shock. The *American Prospect's* Michael Steinberger rightly commented that the 1990s "were only years of repose and sabbatical if you believe that globalization is a myth and that America's position in the world is purely a function of its military prowess."[9] *Washington Post* columnist E. J. Dionne asked incredulously, "Is the assumption here that Americans are better off when we are embattled and less noble when we are at peace? Is this a call for unending conflict and confrontation?"[10]

The short answer was "yes." In their rejection of the Clintonian, soft-power view of the world, the neocons draw a sharp distinction between the corporate and imperial approaches to globalization. Prioritizing U.S. power over the more general interest of global capital, they envision a far bloodier world than most corporate executives would prefer. The neocons argue that although an international order based on peacetime commerce might be nice to imagine, the real world doesn't work that way. To prove the point, they draw on historical evidence from an earlier period when globalization was on the rise—the late 1800s and early 1900s.

In the decades leading up to the First World War, international trade was swiftly expanding. Many members of a rising class of global capitalists argued that the bonds of business would avert international conflict. Since war hurt everybody's bottom line, the economic liberals of the time believed that nations would look to more peaceful means of resolving their disputes. Of course, they found out the hard way that the new technology of the industrial revolution, not only fostered freer trade, but it also facilitated ever more vicious forms of combat. Ultimately, it led to conflict on a previously unimaginable scale. Hard power, in the end, remained decisive.

Robert Kagan, who served in the Reagan administration before becoming a leading PNAC member, promoted this reading of history in a 1997 article in the *New Republic*, where he emphasized its relevance for the contemporary era of globalization. "Not since the nineteenth century has international trade been so exalted as the single cure for all of humanity's most persistent maladies, from tyranny and oppression to international disputes and war," Kagan contended. "We forget, because the theory was so discredited by the two world wars of the twentieth century."[11]

Applying the lesson to today, the neocons reject the notion that "free trade" can serve as a paradigm for governing world affairs. When the world is running smoothly, when corporations are able to go about their business, it is because military power has created stability. Economics itself is powerless to stop war or dictatorship, and it cannot be the driving force in international affairs. During the Cold War, this idea appeared self-evident, as Kagan explained in his article:

> When Occidental Petroleum's Armand Hammer and Pepsico's Donald Kendall insisted that their business interests in the Soviet Union coincided with the nation's interest in détente, they were regarded as disingenuous. Not many believed that selling Pepsi in the Soviet Union would hasten the fall of communism. It was not that businessmen were bad; their legitimate goal of maximizing profits merely conflicted sometimes with the nation's moral, strategic and even economic aspirations.[12]

Neocons feared that in the new age of globalization this perspective had been lost. As in the early 1900s, businesspeople were once again held up as world-historical actors. President Clinton hobnobbed with corporate elites at the annual World Economic Forum in Davos, as everyone in attendance imagined that they were shaping global politics with their entrepreneurialism. For the neocons, it was a perilous illusion.

To those who are accustomed to thinking about the war in Iraq as an endeavor undertaken for the benefit of Bush and Cheney's friends in big business, the imperial globalists' attitudes toward corporate America will sound startling. The government's allegiance to the business community, Kagan flatly stated, should go only so far:

> The fundamental facts of international relations have not changed that much in a century. Then as now, the United States has broad strategic and moral interests which cannot be pursued on the well-tailored backs of American businessmen. Although corporate leaders can be expected to ask the government to help them out abroad, it is still the job of our political leaders sometimes to say no. The unwillingness of recent American governments to keep business interests in their place has become dangerous.[13]

THE BUSH DOCTRINE:
A NEO-REAGANITE FANTASY COME TO LIFE

If corporate-led foreign policy presents a danger to U.S. dominance, what is the neocons' alternative? As it turns out, the vision of foreign policy promoted by institutions like the Project for a New American Century is, in large part, what became official dogma for the Bush administration after 9/11. What has become known as the "Bush Doctrine" envisions a world order with a deregulated, "free market" global economy. However, economic policy in this worldview is secondary to an aggressive, moralistic defense of U.S. power. A strong American nationalism is the foundation of global affairs, and promoting it is the primary task of international relations.

In one of their most famous and influential essays, a 1996 piece titled "Toward a Neo-Reaganite Foreign Policy," William Kristol and Robert Kagan argued that the U.S. role in the world should be one of "benevolent global hegemony." As they explained: "Having defeated the 'evil empire,' the United States enjoys strategic and ideological predominance. The first objective of U.S. foreign policy should be to preserve and enhance that predominance by strengthening America's security, supporting its friends, advancing its interests, and standing up for its principles around the world."[14]

For a statement written in the latter half of the 1990s, the neo-Reaganite proposal had some notable omissions. Economics was hardly mentioned, clearly treated as secondary to military strength and geopolitical strategy. As Steinberger commented in the *American Prospect*, "Not once in their essay did they use the word 'globalization,'" a remarkable omission, given that globalization was becoming the center of foreign policy discussions at the time the article was published.[15] The real concern for the authors was how American military muscle should be flexed—proactively and without apology—to enforce U.S. dictates.

First and foremost, the new foreign policy would necessitate increased Pentagon spending. Beyond that, Kristol and Kagan argued that it would require both "citizen involvement" and "moral clarity." Americans would have to be motivated by more than padding their bank accounts. They would need to embrace an "elevated patriotism" of a very particular sort—one that would lead them to shun isolationist feelings and support a commanding imperial role for their country. In the mid-1990s, all this seemed rather far-fetched, and few politicians were willing to embrace overt imperial sentiments. For the remainder of the decade, neocon foreign policy took shape only in discussion groups at think tanks like PNAC and in the pages of magazines like the *Weekly Standard*. Even in the opening year of the Bush administration, U.S. foreign policy, while generally unilateralist and adverse to UN treaties, lacked a distinct focus. It incorporated disparate strains of Republican foreign policy thinking, accommodating traditional realists as well as the neocon militarists.

The attacks of September 11, however, changed things. On one level, the White House response seemed inhospitable to neocon thinking. Notably, the Bush administration did not call for the type of sacrifice that Kristol and Kagan might have envisioned. "I encourage you all to go shopping more," President Bush said as the 2001 holiday season began.[16] He further called on citizens to "Do your business around the country. Fly and enjoy America's great destination spots." He even implored Americans to "Get down to Disney World in Florida."[17] Such petty affairs, it appeared, were necessary to keep the economy afloat.

Nevertheless, neocon pundits detected the conditions that would allow for a more forceful American role in the world. They commented excitedly on how the country's mood had changed. They observed a new sense of patriotism and moral purpose animating civic affairs. David Brooks approvingly noted the nonmarket qualities of this mood, commenting that "commercial life seems less important than public life. . . . When life or death fighting is going on, it's hard to think of Bill Gates or Jack Welch as particularly heroic."[18]

Indeed, the post-9/11 political climate was an invigorating one for the neocons. In the words of Corey Robin, these thinkers had entered "a heady time, a moment when their ambivalence about the free market— not about capitalism per se, which they refuse to challenge, but about the culture of capitalism, the elevation of buying and selling above political virtues like heroism and struggle—may finally be resolved."[19] In a return to Cold War form, moral language could be reintroduced into foreign policy. The decadence of the previous decade could be overcome. A new good-versus-evil struggle could be defined. And in this context, they reasoned, the need for an American empire would become clear.

The imperial foreign policy of George W. Bush began to take shape in a series of key statements. In a June 2002 speech at West Point, the president stated that America would maintain "military strengths beyond challenge," and he asserted the country's right to launch preventive war: "We must take the battle to the enemy, disrupt his plans and confront the worst threats before they emerge."[20] For international observers, these statements suggested a troubling new declaration of American dominance, an assertion of a right to intervene whenever and wherever it saw fit, regardless of international agreements. They were signs of things to come.

A much fuller expression of this outlook came with the release of a new National Security Strategy (NSS) by the White House in September 2002. The NSS serves as an official, public statement of America's aims in international affairs. Filled with lofty moral language about the U.S. role in bringing freedom to the world, the document laid out several key ideas that represented radical departures from established diplomatic norms. First, it explained that U.S. military dominance would provide the foundation for global order and that no other country would be allowed to emerge as a rival military power: "Our forces will be strong enough to dissuade potential adversaries from pursuing a military build-up in hopes of surpassing, or equaling, the power of the United States." Second, flouting the standards set by international law, the NSS insisted on America's right to intervene at will, asserting that the United States "will not hesitate to act alone, if necessary, to exercise our right to self-defense by acting preemptively."[21]

The *Washington Post* dubbed the NSS a landmark document that "shift[s] U.S. foreign policy away from decades of deterrence and containment"[22] and "gives the United States a nearly messianic role"[23] in remaking the world.

Interestingly, the central ideas in the NSS had appeared a decade earlier as proposals for U.S. policy, but they were rejected at the time by Congress, the public, and the press as far too extreme to be adopted. In

1992, a handful of officials and advisors in the George H. W. Bush administration—figures such as Paul Wolfowitz, I. Lewis "Scooter" Libby, and then Secretary of Defense Dick Cheney, all of whom would later join Kristol and Kagan in the Project for a New American Century—drafted a secret Defense Planning Guidance (DPG) document for the Pentagon. Because it was meant to be a classified statement, the DPG was not filled with the same diplomatically sensitive language as the 2002 National Security Strategy. Hence, it was much more forthright in promoting U.S. unilateralism and justifying preemptive war.

In addition to foreshadowing the themes of the 2002 NSS, the 1992 DPG redefined America's attitudes toward its allies. It argued that the country must be prepared "to act independently when collective action cannot be orchestrated," and it envisioned future alliances as "ad hoc assemblies, often not lasting beyond the crisis being confronted, and in many cases carrying only general agreement over the objectives to be accomplished."[24] This conception of international coalitions was very different from the type of long-term alliance-making that had defined American diplomacy during the Cold War. Yet it accurately expressed the attitudes that would guide the effort to create a "coalition of the willing" to invade Iraq in 2003.

When it appeared in 1992, the DPG was met with widespread dismay. The secret document became a public relations fiasco for the first Bush administration when a draft was leaked to the press in March 1992. Members of both political parties, as well as outraged foreign allies, denounced the DPG. Even members of George H. W. Bush's political team, whose foreign policy orientation tended to be traditional and realist, seemed dismayed by the brash arguments of the Pentagon group. The backlash forced Secretary of Defense Cheney to revise the draft DPG—softening the document's extreme language. And even then, the revised document, dubbed the "Defense Strategy for the 1990s," was released only in the last days of the senior Bush presidency, when the lame duck administration no longer had anything to lose.

The document would essentially lie dormant for a decade. Yet, it would ultimately prove very influential. A statement that openly envisioned the United States unilaterally intervening across the world to defend its unrivaled power was too radical to be accepted in public debate in 1992. But just a decade later, under George W. Bush, it would become the order of the day.

Free Enterprise as America's Gift to the World

The militarist mind-set of the Bush administration is at the core of the imperial globalization agenda. On the one hand, this agenda promises a continuation of the neoliberal policies of the Clinton era. On the other, it carries the neocon suspicion of "free trade" as a governing ideology and subordinates economics to a secondary role. By insisting that American foreign relations be based on a proactive, interventionist militarism, imperial globalization breaks not only from the Clintonian philosophy of how to rule the world but also from earlier Republican traditions of how to conduct business. It regards a healthy global capitalism not as a key end in itself but as the by-product of U.S. dominance.

One of the few people to take a hard look at the economic aspects of documents like the 2002 NSS and the 1992 DPG is Antonia Juhasz, foreign policy analyst and author of *The Bush Agenda: Invading the World One Economy at a Time*. She concludes that Bush's national security agenda, as expressed in the NSS, "is, in fact, almost as much about corporate globalization as it is about war."[25] Although Juhasz's analysis sheds light on some interesting aspects of the document, I ultimately disagree with her conclusion.

Juhasz's argument is founded on several important facts. The NSS makes abundantly clear that the New American Century will be a capitalist one and that continued advocacy of "free markets" will be a critical part of U.S. policy. The document asserts that there is "a single sustainable model for national success: freedom, democracy, and free enterprise." Freedom and free enterprise are regarded almost as one and the same. Moreover, the NSS includes a detailed section laying out America's efforts to "Ignite a New Era of Global Economic Growth Through Free Markets and Free Trade," which outlines many of the central economic tenets of neoliberalism. It calls for "pro-growth legal and regulatory policies to encourage business investment, innovation, and entrepreneurial activity"; it repeatedly lauds "free trade"; and it demands lower taxes on businesses. Furthermore, the NSS pledges to continue U.S. support for the IMF and to develop new trade deals. Certainly, anyone concerned with creating a fairer global economy should be dismayed that these economic mandates are included in a document defining America's "security" agenda and outlining its military vision.

Juhasz and others who emphasize the extent to which the Bush Doctrine vows to advance U.S. corporate interests do a valuable service in explaining how many extremist "free trade" economic policies have become an enshrined part of the "war on terror." There is a question, however, about how to interpret the inclusion of economic recommendations in the Bush administration's national security agenda. In the end, there is reason to doubt that the authors of documents like the NSS truly view the drive for corporate globalization as being on a par with military power.

Although Juhasz regards the NSS as the definitive policy statement defining the Bush Doctrine, its language is actually watered-down. Far more subdued than the 1992 DPG or the influential statements of the Project for a New American Century, the 2002 NSS is filled with diplomatic language designed to reassure allies and downplay the radical unilateralism and militarism of the new foreign policy. The NSS includes flowery language on supporting the global fund for HIV/AIDS, aiding the "half of the human race [that] lives on less than $2 a day," and retraining workers who need new skills to compete in the global economy.[26] In other words, there is plenty in the document that is peripheral to its central vision. In this context, the sections on U.S. trade and development policy can be seen as mere restatements of positions that had long been on record, championed at every trade summit by U.S. negotiators. Admittedly, they show that neoliberalism still defines the economic orientation of U.S. policymakers. But to regard them as central elements of the new security agenda is suspect. Considered broadly, the economic sections in the NSS are exceptions to the neocons' relentless focus on hard power. Juhasz notes that in the other documents that define the Bush Doctrine "economic policy is mentioned mainly as an afterthought to military strategy."

Some of the economic passages in the NSS draw on the boilerplate language of American triumphalism. At least since the Cold War, bipartisan praise for the "free enterprise" system has been a way of celebrating U.S. hegemony and exceptionalism; it hardly marks a unique departure in vision. The distinctive feature of the Bush Doctrine is not that it continues U.S. advocacy of "free enterprise" and "free trade" but rather that it views global capitalism in a special way: as a gift from the United States to the world. This idea is common to many neocon statements, including the founding principles of the Project for a New American Century. As PNAC explains it, policymakers must "accept responsibility for America's unique role in preserving and extending an international order friendly to our security, our prosperity, and our principles."[27] Without American leadership, the imperial globalists simply cannot conceive of a successful global marketplace. And, of course, preserving America's "unique role" requires a heightened level of U.S. interventionism.

This position marks a dramatic departure from earlier Republican stances of realism or isolationism in foreign affairs. Although those who have driven the Bush agenda of imperial globalization are not all neocons (indeed, many key neocon thinkers were exiled from government in the wake of the Iraq War's failures), these ideologues left a distinctive mark on White House policy. In terms of his personal philosophy, George W. Bush did not bring a fully formed vision of foreign affairs with him to the White House. Rather, he brought a set of biases and instincts: a moralistic sense of America's purpose in the world, influenced by his evangelical religious beliefs; a distrust of multilateralism; and a faith that decisive action is preferable to the subtle, restrained calculations of *realpolitik*. Likewise, some analysts have classified Dick Cheney and Donald Rumsfeld as "aggressive realists" rather than neocons—more concerned with defending presidential power and America's unilateral prerogatives than with any grand idealist vision of reshaping the world. However, in the post-9/11 context, these instincts meshed nicely with the neocon agenda.

Precisely because of the moral conviction and broad sweep of their political thinking, the neocons were able to lead the administration down a path that many corporate-minded, pro-business Republicans regard as reckless. Back in the early 1990s, foreign policy realist and elder Republican statesman Brent Scowcroft advised the first President Bush to steer clear of the neocons, telling him to "Keep these guys at arm's length."[28] In 2002, he wrote an op-ed in the *Wall Street Journal* arguing against a war in Iraq, which he said "undoubtedly would be very expensive—with serious consequences for the U.S. and global economy."[29] Meanwhile, among isolationists, Pat Buchanan, past candidate for the Republican presidential nomination, stands as a steadfast critic of the neocons. He laments the "disproportionate power" of these thinkers in setting the agenda for the Bush years. Writing in advance of the 2004 election, Buchanan went so far as to contend that President Bush "will not deserve re-election if he does not jettison the neoconservatives' agenda of endless wars on the Islamic world."[30]

REAL REASONS FOR THE IRAQ WAR

The adventurist nature of neocon ideology, rather than its latent capitalism, produced the central reasons for the Iraq War. There were many personalities and motivations that propelled the invasion, and certainly there were some influential businesses, like Halliburton, that helped the push for war. But far more than Halliburton or Bechtel's bottom line, the war was about securing U.S. hegemony for the next century. It was but one piece of a radical plan to reshape the world—a plan that might have swiftly moved beyond Iraq had the removal of Saddam Hussein not turned into a quagmire. It *was* a war for oil, but one more concerned about the geopolitical significance of oil resources than the short-term profits of U.S. energy corporations. And it was part of a geopolitical vision that would result in imperial overstretch and, ultimately, invite financial disaster.

Filmmaker Michael Moore and others promoting the "war for profit" thesis often highlight Bush administration officials' ties with big business.

They then speculate that these connections created sinister, hidden motives for the Iraq War. But such speculation may not be necessary. In their public statements, op-eds, and strategy papers, the architects and principal apologists for the war explicitly laid out a vision that is plenty sinister by itself. Any attempt to grapple with the predicament that the United States now faces in the Middle East should begin by taking them at their word and understanding their plan for American imperial domination in the twenty-first century.

In their book, *The War over Iraq*, William Kristol and Lawrence Kaplan affirm, "The mission begins in Baghdad, but it does not end there."[31] Instead, the Iraq War is meant to be an opening salvo in a much larger effort to restructure the geopolitically sensitive Middle East. The neocons believed that with Iraq established as a democratic foothold, America could go on to overthrow a variety of hostile states, creating governments sympathetic to U.S. hegemony. Their convictions were echoed by the U.S. military officials that reporter Laurie Garrett heard in Davos in 2003. Recall that these officials argued, in Garrett's words, "We need to attack Iraq not to punish it for what it might have, but preemptively, as part of a global war. Iraq is just one piece of a campaign that will last years, taking out states, cleansing the planet."[32]

In their militaristic vision for reshaping the Middle East, the neocons have consistently aligned themselves with extreme elements of Israel's right-wing Likud party. To the dismay of a substantial portion of the Israeli population, Likudniks and neocons alike have unflinchingly advocated the most hard-line, hawkish positions on the Arab-Israeli conflict and have favored "regime change" in a wide range of nearby countries.

The list of countries slated to fall varies in different neocon documents, but Syria, Iran, Lebanon, and Saudi Arabia are commonly mentioned, along with the African countries of Egypt, Libya, Sudan, Somalia, and Yemen. One after another, each of these nations would succumb to U.S. force or the threat of force. With America on the march, the entire region would have reason to compromise with Washington and purge radical Islamist elements. As Michael Ledeen, a former Reagan administration consultant and current American Enterprise Institute scholar, forthrightly explained to journalist Robert Dreyfuss, the effort "may turn out to be a war to remake the world."[33]

One of most controversial aspects of this plan is the suggestion that the U.S. restructuring of the Middle East should include regime change in Saudi Arabia, a country that is ostensibly a vital American ally in the region. In the neocon vision, establishing a pro-U.S. regime in Iraq would allow the United States to shift its military bases there and begin cutting ties with the Saudis. Writing in the *National Review*, conservative pundit Jonah Goldberg explained: "The Saudis dread the idea of our toppling Saddam, even though Saddam wanted to invade Saudi Arabia. Why? Because the notion that authoritarian regimes can be changed terrifies these overfed and fanatical monarchs. The Saudis have been financing and exporting precisely the sort of extremist ideology which created Osama bin Laden and his cadres, including in this country. So if the Saudis were to tumble in the years to come, I would not weep."[34]

Goldberg's phrasing is mild compared with that of his peers. The barrage of threats directed toward Saudi Arabia from the neocons became a diplomatic embarrassment to the Bush administration. The White House scrambled to distance itself from one notably impolitic statement in June of 2002, when the *Washington Post* leaked a briefing distributed to the Defense Policy Board, an influential advisory body for the Department of Defense. The briefing dubbed Saudi Arabia "the kernel of evil" and, as the British *Daily Telegraph* reported, "predicted that the overthrow of Saddam Hussein, and the installation of a friendly regime in Iraq, would end U.S. dependence on Saudi oil, and would allow America finally to confront Saudi support for extremist Islam."[35] Even as the White House scrambled to contain the damage, an anonymous administration official supported the briefing's views. "The road to the entire Middle East," he told the *Washington Post*, "goes through Baghdad."[36]

THE LEDEEN DOCTRINE

With such a large list of targets, it did not necessarily matter to the imperial globalists where the United States began. Asserting U.S. dominance itself was the key first objective. Jonah Goldberg calls this idea the Ledeen Doctrine. The principle is named after a neocon godfather with a particularly unsavory past. Michael Ledeen is the resident scholar in the Freedom Chair at the American Enterprise Institute and a past consultant to the Pentagon, State Department, and White House under Ronald Reagan. Working with National Security Advisor Robert McFarland in the 1980s, Ledeen became an important figure in the Iran-Contra scandal, helping to establish links between Israeli officials and Iranian arms dealer Manucher Ghorbanifar.[37] Ledeen has consistently been one of the most hawkish voices in the conservative foreign policy establishment. He is longtime advocate of regime change in both Iraq and Iran, as well as a prominent admirer of Machiavelli. In 1999, Ledeen penned a book titled *Machiavelli on Modern Leadership*, where he contended that war "provides a real test of character" and "creates a pool of leaders for the nation." Peace, on the other hand, "increases our peril, by making discipline less urgent" and "encouraging some of our worst instincts."[38]

As Jonah Goldberg explained, the Ledeen Doctrine essentially means that "every ten years or so, the United States needs to pick up some small crappy little country and throw it against the wall, just to show the world we mean business." For Goldberg, this behavior makes perfect sense. "There are plenty of excellent geostrategic, legal, and political arguments in favor of regime change in Iraq," he wrote in 2002. For example, the British understood that the second-largest oil producer in the region needed to be, if not a client state, then at least allied with the West." But, in the end, none of these justifications were really necessary. The neocons believed that the Ledeen Doctrine alone was sufficient: "The United States needs to go to war with Iraq because it needs to go to war with someone in the region and Iraq makes the most sense."[39]

A year after the invasion of Iraq, in the midst of the public debate about Iraq's missing weapons of mass destruction, apologists for the war could be found nakedly explaining that the real issue at stake was not security but U.S. power. "WMD was never the basic reason for war. Nor was it the horrid repression in Iraq. Or the danger Saddam posed to his neighbors," wrote Daniel Pipes, a conservative columnist for the *New York Post*. These statements might have come as a surprise to the American people, who were called upon to invest confidence in each of these ideas. But having ruled out such leading justifications, Pipes went on to explain, "The campaign in Iraq is about keeping promises to the United States or paying the consequences."

His point was that since Saddam Hussein had played cat-and-mouse with weapons inspectors for years, the United States had a right to take him out. Regardless of whether Hussein actually had an arsenal, his defiance alone set a precedent that was incompatible with the neoconservative aim of projecting U.S. dominance. "Keep your promises or you are gone. It's a powerful precedent that U.S. leaders should make the most of," Pipes wrote.[40]

Interestingly, the *New York Times* columnist Thomas Friedman, although far more moderate than the neocons, offered a liberal-interventionist corollary to their line of thinking. In the summer of 2003, a few months after the invasion of Iraq, he, too, argued that the "real reason" for the war was America's need to send a message to "the Arab-Muslim world."

"Smashing Saudi Arabia or Syria would have been fine," Friedman wrote. "But we hit Saddam for one simple reason: *because we could*, and because he deserved it and because he was right at the heart of that world." Friedman admitted that this rationale contradicted the "stated reason" for the attack: "I argued before the war," he wrote, "that Saddam posed no [immediate] threat to America, and had no links with Al Qaeda, and that we couldn't take the nation to war 'on the wings of a lie.'"[41] Of course, the Bush administration did just that, with Friedman's support. It is doubtful that the war could ever have been sold to the public if the administration had been more honest, followed Friedman's advice, and proposed launching a war "because we could."

A WAR FOR OIL?

A final factor that must be counted among the real reasons for the war is oil. Petroleum resources undoubtedly play a critical role in America's interest in Iraq. According to the U.S Department of Energy, the country holds 115 billion barrels of proven oil reserves, with as many as 100 billion yet to be discovered.[42] At a June 2003 summit in Singapore, when then Deputy Secretary of Defense Paul Wolfowitz was asked why America had not responded to North Korea's potential threat in the same way as Saddam Hussein's, he candidly replied: "Let's look at it simply. The most important difference between North Korea and Iraq is that economically, we had no choice in Iraq. The country swims on a sea of oil."[43]

Yet while oil cannot be overlooked as a motivation for the war, this factor, too, must be put in context. The invasion of Iraq was indeed a war for oil, but not for the short-term profits of energy corporations. Rather, the control of oil is a piece of a larger geopolitical strategy that progressives often overlook. While activists rightly demand "no blood for oil," they commonly focus too narrowly on Iraq's oil fields as corporate plunder rather than a source of imperial power and thus miss the wider agenda of U.S. dominance.

A strategy that views Middle Eastern oil as a tool for controlling international relations is both consistent with the thinking perpetuated in outlets like the *Weekly Standard* and reflected in official policy. In the imperial globalists' vision, having some of the world's largest oil producers within a U.S. sphere of influence is a key to sustaining America's "benevolent hegemony." Control of Persian Gulf oil allows America to check potential adversaries.

As journalist and long-time national security analyst Robert Dreyfuss concluded:

> While the [energy] companies hope to cash in on an American-controlled Iraq, the push to remove Saddam Hussein hasn't been driven by oil executives, many of whom are worried about the consequences of war. Nor are Vice President Cheney and President Bush, both former oilmen, looking at the Gulf simply for the profits that can be earned there. The administration is thinking bigger, much bigger, than that.[44]

Political analyst Michael Klare, author of *Blood and Oil: The Dangers and Consequences of America's Growing Dependency on Imported Petroleum*, concurred: "Controlling Iraq is about oil as power, rather than oil as fuel. . . . [C]ontrol over the Persian Gulf translates into control over Europe, Japan, and China. It's having our hand on the spigot."[45]

An examination of U.S. policy in the Middle East over the past thirty years supports these conclusions. America's strategic designs began to form in the aftermath of the 1973 oil crisis, which laid bare the perils of U.S. dependence on Saudi Arabia and other potentially unfriendly states. In his 1980 State of the Union address, President Jimmy Carter famously declared that the Gulf would be regarded as within America's sphere of influence. If necessary, the United States would ward off geopolitical rivals with hard power: "Let our position be absolutely clear," he said. "An attempt by any outside force to gain control of the Persian Gulf region will be regarded as an assault on the vital interests of the United States of America, and such an assault will be repelled by any means necessary, including military force."[46]

In the 1970s, the United States had a minimal military presence in the Middle East. Since then, however, the country has established several military bases in the region and stepped up naval operations in the Persian Gulf in an attempt to control access to critical resources. This trend accelerated in the wake of the first Gulf War, which helped the United States to cement a presence in a number of Middle Eastern countries, including Saudi Arabia. (Indeed, the siting of bases in Saudi Arabia was a significant grievance fueling Osama bin Laden's war against America.)[47] After 9/11, White House militarists believed that ousting Saddam Hussein and installing a friendly Iraqi regime would solidify control and ensure U.S. hegemony in the region.

America's primary interest in Persian Gulf oil is not based on a pressing need for fuel. Although Middle East oil is undoubtedly important in the long term, the United States currently relies more on imports from Canada, Mexico, Venezuela, and Nigeria for its domestic oil supply. However, for rival powers, access to Gulf oil is critically important, making control over it a trump card at the foreign policy table. Power over oil has been a constant geopolitical concern across diverse administrations, even under the more multilaterally oriented Clinton administration. However, the primacy of this strategic objective has become much more pronounced under imperial globalization.

Elusive Profits

It is important to keep the overall argument about the nonmarket aspects of neocon thinking in perspective. To highlight their military focus and reservations about corporate thinking is not to suggest that the imperial globalists are not capitalists. They certainly are, and their vision of long-term U.S. dominance ultimately aims to bolster American business interests. But they nevertheless have a set of perspectives and priorities that is very different from that of the typical Wall Street broker. In the short term, they are willing to accept a level of instability and risk that would make most CEOs shiver. In the view of the neocons, businesses are inherently short-sighted, and it would be folly to let corporate preoccupations with quarterly earnings statements override the imperatives of national security and geopolitical power. As a result, their outlook on creating and defending a global "free market" diverges markedly from that of the majority of business executives—especially those working outside the market sectors that are most closely linked with national policy, such as arms and oil.

An interesting and little-noted fact is that even U.S. oil companies were ambivalent about the invasion of Iraq. Reuel Marc Gerecht, former CIA officer and prominent neocon thinker, noted with disdain that both energy executives and foreign policy realists, lacking proper moral fervor, were long happy to be doing business with Saddam Hussein. In the late 1980s, Gerecht reported, "American oilmen were clogging every first-class Baghdad hotel, eager to show how they'd tap Iraq's immense, undeveloped energy resources. American 'realists' were thus certain they'd found an Arab strongman with whom they could deal."[48]

In advance of the 2003 invasion of Iraq, oil executives feared that war would destabilize the region and fuel anti-Americanism, making it difficult for them to do business in Arab states. Of course, they also saw the possibilities for big profits if they could gain access to Iraqi oil. "It's greed versus fear," David Long, a diplomat who served in Saudi Arabia in the 1980s, told reporter Robert Dreyfuss. Georgetown University professor and energy industry consultant Ibrahim Oweiss concurred: "I know that the oil companies are scared about the outcome of this. They are not at all sure this is in the best interests of the oil industry."[49]

With a new Iraqi oil law still pending before the Iraqi Parliament as of late 2007, it remains to be seen whether U.S. oil companies will secure lucrative "production sharing agreements" that would effectively mark the privatization of Iraq's formerly public oil industry. But even if they do succeed, they face the burden of doing business in a country spiraling into an ever-deeper civil war and protecting a sprawling network of pipelines and refineries from sabotage. Their greed might yet be stymied, and their fear proven justified.

The oil companies are not alone in finding profits to be more elusive than anticipated. The fiasco in Iraq has limited the profiteering ventures of even those companies that embraced the war and sought to benefit from it. Both advocates of the "war for profit" thesis and its critics can agree on one thing: To the extent that the Bush administration's plans were pro-business, they were largely thwarted when the neocons' fantasy that Iraq would be a quick and relatively simple step on the road to a wider regional transformation met with the unanticipated reality of sectarian war in Iraq.

Naomi Klein insightfully explained:

> The great historical irony of the catastrophe unfolding in Iraq is that the shock-therapy reforms that were supposed to create an economic boom that would rebuild the country have instead fueled a resistance that ultimately made reconstruction impossible. . . . These forces have transformed Year Zero in Iraq into the mirror opposite of what the neocons envisioned: not a corporate utopia but a ghoulish dystopia, where going to a simple business meeting can get you lynched, burned alive, or beheaded.[50]

The experience of the San Francisco–based Bechtel Corporation, one of the largest engineering companies in the United States, is illustrative. In late 2006, the company announced that it was leaving Iraq after a three-year stay during which it was awarded more than $2 billion in cost-plus contracts by the U.S. government. It might appear that Bechtel bailed out after having made a hefty profit, abandoning its obligation to repair the country. But while the company deserves criticism for its profiteering, it should also be noted that the Iraq War proved not to be the source of easy money it initially appeared to be. Fifty-two Bechtel employees were killed in war-torn Iraq, and another forty-nine were wounded. Amid the chaos, hundreds of millions of dollars from Bechtel's contracts were shifted by U.S. government officials away from reconstruction and toward security. The income Bechtel earned in Iraq constituted only a small percentage of the gigantic earnings from its global operations (the company generated almost $52 billion in revenue between 2003 and 2005). Ultimately, it decided that the Iraq inflows were not worth the costs.[51] Describing an interview with Cliff Mumm, president of infrastructure work for Bechtel, David Baker of the *San Francisco Chronicle* explained, "He once hoped the new Iraqi government would turn into a steady Bechtel client, bringing the company lucrative new contracts in a country where virtually every road, power plant and waterworks needs repair."[52] These hopes dissolved, and the war became a great disappointment for the company.

The elusiveness of Iraqi profits is only one part of the dilemma that imperial globalization has helped to create. As we will see, not only do defenders of corporate globalization face an international rebellion against the failures of economic neoliberalism, they must also reckon with an overextended U.S. empire teetering on the edge of bankruptcy.

3

THE NEW TERRAIN OF
GLOBALIZATION DEBATE

During the Bush years, the context for arguments about globalization shifted in significant ways. Pursuing an aggressive vision for reshaping the world, the neoconservatives produced a war that has inflamed resentment and damaged U.S. credibility across the globe. In the next decade, members of a new administration, CEOs trying to do business in the international marketplace, and citizens promoting a more democratic global order will have to contend with this bitter legacy. But the Bush administration's recklessness is not the only source of tension in the international system. The shift from corporate globalization to imperial globalization coincides with several other major geopolitical changes as well. Together, these are creating a setting for the global justice debate that is very different from the one that existed in the wake of the Seattle protests at the end of the Clinton years.

No one person has done more to illuminate the overlapping crises currently facing the global system than a soft-spoken professor from the Philippines. After a long career of taking fearless stands for social justice, Walden Bello continues to offer invaluable insights into the challenges facing grassroots movements. Indeed, his personal history has helped him to grasp the deep connections between militarism and economic policy, as well as the power of democratic resistance. Bello was born in Manila in 1945, and his political sensibilities started forming early in his life. He was educated in Jesuit-run schools that generally served the children of the country's wealthy. Aware of the vast divide that separated his elite classmates from the majority of Filipinos, Bello developed a hatred for the class divisions he saw being reproduced at his school. He carried this consciousness with him through his university life. In the late 1960s he migrated to the United States, studied for his doctorate in sociology at Princeton, and became active in organizing protests against the Vietnam War. As mass protests helped to force an end to that war, chaos erupted in his home country. When Ferdinand Marcos took power in 1972 and declared martial law, Bello immersed himself in working with Filipino exile communities opposed to the dictatorship.

Bello's passport was revoked by the Marcos regime due to his activism, and he was forced to endure a long exile. Based in the United States in the 1970s and 1980s, Bello was a leader in organizations such as the Anti-Martial Law Coalition and the Philippines Human Rights Lobby. In 1978, he helped organize a nonviolent occupation of the Philippine consulate in San Francisco, and after his arrest, he undertook a weeklong hunger strike in jail to draw attention to the repression of democracy in his native land.

Bello's work for democracy in the Philippines led to him to make connections between the international financial institutions and human rights abuses abroad. "It was when we were researching the question of U.S. bilateral aid to Marcos that we realized how much of it was being channeled through the World Bank," Bello explained. "The role of multilateral institutions—and the Bank in particular—in the Philippines dwarfed direct American support. That's where my own interest began."[1] Well over a decade before mass protests against corporate globalization erupted in places like Seattle, Genoa, and Quebec City, at a time when few Northern progressives had little, if any, awareness of the IMF or World Bank, Bello was highlighting the nefarious roles of these bodies in international affairs.

Defying the stereotype of evolution from 1960s youthful idealism to midlife conservatism, Bello has maintained a determined anti-imperial commitment to building social movements for genuine democracy. After the fall of Marcos in 1986, he returned to the Philippines, settling in his home country for the first time in nearly twenty years. He now serves as the founding director of Focus On the Global South, a highly regarded progressive think tank based in Bangkok, Thailand. In 2003, he was selected for the Right Livelihood Award, an honor commonly referred to as the "Alternative Nobel Prize," for his contributions to global justice. To some, he may seemed like an odd model for a firebrand activist—he is neat, quiet, and professorial. But he advances his theories with an intellectual boom. You wouldn't know it by looking at him, but Bello is one of the global South's most outspoken crusaders, and one of the leading observers of the changing terrain of globalization debate.

Overlapping Crises

Part of Bello's genius is his understanding of how several distinct but interconnected crises are remaking the politics of the global economy. Each of these areas of concern is a significant and complicated issue that could fill a book of its own. But any such account would necessarily miss the wider panorama. Bello contributes an integrated perspective that a micro-analysis of any given issue could never provide. Few theorists have done more to sketch an overarching picture of how different geopolitical pressures are combining to create unique possibilities for global justice advocates. Although I contend that Bello and other theorists of American decline are sometimes overly pessimistic about the United States' prospects to maintain economic power in the coming decades, they nevertheless provide an important account of the consequences of past economic strategies.

Three crises, in particular, are affecting how corporate CEOs, government leaders, and social movement activists will approach international politics in the coming years. Bello labels these the "crisis of legitimacy," the "crisis of overproduction," and the "crisis of overextension."[2] These crises do not constitute the whole of the geopolitical picture; the influence of religious fundamentalism, for example, is a major topic that falls largely outside the purview of this analysis. Nevertheless, these three crises have serious implications for the global economy.

The first crisis—the crisis of legitimacy—pertains to the ideologies that guide the governing of the world. For our purposes, I will focus on neoliberalism, which has served as the dominant economic program over the past twenty years. Neoliberalism has defined the policies that the IMF and World Bank have attempted to impose on countries throughout the world, and—especially under the Clintonian model of corporate globalization—it has been an important part of U.S. foreign policy. In recent times, however, this dogma has come under fire. Several factors have combined to pose a serious challenge to neoliberalism's legitimacy. For those of us who oppose both empire and corporate rule, this is a good thing. With neoliberalism being displaced as a central force in international economics, there is now space for new ideas to come to the fore. However, there is no guarantee that a more just and democratic economic order will emerge as the old order fades. Uncertainty presents challenges as well as possibilities for change.

This is even truer with regard to the second area of concern: the crisis of overproduction. The U.S. economy is facing long-term difficulties that may hamper the country's ability to remain an unrivaled economic superpower. For several years, critics from both the left and the right have expressed concern over the most visible manifestation of U.S. economic problems: the overvalued dollar. In recent years there has been a steady stream of news stories about the dollar's coming decline and the economic pain it would produce. Although there are differing theories on the root causes of U.S. economic woes, Bello and other leftist analysts contend that America is competing in a global economy where there is ever more capacity to produce goods but not enough demand to go around. Whatever the root cause of America's economic challenges, the falling value of the U.S. dollar concerns everyone. A serious downturn in the U.S. economy would have significant consequences for the future global order.

The third crisis is the crisis of overextension. Today, it is not uncommon to see the title of historian Edward Gibbon's famous work being paraphrased as "The Decline and Fall of the American Empire."[3] Like Rome, the United States has its military forces scattered far and wide, and it is paying a steep price for its imperial deployment. As we will see, many observers have predicted that despite the country's vast wealth, America's military ambitions may have outstripped its available resources. Although that contention is debatable, it is beyond doubt that the imperial globalists of the Bush administration have greatly worsened overextension by immersing U.S. forces in the quagmires of Iraq and Afghanistan. By squandering the sympathy of America's allies and damaging its credibility among rivals, the White House has made its reliance on hard power ever less tenable. Maintaining a global military deployment is far more expensive when allies are unwilling to help bear the costs and when one's forces are regularly subject to guerrilla assaults. While the U.S. military has enough firepower to destroy the world many times over, and while it may be bankrupting itself by continually augmenting its arsenal, it has been unable to exercise control even in limited, regional conflicts. The world has taken notice.

Together, these three crises have created a critical moment in the politics of the global economy. Some analysts have gone so far as to argue that they will soon bring an end to American hegemony. I do not believe that this is the case. Those who predict a sharp decline in U.S. power in the near future, I believe, tend to underestimate the adaptability and resilience of American capitalism. I also disagree with observers who have suggested that a shift toward increased militarism in the Bush administration was motivated by these crises—that the imperial approach is a result of these problems as much as a cause of them. I believe that view is also too deterministic in its assessment of how structural issues have influenced U.S. policy. It underappreciates the way in which that invasion of Iraq was indeed a war of choice, and it is too quick to overlook the nonmarket aspects of neoconservative thinking.

However, if these overlapping crises did not cause the shift to imperial globalization, they will certainly constrain the next administration's ability to easily switch back to a corporate-led vision. And these changes will also determine what space is open for alternatives. For those who want the fast-changing international order to move in a more just and democratic direction, understanding the tensions in the current system is a vital first step.

Neoliberalism on the Rocks

Supporters of corporate globalization have long contended that the march toward deregulation, privatization, and increased market access is inevitable and irreversible. Today, that assumption is under assault. As it becomes ever more clear that neoliberal policies create economies that are unstable, slow-growing, and rife with socioeconomic inequality, governments in the developing world are increasingly rejecting Washington Consensus advice. Trade and international commerce are not going away. But the ground rules for managing them can and will change. Neoliberal ideology, which seemed like an unstoppable juggernaut when global protests erupted only a short time ago, is now facing a crisis of legitimacy.

Neoliberal policies are still in place throughout much of the world, and they are only starting to be replaced. But the justifications for these policies have eroded. A number of forces have combined to dethrone neoliberal economic thinking. The first is the ideology's long-term failure to serve the majority of people in the places it has been implemented. Recall that per-capita income in the countries where the IMF and World Bank held the most sway barely increased in the neoliberal years of the 1980s and '90s. As economist Mark Weisbrot pointed out, "Over the last 25 years, Latin America," a region where the Washington Consensus was perhaps most influential, "has had its worst long-term economic growth performance in more than a century."[4] In contrast, the success stories of the developing world—countries like China and the "Asian Tiger" economies—did best when they defied IMF mandates: They protected infant industries, maintained capital controls, and were very careful about the way they opened their economies to greater trade. Now that neoliberalism has a track record more than two decades long, faith-based proclamations that "trickle-down" economics will benefit everyone are losing credibility in the face of steadily mounting evidence to the contrary.

Beyond the disastrous long-term performance of the IMF and its neoliberal ideology, the institution's role in precipitating and exacerbating acute financial crises has helped to undermine the Washington Consensus. Argentina, which had been considered a model pupil of the IMF, experienced a painful economic meltdown in 2001. But that fate was not limited to one Latin American country. Several previous financial collapses had already served as damning indictments of IMF policy—none more prominently than the Asian financial crisis that began in 1997.

The IMF's mandates had a hand both in causing the Asian crisis and in aggravating it once it was underway. One policy at the root of the crisis was the elimination of controls on capital flows. These regulations limit the amount of local currency that can be exchanged or require investors to keep their money in a country for a minimum amount of time once they choose to invest. Such controls quell turbulent capital markets and give countries time to respond to sudden changes in the international climate. Although there was little economic evidence showing the benefits of liberalizing capital markets, the IMF pushed countries to open their markets to foreign investment and to remove measures that would restrict how and when investors could transfer their money. A liberalized capital market encourages speculation, something Wall Street firms were eager to engage in.

Speculation is different than traditional capital investment. It does little to build infrastructure, develop the workforce, or generate productive economic activity. Rather, it is a short-term form of economic gambling. It aims at generating quick profits, and it is made possible by computers that can shift billions of dollars at the push of a button. One form of speculation is currency trading, in which money managers make bets on whether a given country's currency will rise or fall relative to the value of other currencies. In one notorious instance, investor George Soros bet $10 billion in September 1992 that the British pound would decline in value. He was right. In a single night he made $1 billion in profit and earned the nickname "The Man Who Broke the Bank of England."[5] Although the social benefit of such economic activity is highly questionable, it has made a few individuals extraordinarily rich.

According to the IMF, removing controls on speculative capital would increase developing countries' access to funds and help to spur development. Leaders of many Asian countries didn't buy it. Along with critics of the Washington Consensus, they worried that speculation could produce instability. But after many years of resisting IMF demands, most countries relented. This proved to be a fateful mistake.

In the 1990s, short-term capital rushed into Thailand when it looked like easy profits could be made on speculative real estate investments. But it rushed out just as quickly in the summer of 1997, when there were rumors of economic trouble. In a matter of months, the Thai currency lost over half of its value. Panicked fund managers began to pull their money out of the whole area, provoking a regionwide crisis. Without capital controls, governments in affected countries had few tools available to them to stop the run on the bank. Thailand's woes swiftly spread to Malaysia, Indonesia, and South Korea. Eventually the crisis would rattle much of the world economy.

Amid the panic, the IMF responded to the Asian countries' cries for help with its standard packages of short-term loan dispatches, made on the condition that recipients implement neoliberal austerity policies. These policies were ostensibly designed to control inflation and resurrect business confidence. But they had the opposite effect. Limiting the supply of money caused more local businesses and banks to fail—and caused food riots in places like Indonesia—heightening the sense of meltdown. The idea of combating recession with budget cuts recalled Herbert Hoover's economic thinking, and it never would have flown in the United States. But in Asia, the IMF callously argued that the pain of social unrest was part of the bitter medicine that the countries would have to swallow.

Sometimes a picture says it all. One of the most famous images from the crisis was a photo of IMF Managing Director Michel Camdessus standing over the president of Indonesia, watching him sign a letter agreeing to the Fund's harsh bailout package. Camdessus, with his dark suit buttoned and his arms folded across his chest, towers above the cowed and humiliated Third World leader. For people throughout the global South, all too familiar with the indignities of colonialism, the im-

© Agus Lolong/AFP/Getty Images

age became an emblem of their continued subjugation within the global order.[6]

In the end, the social impact of the crisis was horrific. Over the course of the meltdown, a million people in Thailand and some 22 million in Indonesia were thrown into poverty, doubling the country's poverty rate.[7] By August 1998, 15 percent of those who had been working in Indonesia the previous year had lost their jobs.[8] Money from the IMF bailout did not go to assist these people but rather went to pay off foreign lenders—many of them the same speculators whose reckless gambling helped to provoke the crisis in the first place.

Neoliberalism came under fire not only from critics in the developing world but from an increasing number of mainstream U.S. economists as well. Walden Bello contends that the Asian financial crisis represented a tipping point for the Washington Consensus:

A paradigm is really in crisis when its best practitioners desert it, as Thomas Kuhn pointed out in his classic *The Structure of Scientific Revolutions*, and something akin to what happened during the crisis of the Copernican paradigm in physics occurred in neoclassical economics shortly after the Asian financial crisis, with key intellectuals leaving the fold—among them Jeffrey Sachs, noted earlier for his advocacy of "free market" shock treatment in Eastern Europe in the early 1990s; Joseph Stiglitz, former chief economist of the World Bank; Columbia Professor Jagdish Bhagwati, who called for global controls on capital flows; and financier George Soros, who condemned the lack of controls in the global financial system that had enriched him.[9]

Backlash from Below

The Asian financial crisis hit in 1997, and for well over a year its aftershocks reverberated in the global economy. Then, in 1999, just as the defenders of the Washington Consensus might have thought that the worst of their troubles were behind them, another bombshell exploded: Seattle. Beyond producing defectors in the ranks of mainstream economists, the failures of neoliberalism prompted a major public backlash. Massive protests against institutions like the WTO, IMF, and World Bank served as a last important manifestation of the assault on the ideology's credibility. And no confrontation better symbolized the wave of discontent than the dramatic showdown at the WTO's third ministerial meetings in Seattle in late November and early December of 1999.

Major protests against the international financial institutions had been taking place for years in the global South, but the international media establishment, based in the advanced industrial countries, hardly took notice. That changed when protests spread to the North, seizing the media spotlight even within the centers of economic power. In Seattle, tens of thousands of demonstrators flooded the streets as the WTO meetings were set to begin. The images of protest there have since been so often recalled and the street theater so often imitated that they now seem like clichés. Yet Seattle's juxtaposition of diverse activists—many from constituencies traditionally at odds with one another—was truly extraordinary: environmentalists dressed like sea turtles mixed with steelworkers in their union jackets, vegan youths with piercings and tattoos, and family farmers from the Midwest. Together, the parties of the broad protest coalition forcefully asserted that the WTO and the agenda of corporate globalization were undermining workers' rights, endangering the environment, and transferring democratic decision-making to unaccountable economic bodies.

In response to the colorful expressions of dissent and to the nonviolent activists who chained themselves around the convention center, police clouded the air with tear gas. The Secret Service refused to let Secretary of State Madeleine Albright leave her hotel room, and President Clinton declared a state of martial law.

While demonstrations continued in Seattle's streets, delegates inside the conference from the global South—frustrated, in the words of a statement released by the Organization of African Unity, at "being marginalized and generally excluded on issues of vital importance for our peoples and their future"—took their own stands of protest.[10] They railed against the inequities of the previous Uruguay Round of trade talks and denounced U.S. and European hypocrisy in refusing to open their agricultural markets. The demands of the developing country governments, many of which were run by conservative elites, were not the same as those of the outside protesters. These groups held opposite views, for example, on whether there should be enforceable standards for workers' rights included in trade deals. However, they did agree on some key points. Expressing his disgust for how the WTO negotiations had been conducted, Sir Shridath Ramphal, Chief Caribbean Negotiator, argued: "This should not be a game about enhancing corporate profits. This should not be a time when big countries, strong countries, the world's wealthiest countries, are setting about a process designed to enrich themselves."[11] With criticisms coming from inside and out, the WTO's plans for an ambitious new round of "free trade" agreements collapsed by the end of the week.

It was a stunning upset. The Seattle protests, along with allied demonstrations taking place throughout the world, left the previously high-flying corporate globalizers of the Clinton years scrambling to play defense.

Trade and financial ministers, who had grown accustomed to meeting in secretive sessions behind closed doors, were suddenly forced to defend their positions before the public. During the April 2000 meetings of the IMF and World Bank, Walden Bello and fellow global justice advocate

Njoki Njoroge Njehu participated in a open debate against two officials from the international financial institutions: Michael Bell, an IMF external relations spokesperson, and Michael Walton, a World Bank economist who had served as chief economist for the East Asia and Pacific region. The debate took place in a packed community center before an overflow crowd of five hundred people, with several hundred more listening over a public address system. In the face of such scrutiny, the institutions' representatives hardly offered a defense of IMF and World Bank policies. Instead they spent most of their time trying to convince the audience that they, too, cared about poverty. Coming from institutions that in past years had zealously trumpeted the importance of structural adjustment in promoting business stability and creating growth in developing countries, this was a remarkable change in tone. But perhaps even more remarkable was that the debate was even happening. Bello and Njehu, two critics who had previously been discounted as representatives of the radical fringe, could no longer be ignored. Their views, the chiefs of the financial institutions knew, were becoming increasingly accepted even among mainstream economists previously sympathetic to the Washington Consensus.

With the curtains drawn, the wizards of neoliberalism looked considerably less intimidating, and the demonstrations that amassed to greet delegates at a series of their major meetings had lasting repercussions for the international financial institutions. The WTO, for one, has yet to recover from the backlash so vividly put on display in Seattle. Moreover, Northern protests represented only a faint echo of the upheavals in the global South. The backlash in Latin America has led to the ousting of neoliberal governments in countries large and small, producing a major political realignment on the continent.

Combined with neoliberalism's long-term record of failure and its propensity to provoke crises, widespread public resistance has eroded the previous authority of the Washington Consensus. The policies of neoliberalism cannot be ruled out altogether, however. There are many people, especially within the IMF and World Bank, who would still like to preserve the core of the neoliberal model, albeit with a softer, "reformed" façade. They will take advantage of the fact that the core policies of this model, while coming under increasing attack, remain in place throughout much of the world. Nevertheless, it is clear that the ideology of neoliberalism will never again reign with the sort of unquestioned hegemony it enjoyed in the 1980s and 1990s.

STRAINS ON THE SUPERPOWER ECONOMY

With neoliberalism's fall from dominance, an exciting space has opened for ideas on how to restructure the global economy to value people before profit. But the decline of neoliberalism is not happening in isolation. It is only one of the major developments that will affect both the debate among elites about how to rule the world and the efforts of social movements to create a more democratic international order. To appreciate its full implications, the fall of neoliberalism must be considered alongside the U.S. problems of an overvalued currency and an overextended military.

A second area of crisis has consequences that are less clear than neoliberalism's decline. This area involves challenges to the strength of the U.S. economy, which most visibly take the form of an overreliance on the financial sector and an overvalued dollar. Economists from a wide variety of political backgrounds have expressed concern with these trends, although they disagree about the fundamental causes. Ultimately, many analysts argue that long-term economic difficulties will threaten America's standing as an unrivaled superpower. These challenges are likely to foster a multipolar geopolitical order, one in which several regional blocs compete for power. For those struggling to create a more democratic world, these changes do not guarantee progress. But all those seeking to influence the international system in coming years will certainly be affected by them.

One explanation of U.S. economic woes that is worth exploring—a theory advanced by Bello and by progressive economists like Robert Brenner—sees the root of these troubles in a "crisis of overproduction."[12] After the Second World War, the American economy revved into high gear, creating a plethora of new industrial and consumer goods. At the same time, the United States sent aid to rebuild the economies of Europe and Japan. With time, those countries began to produce significant exports, reemerging as economic rivals. By the 1980s, "Asian Tiger" economies such as South Korea and Taiwan also became global players by actively competing for larger shares of export markets.

But while the global ability to produce was increasing, demand became stagnant. Real wages of working people in the United States failed to rise between the early 1970s and late 1990s, limiting consumption. Meanwhile, neoliberal policies in the developing world failed to lift people out of poverty, curtailing the creation of new consumers.

Excess industrial capacity made it harder to make money. As more and more goods were produced, prices declined. Exporting economies had to compete ever more assertively for a limited supply of consumers. As a result, profits fell. Overall worldwide GDP growth followed. Tracking what he calls "the long downturn," economist Robert Brenner has shown that net profit rates for manufacturing in the G7 advanced industrial countries dropped from about 24 percent in the period between 1950 and 1970 to under 15 percent between 1970 and 1993. Net profit rates for private business as a whole fell by more than 25 percent during the same period.[13] Likewise, annual GDP growth in the G7 countries fell from 5.1 percent in the 1960s, to 3.6 percent in the 1970s, to around 3 percent in the 1980s and '90s.[14]

Across almost every industry, more products have been produced than firms can sell. Bello has noted that automakers in the 1990s produced some 70 million cars every year but could sell only 53 million.[15] The *Economist* has reported that "the world is awash with excess capacity in computer chips, steel, cars, textiles, and chemicals." The magazine concluded, "The global glut is pushing prices relentlessly lower." Indeed, it has created a disconnect between capacity and sales reminiscent of the 1930s.[16] Theorists of overproduction hold that this intensifies cutthroat competition between nations. Additionally, it helps to increase the importance of speculative finance: As traditional sectors like steel, electronics, and autos became less profitable, investors began to look elsewhere for returns. Often they have bet on short-term investments in the developing world and in high-tech industries.

Whatever its cause, the rise of speculation as a leading force in the world economy is a truly disconcerting trend. We have already seen the role of speculative investing in provoking economic crises. Aided by advanced computer technology and by IMF-driven deregulation of financial sectors, trillions of dollars a day now race around the world in cross-border financial transactions, many for wagers that do little to stimulate productive economic activity.

As other parts of the American economy have struggled to function profitably, the United States grows ever more dependent on its financial sector. The dangers of this trend have long been recognized. Economist Robert Pollin cited the warning of John Maynard Keynes in his landmark 1936 book, *The General Theory*: "Speculators may do no harm as bubbles on a steady stream of enterprise," Keynes wrote. "But the position is serious when enterprise becomes the bubble on a whirlpool of speculation. When the capital development of a country becomes a by-product of the activities of a casino, the job is likely to be ill-done."[17]

This is precisely the dilemma we face today. Finance capital is supposed to be secondary to the core economic activities of production and consumption. But increasingly, financial gambling is taking a primary role in steering the global economy. And as finance becomes more and more dominant, speculation leads to panics like those that crippled East Asia. It produces distortions such as the fevered dot-com bubble that burst in 2001, driving the U.S. economy into recession, as well as the housing bubble that began to have a strongly negative impact on the economy in 2007. Moreover, it creates an atmosphere conducive to fraudulent enterprises like Enron, which became a huge multinational power based on virtual profits that were made up of hype, wishful thinking, and cooked books rather than actual economic production.

THE FALL OF THE DOLLAR

As the world's largest economy and dominant leader, America may yet succeed in maintaining its prime economic standing over the next several decades, even if the global system falls on hard times. But it won't be easy. According to Brenner, the prospects for the United States breaking from its long-term decline look grim. "Neither the transcendence of the long downturn, nor indeed the avoidance of deepening stagnation or worse, can be expected in the foreseeable future," he wrote.[18] Put simply, the stock market bubble that helped to temporarily reverse U.S. economic woes in the second half of the 1990s was clearly unsustainable. Absent the sort of stimulus provided by that frenzy, competition among the major industrial powers will tend to intensify. It is dog-eat-dog in the global economy today. And burdened by the "enormous financial imbalances that have been left over from the bubble," there is reason to doubt that the United States can emerge unscathed.[19]

Of these financial imbalances, two of the most pressing are trade deficits and the dramatically overvalued dollar. In 2006, the U.S. trade deficit rose to $765.3 billion, setting a record for the fifth consecutive year. Americans are buying far more from the rest of the world than other countries are buying from the United States. The imbalance with China was particularly severe, reaching an unprecedented high of $232.5 billion.[20] For every dollar in goods and services that Chinese consumers bought from U.S. manufacturers, Americans bought almost six dollars worth of imports from China. While economists endlessly debate the ramifications of this imbalance, it's not hard to see how it can create problems. Chinese exporters are opening new factories and expanding operations with the money pouring in from U.S. consumers. Factories in the United States, in contrast, are closing their gates.

In the broad picture, the United States is living beyond its means. The government is relying on foreign investors to pay for its excessive military spending. And on the consumer level, families are going into credit card debt and are borrowing against the value of their homes to keep spending.

Normally, a country would not be able to maintain this situation. The IMF would rail against wanton economic mismanagement and warn creditors not to invest in that country unless the government promised sweeping reforms. Even without the institution's influence, textbook economics holds that upon seeing such signs of economic weakness, investors would shy away from the country, its currency would fall, consumers would no longer be able to afford as many foreign goods, and the economy would undergo a necessary, if painful, "correction."

What makes the United States different? As the world's political superpower and largest economy, America's dollars serve as the reserve currency for the rest of the world. Foreign countries keep their money in dollars because they believe they are more dependable than any alternative. As long as other nations are willing to keep pouring money into the dollar, the currency will remain strong, imports will remain relatively cheap, and the United States can finance ever-larger deficits. The dollar has been sinking in the Bush years and fell sharply in 2007, but most economists believe that it is still significantly overvalued and could fall further. Foreign governments are paying much more to invest in dollars than market logic would warrant; other currencies, such as the euro, would seem to be a safer bet, based on the relative strength of European economies.

The reason foreign nations are willing to keep buying dollars is that they have based their own economic strategies on the strength of the U.S. currency. So far, foreign creditors—especially the central banks of China and Japan—have propped up the dollar because it helps them to keep their exports strong and to boost their economies. After all, if the dollar is worth more, Americans can buy more Chinese and Japanese goods. Consistent with this economic strategy, these two countries each have reserves of U.S. treasury bills worth nearly a trillion dollars. Whether a Democratic administration would have managed this situation any better than the Bush administration is not clear. But liberals are finding solace in a certain irony. As Michael Steinberger of the *American Prospect* pointed out, "An administration determined never to surrender an inch of American sovereignty has now, through its fiscal recklessness, created a situation in which several Asian central banks control the fate of the dollar and, to a large extent, the U.S. economy."[21]

RISING RIVALS

The failure of the White House to combat these trends produced a series of blunt economic assessments from corporate globalists, who like to blame U.S. woes on Bush administration incompetence. "There's nobody home on economic policy in America right now," Stephen Roach, chief economist at Morgan Stanley, told an audience in Davos in 2005. "The twin burdens of household and public debt in the United States are unsustainable. This is an insane way to run the world economy. You know that, we know that, but the Federal Reserve is in denial."[22]

Yet while Democrats and corporate globalists from Wall Street like to put the sole blame for outsized trade deficits and dollar imbalances on the Bush administration, the White House's decision to maintain the high dollar in the early years of the millennium was a continuation of Clinton-era policy. In recent years, especially in 2007, the value of the dollar has started to decline relative to the euro, and Washington has tried to pressure China to stop keeping its currency artificially low. But so far, it has had little success.

To some extent, the situation is a Catch-22. The dollar needs to fall further if the United States is to have any hopes of rejuvenating its export sector. At the same time, the dollar's decline could lead to high interest rates that choke off economic growth. Moreover, if the retreat from the currency goes too far and the dollar is displaced as the preference of the world's central bankers, it could have daunting long-term implications. If and when one of the major central banks in Asia decides that it would do better with its money in, say, euros and starts to cut its losses, it could provoke a mass exodus. The result would be a sharp contraction of the U.S. economy and a deep recession that would spread internationally. A more desirable alternative would be an intentional, managed deflation of the dollar—something that is still likely to have painful, if less cataclysmic, consequences for the U.S. economy.

Washington need only consult London about the gravity of this problem. As many historians have observed, the unraveling of the British Empire came quick on the heels of the shift away from pounds sterling as the world's dominant currency.

Since a global recession sparked by a falling dollar would hurt everybody, and since the Asian central banks stand to lose a lot of money if they have to sell their massive dollar holdings at cut-rate prices, other countries have an incentive not to start a rush for the door. Nevertheless, an increasing number of foreign banks are starting to diversify their holdings, and the U.S. predicament is giving China and the European Union geopolitical leverage. Serious rivals will not emerge overnight. But over the next twenty years, the trend of regional powers displacing the United States in power and influence among their neighbors is likely to increase. Economist Jeffrey Sachs described the economic changes that are looming on the horizon: "China will have an economy larger than the U.S. economy within 25 years—potentially 50 percent larger by 2050. India, considerably poorer on average than China, will also close the wealth gap. By 2050, India will conceivably have an economy the size of America's, with four times the population and roughly one-fourth of the average income level per person."[23]

Even U.S. government intelligence sources predict a major realignment over the next two decades. In early 2005, the National Intelligence Council released a 119-page report, "Mapping the Global Future: Report of the National Intelligence Council's 2020 Project," which was made publicly available through the CIA's Web site. As the online magazine *Slate* reported, the analysis predicted significant changes in U.S. stature by 2020: "The United States will remain 'an important shaper of the international order'—probably the single most powerful country—but its 'relative power position' will have 'eroded.' The new 'arriviste powers'— not only China and India, but also Brazil, Indonesia, and perhaps others—will accelerate this erosion by pursuing 'strategies designed to exclude or isolate the United States' in order to 'force or cajole' us into playing by their rules."[24]

All of these trends imply that a major shift in the distribution of world power is likely to occur over the next decades, with the United States having to accept a demotion from almighty hegemon. Of course, it is impossible know how changing geopolitics will shape up in reality. Still, the challenges to American dominance are sure to provide an important backdrop during the next phase of the global justice struggle, when nations, corporations, and social movements battle to determine what comes after Bush-era imperial globalization.

Stretching Empire to Its Limits

Any government in power in the United States—whether pursuing a multilateralist program for corporate globalization, nakedly pursuing American dominance, or looking to altogether redefine the country's role in the international order—would have to wrestle with issues like the fall of the dollar. In that sense, these are not dilemmas unique to the Bush administration. However, the aggressive program of imperial globalization implemented under Bush has made the U.S. predicament much worse. By neglecting economic problems, disregarding the importance of "soft" power, and overrelying on military force—miring U.S. troops in Iraq and Afghanistan in the process—Bush's policies have greatly intensified the third area of crisis that Walden Bello identified: the crisis of overextension.

Also called "overreach" and "overstretch," this problem was perhaps most famously described by historian Paul Kennedy in *The Rise and Fall of the Great Powers*, published in 1988. Although Kennedy was not well known at the time, his book received tremendous attention, sparking heated debate in Washington and beyond. Kennedy's basic argument is that throughout history dominant world powers doomed themselves by engaging in overseas adventures that drained their strength and strained their finances. He called this weakness "imperial overstretch," a term that quickly became a fixture in mainstream political discussion.

American conservatives fumed. They argued that the British-born professor was a doomsdayer who did not appreciate America's unmatched power and asserted that although the Soviet Union might suffer from the problems of empire, the United States would not. When the USSR collapsed and the American economy took off in the 1990s, they considered themselves vindicated. What the critics failed to appreciate was that Kennedy was not predicting an immediate disaster, but rather a twenty-year trend toward overextension that would come to a head by 2010. Today it appears that the historian may yet have the last word.

"U.S. Army generals would definitely say that America is overstretched," Kennedy said in a 2006 interview.[25] Indeed, there are ample signs that the same tendencies toward overreach that afflicted previous empires are damaging the United States. Worries about troop levels are a first sign. The military's top commanders have repeatedly expressed anxiety about having enough troops to meet the need created by the White House's grandiose ambitions. Right now, the United States is struggling to staff a vast military deployment that is spread across the globe and engulfed in at least one bloody conflict that seems impossible to win.

In recent years, the number of troops the United States has stationed abroad has hovered between 250,000 and 300,000.[26] This includes the roughly 140,000 troops in Iraq (as of early 2007) plus forces in Afghanistan, South Korea, and elsewhere. Indicative of the pressure these deployments put on U.S. capabilities, reserves and members of the National Guard have consistently made up over a third of the forces in Iraq. As re-enlistment rates fall, troops are being involuntarily reassigned to repeat tours of duty. Young people who might have seen the armed forces or reserves as a good source of money for college are looking elsewhere, and military recruiters have to go to extreme lengths to meet quotas for new soldiers. Yet, despite calls for withdrawal from across the political spectrum, America will likely have a substantial force in Iraq for years to come.

In an interview with the *Christian Science Monitor* in April 2007, retired four-star general Barry McCaffrey noted the decline in recruitment and flatly stated, "There is no argument of whether the U.S. Army is rapidly unraveling."[27] Similarly, military expert and retired Army officer Andrew Krepinevich concluded in a report conducted in early 2007 under a Pentagon contract that the military was at risk of breaking under the pressures of war. He warned that the Army could fall into "a catastrophic decline" should changes not be made.[28]

The pressures on troop deployment capabilities are matched by the military's financial burdens. The ever-increasing yearly budget for the Pentagon now hovers around $440 billion. As defense analyst William Hartung has noted, this far exceeds America's combined spending on education, the environment, housing, agriculture, transportation, energy, economic development, and the administration of justice.[29] Still more alarming, this huge sum does not even include funding for the wars we are actually fighting. Those are appropriated separately. In recent years, the White House has requested, and Congress allocated, some $120 billion annually for military operations in Iraq and Afghanistan. If you factor in costs for nuclear weapons facilities, plus hospital and disability expenses for veterans, U.S. military expenditures total nearly three-quarters of a trillion dollars per year.[30]

Such vast sums are necessary if the United States wants to maintain its "Baseworld." This is what author and foreign policy analyst Chalmers Johnson has dubbed the country's sprawling network of overseas encampments, rarely noticed by citizens at home but bitterly resented by much of the world. The United States officially maintains 737 bases worldwide, worth more than $127 billion and covering at least 687,347 acres in some 130 foreign countries. "Once upon a time, you could trace the spread of imperialism by counting up colonies," Johnson observed in his 2007 book, *Nemesis: The Last Days of the American Republic*. "America's version of the colony is the military base."[31] For local populations exposed to the pollution, bar fights, and brothels that surround such encampments, they are wounds that constantly fester.

The vast complex of U.S. bases breeds resentment and damages U.S. "soft" power—and to what end? Johnson explained: "The purpose of all these bases is 'force projection,' or the maintenance of American military hegemony over the rest of the world. They facilitate our 'policing' of the globe and are meant to ensure that no other nation, friendly or hostile, can ever challenge us militarily."[32] This, of course, is an ambition that will sound familiar to any student of neoconservatism. But, as the historians of empire tell us, it is not a sustainable proposition.

The Price of Dominance

Chalmers Johnson, like many analysts, has declared that the hard costs of militarism will eventually lead the United States to bankruptcy. But a focus on direct military expenses is too narrow to reveal the true price of trying to remain an unchallenged hegemon. According to economist James K. Galbraith, "The real economic cost of Bush's empire building is twofold: It diverts attention from pressing economic problems at home and it sets the United States on a long-term imperial path that is economically ruinous."[33]

For those who would like a world in which the United States no longer acts as a sole bullying superpower, there is a certain satisfaction in seeing arrogant hawks being forced to face the unsustainability of empire. But an imperiled titan can also be a very dangerous one, and economic catastrophe in the United States could create severe hardship throughout the global economy—something that does not necessarily help democratic movements. Moreover, an economic downturn in the United States would no doubt hit working people the hardest.

In their emphasis on hard power, Bush and the neocons have not only failed to address the country's mounting economic woes but exacerbated the dangers that these troubles present. Aware of the potential costs, Galbraith chaired a group of economists who opposed the invasion of Iraq from the start. He described their concerns about the war: "As far back as 2002, we understood—as the economically illiterate neo-imperialists did not—that a world system very favorable to America was on the line. And it was not, as they seemed to think, just a matter of military might. We knew that if the war undermined confidence in the power, good faith and common sense of the United States, that could lead toward disastrous changes on the financial front."[34]

A commitment to maintaining military superiority despite evident overextension will limit U.S. prospects of escaping long-term industrial decline. Yale sociology professor and theorist Immanuel Wallerstein explained the dilemma: "A superpower whose only important claim to superiority in the world arena is military must (and will) emphasize continuing investment in military hardware. From the point of view of long-term economic development," the benefits of such investments are "less than the benefits of using the same money to create more long-term productive enterprises."[35]

The fact that foreign rivals cannot hope to compete with the U.S. militarily ends up working to their advantage. This, Wallerstein argues, "embodies the oldest story in the history of hegemonic powers. The dominant power concentrates (to its detriment) on the military; the candidate for successor concentrates on the economy. The latter has always paid off, handsomely."[36] In this case, "the fact that non-military development is given a far higher priority by Western Europe and Japan" will likely provide significant dividends over the next twenty to thirty years.[37]

Ironically, as the imperial globalists place ever more stock in America's military power, they only end up demonstrating its impotence. In Iraq and Afghanistan, the United States has shown itself unable to create stability or suppress insurgency with its might. Like its failure in Vietnam, the fiasco in the Middle East has only emboldened opposition. The neocons dreamed of Iraq as a democratic ally and platform for U.S. power in the region. Instead, the country is now a symbol of the superpower's weakness. Intelligence reports consistently show that the war has increased the risk of further terrorist attacks, bolstering Islamic extremism. By any measure, this is hardly a sound plan for securing a New American Century.

Crisis and the Coming World Order

So what are the ultimate implications of the three overlapping crises that Bello has identified? Looking at the tensions straining the current international order, it is tempting to conclude that the end of American hegemony is near. Many analysts have done so. Some, like Chalmers Johnson, have voiced extreme and ominous warnings about the death of the republic.

I disagree with the theorists of decline—particularly the most alarmist ones, such as Johnson—for being too eager to declare the demise of American empire. It is worth noting that the U.S. economy also has its defenders. In a consideration of how Paul Kennedy's thesis fares today, the *Economist* argued, "The burdens of America's world role are large and expanding, but not overwhelming." The magazine noted that U.S. military spending in the Vietnam era reached 9 percent of GDP at times. During the Reagan years, it was 6 percent. Today the U.S. economy is much larger, and Defense Department appropriations in coming years will likely constitute only around 4 percent of GDP. "That spending will exceed the military budgets of the next 14 biggest defense spenders combined," the magazine's editors remarked, "but will still be readily affordable."[38]

The *Economist*'s accounting includes only the annual Pentagon budget and not the "supplemental" expenses of war in the Middle East or costs of veterans' services. Moreover, the magazine's editorial bias is to present a sunny view of the forward march of the market system. Yet it is also true that a certain deterministic impulse within the Marxist tradition has often led to premature or overstated predictions of crisis with the U.S. economy and that American capitalism has regularly proved to be more dynamic than many of its critics had expected. We should remember, too, that in the 1980s many geopolitical observers across the political spectrum argued that the rise of Japan spelled the end of U.S. dominance. This contention quickly fell out of fashion in the 1990s, when Tokyo was struggling with economic stagnation.

Another problematic conclusion some analysts draw from the crises now facing the U.S. economy is that America was forced into its hyper-aggressive military posture because corporate globalization had reached a dead end. The International Forum on Globalization, a group of scholars that includes Bello and draws on his analysis, assert in their book *Alternatives to Economic Globalization*: "The war in Iraq is primarily an attempt to keep an overstressed U.S. economic juggernaut, one now gasping to sustain its huge need for resource flows and supply lines, breathing a little longer. It's a kind of CPR for a system that's having a hard time breathing for itself."[39] This position has several flaws: It underestimates the extent to which the invasion of Iraq was a war of choice; it skirts the way in which Middle Eastern oil is more an instrument of power for neocon warmongers than a directly consumed resource for the United States (especially given that other viable oil suppliers will continue to fuel the country for some time); and it disregards the resistance of business elites who correctly argued that neoliberalism would be ill-served by the attack.

I contend that the crises of neoliberal legitimacy, economic overproduction, and military overextension had less influence on President Bush's shift to imperial globalization than they will on what comes next.

The next administration will not be able to approach the world with the same arrogance that the neocons oozed at their prime. Yet the three overlapping crises now affecting the global economy will make it difficult to carry out a simple return to Clinton-style policy.

Those who oppose both U.S. imperialism and corporate power are entering a moment of uncertainty and openness. The fall of neoliberalism and a potential weakening of imperial influence create dangers but also make space for alternative visions of the international order to emerge. As we will see, many proposals for a more just and participatory world order have already begun to assert themselves—and can be pushed further by renewed social movement efforts. But such movements will have to deal with a set of international bodies that are also scrambling to adjust to changing geopolitical circumstances. These institutions, the embodiments of the Bretton Woods order of the past fifty years, were the leading targets of globalization protests in the post-Seattle period, and they remain the hope of many neoliberals who believe that corporate globalization should rule the world. They are the World Bank, International Monetary Fund, and World Trade Organization.

PART TWO

Ending the "Washington Consensus"

4

THE BESIEGED WORLD BANKERS

In 1994, a collection of activist groups came together to form a unified campaign against the World Bank and its sister organization, the International Monetary Fund. The two institutions were then celebrating a half-century in business. They were originally founded by delegates from more than forty Allied nations to a July 1944 conference in Bretton Woods, New Hampshire. The Bretton Woods conferees, coming together as the Second World War continued to rage in Europe and in the Pacific, wanted to speed postwar reconstruction and mitigate the possibility of another Great Depression. Fancying themselves altruistic internationalists, they set out to create institutions that could foster development, facilitate trade, and create stability in a renewed global economy.

Yet despite the noble rhetoric of the Bretton Woods conference, the institutions it ultimately spawned were always dominated by the United States and its Western European allies. By the 1980s, they had become leading mechanisms for compelling developing countries to adopt neoliberal economic policies. Citizen activists, especially in the global South, cried foul. When they banded together in the mid-1990s, they named their coalition after their slogan: "50 Years Is Enough."

The group's call to action against the international financial institutions seemed to come at an inopportune moment. The mid-1990s were high times for corporate globalization. Enthusiasm for the expanding "New Economy" was rising. The Clinton administration placed structures like the World Bank, the IMF, and the WTO at the center of its foreign policy. The march of neoliberalism seemed unstoppable.

By the institutions' sixtieth anniversary in 2004, however, things had changed. The Asian financial crisis sent shock waves through the global economy in 1997 and 1998, and Argentina's economy collapsed in 2001. Each episode was a damning blow to IMF credibility. Meanwhile, the left's critique of the World Bank—which challenged the institution's practice of forcing structural adjustment on countries needing loans, its support for environmentally destructive dams and other megaprojects, and its undemocratic governance structure—drew mass protests to its previously inconspicuous meetings. In response, the World Bank was compelled to launch a major PR offensive promoting its righteous mission of ending poverty.

Perhaps more disconcerting still for the IMF and World Bank's defenders, influential conservative economists and Bush administration officials were also ready to declare "enough." In recent years, the international financial institutions have faced escalating attacks from all sides. The IMF is now groping to find a reason for its continued existence. Meanwhile, the World Bank maintained at best a lukewarm relationship with the Bush White House—and at times has found itself abandoned altogether.

Any attempt to understand the evolution of the global justice movement in the years since it seized the spotlight in Seattle in 1999 must start by addressing the militarism of George W. Bush and his administration. The reckless and opportunistic response of White House ideologues to the attacks of 9/11 and the disastrous outcomes of their wars have set the stage for the debate about what values should now define the world order. The first part of this book focused on the rise of imperial globalization. It discussed why activists have sometimes been slow to see the break in Washington's foreign policy, it examined the nonmarket aspects of the imperial globalist vision, and it explained how a militarized agenda has heightened geopolitical tensions. Finally, it explored the three interconnected crises surrounding neoliberalism's legitimacy, problems with the declining dollar, and the dilemma of U.S. overextension.

Yet even as wars in Iraq and Afghanistan have monopolized political space, the debate about trade and development policy—the issues that drew the media spotlight in the post-Seattle moment—has continued. The connection of trade and development issues to our everyday lives can often seem abstract. But for billions of people across the globe, decisions made by trade and finance ministers at international meetings determine whether neighborhoods will have public access to clean water, whether families will be able to afford to send their kids to school, and whether communities will have a say in their own economic affairs. For those of us in wealthy nations, the outcome of the debate means the difference between locking in a worldwide version of Ronald Reagan's "trickle-down" system of market fundamentalism on the one hand and, on the other, creating a global order that values human rights and a healthy environment over the unimpeded drive to maximize profits.

The second part of this book focuses on how struggles over trade and development have unfolded—and the consequences they will have in the post-Bush era. In particular, I examine the dramatically altered standing of the international financial institutions. During the 1990s, global justice activists highlighted three institutions as the linchpins of the neoliberal system: the World Bank, the IMF, and the WTO. Each one had an important role in expanding and propagating corporate globalization. Although they continue to influence the global economy, the recent history of these institutions shows how a shift in American foreign policy has altered the setting for international debate.

The three Bretton Woods institutions have received relatively little attention in recent times, as social movements have focused instead on rallying against the invasion and occupation of Iraq. Especially in the United States, activists have been concerned with denouncing the Bush administration's arrogant warmongering, its regressive domestic agenda, and its shredding of the Constitution. The urgency of these pressing challenges have taken the spotlight off the World Bank, IMF, and WTO.

But unexpectedly, even as protests against these bodies have made fewer headlines, those who have argued that the institutions should be abolished have come ever closer to realizing their goal. The WTO, which is examined in more detail in chapter 6, has run into serious roadblocks, and trade ministers have been forced to put their negotiations on hold. Meanwhile, as criticisms have mounted over the years against the IMF and World Bank, governments of developing nations—often under pressure from vibrant citizen groups—have increasingly stood up to the Washington Consensus. The aura of invincibility surrounding these bodies has dissipated. As a result, the institutions have lost much of their power in the Bush years. If the call for the end to the IMF and World Bank after "50 Years" seemed premature to many, the idea that the institutions might now be headed for early retirement does not seem nearly as incredible.

The current travails of the World Bank seem most paradoxical. When Democrats held the White House and the World Bank's president was liberal internationalist James Wolfensohn, protests challenging the Bank from the left flourished. More recently, challenges to the institution have also mounted from the right, even after George Bush's first appointee, neocon Paul Wolfowitz, took over as head of the institution in 2005. How did the World Bank attract such a diverse array of critics? What do their arguments tell us about the wider debate over who should rule? And what possibilities exist for international economics after the dissolution of the Washington Consensus?

A good place to start finding answers is the story of an initiative known as the Structural Adjustment Participatory Review Initiative, or SAPRI.

THE WORLD BANK'S ONE-WAY DIALOGUE

In April 2000, as protests raged in Washington, D.C., World Bank President James Wolfensohn presented himself as a reasonable man facing an unreasonable mob. "[I] invite the critics to come in," he said, "but I do not think it helps to close down the meetings." Highlighting his ties with nongovernmental organizations (NGOs), he added, "Fortunately there are many international institutions, NGOs, and certainly local NGOs with whom we have a very deep and ongoing dialogue."[1]

Wolfensohn's indignant position was part of the World Bank's reinvigorated—some said desperate—defense of its public image. Faced with increasingly vocal opposition from the global justice movement, the Bank claimed as a point of pride its cooperation with the organizations of "civil society." Words like "interface," "engagement," and "partnership" began to litter the institution's reports and press releases. It was all part of an effort to rebrand the Bank as less a heavy-handed, unaccountable financial institution and more a noble crusader against world poverty.

Wolfensohn was not completely dishonest in claiming that the Bank had started some dialogues with its critics in civil society. However, these initiatives ended up showing precisely the opposite of what he wanted to demonstrate. Those outsiders who took seriously the Bank's desire to reform and decided to work with it to review its methods of doing business found that the institution was still firmly entrenched in neoliberal dogma. Contrary to its cooperative rhetoric, it had little desire to change its ways. In fact, its "partnerships" almost perfectly illuminated what global justice activists found problematic about the World Bank in the first place. To understand why the Bank has drawn denunciations from across the globe, one need look no further than the project known as SAPRI and the grassroots coalition spawned by this initiative, called SAPRIN.

SAPRI was born in 1996, shortly after a network of NGOs launched the "50 Years Is Enough" campaign. The coalition of international organizations challenged newly appointed World Bank President Wolfensohn to reevaluate the Bank's structural adjustment policies on the basis of local knowledge from Southern countries. Eager to answer his critics, Wolfensohn accepted. In statements released that year, he offered a limited acknowledgment of problems with the adjustment process: "Policy reform has had a mixed track record. . . . Adjustment has been a much slower, more difficult and more painful process than the Bank recognized at the outset." He pitched the SAPRI initiative as a way to help shape "a different way of doing business in the future."[2]

In signing on to the initiative, the Bank agreed to work with the NGOs to decide how the research would be gathered and presented, and it took responsibility for securing the cooperation of governments in the initiative's target countries. Although funding was to come from outside parties, including European governments, the European Union, the United Nations Development Program, and private foundations, the Bank would be a fund-raising partner for several SAPRI solicitations—helping to raise a substantial portion of the project's $4.1 million total budget.[3] Finally, Bank officers vowed that the exercise would "identify specific actions" to be used in formulating the institution's future policies.[4]

The openness expressed by James Wolfensohn at the time was quite remarkable. In an April 1996 letter, he wrote to the grassroots advocates: "What I am looking for—and inviting your help in—is a different way of doing business in the future. My objective is to ensure that economic reform programs make maximum contribution to poverty reduction, that we fully appreciate the impact of reform on disparate population groups, that we promote measures which narrow income differentials . . . ."[5] Probably never before had a World Bank president offered such an open invitation for review of the institution's practices. The next five years would test the sincerity of his offer.

On the grassroots side of the equation, SAPRI spawned an impressive coalition of local groups that became known as SAPRIN (the Structural Adjustment Participatory Review International Network). SAPRIN members carefully negotiated the methodology of the initiative with Bank officials to ensure that it would not be a mere public relations exercise. They planned a multiyear project with field investigations in Bangladesh, Ecuador, El Salvador, Ghana, Hungary, Uganda, and Zimbabwe. Mexico and the Philippines were also on the original list, but civil society groups in those countries were forced to undertake investigations there independently after their governments ultimately refused to participate in the official review.

The research methodology that SAPRI established was very innovative, bringing voices to the review process that would never be heard in a regular economic study. For each location, SAPRIN planned two national forums, designed to invite public discussion of the field research taking place. Individuals affected by structural adjustment could testify on the impact that different policies had in their communities. In the words of the final report, the events highlighted "local knowledge and analysis related to the impact of adjustment programs."[6] Dozens of organizations worked to coordinate SAPRI, and hundreds of others in each country contributed to the public forums and participatory research.

The SAPRIN Global Steering Committee was made up of representatives from each of the countries involved in the initiative, including Helen Wangusa of the African Women's Economic Policy Network in Uganda, Nina Torres of Equipo Pueblo in Mexico, and Mahbubul Karim of PROSHIKA in Bangladesh. According to this committee, the research process they negotiated with the Bank was designed to "level the playing field" between the Washington institution and civil society groups in the global South. The forums allowed local populations to become equal partners in the venture.

The idea behind the methodology was at once challenging and commonsensical. SAPRIN maintained that understanding structural adjustment policies required perspectives coming from a different "location in life" than that of Northern elites. "A major policy shift taken by a country of the South to meet a World Bank or IMF loan condition may look benign and, in fact, universally beneficial to a banker sitting in London," the committee wrote, "but to a poor Third World farmer who has come to understand how local, national and even global systems, structures and institutions work to reward the more powerful and influential, expectations may be much lower."[7]

Not all SAPRIN members were convinced that Wolfensohn's offer of collaboration was genuine. Nevertheless, the groups decided that a show of good faith toward Wolfensohn would create a valuable opportunity to publicize and legitimate the concerns of communities affected by structural adjustment. "Our expectations for working with the Bank were modest," said Doug Hellinger, SAPRIN's global coordinator. "But we had faith that if this work on the ground was done professionally and objectively, the truth of what people were living would come out."[8]

Undertaking a joint project with the World Bank was appealing for another reason as well. The institution had long been confronted with studies documenting the harmful impacts of its policies. Normally, Bank officials dismissed these critical reports out of hand, citing their own research to defend their initiatives. However, refuting the validity of SAPRI would be a far more difficult task. Since the Bank participated in choosing the countries that would be involved, determining the procedure that the initiative would follow, and hiring researchers to carry out field investigations, it acted as a full partner in the initiative. Economists at international financial institutions thus would have to contend with the credibility of a report from the World Bank itself.

The Impact of Structural Adjustment

Over the course of the initiative, SAPRI research on structural adjustment revealed a reality that was starkly different from that portrayed in any previous World Bank study. Originally released in draft form in 2002, the initiative's findings were later collected into an independently published book called *Structural Adjustment—The SAPRI Report: The Policy Roots of Economic Crisis, Poverty, and Inequality*.[9] The final report "identified four basic ways in which adjustment policies have contributed to the further impoverishment and marginalization of local populations, while increasing economic inequality."[10]

First, trade and financial sector reforms, the research concluded, destroyed domestic manufacturing, throwing local employees and small producers out of work. "Instead of helping producers that need capital to maintain or expand their operations," the report observed, "financial intermediaries have directed financing toward large (usually urban) firms and extended the largest share of loans to a few, powerful economic agents. This has hindered the development of small and medium-size enterprises, an important source of employment generation."[11]

Second, the promotion of export-oriented agriculture threatened food security, particularly in rural areas, and it worsened prospects for small farmers. In the words of the report, "Where exports have expanded and earnings increased . . . much of the economic benefits has accrued only to large-scale producers, as small farmers have lacked equal opportunity to enter and gain within a liberalized market."[12]

Third, privatization and labor market reforms suppressed wages and weakened workers' bargaining power. After changes to the labor code in Ecuador in the 1990s, for example, "72 percent of large and medium-sized businesses and 16 percent of small businesses have turned to employing temporary workers, and 38 percent of them laid off permanent staff," creating job insecurity and depressing real wages.[13]

Finally, the cutting of state services reduced poor communities' access to utilities, health care, and education in the SAPRI countries. "The establishment of user fees for health-care services" in such places as Zimbabwe and Ghana "has led an increasing number of people and families to resort to self-medication and home care instead of visiting clinics and hospitals. This has especially been the case for women," the report asserted. As a result, these countries witnessed "an increase in the number of people who die in their homes from curable diseases" as well as the unnecessary spread of diseases that endanger public health.[14]

"What one realizes when reading the report is that all is interlinked," said Swedish activist Johanna Sandahl upon release of the SAPRI findings. "Even as very different countries are being assessed, their experiences are very similar. The same model was being implemented everywhere, and it appears that it didn't work anywhere."[15]

Indeed, the SAPRI findings called into question whether structural adjustment processes were ever intended to help the poor in the first place. *Dagens Nyheter*, the national newspaper of Sweden, summed up the findings with an article headlined "World Bank Policies a Fiasco."[16]

STRATEGIES OF BUREAUCRATIC RESISTANCE

As important as the research findings SAPRI produced were the experiences that NGOs had in working with the Bank. Long before the findings were released, harmonious cooperation between the financial institution and its civil society partners had deteriorated. Early in the SAPRI process, various government and World Bank participants realized that the outcomes of the initiative would not reflect well on the policies they had implemented. In fact, they faced serious dilemma. If they allowed critical findings to emerge, people would expect them to change their policies. The IMF and the U.S. Treasury, however, would never allow that to happen. The only solution was to sandbag the SAPRI process. El Salvador's government went so far as to back out of the review, while various Bank officers tried their hand at more subtle forms of noncooperation.

One of the first problems was getting the Bank to release information about specific adjustment conditions demanded by their loans. Obviously, this information would provide an essential foundation for the review. Yet, despite the fact that Wolfensohn had agreed in March 1996 to make all necessary documents available to SAPRIN, Bank officers did their best to resist. Even after the NGOs reached a compromise with Bank staffers, nearly a year passed before the Bank's legal department consented to the release. They also stonewalled on funding for the initiative. In one instance, the Bank refused, until challenged, to release approximately $200,000 that had been donated by a European government for the NGO network.

In the countries where SAPRI was taking place, such as Ecuador, local Bank staff members praised the research methodology and the quality of the study.[17] But back in Washington, Bank officers told members of the SAPRIN Global Steering Committee that they did not intend to use the initiative's findings to reformulate their approach to poverty reduction. The activists were taken aback. In a letter that radiates a sense of betrayal, the committee made a personal appeal to Wolfensohn: "[W]e do not believe that the message we have been receiving from Bank staff could possibly be your position," they wrote. "Failure on the part of the Bank to fulfill its commitment to the original SAPRI agreements would send a clear signal to thousands of organizations—which, upon your word, invested heavily in SAPRI in terms of time, resources, and expectations."[18]

Unfortunately, Wolfensohn did not step up to rectify the situation. When the time came for the final presentation of the SAPRI findings, Bank leaders shied away from scheduling a large-scale public event, which it had previously committed to support. Wolfensohn even failed to show up for a smaller roundtable discussion. "Our expectations were not high," said Iván Cisneros, coordinator of SAPRIN in Ecuador. "We were surprised, however, not only by how unforthcoming the Bank was, but also by how unprofessional its Washington leadership was and has been throughout this endeavor."[19]

The institution's response to the far-reaching SAPRI field research was also revealing. Rather than engaging with the information in a serious way, Bank officials preferred to remain in their own echo chamber. The Bank declined to collaborate with SAPRIN on a final global report, choosing to prepare its own document. Totaling only forty pages, the Bank's paper, called "Adjustment from Within," barely considered the extensive SAPRI research.[20] Rather, it leaned heavily on previous World Bank studies. This allowed the authors to reach banal and erroneous conclusions—for example, "The impact of financial sector reforms implemented in SAPRI countries has been generally positive, but less impressive than expected."[21] Bank staff provided no response to the comprehensive draft report that SAPRIN provided. Despite having cooperated in designing the SAPRI methodology, the World Bank simply could not accept results that contradicted its deeply ingrained ideological biases.

Lidy Nacpil of the Freedom from Debt Coalition in the Philippines and a member of the SAPRIN steering committee concluded from these interactions: "It is clear that the Bank is incapable, for political and bureaucratic reasons, to hear, much less respond to, the insights and priorities of people around the world affected by its policies. Many of us have also been in the streets, in the South and the North, to bring public attention to the social, economic and environmental devastation it has wrought. We now know that this is the only way, other than cutting its resource base, to put an end to its calamitous and undemocratic processes."[22]

After the Bank ignored the SAPRI results for nearly a year, media attention forced Wolfensohn back to the table following the release of the initiative's final report in 2002. In subsequent meetings with SAPRIN organizations, he acknowledged that their findings were "important" and "legitimate." However, during the remainder of his time in office, Wolfensohn failed to take any action based on those findings. "I wouldn't say we were hopeful, but SAPRIN was willing to take a chance given the critical importance of the issue," said SAPRIN coordinator Doug Hellinger. "In the end, the Bank once again demonstrated, this time quite publicly, that it isn't about to change course regardless of the evidence."[23]

SAPRI was the most thoroughgoing of the Bank's engagements with grassroots critics, and it provided probably the most important illustration of the Bank's unwillingness to engage in honest dialogue. At the same time, it was not unique. A similar pattern emerged with other endeavors, such as the World Commission on Dams and the Extractive Industries Review. Upbeat press releases publicized the launch of each new "partnership," emphasizing the World Bank's willingness to work cooperatively with its detractors. Official enthusiasm then waned markedly when the initiatives suggested that policy-as-usual was unacceptable.

Patrick McCully of the International Rivers Network cited the example of the World Commission on Dams (WCD), which criticized many Bank-funded projects. "The World Bank, as a key sponsor of the WCD, should be actively incorporating the Commission's findings into its own policies and practices and encouraging others to do so," he maintained. "Yet the Bank has refused to adopt any of the WCD's recommendations into its binding policies." Moreover, "the Bank is also misrepresenting or ignoring the Commission's findings on the Bank's role in promoting poorly performing and destructive dams."[24]

The words of Lidy Nacpil fairly sum up the situation: "Thousands of groups around the world have involved themselves in various dialogues with the Bank, but all our words have fallen on deaf ears. The Bank continues to push countries into the same old programs which have failed."[25]

The Limits of Reform

Despite the failure of these partnerships, the World Bank and the IMF claim to have made major changes in their lending practices. In 1999, the two organizations announced that they were moving away from aid conditionality—that is, making needed loans contingent on the adoption of neoliberal policies. In the rhetoric of these institutions, "structural adjustment" is no more. Instead, they have adopted a new lending strategy, centered on what they call Poverty Reduction Strategy Papers (PRSPs).

Stressing the language of "ownership" and "participation," the IMF describes PRSPs as economic strategies "prepared by the member countries through a participatory process involving domestic stakeholders as well as external development partners."[26] Theoretically, instead of having the Washington institutions mandate a slate of economic policies in top-down fashion, poor countries create policy strategies themselves. The World Bank and the IMF then choose whether or not to endorse these strategies. According to the institutions, "the poor become active participants, not just passive recipients."[27]

For most of the grassroots groups that had engaged critically with the Bank, the new process was suspect from the start. Under the supposedly revamped regime, the World Bank and IMF still stand in judgment of a country's ostensibly sovereign decisions about how to govern its own economy. And the institutions base their criteria for acceptable policies on the same neoliberal ideology as before. As a result, the "poverty reduction" framework looks very much like structural adjustment with a different name. In a joint assessment of PRSPs implemented before November 2001, Shalmali Guttal of Focus on the Global South, Alejandro Bendaña of Jubilee South, and Helen Wangusa of the African Women's Economic Policy Network concluded that in the revised process, "fighting poverty becomes the newest justification for the aging prescriptions" that have guided decades of corporate globalization.[28]

Interestingly, an internal report issued and made public by the IMF's Independent Evaluation Office in early 2007 confirmed many of the charges leveled by outside critics. Coming from the institution's own auditors, the report provided an unusually strong indictment. It confirmed that the Fund's efforts under the guise of "poverty reduction" differed little from its earlier work promoting "structural adjustment." Specifically, it noted a problematic "disconnect between the IMF's external communications on aid and poverty reduction, and its practice in low-income countries."[29] In plain English, the evaluators charged the IMF with lying—saying one thing in its rosy press releases while in practice doing quite another. The report concluded that the IMF has "done little to address poverty reduction and income distributional issues, despite institutional rhetoric to the contrary."[30]

Calling Bad Business Good

Few examples illustrated the IMF and World Bank's continued allegiance to neoliberalism so clearly as a report the Bank issued in September 2006, titled "Doing Business 2007: How to Reform." The annual report ranked 175 countries in terms of the "ease of doing business" within their borders. It evaluated nations based on ten categories related to taxation, licensing, financial and trade regulation, legal infrastructure, and labor.[31] All this might look fine on the surface. But unfortunately, a nation's success in the rankings was not necessarily based on what working people anywhere would call good business practices. In fact, a group of prominent Democratic senators sent a letter to the then president of the World Bank, Paul Wolfowitz, charging that the report encouraged countries to violate internationally recognized labor standards.

The senators' letter decried the report's favorable ranking of countries that lack minimum wages, fail to regulate overtime, and condone union busting. "Rewarding lax or non-existent labor standards," the senators wrote, "contradicts ILO [International Labor Organization] policy, which encourages countries to establish a minimum wage and regulate hours of work and to pass and enforce laws protecting freedom of association and collective bargaining."[32] The senators pointed out that the State Department officially uses respect for ILO principles as a factor in gauging a country's commitment to human rights. Nevertheless, the World Bank report gave high marks to countries that disregard these standards.

Saudi Arabia, a country that denies freedom of assembly and does not permit workers to organize, received the best possible score from the Bank on indices measuring "difficulty of hiring" and "difficulty of firing" employees. The report also praised the country of Georgia for reforms that reduced the number of hours counted as overtime and decreased companies' required contributions to the social security system.

Perhaps most telling was the country that stood at the top of the rankings: Singapore. During the same month the World Bank unveiled "Doing Business," the international press blasted this country for its repressive policies. In mid-September 2006, the World Bank and the IMF held their ministerial meetings in Singapore. To prevent protests, the government denied critics permission to hold a countersummit or a public march. It also banned several dozen high-profile NGO representatives from the island altogether—even though these activists had been accredited by the Bank to attend the meetings. An embarrassed Wolfowitz dubbed the move "authoritarian." Yet his institution simultaneously lauded Singapore as an ideal place to do business.

THE RIGHT-WING ASSAULT

The harmful impacts of structural adjustment, the persistence of neoliberalism as the guiding ideology of World Bank policy, and the failure of the institution to seriously reform explain why global justice advocates criticized the organization, even in the "liberal" Wolfensohn era. Over time, these criticisms have taken a toll on IMF and World Bank credibility. Often under pressure from vocal social movements, governments of developing countries are increasingly seeking to break from the Washington Consensus. In this context, the international financial institutions can no longer function with the same unencumbered power they held before.

In more recent years, the institution's woes have been compounded by challenges from the right. A number of conservative economists have long critiqued the Bretton Woods institutions' effectiveness and questioned their benefits for the United States. With the shift to imperial globalization in the Bush White House, these critical voices became increasingly influential. Disregard for U.S. "soft" power and willingness to sidestep or even undermine the multilateral structures of corporate globalization are two defining features of the imperial approach to globalization. The United States has a disproportionate share of power in multilateral bodies. Nevertheless, making these institutions work requires compromise and diplomatic savvy—things the militant unilateralists never particularly valued.

The first of the Bretton Woods institutions affected by the shift to imperial globalization was the WTO. I examine the unique role and recent travails of the WTO in chapter 6. For now, it is important to note that even under Clinton the United States was more interested in opening other countries' markets than submitting itself to "free trade." But under Bush, defense of national interests grew even more aggressive. Unwilling to sacrifice powerful economic interests—such as Florida sugar growers—that benefit from U.S. protectionism, the administration offered little in international trade negotiations. In advance of the WTO's September 2003 Ministerial Conference in Cancún, Shefali Sharma of the Institute for Agriculture and Trade commented, "[B]efore, the European Union was the biggest sinner" in terms of refusing to compromise, "but the United States is [now] making Europe look good."[33] Since then, trade talks have deadlocked, and although the WTO still has power to mediate many disputes, boosters have been forced to scrap their visions for its expansion.

As an alternative to stalled multilateral trade deals, the Bush administration has pursued bilateral, one-on-one agreements with individual countries. Negotiating on their own, less powerful trading partners lose the ability to join a trading bloc to resist U.S. demands (which, as we will see, is precisely what happened with the formation of the G20+ in Cancún). The administration has successfully used the bilateral method to negotiate favorable agreements with countries, including Australia, Morocco, Singapore, and Chile.

The imperial globalists of the Bush administration sidestepped the WTO first, in part because it is the most democratic of the international financial institutions, in principle operating on a one-country, one-vote model. The IMF, meanwhile, proclaims itself "accountable to its shareholders." Its voting structure is weighted based on each country's economic heft and financial contributions to the institution. As a result, the United States alone holds 17 percent of the voting power; Europe holds approximately 40 percent; and developing countries as a whole have only 37 percent of IMF votes. China and India are dramatically underrepresented. The different branches that make up the World Bank operate on a system similar to the IMF's—and the fact that an 85 percent supermajority is required for major decisions effectively gives the United States veto power.

Nevertheless, these institutions fell out of favor with White House unilateralists. The neocon vision of foreign aid sees it as funding that should be doled out directly by the United States to get other countries to act in accordance with America's geopolitical objectives. The Bush approach to the World Bank reflected this orientation. From the start, the World Bank experienced significant neglect from the Bush administration, especially relative to the attention it had received from the Clinton White House. Rather than focusing on using loans from the multilateral institution to promote neoliberal development, President Bush preferred using bilateral foreign aid—and tying aid packages to specific political and military objectives of the United States. Such bilateral aid deals played a large part in the effort to mobilize a "coalition of the willing" to invade Iraq.

In 2005, foreign policy analyst Tom Barry described the strategic alignment of assistance in the Bush administration: "The 2004–2009 strategic plan produced by the State Department and USAID (U.S. Agency for International Development) defines 'security' as the main goal of U.S. foreign assistance. The strategic plan aims to 'align diplomacy and development assistance' with the president's National Security Strategy of September 2002—the document that lays out the case for preventive war and for building the capacity for global military intervention."[34]

Early in 2006, the administration moved to further politicize USAID by reducing its formal independence and more closely aligning its operations with the overall aims of the State Department. With this arrangement, the White House made the political use of aid more overt than ever. Although the changes are being implemented in the name of efficiency and accountability, Oxfam America identified USAID reorganization as a further step in "a drastic shift in U.S. foreign assistance" since the attacks of 9/11 "that has blurred the lines traditionally separating development and humanitarian aid from political and military action."[35] Under Bush, significant increases in U.S. foreign aid were channeled not through the World Bank but rather through new go-it-alone American initiatives, such as the Millennium Challenge Account.

Bucking the Bank

Even as it pushed development aid through its own bilateral mechanisms, the Bush administration, in key moments, effectively advocated
defunding the World Bank. One such instance took place in discussions
leading up to the G8 agreement on debt relief in the summer of 2005.
There, debate centered on how billions of dollars worth of debt cancellation for eighteen heavily indebted countries would be financed. The
United States argued that the World Bank and the IMF should use their
own resources to pay for the cancellation. If the World Bank stopped collecting payments on outstanding debts from poorer nations, it would
simply have less money for future loans, the White House contended.

Many European groups objected, arguing that this change would
amount to giving to developing countries with one hand while taking
with the other. They argued that "additionality," or a net increase in aid
funds from wealthy nations, was absolutely necessary. From the perspective of the European advocates, subsidized World Bank loans were a
form of aid to the poor; they did not believe that debt relief should come
at the cost of cutting back these loans. The end result was a role reversal
for many activists who traditionally opposed the World Bank; the NGOs
essentially advocated holding up a debt deal until G8 governments
agreed to extra financing for the much-scorned institution and its "development" loans.

This is not the only case in which progressive responses to the new
context of imperial globalization were muddled. The downgraded status
of the World Bank in the eyes of Bush administration officials also contributed to some questionable analysis upon the appointment of Paul
Wolfowitz as the Bank's new president in early 2005. Even as liberals
warned that Wolfowitz could destroy the World Bank, critics further to
the left argued that the move showed the continued centrality of the institution in promoting U.S. policy. Few considered that from a neocon perspective, being shipped off from a key post at the Department of Defense
could be considered a demotion—or more importantly, that undermining the World Bank could be part and parcel of the administration's imperial doctrine.

One exception was British journalist and *Guardian* columnist George Monbiot. In an April 2005 column, he acknowledged the shift at hand and wished Wolfowitz well in his new position. The appointment, he asserted,

> illustrates the unacknowledged paradox in neocon thinking. They want to drag down the old, multilateral order and replace it with a new, U.S. one. What they fail to understand is that the "multilateral" system is in fact a projection of U.S. unilateralism, cleverly packaged to grant other nations just enough slack to prevent them from fighting it. Like their opponents, the neocons fail to understand how well Roosevelt and Truman stitched up the international order. They are seeking to replace a hegemonic system that is enduring and effective with one that is untested and (because other nations must fight it) unstable. Anyone who believes in global justice should wish them luck.[36]

Sadly, this viewpoint was drowned out by liberal denunciations of the Wolfowitz selection and retroactive celebrations of the Wolfensohn years.

THE CONSERVATIVE CRITIQUE

There is more to right-wing aversion to the World Bank than just a general unilateralist disposition. A critique of the institution developed by several conservative economists has become influential within the Bush administration. First put forth in the early 1990s by Harvard economist Kenneth Rogoff and Stanford economist Jeremy Bulow, this analysis denounces the Bank's inefficiency and ineffectiveness. This critique has since been prominently advanced by a congressional committee headed by Carnegie Mellon University economist Allan H. Meltzer, which released its findings in March 2000, and by Adam Lerrick, a visiting scholar at the American Enterprise Institute.

The conservative stance provides a rationale for dramatically downsizing several branches of the World Bank. The Bank, properly named the World Bank Group, actually consists of several allied financial bodies. These include the International Development Association (IDA), which finances the poorest countries, and the International Bank for Reconstruction and Development (IBRD), which provides loans to middle-income countries. Additionally, the International Finance Corporation (IFC) and the Multilateral Investment Guarantee Agency (MIGA) promote private-sector investment.

As part of their radical plan for reordering the World Bank, conservatives argue that the IDA should stop making loans, given that poor countries are consistently unable to pay them back. Instead, the economists argue, the institution should make "performance-based" development grants to countries in need. The World Bank boasts that the recipients of its assistance never default on their loans. Economists like Meltzer and Lerrick charge that this claim is based on financial practices that would never be accepted in the private sector. When developing countries fail to pay off their loans, a private bank would be forced to declare a default. The World Bank, in contrast, simply distributes new loans that allow indebted countries to keep paying. Although few countries ever fully pay off their obligations, the Bank can count on some steady income trickling in from the debtor countries. In addition, having a large loan portfolio adds to the Bank's clout. Conservative critics consider this a sham.

"For more than two decades, the bank has played a shell game with worthless developing nation loans by recirculating funding in what even the UK Treasury describes as 'balance sheet fantasies,'" Lerrick declared. "The bank must accept that it is in the development business, not the banking business."[37] Being in the development business means being willing to give away money and not pretending that irretrievable loans are still good. It means ending the perpetual reloaning cycle and adopting a more efficient mechanism of development grants—similar to that of Bush's bilateral Millennium Challenge Account.

Right-wingers make even more drastic proposals for the IBRD. They argue that the Bank's role as a lender to middle-income countries is obsolete in a world that is now awash in private capital. Although the Bank's status as a dominant funder is declining, it is "struggling to maintain market share," according to Lerrick, and acting like a failing business that refuses to let go of its visions of grandeur.[38]

Conservatives would prefer that the Bank give up. The report of the Meltzer Commission contends that the World Bank should be "transformed" into something that is hardly a bank at all, "from capital-intensive lenders to sources of technical assistance, providers of regional and global public goods, and facilitators of an increased flow of private sector resources to the emerging countries."[39] In short, the Bank would remain an overseer of neoliberal policy, while the private sector would handle most of the cash.

Money in the Bank

Seeking to curtail the World Bank's most profitable activities, right-wing critics want not only to transform the World Bank but also to defund it. Because the Bank makes loans at market-based rates to middle-income countries, and because those clients have the greatest ability to pay their debts, the "IBRD has become a crucial source of financial support and clout for the development community," explained Jessica Einhorn, a former managing director at the World Bank. "IBRD income helps sustain the World Bank's administrative budget of $2 billion."[40]

When coupled with the loss of revenue that previously came from the poor countries that have now been granted debt relief, conservative plans would make the World Bank more dependent on "replenishment" funding supplied by donor countries. This funding can be precarious, especially if ideological opponents of the Bank hold sway in donor countries' parliaments. Lawrence Summers, who was Clinton's secretary of the treasury at the time of the Meltzer report and a World Bank defender, argued that the commission's recommendations "would dramatically reduce the total amount of resources that can be brought to bear in [developing] economies and require an unworkable system for delivering such assistance."[41]

In response to the conservative attack, liberal and centrist defenders of the Bank proposed various schemes to tweak the institution's function and governance. In the wake of the Meltzer report, Summers himself promoted a series of modest reforms designed, in part, to create a "clearer delineation of the respective roles of the World Bank and the IMF."[42] Ultimately, though, such defenders continue to hold up the Bank as an important foreign policy instrument, and they are loath to risk losing it.

Sebastian Mallaby, *Washington Post* columnist and author of *The World's Banker*, has argued that by paying the small cost of keeping the institution involved in lending, "the United States and its allies keep the World Bank active in strong developing countries, allowing it to earn a profit on its loans and therefore to sustain the professional standards that make it an important tool of U.S. and European foreign policy." He contended, "Once you start picking at the bank's intricate mechanism for financing soft loans, it is not hard to imagine the whole system unraveling."[43]

Strange Bedfellows

In this contentious context, progressives must figure out how to express the distinct nature of their criticisms—and decide whether they want to make common cause with their conservative anti-Bank counterparts. Clearly, there are several points on which left and right agree. Many progressive advocates of debt relief, in Africa as well as the United States, support the shift from World Bank loans to grants. Likewise, Lerrick's description of Bank efforts at poverty reduction as "fifty years of failure" echoes the call of "50 Years Is Enough." And when Allan Meltzer's followers propose downsizing key functions of the World Bank and the IMF, they hold much common ground with street protesters chanting that the institutions have "got to go."

Indeed, this type of alliance has already made a political impact. In late 1998, an unusual coalition of conservatives and liberals in the U.S. Congress very nearly denied the IMF some $18 billion in funding. Although the funding ultimately went through, their dissent forced the creation of the Meltzer Commission.

The left must recognize some pitfalls in bolstering the conservative critique, however. While Meltzer and Lerrick would displace the World Bank, they would hand over any profitable development lending to private bankers. In other words, rather than abolish the World Bank, the right would privatize it. At the same time, they might keep the remnants of the multilateral institutions on hand to continue evaluating the credit-worthiness of poorer governments. In the past, this "gatekeeper" role has given the IMF and the World Bank much of their power to dictate economic policy in the developing world.

In a critique of the Meltzer Commission's findings, Sarah Anderson of the progressive Institute for Policy Studies pointed out that under the right-wing restructuring, "the IMF would terminate long-term assistance tied to structural adjustment conditions but would maintain tremendous influence by requiring that countries meet free market-oriented 'preconditions' to qualify for emergency assistance."[44] For the poorest countries, grants from the World Bank's IDA would also remain highly conditional.

One of the Meltzer Commission's key findings was that the World Bank has a terrible track record of reducing poverty, its stated mission. After examining Bank documents and interviewing experts, the commission concluded that the Bank's failure rate is 55 to 60 percent for projects in all developing countries, and even higher in Africa. Critics on both the left and the right cite these figures, but they hold very different understandings of why projects have failed. Conservatives point to corruption and lack of accountability in developing nations. Unlike progressives, they do not recognize flawed macroeconomic assumptions or the rigidity of neoliberal structural adjustment as integral to the problem. If conservatives had their way, eviscerating the World Bank and relying on private financing (plus a system of politicized, bilateral grants) would further entrench U.S.-backed neoliberalism.

APPROACHING THE POST-BUSH MOMENT

As the Bush era comes to a close, the World Bank and the IMF have both been pushed to publicly argue for their continued existence. Traditionally, the two institutions have worked in tandem to promote neoliberalism. Although the World Bank loans much more money, the IMF has a greater role in setting policy. In recent decades, if developing countries did not meet the Fund's highly ideological standards for good economic governance, they would be disqualified from World Bank loans. They would also lose funding from regionally based multilateral development lenders, such as the Asian Development Bank and the Inter-American Development Bank. Furthermore, many private-sector lenders took their lead from the IMF, so that countries not eligible for public funding found it very difficult to get private money.

Finally, the IMF derived power from its role in managing financial crises. When times got hard for a developing country, the United States and its European allies would engineer bailout packages through the IMF, making the institution the world's "lender of last resort." Thus, few countries in the global South could afford to fall out of favor with the Fund. For this reason, some economists saw it as the head of what they dubbed a "creditors' cartel"; when the Fund offered its guidance to a country, the nation's leaders were presented with "an offer they couldn't refuse."[45]

While the World Bank has been besieged by critics of both the left and the right, the IMF faces struggles of its own. Just as they would scale back the Bank, many conservatives would limit the IMF mostly to gathering and disseminating information about financial markets. But the Fund's bigger problem is that its supposed beneficiaries are in revolt. Asian countries burned by the region's neoliberal financial crisis in 1997 are building large cash reserves to prevent a return to the Fund in times of economic downturn. And many countries are paying off their IMF debts early to escape the institution's oppressive oversight, as noted by Adam Lerrick: "One after another, developing nations—Brazil, Argentina, Uruguay, Indonesia, the Philippines—paid off their loans early. Finance ministers across the globe, who'd trained at Harvard and the University of Chicago, had figured out that it was better to give up the Fund's subsidies than to cede control over their own economic destinies. . . . Desk managers at the Fund once micromanaged 50 different economies. But those days are now gone."[46]

The International Monetary Fund is no longer the intimidating bully it once was. Indeed, it has been forced to contemplate a future of reduced global sway. Moves from the global South are sapping both IMF revenue streams and the institution's influence. Its loan portfolio, which had soared to nearly $100 billion in 2004, fell to under $20 billion by early 2007.[47] A single country, Turkey, accounts for much of the remaining sum. The IMF's dramatically curtailed lending is also producing funding shortfalls for the institution. Three of the IMF's four largest clients—Argentina, Brazil, and Indonesia—used currency reserves and financing from other countries, such as oil-rich Venezuela, to pay off their IMF debts early. This early payback has deprived the institution of lucrative interest payments, making a sizable dent in the institution's operating budget. The IMF anticipated a $116 million shortfall in fiscal year 2006.[48] Turkey, the largest remaining client, is also considering buying its way out of IMF oversight in the near future, which would put an even tighter squeeze on the institution's finances. Of course, it should be noted that the Fund is not going broke; among other assets, the institution sits on some $75 billion worth of gold. Nevertheless, the enterprise cannot hemorrhage money indefinitely.

In a belated attempt to regain credibility—and to answer critics who charge that the voices of developing countries are dramatically underrepresented in its decision-making—the IMF has spent much of 2006 and 2007 concocting schemes to slightly adjust its voting system. Although such tinkering would give somewhat greater weight to some countries, such as China, India, and Mexico, it would not affect the dominant role of the United States in the institution. Ultimately, the altered voting plans reek of too little, too late. The global South already voted with its feet.

THE BANK'S "GOOD GOVERNANCE"?

Unlike some other conservatives, Bush appointee Paul Wolfowitz probably wasn't interested in intentionally undermining the World Bank when he took over as the institution's president. Nevertheless, he succeeded in doing a pretty good job of it. From the start, European governments were offended that the Bush administration would assign a leading U.S. war-planner to lead the World Bank. Wolfowitz added insult to injury by brushing aside Europe's concerns that poverty reduction should be the dominant focus of the Bank's work and instead making anticorruption his flagship initiative. No doubt, corruption is a genuine concern. However, Wolfowitz's zeal for fighting it became notably muted when it came to such countries as Afghanistan, Iraq, and Pakistan, which the White House had a vested interested in funding. On his watch, World Bank funding for key countries that had supported the U.S. "war on terror" increased markedly, whereas countries such as Uzbekistan—which had declined to let American warplanes use its territory as a landing strip—saw Bank-funded projects suspended.[49] All this heightened the perception that the neocon-in-chief had again put nationalism first and betrayed the transatlantic alliance that had previously sustained corporate globalization.

Under pressure to distance itself from an increasingly unpopular Bush administration, the Blair government in the United Kingdom signaled that it would not go along with Wolfowitz's initiatives at the World Bank. During the IMF and World Bank's Singapore meetings in fall 2006, Britain announced that it would withhold approximately $93 million worth of payments to the World Bank to protest the institution's continued practice of making poor countries undertake onerous, and often antiworker, economic "reforms" as a condition of receiving loans for development.[50]

Such troubling developments should have sparked public debate by the time the spring 2007 meetings of the IMF and World Bank rolled around. But, as it turned out, discussion of the institutions' funding problems and lack of democratic representation was overshadowed by a personal scandal. When Paul Wolfowitz took the reins of the institution, he faced a conflict of interest involving his romantic partner, Shaha Ali Riza, who worked in the Bank's Middle East section. Wolfowitz arranged a deal by which Riza was transferred to the State Department and awarded a hefty raise, her salary jumping from $132,600 to $180,000, with guaranteed annual increases. As details of the deal came to light, it not only became a great public embarrassment but also prompted the Bank's staff to call for the president's resignation. An internal review panel found that contrary to his claims that the arrangement had been approved by in-house ethics officials, Wolfowitz had sidestepped proper procedures in setting the exorbitant raise, worked to silence skeptics who disapproved of the arrangement, and attempted to keep the Bank's legal department from being involved in the negotiations.

It was the last straw for Wolfowitz at the Bank. Well before the Riza incident exploded into scandal, he had thoroughly alienated his staff. Some felt wary of working with an architect of the Iraq War. But Wolfowitz's bigger sin as a manager was ignoring established fiefdoms within the Bank and instead empowering aides that he brought with him from the Bush administration. Bank staffers resented being forced to defer to the notoriously abrasive Robin Cleveland, imported from the White House Budget Office, and Kevin Kellems, previously an aide to Dick Cheney. Both of these senior advisors garnered jobs normally reserved for PhDs with decades of development experience—and secured salaries of over $200,000 per year, tax-free. Needless to say, the aides were rewarded with these plush positions based not on their academic credentials or their knowledge of development but rather on their proven loyalty and effectiveness as partisan attack dogs.

Even World Bank defenders became aware that such blatant cronyism made it impossible to publicize its newly released anticorruption manual, "The Many Faces of Corruption," for fear that the institution would become a global laughingstock.[51] After a bitter six-week battle, Wolfowitz resigned. Ultimately, it should have been evident long before the Riza scandal that the World Bank and the IMF, two of the least transparent and democratically accountable of public bodies, were hardly qualified to lecture the world about good governance.

Bush's second appointee to head the World Bank, former U.S. Trade Representative Robert Zoellick, will likely do better than his predecessor at managing the institution's staff and quelling internal dissent. However, he brings to the role a history only slightly less problematic than Wolfowitz's. Zoellick was a leader in opportunistically equating "free trade" with "freedom" in the wake of 9/11 and in using the terrorist attacks to bully Democrats into supporting Bush administration trade policy. Perhaps most troubling for progressives, Zoellick remarked, just two weeks after the attacks, "It is inevitable that people will wonder if there are intellectual connections with others who have turned to violence to attack international finance, globalization, and the United States," implying a connection between nonviolent activists and terrorists. If he is meant to be a more conciliatory choice for leadership, few critics on the left should be placated. At the same time, Zoellick may well fuel the right-wing hopes of restructuring the World Bank. The *New Republic*, citing Columbia University economist and defender of corporate globalization Jagdish Bhagwati, reported: "Zoellick's tenure as U.S. Trade Representative involved a much heavier focus on bilateral deals with developing countries than on broad multilateral trade agreements. The idea, Bhagwati says, was to allow the United States to negotiate with poorer countries one-on-one in order to force them to accept demands unrelated to trade."[52] Many anti-Bank conservatives would approve if Zoellick were to bring this same America-first attitude to the financial institution.

The World Bank and the IMF have never been laid so low as in the waning days of the Bush administration. But although they are down, they are not yet out. Liberal defenders of the Washington Consensus still hope that the bodies might rebound. It is possible that a new White House, more mindful of the need to put an internationalist face on U.S. foreign policy, might again use multilateral bodies to pursue its objectives. Moreover, the institutions, albeit diminished, still have more power than they should in dictating how sovereign countries run their economies.

There is no doubt, however, that the current trend is one of decline. Anyone wishing to slow the World Bank and the IMF's drift toward obsolescence will be paddling against the current. The global justice movement, aided by independent-minded governments and anti-Bretton Woods conservatives, won the fight to push the IMF and the World Bank from the center of global economic decision-making. Its next challenge will be exposing the myths of "free trade."

5

"Free Trade's" Broken Promises

When most people think of Costa Rica, they don't imagine oil rigs stationed off the pristine beaches. Nor do they envision pit mines cutting into the cloud-forested mountains. But, despite the country's noteworthy conservation efforts, its scenic vistas and extraordinary biodiversity have faced real threats from extractive industries—and are now endangered by international trade deals. A long-standing dispute between Costa Rican environmentalists and Harken Energy, a Texas-based oil company with close ties to George W. Bush, provides a vivid illustration of what campaigners in global justice movement have denounced as the exploitative and undemocratic aspects of the "free trade" agenda.

"Free trade" is one of the most carelessly repeated, and most ideologically loaded, phrases in politics. As with globalization, elected officials from a wide range of political backgrounds claim to support it, and they brand those who object as hopeless Luddites. In truth, the term "free trade" is tremendously misleading. In the past fifteen years, as grassroots opposition has confronted proposals such as the Free Trade Area of the Americas (FTAA), the Central American Free Trade Agreement (CAFTA), and the expansion of the World Trade Organization (WTO), the term has generated a number of confusing contradictions. First, "free trade" is not free; it includes protectionist measures that benefit select industries. Second, the most significant and controversial parts of the agenda often involve issues that lie far outside the traditional definition of "trade." Those who oppose the "free trade" agenda are not necessarily against trade at all. Finally, the term "free trade" elides important political differences among ruling camps. Despite using similar terminology, imperial globalists of the Bush administration have adopted an approach to trade politics that is different from that of their corporate-minded predecessors in the Clinton White House.

Today, the politics of trade affect the kinds of jobs that are available in our economy, the conditions we work under, and the type of environment we live in. To understand the potential for creating a more democratic global order in the post-Bush era, we must cut through the confusion created by "free trade" rhetoric. The shift between the different visions of globalization that profoundly affected the World Bank and the IMF has also altered trade politics. In the years since the Seattle protests of 1999, negotiations at the WTO have deadlocked, and other sweeping deals, such as the FTAA, have fallen apart. These new developments are the focus of chapter 6.

But first, we must understand why grassroots movements have opposed neoliberal trade policies to begin with. NAFTA and CAFTA are models of "free trade" deals that undermine workers' rights, public health, and environmental protections. Both the content of these deals and the objectionable political maneuvers that brought them to life were mirrored in the creation of the WTO—and they were reflected again as the Bush administration shifted to bilateral trade negotiations. Because NAFTA and CAFTA continue to impact the lives of millions, it is important to examine their legacies. To do this, we turn to the beaches of southeastern Costa Rica.

RED ALERT IN TALAMACA

The history of the environmentalist battle against Harken Energy in Costa Rica goes back more than ten years. In 1994, as part of a series of measures designed to comply with a structural adjustment program sponsored by the World Bank and the IMF, the Costa Rican legislative assembly opened the way for foreign corporations to win concessions on oil exploration in the country, passing what is known as the "hydrocarbons law." Isaac Rojas, board member of *Comunidades Ecológicas La Ceiba*, a Costa Rican affiliate of Friends of the Earth, said that the neoliberal reforms "took the country's advances in the area of environment back about thirty years" by exposing previously sheltered ecosystems to drilling and mining.[1] After the law was passed, a little-known Louisiana-based company named MKJ Xploration successfully bid to prospect in several blocks on the nation's Caribbean coast. The company later sold its Costa Rican interests to Harken Energy, a company whose board of directors previously included George W. Bush.

The location that Harken-MKJ group selected for its activities was the Talamaca region of southeastern Costa Rica, a naturally stunning area resting between several protected wilderness preserves. Among residents in the area, there was an immediate awareness that oil rigs could damage coral reefs and mangrove swamps and threaten the sea life offshore, including endangered sea turtles. Locals felt shocked and betrayed by the lack of consultation involved in the deal. "We saw an announcement in the national newspaper saying that the government had approved concessions for oil exploration," said Enrique Joseph, a thirty-eight-year-old tour guide and restaurateur who grew up in the area. "Within two or three days, we raised a red alert."[2]

Dozens of groups—ranging from farmers' organizations and the fishermen's union to small-business owners, religious groups, and marine biologists—came together in the following months to form *Acción de Lucha Anti-Petrolera*, or Anti-Petroleum Action (ADELA). In December 1999, they convened a meeting with about 250 people. Participants drafted a declaration opposing the concessions and declaring a moratorium in Talamaca. Their declaration received national attention, and the legal strategy they launched bore fruit. In September 2000, the Costa Rican Supreme Court ruled the oil concessions null and void because indigenous communities had not been properly consulted.

Harken-MKJ would soon strike back, however. Two months later, after the company appealed the ruling, the court allowed the oil interests to continue their activities in the offshore blocks where no indigenous communities exist. The corporate executives were pleased with this outcome because their main targets for exploration were offshore, near Puerto Moin. As Harken Vice President Stephen Voss explained months earlier, "The Moin prospect is the largest structure that the company has ever tested, and it offers great exposure to Harken shareholders for the discovery of significant reserves."[3] Unfortunately, the project's prospects for environmental sustainability were not nearly so promising as its anticipated profits. ADELA set out to amplify the message that, as Isaac Rojas said, "local people had declared firm opposition to extractive activity. They said that this could not be done."[4]

ADELA's efforts to organize opposition faced several difficulties. First, the locals were clearly outfunded. "We discovered that the talks we would give on the radio weren't very effective, because the oil companies bought up most of the space available," explained Joseph. "Or, if we drove around in a truck with a megaphone, we'd later see the company rent three cars to do the same."[5] Activists complained of the *compadrazgo*—the sense of comradery—that seemed to exist between Harken executives and government officials. And they saw some communities, particularly in the city of Limón, come to advocate the economic benefit of resource exploration. "The companies promise clouds of gold," Rojas said of his experience with extraction projects, "and some people believe them."[6]

"Seeing our brothers in Limón against us, because of their false expectations," noted Joseph, "that was the hardest part of the campaign."[7]

By January 2001, international groups, including the Natural Resources Defense Council (NRDC) and the Environmental Law Alliance Worldwide, began to bolster the local organizing with financial support, research, legal resources, and international exposure. In what Jacob Scherr, director of NRDC's International Program, described as "probably one of the largest deluges of mail they'd ever seen," supporters sent the oil companies and the Costa Rican government some twenty-seven thousand e-mails, faxes, and letters of protest.[8]

That same year, ADELA's campaign to raise public awareness made it politically risky for presidential hopefuls in Costa Rica to support oil exploration. Candidate Abel Pacheco was outspoken in his pro-environmental stance; he had drafted a proposal to repeal the hydrocarbons law while serving in Costa Rica's legislative assembly. Local environmentalists also made progress in the communities. According to Enrique Joseph, things shifted in Talamaca at a meeting between ADELA and Harken officials. "People were offended to see the oil executives come in and act rudely toward residents who were well-respected. Many people started to doubt the companies' promises."[9]

Victory came soon afterward. In February 2002, a national board rejected Harken-MKJ's plans for offshore drilling. Several months later, the environmental ministry denied an appeal from the oil companies. Its decision noted more than fifty reasons why the environmental impact statement for the project was insufficient—a list that mirrored the meticulous documentation presented by ADELA and its international allies. Responding to the large-scale mobilization of the country's environmentalists, legislators began working to repeal laws that exposed the country to extractive industries. And when Abel Pacheco was inaugurated as the president of Costa Rica in 2002, he proudly announced a moratorium on hydrocarbon exploration in the country, declaring that the country would "not be an oil enclave or land of open pit mining." He vowed, "The true fuel and the true gold of the future will be water and oxygen, our aquifers and our forests."[10]

"From the beginning," said Enrique Joseph, "I felt that we were going to do all right in this fight. The companies weren't willing to debate us, but our arguments were strong. Latin Americans have endured much suffering. At least this is a guarantee that, at my age, I can continue living in a beautiful place. I want my children and their children to run on the beaches and see the trees still there."[11]

The Right to Drill Oil

Unfortunately, community organizers had not yet won the war, and they would have been hard-pressed to see the direction the dispute would take next: The company would turn to "free trade" agreements to assert its right to drill oil. Harken was furious with the court rulings upholding Costa Rica's environmental impact guidelines. Arguing that it had already invested more than $12 million in the deal, it turned to international investment treaties to sue Costa Rica—for $57 *billion*.[12]

The number caused many people to do a double take. Fifty-seven billion dollars is almost five thousand times the amount that Harken claims to have invested in Costa Rica. It is also several times larger than the whole of the country's economy. According to the World Bank, Costa Rica's annual GDP for 2005 was $20 billion, and the government's total revenue was less than $5 billion.[13] To put this sum in context, a $57 billion settlement would be the equivalent of sending $1 million to Harken every day for the next 156 years. The company argued that the $57 billion figure represented its total projected profits of the scuttled deal. Hallmarks of many "free trade" agreements—most famously embodied in the notorious Chapter 11 of NAFTA—are provisions that allow companies to sue for lost profits if a country erects trade barriers that interfere with their commerce. In this case, the "barriers" in question were Costa Rica's environmental laws.

Harken attempted to extort the enormous payment by employing the World Bank's International Center for the Settlement of Investment Disputes. But Costa Rica would have none of it. In late September 2003, soon after the Center notified the Costa Rican government of Harken's claim against it, Pacheco announced that his country would not submit to international arbitration. He refused to acknowledge any decision made by the World Bank's body, insisting instead that Costa Rica's national court system was the legitimate venue for the dispute. Although the United States has since tried to pressure Costa Rica to reach an out-of-court settlement and pay millions to Harken, the case remains unresolved.

Costa Rica has been able to stick by its environmental laws thus far in part because the World Bank's dispute mechanisms are not particularly strong. But the final fate of the Harken dispute, and other cases like it, could change when the country becomes part of CAFTA. This trade deal narrowly passed through the U.S. Congress in the summer of 2005.

CAFTA became a reality in 2006, after neoliberal governments in Guatemala, Honduras, Nicaragua, El Salvador, and the Dominican Republic beat out popular opposition and ratified the treaty. The agreement is now in effect among those countries and the United States. Intense controversy in Costa Rica forced a public referendum on CAFTA in the fall of 2007. The trade deal passed on a narrow 52 to 48 percent vote and will go into effect in March 2008, provided that Costa Rica's legislature passes a series of complementary laws required for the agreement.

For opponents of CAFTA, the Harken case is a paradigmatic example of how corporations use international agreements to bully countries into dropping environmental protections. CAFTA's investor protections are modeled after NAFTA's Chapter 11, which allows companies to bring their complaints about unfair "trade barriers" directly to international tribunals. Under the new agreement, Costa Rica would not be able to rebuff efforts to bypass its national courts. Instead, it would have to allow deliberations about Harken's astronomical $57 billion "compensation claim" to move forward on the international level.

Regardless of whether such corporate claims are upheld, the threat of a multibillion-dollar lawsuit is enough to persuade many states to back down on enforcing their environmental laws. The example of NAFTA shows that even powerful countries are susceptible to what activists dub "environmental blackmail." In one famous 1998 case, the Ethyl Corporation sued Canada over its public health ban on MMT, a fuel additive. Canada chose to overturn its environmental provision and pay $13 million to Ethyl rather than risk $251 million in damages.[14] In the United States, the State of California came under similar attack for its ban on MTBE, a documented water pollutant that poses risks to human and animal health. With such cases on record, Australia refused to include a provision in its trade agreement with the United States that would let investors bypass national courts and take disputes to international bodies. But poorer nations, who feel they cannot afford to risk losing access to U.S. markets, rarely have the power to make such demands.

Many elected officials may not even know what they are agreeing to when approving neoliberal trade deals, the texts of which are shaped by a revolving cast of trade lawyers and corporate lobbyists. Remarkably, Joseph Stiglitz, who served as chairman of the Council of Economic Advisors during Clinton's first term, has claimed that the president and his staff were not even aware of Chapter 11 and its potential impacts when they so forcefully promoted NAFTA. "Anti-environmentalists," Stiglitz asserted,

> had succeeded in burying in that chapter a provision designed to halt regulation by making it too expensive, by forcing compensation for loss of market value as a result of regulation, including regulations protecting the environment and public health. The irony was that the Clinton administration had devoted enormous energy to stopping the enactment of congressional legislation that would have done this—and had succeeded; Clinton and U.S. Trade Representative Mickey Kantor may have known this was part of the fine print in the NAFTA agreement they were simultaneously pushing, but if so, they neither talked about it publicly nor discussed it privately in the White House NAFTA meetings.[15]

Such an oversight would be especially notable given Clinton's sharp eye for policy detail. But whether he missed the chapter or merely kept quiet about it, the damage has been done. By 2006, over $13 billion in legal claims had been filed under Chapter 11.[16] And CAFTA's investor protections will now extend its reach beyond Mexico to Central America.

The office of the U.S. Trade Representative claims that CAFTA contains strong protections for the environment. It is true that the agreement includes provisions for citizens to submit charges regarding violations of environmental laws. However, although there are clear consequences for violating the agreement's investor provisions, there is no clear enforcement mechanism to ensure action on environmental complaints. The deal may also make it impossible for Costa Rica's legislative assembly to easily repeal the 1994 hydrocarbons law.

"Costa Rica of course can repeal its hydrocarbons law," explained Lori Wallach, director of Global Trade Watch at Public Citizen in Washington, D.C. "But under the final CAFTA text, the oil companies would be empowered to sue for lost profits. Plus, governments could claim that a repeal would infringe on their rights to market access in the service sector."[17] The fate of the Talamaca victory is now uncertain. And the implications extend beyond Costa Rica: If a government in one of the countries that has already ratified CAFTA decides to forgo drilling for oil in the coming years, its decision may be nearly impossible to implement.

Not "Free," Not "Trade"

The debate about CAFTA's impact reveals many problematic features of the "free trade" agenda as a whole. First, the neoliberal agenda extends far beyond traditional "trade." The primary economic impact of CAFTA is not in regulating shipments of goods between the United States and Central America—the activity most people think of as trade. The deal offered little to poorer countries in that respect: 75 percent of all goods sent from the region to the United States already entered duty-free as a result of the previously implemented Caribbean Basin Trade Partnership Act of 2000.[18]

Economically, the agreement's real impact is in opening up other sectors of the Central American economies to foreign investment. CAFTA provisions mandating access to the service sectors of Central American countries will protect corporate interests in cases like the Harken dispute. And such measures are increasingly being used to compel poorer nations to privatize utilities and other public enterprises, leading to large-scale protests.

The other main economic impact of CAFTA demonstrates how neoliberal trade deals are not very "free" either. The deal will create tougher intellectual property regulations to protect corporate copyrights and patents. Large pharmaceutical companies stand to benefit immensely from CAFTA's intellectual property provisions, which stop Central American countries from producing inexpensive, generic drugs. Dr. Karim Laouabdia of the Nobel-prize-winning organization Doctors Without Borders—which, before CAFTA, had been providing generic antiretrovirals to Guatemalan AIDS patients—has argued that new patent protections "could make newer medicines unaffordable." For his group, this "means treating fewer people and, in effect, sentencing the rest to death."[19] By any economic standard, such controls signify a move toward protectionism, not "liberalization." But since they allow drug exporters—whose lobbyists have been famously influential in recent years—to reap a windfall on their monopolized goods, the U.S. trade office has not dwelt on the contradiction.

At its core, the argument over agreements like CAFTA, NAFTA, and the WTO is a debate about whose interests the rules of trade should protect. Yet some people have a much greater voice in the debate than others. If "free trade" is not free (and often reaches far beyond the realm of traditional trade), it is also not very democratic. Instead, the agenda has been carried out in a manner that lets corporate lobbyists in but keeps the public out. While working to pass CAFTA, the White House claimed that its efforts to open markets throughout the hemisphere would serve to "strengthen democracy" abroad and commit Central American nations to "even greater openness and transparency."[20] Ironically, despite demands from watchdog groups, drafts of the CAFTA text were not made available to the public during the negotiations, stifling open, transparent, and democratic discussion about how to shape the global economy.

When the deal was made public and presented for a vote in Congress, U.S. legislators were not able to use amendments to strike out offensive planks like CAFTA's Chapter 11–style investor protections. In July 2002, President Bush had pushed "fast-track" trade negotiating authority through the House in a tight, 215 to 212 vote. The president's "fast-track" authority requires Congress to accept or reject trade policies wholesale. As Congressman Sandy Levin explained, this leaves "a minimal, meaningless, and last minute role for Congress at a time when trade policy is increasingly intertwined with all areas of domestic policy."[21]

Wanton corporate interference has become an entrenched part of trade negotiations. Representative Billy Tauzin, who was the chairman of the House Energy and Commerce Committee during the CAFTA debate, perfectly illustrates the "revolving door" between Capitol Hill and the corporate lobbying firms on Washington's K Street. Tauzin worked closely with the Pharmaceutical Research and Manufacturers of America (PhRMA) in making sure that NAFTA and CAFTA passed with intellectual property protections designed to the industry's specifications. Among other things, Tauzin's powerful committee was responsible for overseeing the drug industry. Yet promptly after retiring from Congress in 2004, he accepted a position as head of PhRMA, reportedly earning more than $2 million a year.[22]

In taking the job, Rep. Tauzin declined an offer from the Motion Picture Association of America, the lobbying organization of the film industry, which was willing to pay more than $1 million a year for his services. The entertainment industry was another business sector regulated by Tauzin's committee—and another beneficiary of the protectionist intellectual property measures in NAFTA and CAFTA. The conflicts of interest revealed by Tauzin's plush private sector appointment are obvious. But such arrangements are hardly unusual in Washington. Upon leaving their posts, powerful elected officials and their staffers can usually rely on lucrative positions from firms that seek to influence government.

Even by Beltway standards the politics of "free trade" have been notoriously crass. Up until the very eve of the House vote in July 2005, the White House did not have the support it needed to pass CAFTA. Environmentalists in Congress and pro-labor Democrats joined with conservatives whose districts were home to trade-sensitive industries like sugar and textiles to form a bloc against the deal. But in the end, the agreement squeaked through the House in a historically close vote of 217 to 215. At the last minute, the Bush administration was able to reverse several key votes with a series of unusually blatant pork barrel buy-offs.

Rarely has Washington's unsavory wheeling and dealing been made so clear as in a remarkable article in the *Kansas City Star* that told the story of how Senator Kit Bond of Missouri was essentially bribed by the White House into supporting CAFTA. It explained:

> The danger for the White House of not having enough votes for CAFTA means opportunity for Bond.
>
> Bond has pushed legislation for new locks and dams along the Mississippi. The Bush administration has, in Bond's words, "sent signals" that it opposes Bond's bill.

But Bond figures trade requires infrastructure, and getting U.S. produce to overseas markets in an efficient manner requires modernized
locks and dams.

So it's quid pro quo time.

Bond has told senior White House officials that he would support
CAFTA if they drop any opposition to his bill.

"We're in the process of negotiations and discussions," Bond said.
"Several top people have said they're coming over to talk. . . . We've got
to get them to drop their opposition and do it publicly."

And if they don't?

Bond grinned and gave a big thumbs-down sign.

"That's how it works, isn't it?" Bond said. "It's simple."[23]

In the end, the White House got Senator Bond's vote. In return, Bond,
blessed with White House support for his legislation, got $1.95 billion in
federal funding for a series of seven locks to be constructed on stretches
of the Mississippi River bordering his home state, plus an additional
$1.72 billion for "environmental restoration."[24]

Bond was not the only elected official to be similarly persuaded. The
watchdog group Public Citizen examined corporate ties to the elected
officials who cast the decisive CAFTA votes and reported that from January to September 2005, a handful of key representatives received $2.8
million in campaign contributions from political action committees
representing industries that will benefit from the trade deal.[25] Of particular note are the Democratic members of Congress who broke ranks to
side with the Bush administration, a group known as the CAFTA 15. The
report released by Public Citizen includes a copy of an invitation to a
$1,000-per-plate fund-raiser held on September 7 in honor of these De-
mocrats. The event was sponsored by the PACs of corporations, such as
Pfizer, Procter & Gamble, and Motorola.

On its face, it seems unusual that the Bush White House, which was
abandoning many multilateral trade deals, would make such a concerted
push to pass CAFTA. However, this agreement more closely resembles
the bilateral agreements the United States is now actively brokering than
it does the sweeping trade frameworks of the WTO or FTAA. Perhaps the

most crucial difference is that CAFTA does not include any major economy, such as Brazil, India, or China, that could stand up to U.S. demands and provide the shelter of a coalition for smaller countries. Instead, as with the bilateral deals, the small countries in CAFTA have little bargaining power, even as a regional bloc.

The process of passing CAFTA through the parliaments of Central American countries mirrored the debacle in the U.S. Congress. South of the border, elites rammed CAFTA through their governments despite massive public opposition. In January 2006, Todd Tucker, research director at Public Citizen's Global Trade Watch, cited polls showing that majorities throughout the region objected to the deal: 76 percent of Salvadorans believed that CAFTA would not help their country; 65 percent of Guatemalans said it would worsen conditions; 61 percent of people in the Dominican Republic opposed the deal; and 77 percent in Honduras regarded their pro-CAFTA government as corrupt.[26] Yet "free trade" marched forward nonetheless.

THE FAILURE OF NAFTA

One of the key differences between today's trade debate and that of the 1990s is that neoliberal trade deals are no longer untested propositions. Instead, we can examine the extensive track record of NAFTA. The legacy of NAFTA goes far in explaining why the "free trade" agenda continues to spark resistance internationally.

Since CAFTA was modeled after NAFTA, the U.S. Trade Representative has been eager to declare the 1994 trade deal a resounding success. Overwhelmingly, pundits in the mainstream media are happy to take them at their word. However, the actual results of NAFTA after more than ten years are hardly encouraging. Just as corporations in Costa Rica had promised local residents "clouds of gold," the Clinton White House peddled NAFTA with a series of glimmering promises that the deal has come nowhere close to fulfilling.

Most notably, "free trade" boosters promised that the deal would generate new employment opportunities. "NAFTA means jobs," President Clinton argued in a 1993 C-SPAN appearance:

American jobs, and good-paying American jobs. . . . NAFTA will generate these jobs by fostering an export boom to Mexico. . . . In 1987, Mexico exported $5.7 billion more of products to the United States than
they purchased from us. We had a trade deficit. Because of the free market, tariff-lowering policies of the Salinas government in Mexico, and
because our people are becoming more export-oriented, that $5.7 bil-
lion trade deficit has been turned into a $5.4 billion trade surplus for the
United States. It has created hundreds of thousands of jobs.[27]

NAFTA, Clinton contended, would further the export boom and expand
the trade surplus, creating even more jobs.

It didn't work out that way. After NAFTA was passed, the U.S trade surplus with Mexico swiftly plummeted. Soon it morphed into a deficit. As
economist Jeff Faux has explained, the same logic Clinton used to predict
job creation showed that the expanding trade deficit with Mexico had cost
the United States nine hundred thousand jobs by 2002.[28] The trade deficit
meant that a rising tide of imports from the South had replaced products
that might otherwise have been made by employees in U.S. factories.

Furthermore, measurements of the actual jobs exported to Mexico do
not account for the more profound impact on working people in the
United States: The mere specter of job relocation put significant down-
ward pressure on wages. The threat that a factory could be moved
abroad loomed large in nearly every labor dispute in the manufacturing
sector after NAFTA. A study carried out for the U.S. Department of Labor by Cornell University professor Kate Bronfenbrenner documented
instances where managers went so far as to start packing machinery onto
trucks labeled "Mexico" when workers at a plant refused concessions.[29]
The main effect, Faux reported, was to increase inequality in the United
States. Although worker productivity in manufacturing increased 57
percent between 1993 and 2002, wages rose only 6 percent.[30] The much
larger share of the benefit from these increases went to the owners.

If NAFTA's results in the United States were not good, those in Mexico
were much worse. There, too, a small number of wealthy individuals
profited handsomely from the agreement, while working people lost out.
In the first decade after NAFTA, real GDP growth per capita in Mexico

averaged only 1.8 percent, far lower than in preneoliberal decades.[31] When pro-NAFTA President Vicente Fox took office in 2000 with a vow to continue Washington Consensus policies, he promised his citizens 7 percent growth per year. In fact, the GDP expansion remained stagnant at 1.8 percent through Fox's six years as president. His economy created few new jobs, and for many Mexicans, migration to the North presented the only viable opportunity for escaping poverty.[32] The negative impact was especially acute in rural areas, where NAFTA created a Mexican farm crisis. Between 1993 and 2000, some 2 million *campesinos* were driven off their land after being forced to compete with a flood of cheap, subsidized agricultural products from U.S. agribusiness.[33]

Early on, NAFTA did draw formerly high-paying U.S. production jobs to Mexico—mainly to the *maquiladoras* near the border. Nevertheless, real wages in Mexico's manufacturing sector actually decreased by 13.5 percent between 1994 and 2000, according to the International Monetary Fund.[34] One reason for this decline was the failure of the trade deal to protect workers' rights to organize unions. In practice, the panel established by NAFTA's labor "side agreement" has failed to impose any real penalties on countries or corporations, even in cases of the most egregious abuse of workers' rights. In *The Children of NAFTA*, a powerful exposé by labor reporter David Bacon, dozens of workers from the *maquiladoras* of Baja California and nearby Mexican states testify that the typical conditions in the border factories are horrendous and that the toothless addendum to NAFTA has done nothing to improve workplace standards.

Exhibit A is Han Young, a Tijuana factory making chassis for Hyundai cars. There, workers who tried to form an independent union in the mid-1990s were threatened, harassed, and fired. State police, closely allied with the company's management, sent a SWAT team to intimidate striking workers. Authorities went so far as to concoct criminal charges against union leaders—accusing them of holding managers hostage during negotiations—and to chase them for months as fugitives. "They want to use these charges to keep us under constant threat of arrest, hoping it will stop the union," said José Peñaflor, one of the targeted officials.[35] The abuses were almost comically exaggerated. Yet in late

1997, when workers presented their grievances to the National Administrative Office (NAO)—the labor board created under the NAFTA side agreement—the board delayed for two years. When it finally made a ruling, it merely mandated a seminar on labor conditions.[36] The process became a sad joke. As Bacon wrote in 2004 of the NAO, "In ten years not one fired worker has been returned to their job, and not one independent union has gained legal status."[37]

Even more damning is the story of the *jonkeados*—Mexican workers whom factory managers referred to as "the junked ones." Bacon reported, "They were workers who became so sick, so chronically disabled," from inhaling toxic fumes at two factories in Mexico owned by Florida-based Breed Technologies, that they were unable to work regular jobs at the plant and were pressured by their employers to quit.[38] Bruno Noe Montañez López, who worked in a Matamoros auto trim factory testified at a NAO hearing in 2000 that as a result of his condition, his son was born with no kneecaps and an enlarged heart. However, the doctors would not let him donate blood for his infant, since, they said, Montañez's "blood was contaminated with drugs." He testified, "I have never taken drugs. The only things I inhaled were the glues and solvents I worked with."[39]

Montañez and his co-workers held out hope that their NAO complaint would force governmental action because it focused on health and safety violations, rather than unionization rights. Instead, their case reinforced a distressing pattern. "Hearings were held," Bacon explained. "Workers testified, sometimes at considerable risk." The NAO documented serious violations of the law. "And then—nothing."[40] The NAO confirmed egregious health and safety concerns at the two factories but did nothing to remedy the situation. Breed Technologies won. And its victory, Bacon's interviewees contend, reflects the very logic of neoliberal trade policy. "What makes our country attractive to U.S. [businesses]," affirmed Mexican professor Gema López Limón, "are low wages."[41]

As CAFTA takes effect, it will extend the abuses of NAFTA. When promoting the new trade deal, Bush administration officials claimed that market reforms would produce "improved working conditions" in Central America.[42] The labor records of the *maquiladora* factories in existing free trade zones in the region, however, suggest that a repeat of the Mexican situation is far more likely. Human Rights Watch issued a report in 2002 stating that "efforts to form labor unions in the maquila sector [in Guatemala] have met with devastating resistance from the industry as a whole and, at best, government negligence. Unionization efforts have been countered with mass dismissals, intimidation, indiscriminate retaliation against all workers, and plant closings."[43]

Thea Lee, assistant director of the public policy department at the AFL-CIO, noted that CAFTA diminishes pro-worker safeguards present in the Caribbean Basin Trade Partnership Act. "[Then U.S. Trade Representative Robert] Zoellick says that this agreement includes unprecedented protections for labor. That's a flat-out lie," she argued.[44] While the previous initiative mandated that participating countries uphold internationally recognized labor norms, the new agreement requires only that governments enforce their own laws, which are often far weaker. Thus, it will encourage factory owners to thwart the freedom of association and the right to form a union. That is why CAFTA was opposed not only by the AFL-CIO but also by a wide range of Central American labor organizations.

The White House and "pro-globalization" pundits still argue that the benefits of neoliberal deals trickle down to the poor, and they contend that the labor groups are ignorant of their members' own best interests. More farsighted, in their view, are corporate lobbies like the National Association of Manufacturers, which pushed hard for both NAFTA and CAFTA.

POLITICAL REALIGNMENT

"Free trade" has produced some of the most contentious political debates of our times. As we will see, the injustices of neoliberal trade policy and the hypocrisy of U.S. stances in international negotiations have produced an upheaval in multilateral institutions such as the WTO, and this has helped to transform the debate about the global economy. But trade is also a significant domestic issue. Today, trade policy plays an important role in the battle for the soul of the Democratic Party.

One of the major accomplishments of the Clinton administration was its successful promotion of the agenda of the Democratic Leadership Council (DLC)—a centrist, corporate-friendly faction within the Democratic Party. Working with pro–"free trade" Republicans, Clinton and the DLC made passing NAFTA in 1993 and approving U.S. entry into the WTO in 1994 into bipartisan crusades. The coalition in favor of corporate globalization was always tenuous, however. In recent years, especially as the Bush administration implemented an increasing belligerent foreign policy, the "free trade" coalition has frayed.

The center of gravity around trade issues has been slowly shifting in the Democratic Party throughout the Bush years, as candidates have found that popular disaffection with "free trade" deals can be a potent political force. As a result, trade debates have grown increasingly contentious. The Bush administration's need to resort to desperate measures to pass CAFTA—and the fact that it squeaked through Congress with the smallest possible majority—reflected the conflict.

When the Democrats swept the November 2006 elections and regained control of Congress, many of the victorious campaigns featured prominent pledges to oppose pro-corporate trade policy. In an excellent postelection analysis, Public Citizen's Global Trade Watch documented a major defeat for the "free trade" coalition. Its report tracked seven senate races and twenty-eight House contests in which "fair trade" advocates ousted "free trade" incumbents or won open seats previously held by advocates of neoliberal deals. In contrast, no fair trade incumbents were unseated.[45] Prominent progressive winners included Vermont Senator Bernie Sanders, an outspoken critic of corporate globalization, and Ohio Senator Sherrod Brown, who joined an Ohio union delegation on the streets of Seattle during the 1999 WTO protests and has since authored a book devoted, as its title indicates, to debunking the *Myths of Free Trade*. A *Miami Herald* headline succinctly summed up the electoral results: "Democrats Won Big by Opposing Free-Trade Agreements."[46]

Whether the wave of revulsion against corporate globalization will propel a lasting change in Democratic policymaking will depend largely on figures such as Representative Charlie Rangel, House Speaker Nancy Pelosi, and Senator Max Baucus, the Montana Democrat who became chair of the Senate Finance Committee. These party chiefs may not be "free traders" like Bill Clinton, but neither are they leading fair trade activists like Brown and Sanders. In late 2006, President Bush visited Vietnam the week before Thanksgiving, and he hoped to bring with him news of Congress's approval of Permanent Normal Trade Relations with that country, a measure that would have served as a stepping-stone to a free trade deal and an endorsement of Vietnam's entry into the WTO. But it did not happen. The bill failed to secure the two-thirds majority it needed to pass, with many emboldened Democrats rallying to defeat it. The *New York Times* declared that the vote, which was supposed to have been an easy victory, signaled "a deep disappointment and embarrassment for the White House."[47]

It may prove to be a temporary setback, however. Both Pelosi and Rangel voted in favor of the Vietnam trade legislation, and promoters of the deal intend to introduce a new bill. In May 2007, Democratic leaders announced that they had brokered a deal with the White House to resume the bipartisan push for "free trade" agreements, ostensibly with stronger labor and environmental provisions attached. True to form, the deal was negotiated in secret, without input from environmental, labor, or public interest groups—or even participation from the majority of Democratic lawmakers who view the "free trade" agenda with suspicion. What the agreement will mean in practice, and whether opposition lawmakers and the citizens who put them into office will accept the Bush-Rangel deal, has not been determined as of late 2007.

The ongoing battle in Washington has made it clear that many centrist Democrats who denounce Bush's imperial globalization would be all too eager to return to Clinton's pro-corporate vision for the global economy if given the chance. But it also indicates that their position may not be as politically viable as it once was. A decade and a half after NAFTA moved the trade debate to the fore of political discussion, the broken promises of "free trade" agreements are making neoliberalism's "clouds of gold" ever harder to sell. And while opposition is solidifying within the United

States, corporate globalizers may be even more distressed to survey the international scene. To the dismay of those who worked patiently to build the Washington Consensus and to ensure multilateral acquiescence to its demands during the Clinton era, Bush's imperial globalists have helped to fuel a worldwide revolt against their trade agenda.

6

SINKING THE WTO

Of all the recent changes in the politics of the global economy, perhaps none is starker than the altered fate of the World Trade Organization (WTO). In the mid-1990s, corporate globalizers hailed the institution as the foundation of a new international order, and critics decried it as a juggernaut that would imperil global democracy. A famous 1996 remark from Renato Ruggiero, the first director-general of the WTO, captured the high-flying confidence of the era's neoliberals: "We are no longer writing the rules of interaction among separate national economies," he said. "We are writing the constitution of a single global economy."[1]

A decade after Ruggiero's declaration, the scene looked very different. In 2006, the most widely repeated quote regarding the institution came from India's trade minister, Kamal Nath, who stated that the WTO's collapsing trade talks were somewhere "between intensive care and the crematorium."[2]

The forces responsible for the WTO's reversal of fortune were clearly visible in the sunny resort town of Cancún, Mexico, where trade ministers met for the organization's September 2003 Ministerial Conference. Even in ordinary times, the divisions between rich and poor in Cancún are dramatic. In the beachfront hotel zone, tourists lounge on white sand beaches and dine in luxury hotels, their needs catered to by Mexicans who live in another Cancún—the crowded and run-down inland sections of the city several miles away. During the WTO meetings, the contrast could not have been starker. The hotel zone, where the trade ministers gathered, was turned into a militarized compound. More than ten thousand protesters—farmers' groups, labor activists, students, and environmentalists—marched from downtown Cancún toward the hotel zone, butting against lines of Mexican police.

At the height of the protests, Lee Kyung Hae, a man who had traveled to Cancún as part of a delegation of activists from South Korea, climbed to the top of the ten-foot-tall fence that barricaded the public from the WTO meetings, wearing a sign that read, "The WTO Kills Farmers." To the horror of the crowd, he then pulled out a knife and plunged it into his chest. His ritual suicide became a dramatic representation of the pain and outrage caused by the neoliberal agenda. Throughout the world, WTO policies had inspired massive demonstrations publicizing the negative impacts of "free trade" and shining a spotlight on normally secretive negotiations.

Inside the hotel zone, trade ministers from the global South, some of whom had been appointed by new governments that had risen to power on the strength of antineoliberal social movements, did something different from what they had done in past negotiations: When the United States and Europe refused to cut agricultural subsidies or to open their own markets, the Southern delegates joined together and denounced the double standard. Brazilian Trade Minister Celso Amorim announced the formation of the "Group of Twenty," a bloc of developing countries that combined forces to defend their national interests. Amorim explained that the bloc, which soon added members and became known as the G20+, represented more than two-thirds of the world's farmers and over half of its overall population.[3] Although the countries represented had regularly been silenced, steamrolled, or bought off as individual parties during previous negotiations, they represented a formidable force as a coordinated group. Without their consent, no WTO deal could go forward. And so, when they declared their opposition, the Cancún talks swiftly unraveled.

Something else happened in Cancún, however. As the WTO's conference fell apart, U.S. Trade Representative Robert Zoellick, a middle-aged man with squinting eyes, a thin mustache, and wave of red-brown hair across his forehead, stood before cameras and announced a new U.S. trade strategy. Expressing his frustration with the "won't do" nations that refused to accede to Washington's demands, Zoellick vowed to work with "can do" countries to secure individual trade agreements. As it turned out, the imperial globalists of the Bush administration, too, were willing to break free from the multilateral institution. They announced their intention to forge ahead on their own, without the WTO.

The Cancún Ministerial Conference had lasting implications, and even today it raises many intriguing questions. Why was the WTO, which had virtually disappeared from the media, still inspiring enough passion to drive someone to suicide? How had a group like the G20+ taken shape? And what impact would the Bush administration's new trade strategy have for advocates of democratic globalization? Even among those who closely watched the WTO in the post-Seattle period, the answers are not necessarily clear. Yet, at a time when trade policy significantly affects how democratic countries manage their economies, and when the debate about globalization has become more open than it has been in decades, these answers are more important than ever.

Neoliberal Trade Goes Global

The words "free trade" suggest that neoliberal trade deals are straightforward agreements, allowing for a simple exchange of goods between countries. In fact, the agreements are anything but simple. They are elaborately structured legal documents, sometimes thousands of pages long, which advance the interests of certain groups at the expense of others. In general, the interests they favor are those of wealthy countries and powerful corporations within those countries. No trade agreement illustrates this better than the WTO. Before examining the post-2006 deadlock in

WTO trade talks, it is useful to look at the organization's history. Like U.S. deals with Mexico and Central America, the WTO is a trade pact that propagates neoliberalism, but it aims to do so on a larger scale than ever before. Despite the recent failure to expand its scope and influence, the organization still has a troubling amount of power to regulate global trade and to control the development options available to poorer countries. International trade was already increasing tremendously before the WTO was established in 1995, so the need for the organization was not clear from the sole perspective of trade. In truth, the main purpose of the deal was to protect the interests of investors. Created to replace the previous General Agreement on Tariffs and Trade, the WTO went beyond national treaties to advance, as Ruggiero said, a "single constitution" for the global economy.

Citizens who like their old constitutions just fine have good reason to be worried. At best, the WTO is indirectly democratic, with elite trade ministers representing their populations. The fact that the overwhelming majority of Americans can't name the U.S. trade representative suggests that this person should probably not be designated a founding father for a new world order. But this problem only hints at deeper troubles. In practice, there is little democratic oversight of the institution. Trade lawyers and corporate lobbyists pore over the fine print of the WTO documents, but few elected officials have any idea what the specific planks of the trade agreements entail.

In the fall of 1994, Ralph Nader famously issued a challenge to members of Congress who were about to approve U.S. entry into the WTO. He offered to donate $10,000 to charity on behalf of any legislator who would actually read the dense, several-hundred-page text of the pending bill and answer ten simple questions about it. The only person to take Nader up on his offer was Republican Senator Hank Brown, a proponent of "free trade." Brown read the bill and aced the test. He then voted against the WTO legislation. Encouraging his colleagues to do likewise, he stated, "Anyone who thinks this agreement expands free trade has not read it."[4]

While lawmakers are in the dark, corporate representatives show a much greater familiarity with the details of WTO agreements—and they have excelled at getting protections for their industries included in the texts. Daniel Amstutz, the official in the U.S. trade office who drafted what would become the WTO's Agreement on Agriculture, was a former vice president of the agribusiness giant Cargill. Taking advantage of Washington's "revolving door," he subsequently returned to private practice and cashed in as an agribusiness lobbyist—only to return to service in the Bush administration in 2003 to oversee the "reconstruction" of agriculture in occupied Iraq.[5]

The extent of corporate influence at the WTO became most clear at the 1999 Seattle Ministerial Conference. The most powerful player in the talks, the U.S. trade representative, officially formed its negotiating positions in consultation with seventeen "Industrial Sector Advisory Committees" made up of representatives from corporations in trade-affected industries. At times, the line between governmental officials and business lobbyists was hard to distinguish. Private sponsors donated $9.2 million to Seattle's host committee to help cover the costs of the WTO meetings. As Russell Mokhiber and Robert Weissman reported, companies that contributed at the $250,000 "Emerald Level," including Allied Signal/Honeywell, Deloitte & Touche, Ford, GM, Microsoft, Nextel, and Boeing, were allowed to send five representatives to the host committee's opening and closing receptions for the conference, as well as to an exclusive dinner with trade ministers. The host committee organized special conferences for private-sector donors, provided up-to-the-minute briefings on negotiations, and offered the lobbyists assistance with their accommodations for the event.[6]

The "access" provided to corporate officials fit into a well established pattern: The whole agenda of the WTO has been structured around the interests of the powerful. The institution's promoters currently want to extend WTO powers in areas like investment and service sector liberalization; this would push countries in the global South farther down the road of privatization and neoliberal deregulation. Fortunately, the current collapse of WTO talks has stopped them from getting their wish. A key reason for the deadlock is intransigence on the part of wealthy nations. The United States and European countries have made few sacrifices for the global South and continue to maintain massive subsidies for their agricultural markets. Many observers have noted that the average cow in Europe receives a subsidy of more than $2 a day, while some 3 billion people live on less.[7] Investor protections and intellectual property rights have been chief matters of concern at WTO talks, whereas discussion of workers' rights and environmental protections has taken place either as an afterthought or as a public relations exercise. And like NAFTA's Chapter 11, the WTO's dispute resolution mechanisms allow corporate interests in one nation to challenge environmental and public interest laws of another country. Furthermore, dispute hearings take place before secret tribunals, hidden from public scrutiny.

Lee Kyung Hae's suicide was a reminder that even as global justice activists in the United States tended to focus their energy on targeting the Bush administration rather than the WTO, the institution continued to draw protests in many parts of the world. Before his death, Lee denounced a situation in which "uncontrolled multinational corporations and a small number of big WTO members are leading an undesirable globalization that is inhumane, environmentally degrading, farmer-killing, and undemocratic."[8] While progressives have debated the merits of agricultural subsidies in different contexts,[9] it is clear that the agribusiness giants that are virtually writing large blocks of WTO agreements have done very well in the institution's negotiations, while small farmers have been forced to bear the brunt of the burden—dislocation, hunger, community dissolution, and material hardship—of "adjusting" to the neoliberal global economy.

Given its practices, it was hardly surprising that the WTO would draw protests from an international network of environmentalists, labor organizers, small farmers, and public interest groups. The more unexpected development was that the institution would be abandoned by the right.

Hard Times for the WTO

During the Clinton years, the WTO was on the rise. It embodied the corporate globalizers' dream of a cooperative, rules-based multilateral system that would benefit all participating countries, the United States first among them. Since then, establishment pundits have stood almost unanimously in favor of creating new trade deals and have beat a steady drum of praise for multilateral agreements like the WTO and the Free Trade Area of the Americas (FTAA). Under Bush the rhetoric became part of the administration's promise to spread its particular brand of freedom throughout the word. Yet, despite widespread declarations of support within the Beltway, multilateral "free trade" initiatives have fallen on hard times.

While President Bush has consistently paid lip service to "free trade," he has been more overt and aggressive than his predecessors in placing nationalist concerns above multilateral harmony. Early in his first term, U.S. negotiators gained a reputation for being even more stubborn than their European and Japanese counterparts in their refusal to cut agricultural subsidies. In 2002 and 2003, the White House provoked a bitter trade war with Europe by implementing protective tariffs for the U.S. steel industry. Time and time again, the Bush administration has refused to make the type of compromises in international forums needed to protect the multilateral order.

Even before Bush took office, the WTO was in trouble. The spectacular collapse of trade talks at the Seattle Ministerial Conference in late 1999 not only signaled a new phase of heightened public opposition to the organization but also highlighted long-standing differences between the North and the South on trade issues. Since then, developing countries have rebelled over the wealthier nations' hypocrisy on agricultural subsidies. They have demanded new concessions before agreeing to open their markets further. The Bush administration has been even more hesitant than usual to grant them, and this has created a lasting impasse.

In November 2001, in the wake of 9/11, the WTO met in Doha, Qatar—a remote and repressive Persian Gulf state, conveniently inaccessible to protesters—to try to recover from the damage of the Seattle collapse. Capitalizing on the wave of global sympathy for the United States following the terrorist attacks, Trade Representative Robert Zoellick (who is now the president of the World Bank) was able to convince the assembled nations to adopt the "Doha Declaration," which initiated a new round of trade talks. Sidestepping sensitive agricultural issues, the declaration focused primarily on increasing WTO sway in areas like investment and services. Had it gone forward as planned, the round of trade talks would have represented a significant expansion of the organization's power. The summit's avoidance of agricultural issues and the anxious, conciliatory posturing of the parties involved allowed for at least the possibility that negotiations would move ahead. Doha's success, however, was always precarious, something that became very clear before the WTO's September 2003 Ministerial Conference in Cancún.

Between Doha and Cancún, negotiators met in a series of closed-door sessions to try to resolve some of the knotty agricultural issues that lingered. They made little progress. Not only was the Bush administration unwilling to cut subsidies, but it seemed insistent on expanding agricultural protections to appease domestic interests. Trading partners watched in dismay as President Bush signed a new U.S. farm bill in May 2002 that guaranteed American farmers $190 billion in subsidies over a ten-year period, almost doubling subsidies on some products.[10]

By the time Cancún rolled around, not many trade analysts expected a breakthrough, and few were surprised when the meetings ultimately ended in collapse. The most interesting aspect of the summit was not the deadlock of the WTO negotiations, which was largely expected, but the manner in which this failure occurred. The G20+, led by Brazil, China, India, and South Africa, was an ambiguous ally of social justice organizations. Many of the G20+ trade ministers represented wealthy elites in their own countries, and their objectives did not necessarily coincide with the demands of demonstrators outside the trade meetings. Nevertheless, the emergence of the G20+ was an exciting and unexpected development. The level of coordination among Southern governments had rarely been seen since the 1970s, and it represented a potentially momentous shift in global trade politics. With the G20+ countries united, the United States had little ability to strong-arm poorer trading partners.

DIVIDE AND CONQUER

What happened next took many protesters by surprise. While not pleased with the Cancún collapse, the Bush administration did not show many overt signs of worry. Instead, it unveiled a new divide-and-conquer approach to trade negotiations—a strategy that would allow it to sidestep international bodies like the WTO. Behind the move was a deep distrust of multilateral institutions. Just as many right-wingers dislike the World Bank and would prefer that the United States provide its foreign aid in direct, bilateral payments—allowing Washington to tie its aid packages to its foreign policy interests—these same conservatives consider the WTO to be a burdensome diversion. Unlike elected officials who look after corporate interests in multilateral trade deals and take advantage of Washington's lucrative revolving door (such as former Representative Billy Tauzin), this strand of conservatives is largely made up of think-tank analysts, longtime political staffers, academics, and right-wing magazine editors who are preoccupied with U.S. power. In theory, the WTO operates on the basis of "one country, one vote," which gives the United States no more say than its smallest trading partner. Imperial globalists think this is a ridiculous arrangement—certainly not one befitting the world's only remaining superpower.

In the wake of the Cancún failure, Zoellick declared that the United States would promote smaller regional and bilateral treaties, similar to those that it had recently brokered with Chile and Singapore. Zoellick's vow to work individually with "can do" countries was not unlike Bush's military "coalition of the willing" in Iraq. Predictably, the "can do" countries were generally smaller nations, often led by pro-U.S. neoliberals, which, in any case, had little leverage to make contrary demands when bargaining with a global superpower. The bilateral approach to trade abandoned the corporate globalist dream of a uniform, rules-based economic order in which international capital could thrive. Instead, it represented a bare-knuckles approach to promoting U.S. power, even at the expense of European allies. Diving headfirst into bilateral negotiations, the White House pursued deals with countries including Morocco, Peru, Oman, Australia, Colombia, and Korea.

The WTO was not the only multilateral initiative to falter under this new strategy. Another casualty of the Bush administration's economic nationalism was the Free Trade Area of the Americas (FTAA). The United States once envisioned the FTAA as a hemisphere-wide pact that would extend NAFTA through the southern tip of Argentina. Under Clinton, negotiations for the deal had moved slowly but steadily forward. However, by November 2003, when Florida Governor Jeb Bush hosted an FTAA summit in Miami, the deal had reached an impasse. U.S. negotiating positions had hardened under President Bush. Meanwhile, a new generation of progressive leaders had swept into office in many Latin American countries, propelled by boisterous social movements against neoliberalism. This made the region's leaders far more willing to defy haughty White House demands.

Venezuela's Hugo Chávez was outspoken in his opposition to the FTAA. Also problematic for Washington was Brazil, led by progressive Luiz Inácio Lula da Silva. Although Brazil, alongside the United States, officially served as one of the cochairs of the FTAA talks, it was also one of the countries that forced a stalemate in Cancún. In advance of the Miami talks, its negotiators were in no mood to cave in to Bush administration pressure for one-sided concessions. The *Economist* explained before the Miami talks, "Not only are [Brazil and the U.S.] further apart than ever on the [FTAA] accord's scope and ambition, but they have spent the past few weeks publicly bad-mouthing each other."[11]

Almost a week before the summit, trade officials announced that none of the substantive issues for the agreement would be on the table for discussion. Miami had failed in advance. Yet, to avoid another outright collapse like Cancún, the United States promoted a face-saving "FTAA-Lite" that allowed Jeb Bush to put a sunshine spin on the deadlock and declare the summit a victory for Florida. The "Lite" FTAA was supposed to be a more flexible version of the agreement that forced fewer binding obligations on its participants. Few trade observers were fooled by the ploy, however. They knew that the FTAA was close to death as ministers departed from Miami.

At this time, the Bush administration announced forward progress on bilateral trade agreements with Colombia, Peru, and Bolivia. Yet, with the failure of Miami, the United States lost access to the key economies of the hemisphere: Venezuela, Argentina, and most importantly, Brazil. The Venezuelan delegation, which had blasted the FTAA as colonialist in design, released perhaps the bluntest statement about Miami's outcome:

"This is an extraordinary victory in the struggle against the FTAA," said Edgardo Lander, a member of Venezuela's Presidential FTAA Committee. "They wanted a full-scale, comprehensive agreement, and they didn't get it. They will never get it. This is not the end of the game. But it is a major, major defeat of the U.S. agenda."[12]

The end of the game for the FTAA was not long in coming. At a January 2004 meeting in Monterrey, Mexico, Brazil's Lula da Silva argued in a highly publicized address, "After the '80s—the so-called lost decade—the '90s was a decade of despair," brought about by a "perverse model that wrongly separated the economic from the social, put stability against growth, and separated responsibility and justice."[13] Venezuela's Chávez demanded "a new moral architecture" in Latin America "favoring the weakest."[14] In this climate, hopes of reviving the FTAA languished. By the next major meeting of hemispheric leaders—a November 2005 summit in Mar del Plata, Argentina—all pretense of forward progress vanished. Future Bolivian president Evo Morales and soccer legend Diego Maradona led a protest against President Bush that packed the streets with forty thousand people, and talks were similarly adversarial. This time even the United States was willing to declare the FTAA dead.

It wasn't much longer before talks at the WTO, the gem of the multilateral system, would go on life support. Trade ministers tried to keep WTO negotiations limping along at a December 2005 Ministerial Conference in Hong Kong. On the PR front, they worked to deflect criticism by promoting the Doha round of trade talks as the "Development Round," ostensibly designed to benefit the global South. But the developing countries did not buy it. Their conflicts with the North seemed intractable.

Make no mistake, the WTO is not altogether dead. Previous agreements made at the organization are still in effect, and its trade courts still have the power to force open markets and strike down public interest laws as trade barriers. But at the same time, negotiations designed to expand the organization's reach and solidify a single multilateral framework for trade have indeed sputtered to a halt. This has been a source of great dismay for corporate globalizers. Reflecting their malaise, influential pro–"free trade" columnist Sebastian Mallaby of the *Washington Post*

complained in April 2006, "It's not that the underlying forces of globalization have gone limp; it's that nobody wants to invest political capital in
global institutions."[15] Following another unproductive meeting of negotiators in July 2006, WTO Director General Pascal Lamy announced the
official suspension of trade talks.[16]

Is Market Access the Answer to Poverty?

Given that social movements had long protested the WTO, its troubles
should have been cause for rejoicing. But instead, the shifts in the trade
debate during the Bush years often created confusion and sometimes
conflict among progressives. As the WTO has fallen on hard times,
some would-be critics have backed away from attacking the organization. Fearful that Bush's bilateral strategy would leave the world's poor
in an even worse situation, they have pushed for reforms at the multilateral body.

As early as Cancún, one response to the deadlock at the WTO was to
focus on the double standard created by the wealthy nations and demand access to agricultural markets for poor countries. Some proponents of this position—led by Oxfam, the prominent antipoverty
organization—distanced themselves from protest groups who denounced the WTO as a whole. In doing so, they joined more mainstream
"free trade" advocates: Institutions like the World Bank and the *New York
Times* editorial board argued that first-world market access was a cornerstone for development and poverty reduction.

It is undoubtedly true that the world's wealthiest countries are guilty
of rank hypocrisy; they preach to poorer nations the virtues of open
markets while providing nearly $1 billion dollars a day in subsidies for
their own farmers.[17] But the Oxfam campaigners, by focusing on the issue of agricultural subsidies and distancing themselves from other critics
of corporate globalization, raised a tricky question: Is market access
really an effective way to relieve global poverty?

In 2002 Oxfam released a report titled "Rigged Rules and Double
Standards." The report presented a range of recommendations for im-
proving the terms of international trade and development, but market

access became the clear focus as the document was promoted in the media. Oxfam echoed World Bank rhetoric, arguing: "For [the] engine [of trade] to function, poor countries need access to rich country markets. Expanding market access can help countries to accelerate economic growth, at the same time expanding opportunities for the poor."[18]

Most controversially, in repudiating segments of the global justice movement that disagreed with its focus on market access, Oxfam employed the same language used by conservative arch-critics to condemn activists as a whole. "Current debates about trade are dominated by ritualistic exchanges between two camps," the report read, "the 'globaphiles' and the 'globaphobes.'" Distinguishing itself from the "globaphobes," Oxfam claimed to have a reasonable, middle-ground position. It argued: "[T]he war of words between trade optimists and trade pessimists that accompanies virtually every international meeting is counter-productive. Both world views fly in the face of the evidence—and neither offers any hope for the future."[19]

Social movement representatives from developing countries, who have often criticized the trade positions of their own government elites, were among the first to respond. Walden Bello charged Oxfam with "caricaturing [free trade critics] in the crudest *Economist* fashion."[20] Faced with this backlash, Oxfam later backed away from such gratuitous criticism of allies in the global justice movement. And subsequently, the organization tempered its demands for market access with greater emphasis on resisting the forced intrusion of neoliberalism into poorer countries.

There are good reasons not to uncritically jump on the bandwagon promoting "free trade" and ending subsidies. First, it is not at all clear that basing economic development on agricultural exports will allow countries to "trade their way out of poverty," as proponents claim. Historically, many nations that relied on export-led development were foiled by declining agricultural prices on the world market. As noted in an earlier, 1992 Oxfam report titled "The Trade Trap," "Countries that depend on the export of primary commodities like coffee, sugar, or cotton are caught in a trap: [T]he more they produce, the lower the price falls."[21]

Ending lavish subsidies would help this situation somewhat by reducing the "dumping" of artificially underpriced first-world goods on the international market. It would not help a lot, however, even if the United States, Europe, and Japan were to eliminate their supports entirely—something that is politically out of the question. The typically pro-trade advocate Nancy Birdsall, along with economists Dani Rodrik and Arvind Subramanian, cited IMF estimates in a 2005 *Foreign Affairs* article discussing the elimination of commodity price supports: "[W]orld prices would only rise by 2 to 8 percent for rice, sugar, and wheat; 4 percent for cotton; and 7 percent for beef. The typical annual variation in the world prices of these commodities is at least one order of magnitude larger."[22] In other words, even with total trade liberalization, the notorious instability of agricultural export markets would remain a bane of poor farmers struggling to survive.

Trumpeting the potential economic benefits of forward progress at the WTO, the World Bank claimed that developing countries would increase their overall GDP by $86 billion if all tariffs were eliminated and trade were completely liberalized.[23] However, this represents a GDP increase of only 0.8 percent. Furthermore, the Doha round of WTO talks promise a much more modest liberalization and would produce only a fraction of this already limited increase. Economist Mark Weisbrot pointed out, "Even a very successful Doha round would barely make a dent in poverty rates: according to the [World Bank] study, the number of people living in poverty in 2016 would be reduced by somewhere between 0.4 and 1 percent."[24] Such decreases, while not insignificant, hardly constitute a panacea for developing countries.

Small farmers are in the worst position to actually reap any income gains from liberalization, which are far more likely to be siphoned off by middlemen. Competing against giant agribusiness corporations that dominate markets and enjoy great political influence (not to mention access to deep lines of credit and facilities in which to store commodities when prices are low), small producers find themselves playing a rigged game. Moreover, the continuing fall of the dollar means that U.S. import markets will contract. Countries that have based their development strategies on gaining a piece of that pie will be left to fight with one another over ever-smaller slices.

Politically speaking, following the World Bank and the *New York Times* in their focus on market access draws attention away from alternative policies that would support small producers in a much more direct way—solutions promoted by social movements in the global South. These include using antitrust law to curb the power of agribusiness, pressing for land reform, promoting regional trade, and upholding international provisions for "special and differential treatment" that allow poor countries with vulnerable populations to ensure food security for their people.

Even if developing countries win concessions on agricultural subsidies in the future, the access to markets will come at a cost. In return, wealthy countries will demand that their trade partners open in other ways—forcing poorer nations to privatize services like water and electricity distribution and curtailing their ability to protect infant industries. Thus, their chances of moving beyond dependence on agricultural exports and developing high-tech or value-added products that would make them more competitive in the global marketplace will be limited. A WTO compromise would also mean cutting government safety nets that have helped protect farmers from the unforgiving fluctuations of international markets. Since furthering corporate globalization is not a price that developing countries should be forced to pay for ending U.S. and European stonewalling on agriculture, the prospects for a just solution to emerge at the WTO look dim.

THE BILATERAL DILEMMA

When the Doha round of negotiations collapsed in July 2006, groups like Public Citizen regarded it as a hopeful event. Lori Wallach, director of the group's Global Trade Watch, released a statement arguing, "Governments and civil society around the world now have an extraordinary opportunity to create a multilateral trading system that could actually deliver benefits to the majority."[25]

The opportunity is genuine. Yet a stalemate at the WTO presented new threats as well. Wallach's vision of a better trade system may ultimately be realized, but it won't come easy. Brazilian Foreign Minister Celso Amorim stated that, as the WTO unravels, international trade will operate according to "the law of the jungle"—where the strong lord over the weak.[26] That suits White House unilateralists just fine, but it has given some progressives the chills. In advance of an earlier WTO meeting, British journalist George Monbiot went so far as to publicly proclaim that he was wrong in calling for the abolition of the institution: "The only thing worse than a world with the wrong international trade rules is a world with no trade rules at all," he wrote.[27]

In Bush's bilateral, one-on-one trade agreements with other countries, poorer nations cannot seek strength in numbers. This approach undermines negotiating blocs like the G20+, which stood up to the United States and Europe in Cancún. CAFTA showed the danger of the strategy. When negotiating this smaller, regional deal, Central American countries had few good cards to play against the daunting United States. Those countries with neoliberal governments signed on to the deal willingly, and those with reservations were threatened with exclusion. As Monbiot observed, President Bush "is seeking to negotiate individually with weaker countries so that he can force even harsher terms of trade upon them. He wants to replace a multilateral trading system with an imperial one. And this puts the global justice movement in a difficult position."[28]

Likewise, Nobel Prize–winning economist Joseph Stiglitz has held that for the countries entering into bilateral deals with the United States, "these agreements have potentially been a disaster." Stiglitz went on to describe the hardball character of these "agreements": "I was having dinner the other night with one of the main trade negotiators of the Morocco agreement. He was opposed to it, and pointed out it was hardly a negotiation. The United States made demands, which Morocco had to either accept or reject. Morocco was hopeful that signing it would at least lead to a burst of new growth, but it hasn't. All it did was reduce access to AIDS medicines."[29] Stiglitz fears that more bilateral deals would only spread the damage.

What then, should we make of the shift in trade strategy under imperial globalization? To an extent, Monbiot and Stiglitz's concerns are valid. Confronting the bilateral deals will no doubt present fresh difficulties for activists. Still, that does not mean that saving the WTO is necessarily a worthwhile task for critics of corporate and imperial globalization. Bilateral negotiations were advancing with or without the multilateral body. The progress of talks at the WTO does not prevent bilateral talks from moving forward nor does it mitigate the harm of these smaller deals.

No doubt, the damage wrought by these smaller agreements is real. At the same time, we should not overstate the impact of bilateral negotiations. Although the United States has brokered deals with many countries, the world's largest economies have shunned coercive one-on-one agreements. In the case of Latin America, the region's most significant players—Brazil, Venezuela, and Argentina—remain out of U.S. reach with the demise of the FTAA and the halting of the WTO.

Finally, critics of the Bush administration need not accept that their enemy's enemy is their friend. Efforts to reform the WTO have met with little past success. Monbiot's proposal to "transform it into a Fair Trade Organization, whose purpose is to restrain the rich while emancipating the poor" remains a distant dream.[30] In theory, the WTO operates on a system of "one country, one vote," but in practice the trade ministers do not vote at all. Instead, deals are brokered by "consensus," which involves intricate backroom negotiations between major world powers. Smaller countries generally have two options: begrudgingly go along or be ostracized. Were the body actually to move to an open voting system, the most powerful nations of the world would quickly flee. Those who imagine a better trading system emerging through a democratic renewal within the WTO must reckon with the inherently undemocratic politics that reaches to the very core of the organization.

Toward a New Vision for Trade

Before preparing any eulogies for the WTO, observers of all political stripes should make sure to check its pulse. First, even if talks at the WTO fail to move forward, the earlier agreements made at the institution are still in place; the organization's secretive rulings can still dramatically limit the development strategies available to a great number of countries and can endanger environmental and public health laws throughout the world. Therefore, global justice advocates will still have work to do in curtailing the institution's power. Second, trade talks have collapsed before. The pre-WTO Uruguay round of negotiations was deadlocked in the early 1990s but was later revived and completed. Likewise, negotiators ultimately returned to the table after the WTO's Seattle and Cancún Ministerial Conferences ended in acrimony. Progress on WTO talks before the end of Bush's term in office is unlikely. However, the organization could be resurrected by a future administration that is more multilaterally minded and more committed to corporate—as opposed to imperial—globalization than the current administration. To prevent this, the global justice movement will need not only to take on bilateral trade agreements sponsored by Republicans but to rebuke pro–"free trade" Democrats and push elected officials to support a real alternative to corporate globalization.

While often portrayed as naïve and fearful protectionists, those working to craft a grassroots globalization have in fact proposed a wide range of ideas for creating a fairer system of international exchange. In doing so, they have revealed that the true struggle is over whose interests the rules of trade will protect. Trade will continue with or without neoliberal pacts to guide it. Opponents of agreements like NAFTA, CAFTA, and the WTO first and foremost reject a system designed for the benefit of corporate elites—and insist that a more democratic alternative can be built.

Until such an alternative blooms, advocates can take inspiration from seeing the once-unstoppable Goliath of the WTO lying flat on its back. The organization was poised to cobble together a bad trade deal that would have further punished the poor. That has been averted by the collapse of the Doha negotiations. And now, more than any time in the past quarter century, the field of debate about our global economy is open for new ideas.

7

THE WORLD IS NOT FLAT

The two people who are perhaps most commonly called upon to explain globalization to the American people strike very different public poses. Turn on the TV and flip to a C-SPAN or CNN discussion of the global economy and you are likely to spot the square head and mustachioed face of *New York Times* columnist Thomas Friedman, who probably will be expressing enthusiasm for the business world's newest high-tech innovations. Change the channel and you might find Joseph Stiglitz, a balding and bespectacled economist with a scruffy white beard who has been likened to actor Richard Dreyfuss. Stiglitz exhibits the demeanor of an absentminded professor; his tie tends to be crooked if not missing. Yet his criticisms of institutions like the IMF are as pointed and incisive as Friedman's paeans to corporate globalization are celebratory.

As "globalization" emerged as a media buzzword in the 1990s, a legion of commentators appeared to discuss the phenomenon. Understanding Friedman and Stiglitz's work is important for a simple reason: No one else from this class of pundits has been as ubiquitous or influential. Both authors have written best-sellers that might be displayed on the front table of your local bookstore. And you would be hard-pressed to engage in mainstream debate about globalization without reckoning with their viewpoints. These two individuals are compelling for a second reason as well: Both have followed trajectories in their professional lives that reveal noteworthy facets of the evolving debate about how to rule the world. Having reviewed the shifts in globalization politics that have taken place in the Bush years, I turn in the third part of this book to examine the drive to create a more democratic global economy. But first, it is valuable to examine how two prominent commentators have navigated globalization's changing currents.

Thomas Friedman stepped forward in the late 1990s as a leading cheerleader for corporate globalization, publishing the best-selling *The Lexus and the Olive Tree*. In the wake of 9/11, he made common cause with White House militarists. He became a high-profile "liberal hawk" and supported the war in Iraq—only to distance himself later in the Bush era and return to championing corporate expansion with a second widely read book on globalization, *The World Is Flat*. For better or for worse, his punditry provides an indispensable guide to how mainstream commentators have tried to defend neoliberalism in the face of challenges from worldwide social movements. Moreover, Friedman's renewed emphasis on corporate globalization in the wake of the botched war in Iraq may also be a significant bellwether for how the Democratic Party—especially the more conservative "New Democrat" wing of the party—crafts a vision for international relations after Bush.

Joseph Stiglitz, author of *Globalization and Its Discontents* and *Making Globalization Work*, represents a different viewpoint. A Nobel Prize–winning economist and former vice president of the World Bank, he made his mark when he left the institution in protest and put forth a damning criticism of the ideological dogma propagated by the IMF and the U.S. Treasury. He is an eccentric academic and an unlikely political firebrand, yet, more than any other person, Stiglitz embodies the entry of the global justice movements' arguments into the mainstream of economic debate. He is not an unproblematic emissary, however. Stiglitz is an advocate of only limited modifications to corporate globalization, and he is disconnected from the movements that are creating the real momentum for change. His stance is similar to Democrats from a somewhat more progressive branch of the party who have adopted mild criticisms of corporate globalization, but who would keep the Bretton Woods system fundamentally intact.

Those who reject both corporate and imperial models of globalization will find that Stiglitz, while much more of an ally than Friedman, falls short of offering a viable vision for how to move forward. Nonetheless, anyone interested in the changing politics of globalization can gain much from examining the stories of how these two pundits ended up where they are now.

You Can't Stop the Dawn

You learn a lot about Thomas Friedman from his response to a famous incident that took place in 1996. In December of that year, Federal Reserve Chairman Alan Greenspan gave a speech at the American Enterprise Institute. In the midst of a long discussion about the role of the central bank, Greenspan sneaked in a statement that made financial insiders sit up straight. He commented that the "irrational exuberance" of Internet-crazed investors was driving the stock market to unsustainable levels.[1] Coming from the notoriously guarded chairman, this was an unusually stern warning; it sent tremors through the market. Ultimately, the stock boom would continue for several more years. But after the bursting of the dot-com bubble in early 2000, a downturn that threw the U.S. economy into recession, Greenspan's phrase was often repeated as a sign that mania over the high-tech "New Economy" should have been tempered long before.

For Thomas Friedman, however, the suggestion that high-tech enthusiasts might have been going overboard was not a sensible warning. It was a personal insult. In a *New York Times* column published shortly after Greenspan's speech, Friedman wrote a mock letter that began, "Dear Dr. Greenspan, I have a terrible problem. I'm feeling irrationally exuberant about the U.S. stock market and I just can't shake it. . . . Every time I come to Europe, or Japan, I return home itching to invest more in the U.S. market."[2] Friedman argued that, in fact, there was plenty to be excited about in the globalizing economy—and in the U.S. economy in particular. He went so far as to title a chapter in *The Lexus and the Olive Tree* "Rational Exuberance."

This is the perfect analogy for the author's overall approach to corporate globalization. In Friedman's view, the end of the Cold War left the world with a single, unassailable ideology. "Globalization," he wrote, "means the spread of free market capitalism to every country in the world." He saw this as an unmitigated good: "[T]he more you open your economy to free trade and competition, the more efficient and flourishing your economy will be."[3] He marveled that "computerization, miniaturization, digitization, satellite communications, fiber optics, and the Internet" were bringing about untold wonders.[4]

Friedman's conversion into the church of corporate expansion took place over many years. His academic training is not in economics, but in Middle Eastern studies. During the 1980s, Friedman was a respected *New York Times* correspondent in Israel and Lebanon, winning two Pulitzer Prizes for his reporting from the region. In 1994, just at the beginning of the Internet boom, he switched to a beat covering the intersection of politics and economics, and his excitement for globalization began to mount in earnest. By the time he became the *Times'* foreign affairs columnist the following year, he was perfectly positioned to evangelize about how unregulated markets and new technology were reshaping global affairs.

Friedman purported to be evenhanded, willing to look at the "dark side" of globalization. But any bits of darkness he found were flooded out by his blinding zeal for technological innovation. In his world, "Horatio Alger is not a mythical character but sometimes your next-door neighbor, who just happened to get hired as an engineer at Intel or America Online when they were getting started and ended up being paid in stock options that are now worth $10 million."[5] Evidence that might suggest a less rosy picture rarely entered into Friedman's field of vision, and disparaging suggestions like Greenspan's "irrational exuberance" became challenges to rebut.

Aware that many people saw him as a modern-day Pangloss extolling the best of all possible worlds, Friedman contended in the *Lexus and the Olive Tree* that he was "not a salesman for globalization."[6] But this is precisely what he was. More than any other public personality he was responsible for portraying neoliberalism as an inevitable and laudable march of progress. "I feel about globalization a lot like I feel about the dawn," he wrote. "[E]ven if I didn't care much for the dawn there isn't much I could do about it. I didn't start globalization, I can't stop it—except at a huge cost to human development."[7] By defining "globalization" as a broad, sweeping phenomenon—political, economic, technological, and cultural—he saw resistance as ridiculous. So when massive protests erupted at the World Trade Organization meetings in Seattle in late 1999, he disgustedly derided the demonstrators as "a Noah's ark of flat-earth advocates, protectionist trade unions and yuppies looking for their 1960s fix."[8]

You might think that the deflating of the dot-com bubble that began in March 2000 would have quelled Friedman's fervor, but you would be wrong. In Friedman's view, the end of the 1990s boom only led to more advancement. "[T]he dot-com bust," he later wrote, "actually drove globalization into hypermode by forcing companies to outsource and offshore more and more functions in order to save on scarce capital."[9] Friedman's cheerleading, too, would go into "hypermode," but not before the columnist took a detour into defending imperial globalization.

WAR AND "FLATTENING"

In the wake of 9/11, Friedman served as one of the country's most prominent liberal hawks. As he described it, the attacks on New York and Washington made him angry—"angry that my country had been violated in this way, angry at the senseless deaths of so many innocent people, angry at the megalomaniacal arrogance of Osama bin Laden and his men."[10] For Friedman, the appropriate response to this anger was for the United States to go to war. Through his *Times* column and his public appearances, he insisted that policymakers, even those with reservations about the Bush administration, should support the ousting of Saddam Hussein and the occupation of Iraq. His was a convoluted stance: Although he conceded that White House belligerence was alienating allies throughout the international community, that official claims about weapons of mass destruction were lies, and that the postinvasion management of Iraq was ill-planned, he nevertheless sided resolutely with the war effort.

A good part of his argument came down to support of the Ledeen Doctrine—the idea that the United States needed to exercise its military power if only to the show the rest of the world who is boss. According to Friedman, "sometimes smashing someone in the face is necessary to signal others that they will be held accountable for the intolerance they incubate. Removing the Taliban and Saddam sent that message to every government in the area."[11] He later contended, "Saudi Arabia would have been fine; Pakistan would have been fine. We did Iraq because we could." As he explained it, "My motto here to my liberal friends is that some things are true even if George Bush believes them."[12]

Along with Bush and the neocons, Friedman believed that the U.S. military could be used to reshape the region—that hard power could "create one good example in the heart of the Arab world of a decent, progressive state."[13] Having distinguished himself as a chief ideologue for corporate globalization, Friedman's accommodation with the imperial globalists was always somewhat awkward. Nevertheless, he did the administration a great favor in the years after the invasion by regularly reasserting that good news from the occupation was just around the corner. In November 2003, Friedman wrote in the *New York Times*, "The next six months in Iraq—which will determine the prospects for democracy-building there—are the most important six months in U.S. foreign policy in a long, long time."[14] Yet, as the media watchdogs at Fairness and Accuracy In Reporting (FAIR) documented, Friedman's "six month" deadline ended up being extended for some two and a half years, as the columnist made his prediction with the same confidence in appearance after appearance.[15]

It was an impressive performance: "What we're gonna find out, Bob, in the next six to nine months is whether we have liberated a country or uncorked a civil war," Friedman said to *Face the Nation* host Bob Schieffer in October 2004, almost a year after his first declaration. Then, in another appearance in December 2005, he asserted, "The next six months really are going to determine whether this country is going to collapse into three parts or more or whether it's going to come together." For good measure, he added in March 2006, "I think we are in the endgame. The next six to nine months are going to tell whether we can produce a decent outcome in Iraq."

These were only highlights. In truth, Friedman offered his same insight again and again until he was finally forced to conclude, in August 2006, "It is now obvious that we are not midwifing democracy in Iraq. We are baby-sitting a civil war." At last, he allowed that "'staying the course' is pointless" and that "we can't throw more good lives after good lives."[16]

Friedman never accepted responsibility for his role in promoting the war, but he did rebuke the model of imperial globalization. "I believe that history will make very clear that President Bush shamelessly exploited the emotions around 9/11 for political purposes," he wrote. "He used those 9/11 emotions to take a far-right Republican domestic agenda on taxes, the environment, and social issues from 9/10 . . . and drive it into a 9/12 world. In doing so, Mr. Bush . . . drove a wedge between Americans, and between Americans and the world." More importantly, "[h]is administration transformed the United States into 'the United States of Fighting Terrorism,'" depriving the world of "an America that exports hope, not fear."[17]

For Friedman, exporting hope meant a return to corporate globalization. In his 2005 book, *The World Is Flat*, he wrote that, after 9/11, conflicts in the Middle East "became all consuming for me. I spent almost all my time traveling in the Arab and Muslim worlds. During those years I lost the trail of globalization."[18] But when he did return to the subject, he was once again wowed. Over the course of just a few years, he concluded, "we entered a whole new era: Globalization 3.0."

Fueled now by wireless technology and ever-smaller microchips, this wave of capitalism was "shrinking the world from a size small to a size tiny and flattening the playing field at the same time."[19] Hospitals in the United States were sending CAT scans to India for analysis; other corporations opened bustling call centers there to handle customer service calls, training their new South Asian employees to speak in American accents; globetrotting columnists could file their stories from the middle of golf courses in China by using their Blackberries. The march of progress was back on.

The Language of Neoliberal Triumph

So what does Friedman actually have to say about globalization? To consider the content of his works, you must first reckon with his use of language. There are several aspects of Friedman's writing that lend themselves to parody. Certainly, he deserves some credit as a reporter. He has traveled the globe extensively and spoken with a broad array of entrepreneurs. However, his books are so overweighted with the opinions of high-tech executives that before long a sentence like "I drove . . . out to the Infosys campus, about forty minutes from the heart of Bangalore, to tour the facility and interview [CEO] Nandan Nilekani" makes you roll your eyes.[20]

Likewise, Friedman is known for conveying complicated ideas through the use of colorful metaphors. Yet his metaphors consistently get so mixed and muddled as to require delicate linguistic untangling. In the course of his two books on globalization, Friedman goes from seeing the world in 3-D to, remarkably enough, seeing in at least six dimensions. Technological advance, he tells us, has now accelerated so much that we have gone through Globalization version 1.0, version 2.0, and entered version 3.0. Friedman presents ten "flatteners," four "steroids," and a "triple convergence," plus at least seven releases of "DOScapital." Various steroids and flatteners are factors that have multiplied globalization's effects exponentially. Journalist Matt Taibbi, who has written the most cutting analysis of Friedman's peculiar language, noted, "Friedman's book is the first I have encountered, anywhere, in which the reader needs a calculator to figure the value of the author's metaphors."[21]

As his symbolic descriptions of the global economy grow ever more clouded, his ability to make a serious argument about the nature of the world order increasingly comes into question. If ever Orwell's warnings that "the slovenliness of our language makes it easier for us to have foolish thoughts" and that the world's "present political chaos is connected with the decay of language" apply, it is to Friedman.[22]

The connection between Friedman's hazy writing and his suspect conclusions about the global economy shows up even in the very premise of his second book on globalization. During a meeting between Friedman and Nilekani in Bangalore, the Infosys CEO offers that "the playing field is being leveled." For Friedman, the tired cliché is a revelation. He mulls it over for hours and then suddenly decides, "My God, he's telling me the world is flat!"[23]

Now, it is quite a stretch to take a routine sports metaphor and superimpose it on global geography—and it is not clear that Nilekani would want credit for such a feat. Not only is Friedman's interpretation of this conversation suspect, but there could be few worse metaphors for talking about a global system that is more integrated and networked than ever before. After all, a flat planet is notoriously treacherous to circumnavigate. It is one where, to get from Los Angeles to China, you have to travel east across the Atlantic and then over the whole Eurasian mainland, because trying to cross the Pacific Ocean would mean sailing off the edge of the world.

"Friedman is a person who not only speaks in malapropisms, he also hears malapropisms," Taibbi argues. Nilekani offhandedly mentions a level field, and Friedman attributes to him the radical idea of a flat world. "This is the intellectual version of Far Out Space Nuts, when NASA repairman Bob Denver sets a whole sitcom in motion by pressing 'launch' instead of 'lunch' in a space capsule. And once he hits that button, the rocket takes off."[24]

It would all be funny if it didn't mask a deeper political problem: For the world's poor, the playing field is far from level. Our world is not flat.

Putting on Reagan's Jacket

With the ideology of neoliberalism steadily losing ground in international discussion, it is important to see how a leading apologist mounts a defense. In Friedman's case, he does so by holding on to dogmatic assumptions, training his sights on high technology, conducting his interviews largely within the insular world of jet-setting corporate elites, and ignoring a world of evidence that would contradict his selective viewpoint. Some reviewers have applauded Friedman for acknowledging negative aspects of globalization in his books. But for Friedman, this does not mean looking at the exploitation and environmental destruction that have resulted from corporate expansion. Instead, his caveats boil down to two points: (1) terrorists, too, can use the Internet; and (2) many countries, especially in "unflat" Africa, are too backward to read the signs that would put them on the high-tech, "free trade" superhighway to prosperity. With regard to the latter, it's not that anything is wrong really, but only that the process has not yet gone far enough or fast enough for everyone to benefit.

Needless to say, Friedman's is hardly a biting exposé. As it turns out, his lack of concern about the bursting of the dot-com bubble is typical. In fact, it is virtually impossible to find any evidence that might make him skeptical about the fundamental greatness of corporate globalization. In 1999, even *Business Week* conceded, "The Asian financial crisis of 1997–99 shows that unfettered liberalization of capital markets without proper regulation can lead the world to the brink of disaster."[25] But for Friedman this crisis, too, was all for the best. He asserts, "I believe globalization did us all a favor by melting down the economies of Thailand, Korea, Malaysia, Indonesia, Mexico, Russia and Brazil in the 1990s, because it laid bare a lot of the rotten practices and institutions in countries that had prematurely globalized."[26] He slams the countries for corruption and cronyism, suggesting that they deserved their fates. But by "prematurely globalized" he does not mean that these countries should have been more cautious about linking their fates to speculative international markets. Rather, he believes that they had not done enough to "reduce the role of government" and "let markets more freely allocate resources."[27] Never does he consider that the market itself might have been a part of the problem. Friedman's solution to the dangers of unregulated markets is more deregulation; the remedy for the excesses of unfettered capitalism is even more excess. The argument is airtight.

Missing from this account, of course, is any sense of the social impact of the crisis. In the end, wealthy foreign investors were bailed out by the IMF and lost little. The real losers were an untold number of middle-class families in places like Thailand and Korea whose savings were wiped out overnight, as well as the poor in places like Indonesia who went hungry when the government cut food subsidies. It takes a very twisted viewpoint to say that the Asian financial crisis did these people a favor.

Friedman holds that the Internet age has created a "flat" world with opportunity for all. Yet he freely admits that the system he describes is founded on the Reagan-Thatcher model of extreme, "trickle down" neo-liberalism. This happens to be one of the most unequal methods of dis-tributing social goods ever devised. Friedman states: "Thatcher and Reagan combined to strip huge chunks of economic decision-making power from the state, from the advocates of the Great Society and from traditional Keynesian economics, and hand them over to the free mar-ket."[28] Countries now have one choice for economic policy: neoliberal-ism. They must radically deregulate and privatize their economies. Friedman calls this the "Golden Straightjacket." It's "golden" because the model supposedly creates widespread affluence. But it's a "straight-jacket" because it radically constricts democracy. Sounding a lot like Ralph Nader in 1999, Friedman explains:

> Once your country puts [the Golden Straightjacket] on, its political choices get reduced to Pepsi or Coke—to slight nuances of taste, slight nuances of policy, slight alterations in design . . . but never any major deviation from the core golden rules. Governments—be they led by De-mocrats or Republicans, Conservatives or Labourites, Gaullists or So-cialists, Christian Democrats or Social Democrats—that deviate too far away from the core rules will see their investors stampede away, interest rates rise, and stock market valuations fall.[29]

The difference between Friedman and Nader is that the *New York Times* columnist approves of this situation. He does not condemn it as an assault on democracy; he says it's just the way things are. Of the De-mocrats, he observes, "Mr. Clinton effectively kidnapped the Democratic Party . . . moved it into the Republican economic agenda—including free trade, NAFTA and the WTO for China—while holding onto much of the Democrats' social agenda."[30] Any Democrat who would try to move it back meets Friedman's wrath. In the new global age, all those to the left of Ronald Reagan on economic policy are simply out of luck.

SITTING ON TOP OF THE WORLD

Those being subjected to corporate globalization have good reason to ask if the straightjacket is golden after all. Friedman posits, "Every law of economics tells us that if we . . . promote greater and greater trade and integration, the global pie will grow wider and more complex."[31] Putting aside the question of whether one would want to eat any pie that has been growing "more complex," recent history has shown that economics is more complicated than neoliberal textbooks suggest. In fact, Friedman's contention that everyone benefits when countries bind themselves into market fundamentalism is based less on a careful review of the evidence than on blind faith. In July 2006, he made a startling admission during a CNBC interview with Tim Russert:

> We got this free market, and I admit, I was speaking out in Minnesota— my hometown, in fact, and a guy stood up in the audience, said, "Mr. Friedman, is there any free trade agreement you'd oppose?" I said, "No, absolutely not." I said, "You know what, sir? I wrote a column supporting the CAFTA, the Caribbean Free Trade initiative. I didn't even know what was in it. I just knew two words: free trade."[32]

That a nationally prominent columnist would gloat about such ignorance is a sad statement about the health of our political debate. As we have seen, "free trade" is a pair of incredibly politicized words, with little concrete meaning. CAFTA (which, contrary to Friedman's rendering, stands for the Central American Free Trade Agreement) includes provisions designed to protect the monopoly rights of giant pharmaceutical companies rather than to create "free" commerce.

But the larger point is that neoliberalism does not make winners of everyone. Its global track record for producing GDP growth is dismal. In fact, its main accomplishment may be to produce inequality. Today the gap between the world's rich and poor has widened to obscene proportions. A study by the World Institute for Development Economics Research reported that in 2000, the richest 1 percent of adults worldwide owned 40 percent of the world's wealth, and the richest 10 percent possessed a full 85 percent. The bottom half, on the other hand, owns scarcely 1 percent of global wealth.[33] In terms of income, those at the top are raking in a far greater share than before neoliberalism. In 1980, the average CEO in the United States earned 42 times the salary of his average worker. By 2001, the average CEO made 411 times as much.[34]

Friedman's own position amid this global divide is telling. He regularly represents himself as just an average guy from Minnesota trying to make sense of the world. The real picture is far from average. In July 2006, the *Washingtonian* magazine reported that in the 1970s Friedman married into one of the one hundred richest families in America—the Bucksbaums—who have amassed a fortune worth some $2.7 billion, with origins in real estate development. The magazine noted that he lives in "a palatial 11,400-square-foot house, now valued at $9.3 million, on a 7.5-acre parcel just blocks from I-495 and Bethesda Country Club."[35] Given that the uber-rich, those with huge stock portfolios and investments in multinational corporations, have benefited tremendously from corporate globalization, commentators like David Sirota have suggested that Friedman's vast wealth represents an undisclosed conflict of interest in his journalism. It is as if multimillionaire Richard Mellon Scaife were to write about the repeal of the estate tax without revealing that he stands to profit handsomely from such a policy change.[36]

Whether or not that is the case, Friedman's position at the very pinnacle of global prosperity is certainly reflected in his view of the world. He relates early in *The Lexus and the Olive Tree* that his "best intellectual sources" about globalization are hedge fund managers.[37] This is a telling admission. Hedge funds are elite, largely unregulated, private investment pools that handle money for extremely wealthy individuals. Their managers are among the highest paid individuals in the United States. In 2006, the top twenty-five hedge fund managers in the country made in excess of $240 million each. This means they each pulled in, on average, $27,000 per hour, twenty-four hours per day, whether waking or sleeping, whether at the office or teeing off on the ninth hole at the country club.[38] Corporate CEOs and hedge fund managers may indeed be well informed about certain aspects of the global economy. But if that is where you get your information, you end up with a very subjective view of the world. You get the winner's view.

In an eloquent critique of *The World Is Flat*, Indian eco-feminist Vandana Shiva wrote:

> Friedman has reduced the world to the friends he visits, the CEOs he knows, and the golf courses he plays at. From this microcosm of privilege, exclusion, blindness, he shuts out both the beauty of diversity and the brutality of exploitation and inequality. . . .
>
> That is why he talks of 550 million Indian youth overtaking Americans in a flat world. When the entire information technology/outsourcing sector in India employs only a million out of a 1.2 billion people. Food and farming, textiles and clothing, health and education are nowhere in Friedman's monoculture of mind locked into IT. Friedman presents a 0.1 percent picture and hides 99.9 percent. . . . In the eclipsed 99.9 percent are the 25 million women who disappeared in high growth areas of India because a commodified world has rendered women a dispensable sex. In the hidden 99.9 percent economy are thousands of tribal children in Orissa, Maharashtra, Rajasthan who died of hunger because the public distribution system for food has been dismantled to create markets for agribusiness.[39]

A Race to the Top?

The corporate globalization that Friedman champions has alarming changes in store not just for the poor of the global South but also for working people in the United States and Europe. One of the things that Friedman particularly admires is Reagan and Thatcher's success in breaking unions. "[I]t may turn out that one of the key turning points in American history, going into the millennium, was Ronald Reagan's decision to fire all the striking air traffic controllers in 1981." He notes with satisfaction, "No single event did more to alter the balance of power be-tween management and workers."[40] Echoing the trickle-down, Reaganite logic, he argues that everyone wins from this, since "[t]he easier it is to fire workers, the more incentive employers have to hire them."[41] Because America busted its unions and Western European countries did not, he contends, the United States developed a more dynamic economy.

What Friedman fails to note is that real wages for working people in the United States have been largely stagnant since the early 1970s, while the number of working hours have skyrocketed. When compared with workers in Western Europe, the average American works 350 hours more per year, the equivalent of nine extra weeks. A study by the International Labor Organization reported that in 2000 the average U.S. worker put in 199 more hours than in 1973. Dramatizing such realities, a group of union and nonprofit activists now observe "Take Back Your Time Day" every October 24. On that day, if the U.S. workload were on par with the rest of the industrialized world, Americans would have the rest of the year off.

Friedman utters not a word of protest about the trend toward more work; in fact, he celebrates it. He argues that European social democra-cies are obsolete, even though they are successful capitalist countries. These nations are running on the wrong version on "DOScapital," Fried-man contends, and need to shift to U.S. standards. (Never mind that economies like Sweden's have performed very well over the past decade, all while maintaining a much higher quality of life for their citizens.)

He has a special hatred for the French, who, he writes, "are trying to preserve a 35-hour work week in a world where Indian engineers are ready to work a 35-hour day." In what he calls a "race to the top," Fried-man predicts a turbulent decade for Western Europe, as

aging, inflexible economies—which have grown used to six-week vaca-tions and unemployment insurance that is almost as good as having a job—become more intimately integrated with Eastern Europe, India and China in a flattening world. . . . The dirty little secret is that India is taking work from Europe or America not simply because of low wages.

It is also because Indians are ready to work harder and can do anything from answering your phone to designing your next airplane or car. They are not racing us to the bottom. They are racing us to the top. . . . Yes, this is a bad time for France and friends to lose their appetite for hard work—just when India, China and Poland are rediscovering theirs.[42]

It is unclear what Friedman sees as getting to the "top" if paid vacations, unemployment insurance, and retirement—benefits traditionally regarded as signs of a civilized economy—must be sacrificed. In *The World Is Flat*, he approvingly quotes a Microsoft "team member" in China describing his group of recruits: "They voluntarily work fifteen to eighteen hours a day and come in on weekends. They work through holidays, because their dream is to get to Microsoft."[43]

That Indian and Chinese workers are willing to sell themselves into bondage for Microsoft is, of course, a dubious sign of global progress. But that is the new reality, according to Friedman. His recipe for success in this climate is to "work harder, save more, sacrifice more."[44] To what end is unclear. Bumper stickers remind us that the activists of the labor movement were the "folks that brought you the weekend." In Friedman's account, corporate globalization is the force that will take it away. Yet we are supposed to be happy about it.

Ultimately, the "race to the top" is another of Friedman's botched metaphors. In the long-standing progressive argument that corporate globalization creates a "race to the bottom," it is not Indian or Chinese workers who are doing the racing at all. It's capital. Deregulation allows corporations to wander the globe in search of ever lower wages and environmental standards. The moment workers stand up for their rights, refusing to tolerate a "35-hour day," a company can pick up and move elsewhere. The governments that might curb such abuses are in straightjackets. The unions that workers might have organized themselves into have been busted. All Friedman can offer is this cryptic and seemingly masochistic advice: "When the world goes flat—and you are feeling flattened—reach for a shovel and dig into yourself. Don't try to build walls."[45]

GLOBALIZATION FROM BELOW

An interesting aspect of Friedman's renewed focus on corporate global-ization at the end of the Bush era is that governments and international financial institutions have faded from his picture of the integrating world. Even corporations are becoming less relevant. In his view, the new era of "Globalization 3.0" is all about *individuals*. Today, it is up to all people to pull themselves up by their bootstraps. He declares, "[E]very person now must, and can, ask: Where do *I* as an individual fit into the global competition and opportunities of the day, and how can *I*, on my own, collaborate with others globally?"[46]

Conveniently enough, accepting this idea makes it impossible to op-pose neoliberalism. In a world of extreme individualism, no one in par-ticular is responsible for setting the rules of the world order. It is pointless to protest governments or international financial institutions. Globalization is unstoppable because people want it.

In truth, these arguments are not new. With scant evidence, Friedman has long claimed that there is a "groundswell" of people throughout the developing world demanding corporate globalization.[47] Of course, the massive protests of the past decade would seem to contradict his asser-tion, but he does not see this as a problem. He dismisses global justice activism by arguing, "from its origins, the movement that emerged in Seattle was primarily a Western-driven phenomenon."[48] The backlash that does exist in poorer countries, he asserts, is not rational politics but simple lawlessness: "[W]hat we have been seeing in many countries, in-stead of popular mass opposition to globalization, is wave after wave of crime—people just grabbing what they need, weaving their own social safety nets and not worrying about the theory or the ideology."[49] In the end, Friedman seems ideologically incapable of accepting that people in the global South could organize their own movements or articulate a co-herent politics of resistance.

Today, with much of the world in open rebellion against neoliberal-ism, this fiction is getting harder and harder to maintain. In fact, Seattle was only the moment when mainstream pundits in the United States and Europe could no longer ignore opposition. That Friedman has perpetually failed to spot the vibrant network of grassroots organizations that has built a worldwide campaign against the Washington Consensus is not a sign of widespread support for corporate globalization. It is an indictment of his reporting. Well before Seattle, there had been protests of millions of people throughout the global South against the "Golden Straightjacket."

These have continued into the new millennium. In their book, *Globalization from Below*, authors Jeremy Brecher, Tim Costello, and Brendan Smith note that in just a two-month period, in May and June of 2000, there were six general strikes against the impact of neoliberalism. In India, as many as 20 million farmers and workers struck, protesting their government's involvement with the WTO and the IMF. Twelve million Argentineans went on strike in response to fiscal austerity policies imposed by the IMF. Nigeria was paralyzed by strikes against neoliberal price hikes on fuel. South Koreans demanded a shorter workweek and the full protection of part-time and temporary employees by the country's labor laws. Finally, general strikes in South Africa and Uruguay protested increasing unemployment rates, which resulted from IMF austerity policies.[50] All of these escaped Friedman's notice.

In truth, they are only reflections of wider resistance. As a sign of the movement's depth, SAPRIN, the global network that produced such a damning denunciation of structural adjustment, drew together between one hundred and seven hundred civil society organizations in each of the countries it studied. These groups represented hundreds of thousands of organized voices in the developing world, none of which fit into Friedman's vision of the global economic system. Lastly, the people of Latin America have certainly not joined the groundswell of support for neoliberal ideology. In country after country they have ousted conservative governments since 2000 and elected more progressive leaders, redrawing the region's political map. The columnist has yet to comment.

There is a way in which Friedman perfectly matches the politics of our times. "Like George Bush, he's in the reality-making business," Matt Taibbi argues. "You no longer have to worry about actually convincing anyone; the process ends when you make the case. Things are true because you say they are. The only thing that matters is how sure you sound when you say it."[51]

As much as he might resemble Bush in this respect, however, Friedman also tells us something important about the post-Bush moment. As a new administration takes over, an increasing number of politicians will seek to move the United States away from the aggressive militarism of imperial globalization and back toward a softer approach to ruling the world. Following Friedman, many will look to revitalize corporate globalization as a model for international affairs.

This is especially a danger within the Democratic Party. Never admitting their own complicity in the war, politicians from the more conservative branch of the party will talk about the damage Bush has done and the importance of restoring our traditional alliances. These "New Democrats" will promise a fresh approach to foreign affairs. But in reality, they would return to something old: a Clintonian model of corporate globalization. Like Friedman, many will proclaim it as the best of all possible worlds, a global order both exciting and unavoidable. It will be up to the world's citizens to demand something better.

GLOBALIZATION'S MAD SCIENTIST

As someone well attuned to the changing political winds inside the Beltway, Thomas Friedman stands in contrast to a second leading commentator on globalization. Joseph Stiglitz neither looks nor behaves like a polished politician. The sixty-four-year-old professor of economics at Columbia University fits the stereotype of the rumpled academic, rushing to lectures with his jackets wrinkled and gray hair unkempt. What he says in his public addresses also runs contrary to most policymakers' mannered declarations. Whether out of a willful desire to act impolitic or a simple ignorance of political calculations, Stiglitz has repeatedly violated the decorum of mainstream economic discussion. And in the process he has done more than perhaps any other individual to influence the unfolding debate about globalization.

For the World Bank, Stiglitz's former employer, and the International Monetary Fund, its sister organization and Stiglitz's nemesis, none of the economist's public statements appeared at a less convenient time than his April 2000 article in the *New Republic*. Published immediately before the largest-ever protests amassed outside the institutions' headquarters in Washington, D.C., the piece began with two of the most damning and oft-quoted paragraphs in the literature of globalization:

> Next week's meeting of the International Monetary Fund will bring to Washington, D.C., many of the same demonstrators who trashed the World Trade Organization in Seattle last fall. They'll say the IMF is arrogant. They'll say the IMF doesn't really listen to the developing countries it is supposed to help. They'll say the IMF is secretive and insulated from democratic accountability. They'll say the IMF's economic "remedies" often make things worse—turning slowdowns into recessions and recessions into depressions.
>
> And they'll have a point. I was chief economist at the World Bank from 1996 until last November, during the gravest global economic crisis in a half-century. I saw how the IMF, in tandem with the U.S. Treasury Department, responded. And I was appalled.[52]

Stiglitz has always been intellectually combative, but that he would become a political renegade was not clear early in his prodigious career. He trained at MIT. in the early '60s. By 1970, when he turned twenty-seven, he was a full professor at Yale. He made his mark with groundbreaking research on the economics of information. Subsequently moving between teaching jobs at outposts such as Stanford and Princeton, he was long considered a contender for a Nobel Prize in economics, which he ultimately won in 2001. When President Clinton took office, Stiglitz joined the Council of Economic Advisors, serving as its chair from 1995 to 1997. He then moved into dealing with international policy at the World Bank.

The strident criticisms of the IMF that Stiglitz began voicing during his time in office took many Beltway observers by surprise. In recent years there have been some tensions between the stern neoliberal taskmasters who staff the IMF and the somewhat softer, at times reform-minded economists at the World Bank. General agreement about policy prevails, however. Differences are usually sorted out in private, and broadsides from high-ranking officials are unheard of.

In this context, some have tried to dramatically portray Joseph Stiglitz as a spy who defected across enemy lines, going public with his secrets in a tormented effort to end his complicity in an evil ideology. There are two problems with this story. First, it portrays Stiglitz as far more cunning than he actually is. Writing in the *American Prospect* about the economist's time in Clinton's cabinet, Jonathan Chait noted that Stiglitz "goes about his troublemaking with a bemused detachment, as if he were oblivious to the consequences of his heresy. Though he has become a powerful policymaker, Stiglitz behaves as though he were an obscure academic, writing and speaking for no purpose beyond his own enlightenment."[53] Stiglitz carried this devil-may-care recklessness and disinterest in conforming to the norms of Beltway politics with him from the Council of Economic Advisors to the World Bank.

DENYING THE VIRGIN BIRTH

The second problem with the spy story is that it suggests a sudden ideological conversion that did not, in fact, take place. Economist Ha-Joon Chang, who edited a collection of Stiglitz's speeches from his time as chief economist, titled *Joseph Stiglitz and the World Bank: The Rebel Within*, has demonstrated that the future Nobel laureate was an iconoclast virtually from the start of his tenure.[54]

During his first year as the World Bank's chief economist, Stiglitz kept relatively quiet. But in January 1998 he delivered a lecture in Helsinki, Finland, subtitled "Moving Toward the Post–Washington Consensus."[55] The speech, which Chang contends "now has a near-cult status," questioned neoliberal economic prescriptions of high interest rates, deregulation, capital liberalization, and privatization for developing countries.[56] It noted that many of the most economically successful nations in East Asia were the ones that had long ignored the IMF's mandates. And it suggested that IMF policies helped to fuel the financial crisis that struck the region in 1997. As *Left Business Observer* editor Doug Henwood has remarked, "For a senior World Bank official to say these things is a bit like a Pope denying the Virgin birth."[57]

The speech was just the beginning. World Bank President James Wolfensohn tried to gently rein in his wayward employee and limit Stiglitz's contact with the press. He failed. As Stiglitz's tenure progressed, he became ever more vocal in denouncing the IMF's handling of the East Asian financial crisis and its program of "shock therapy" in Russia. The IMF and the U.S. Treasury were furious. World Bank insiders have claimed that influential and bullying Treasury Secretary Lawrence Summers delivered an ultimatum to Wolfensohn: If he wanted the White House to support him for a second term as World Bank president (and he did, badly), Wolfensohn would have to fire Stiglitz.[58] The chief economist's resignation was announced in November 1999, the same month, coincidentally, that protests rocked the World Trade Organization Ministerial meetings in Seattle.

Anyone who had been listening to activists and progressive intellectuals in the global justice movement would have found little that was novel in Stiglitz's increasingly outspoken challenges to U.S. economic policy. But never had an insider of Stiglitz's reputation so forthrightly assailed neoliberal dogma. The impact was profound. London School of Economics professor and former World Bank staffer Robert Wade explained the importance of Stiglitz's dissent:

> More than just a source of funds to be offered or withheld, the World Bank is a fount of Anglo-American ideas on how an economy—and, increasingly, a polity—should be run. The role of the World Bank's chief economist is a critical one from this point of view. The Bank's legitimacy rests on the claim that its development advice reflects the best possible technical research, a justification readily cited by borrowing governments when imposing Bank policies on their unwilling populations.[59]

Stiglitz's stance undermined this claim and lent a newfound, mainstream respectability to other critics' long-standing arguments. It also signaled a trend. Even as Stiglitz began his assault, other prominent figures in the field, including Paul Krugman of Princeton and Harvard economists Dani Rodrik and Jeffrey Sachs, would voice further misgivings, albeit moderate ones, about the Washington Consensus. The fortress of neoliberal credibility had been breached, and the once-indomitable ideology has never come close to regaining its former authority.

In an interview with the *Financial Times*, Stiglitz confirmed that pressure from Summers influenced Wolfensohn, but he indicated that he was not fired outright. "I was told that I could stay in the Bank," Stiglitz said, "but if I did I would have to circumscribe my thoughts. So I chose to resign."[60] After his departure, the World Bank retained Stiglitz as a consultant and special advisor. That is, until his *New Republic* article appeared. There he flatly stated: "Economic policy is today perhaps the most important part of America's interaction with the rest of the world. And yet the culture of international economic policy in the world's most powerful democracy is not democratic." Moreover, "the older men who staff the fund—and they are overwhelmingly older men—act as if they are shouldering Rudyard Kipling's white man's burden. IMF experts believe they are brighter, more educated, and less politically motivated than the economists in the countries they visit." In fact, Stiglitz asserted, the IMF staff "frequently consists of third-rank students from first-rate universities."[61]

Lawrence Summers was reportedly seething. The World Bank promptly severed all remaining ties with Stiglitz.

A Curious Blend of Ideology and Bad Economics

In his 2002 best-seller, *Globalization and Its Discontents*, the full shape of Stiglitz's critique becomes clear. There, he clearly places his arguments within a framework of general support for globalization, vaguely defined. He affirms: "I believe that globalization—the removal of barriers to free trade and the closer integration of national economies—can be a force for good and that it has the *potential* to enrich everyone in the world, particularly the poor. But I also believe that if this is to be the case, the way globalization has been managed, including . . . the policies that have been imposed on developing countries . . . need to be radically rethought."[62]

One of Stiglitz's more interesting moves is to link his criticisms with his pathbreaking early work on the economics of information. The awarding of the Nobel Prize in economics to Stiglitz in 2001 represented another epic instance of bad timing for defenders of the Washington Consensus. Just as they had hoped to discredit the renegade economist, they were forced to look on helplessly as the Nobel committee heightened his acclaim tremendously. Since Stiglitz's earlier work was unimpeachable, critics were forced to try a different tack. They sought "to portray Stiglitz as a highly respectable 'scientist' gone mad in his old age," according to Ha-Joon Chang. Detractors asserted that he had strayed far from his mainstream research in making his criticisms about the international financial institutions.[63]

Stiglitz explicitly rejects this interpretation. His long-established body of research highlighted ways in which unregulated markets can fail to work properly in real-world circumstances. At the core of neoclassical economics is the assumption that all actors in the market operate with perfect information. As explained by Stiglitz, "My research . . . showed that whenever information is imperfect—where some individuals know something that others do not (in other words, *always*)—the reason that the invisible hand seems invisible is that it is not there." Asymmetric information leads to distortions in supposedly perfect markets. Thus, "without appropriate government regulation and intervention, markets do not lead to economic efficiency."[64]

Stiglitz carries his original critique of textbook economic models into his discussion of globalization. He does not so much reject the specific policies of neoliberalism but rather charges that they have been deployed in a way that was far too rigid and ideological. "I believe in privatization," he explains in one illustrative passage, ". . . but only if it helps companies become more efficient and lowers prices for consumers"—outcomes that are most likely to arise if the government intervenes with "strong competition policies."[65] The IMF leaves little room for such measured views. It bases its prescriptions on a fundamentalist belief in the infallibility of markets and inefficiency of governments. Because markets are not perfect, the results have been disastrous.

"The IMF has made mistakes in all the areas it has been involved in," Stiglitz asserts, "development, crisis management, and in countries making the transition from communism to capitalism."[66] Such errors included "forcing liberalization before safety nets were put in place . . . ; forcing policies that led to job destruction before the essentials for job creation were in place; forcing privatization before there were adequate competition and regulatory frameworks."[67]

Problems with "pacing" and "sequencing" were especially significant in Russia, where the IMF pushed rapid privatization. Without proper banking systems, competition policy, or government regulation, sales of state industries swiftly devolved into a process of "briberization." A new class of criminal oligarchs took over state monopolies, forcefully shut out rivals, and fostered rampant government corruption.

With regard to trade policy, Stiglitz points out that the United States and other wealthy nations long protected their infant industries from foreign competition, and even today, while preaching "free trade," they shield and subsidize domestic enterprise, especially agriculture. The East Asian economies that have most successfully entered the global marketplace did so by carefully controlling the timing of trade liberalization and adopting policies that would ease its social impact.

Beyond questions of pacing, Stiglitz takes the IMF to task for shutting out contrary viewpoints. "Decisions were made on the basis of what seemed a curious blend of ideology and bad economics, dogma that sometimes seemed to be thinly veiling special interests. . . . There was a single prescription. Alternative opinions were not sought. . . . Ideology guided policy prescriptions and countries were expected to follow the IMF guidelines without debate."[68]

The Asian financial crisis provided the key example of the damage that ideology and bad economics could together cause. According to Stiglitz, "IMF policies not only exacerbated the downturns but were partially responsible for the onset," owing to their zealous promotion of financial and capital market liberalization.[69] Contrary to the belief of cheerleading pundits like Thomas Friedman, the East Asian countries affected by the crisis had succeeded for so many years precisely because they were willing to buck Washington Consensus advice. "The IMF and the World Bank had almost conspicuously avoided studying the region," Stiglitz observes, "though presumably, because of its success, it would have seemed natural for them to turn it in to a lesson for others."[70] The international financial institutions rigorously avoided this investigation, of course, because such lessons would not have been flattering for the institutions, suggesting a much more robust role for government in economic planning—counter to Washington Consensus ideology.

When the East Asia economies finally relented to capital liberalization, it quickly proved to be disastrous. In September 1997, before the collapse of the Thai currency had expanded into a regionwide meltdown, the leaders of the world financial community gathered in Hong Kong for the fall meetings of the IMF and World Bank. There, Bill Clinton and IMF representatives insisted that Thailand's troubles were minor, and they continued to pressure other countries to liberalize their capital markets. "Meanwhile, the leaders of Asian countries, and especially the finance ministers I met with, were terrified," Stiglitz reports. They feared a crisis provoked by speculative investment "would wreak havoc on their economies and their societies, and they feared that . . . the policies [the IMF] would insist upon should a crisis occur would worsen the impacts. They felt, however, powerless to resist."[71] In the end, the finance ministers were right, and their economies suffered terrible collapses.

The impact of IMF failures across the globe, Stiglitz tells us, has been great. Country after country ended up suffering social and political turmoil; economic growth slowed dramatically, and the middle class was devastated. "Even those countries that have experienced some limited growth have seen the benefits accrue to the well-off, especially the *very* well-off—the top 10 percent—while poverty has remained high, and in some cases the income of those at the bottom has even fallen."[72] The IMF's original mission was to foster international economic stability. But in this, too, it failed miserably. Despite heralded advances in economic science that are supposedly guiding policy, crises have become more frequent, and have done more damage, than in the period prior to the creation of the Bretton Woods system.

OBSTACLES TO REFORM

The *New York Review of Books* held that *Globalization and Its Discontents* "certainly stands as the most forceful argument that has yet been made against the IMF and its policies."[73] It is hard to disagree. Stiglitz's blows are still sore subjects at the institution, and many of his arguments, particularly those regarding the perils of unregulated short-term capital flows, have become accepted as new consensus positions among mainstream economists.

To supplement his attacks on market fundamentalism, Stiglitz has more recently sought to present a positive agenda, a vision for *Making Globalization Work*—the title of the book he released in the fall of 2006. Yet here the same trait that made Stiglitz dangerously effective as a critic—his disregard for political considerations—limits him as a reformer.

Making Globalization Work is, in part, a nontechnical version of *Fair Trade for All*, which Stiglitz published in 2005 with fellow economist Andrew Charlton.[74] It also expands upon policy recommendations mentioned briefly in *Globalization and Its Discontents*. By the end of that earlier book, Stiglitz makes clear that he fancies himself a modern-day Keynes, an economist willing to use government intervention to rescue the capitalist system from its own shortcomings. In addition to calling for more regulation and improved safety nets, he supports demands for debt relief and increased aid for poor countries. He proposes increased transparency and more democratic representation at the international financial institutions. Finally, in language that sounds rather tepid, especially given the vigor with which he had just slammed the IMF, he advocates "a balanced view of the role of government, one which recognizes both the limitations and failures of markets *and* government, but which sees the two as working together, in partnership."[75]

In his newer book, Stiglitz reiterates his argument that "the problem is not with globalization itself but in the way globalization has been managed." He then presents a more elaborate platform of reforms, many based on the economic idea that government should provide incentives that will guide the market to work in the public interest. For example, Stiglitz proposes that "all the countries of the world impose a common tax on carbon emissions" to control global warming. "Firms and households would respond to this tax by reducing usage, and thereby emissions."[76] States could use the revenue from the tax to reduce taxes in other areas, like income or savings, and thus stimulate the economy. All this would be in the interest of business and government, he explains, because the long-term costs of global warming (more Katrinas, for starters) will be much more expensive than a common tax.

Among other measures, Stiglitz contends that wealthy countries should move away from putting neoliberal conditions on their loans to poor nations and create mechanisms for international bankruptcy. In the realm of trade policy, he contends that the United States and its advanced industrial allies should end their hypocritical subsidies for agriculture. In fact, he argues, they should unilaterally open their markets to imports from poor nations, leading by positive example. Moreover, they should design a "balanced intellectual property regime" that creates prizes to encourage innovation but gives poorer countries more access to new technology and allows them to distribute lifesaving drugs. Most ambitiously, he proposes a common fund to replace the currently unstable global reserve system, a change that would create capital for social initiatives. Once again, Stiglitz's rationale for why these proposals might appeal to policymakers is that they make sense in the long term: Everybody wins from these actions, Stiglitz contends, because "with prosperity, the developing countries will provide a robust market for the goods and services of the advanced industrial countries."[77]

As such proposals suggest, Stiglitz's approach is to tinker with the current economic structure, hoping to increase efficiency and create growth with benefits that are more evenly distributed than in the past. He exhibits a resolute faith that the tools of contemporary economic science can produce better solutions to global problems. Most of Stiglitz's ideas are not bad; they would be welcome suggestions within a moderate, medium-term program for change. In fact, many of his proposals, or versions of them, have been proposed before by social movement activists—but opposed, sometimes vehemently, by government elites and their corporate sponsors.

Stiglitz's distance from this history of struggle is precisely the problem. His reforms are almost dangerously disconnected from real-world politics. Appeals to long-term, enlightened self-interest have never done well in America's capitalist marketplace, which is far more likely to fixate on a company's next quarterly statement. Such appeals are not known to be particularly effective in politics either. On repeated occasions, Stiglitz forthrightly acknowledges that globalization has been managed by and for the rich. "The rules of the game have been largely set by the advanced industrial countries—and, not surprisingly, they have shaped globalization to further their own interests," he charges. "They have not sought to create a fair set of rules, let alone a set of rules that would promote the well-being of those in the poorest countries in the world."[78]

In truth, the rules benefit only a small slice of the population even within the advanced industrial countries. In *Globalization and Its Discontents* Stiglitz insightfully observes that many of the IMF's ideological blind spots formed when it mistook the distinctive interests of Wall Street for the national interest of the United States and the general interest of the international community. Because controlling inflation was a priority of the financial community, it is not surprising that it ranked high among IMF concerns—and that maintaining full employment did not. But because the Fund's economists maintain close ties with Wall Street, and sometimes are "richly rewarded" with lucrative jobs there upon retiring to the private sector, the conflation of interests has only hardened with time.[79]

Yet Stiglitz never seems to take to heart his own recognition that globalization is fraught with special interests. His logic is almost tautological: The advanced industrial nations have not created a fair set of rules in the past, so he proposes that they do so in the future, for fairness's sake. Poor countries are woefully underrepresented in economic decision-making, and big business consistently blocks reforms. Still, Stiglitz chides protesters in *Making Globalization Work* for having a one-sided view of corporations and for portraying them as villains. It is as if his slogan for action is "even-handedness gets the goods."

Stiglitz's perceptions of the changes that have already taken place also seem to be askew. Interestingly, while he furiously denounces the IMF, he rarely says a bad word about the World Bank. Instead, he takes at face value the institution's claims that it has abandoned structural adjustment, moved away from imposing neoliberal reforms as a condition of receiving aid, and opened a much wider debate about the goals of "development," one that welcomes dissenting viewpoints. Social movement critics have convincingly demonstrated that these changes are more rhetoric than substance. Still, Stiglitz believes that he helped set the institution on a more humane and open path. Ha-Joon Chang succinctly notes, "Unfortunately, the subsequent events, including his own expulsion, have revealed that this [is] an overly optimistic view."[80]

Upton Sinclair once famously remarked, "It is difficult to get a man to understand something when his salary depends upon his not understanding it." The wisdom in this maxim bears heavily on Stiglitz's drive to create a "change in mind-set" among finance ministers and other international elites.[81] As *Making Globalization Work* progresses, the author's dance between acknowledging political barriers and retreating into wishful thinking grows tiresome. During one such two-step, he explains: "Those who benefit from the current system will resist change, and they are powerful. But forces for change have already been set in motion." The passive voice in the second sentence is not incidental. A sense of uncertain passivity pervades his political thinking; he has trouble understanding or often even identifying the forces that can make change possible. And so he writes in blurry strokes: "There will be reforms, even if there are piecemeal ones. . . . There are many things that must be done."[82]

If only we could sidestep politics, Stiglitz's prescriptions suggest, then impartial policymakers could weigh the objective merits of different ideas, adopt the best ones, and make the global economy work for all. This liberal scientific fantasy underlies Stiglitz's political program and is its core weakness.

One might propose a corollary to Stiglitz's thesis about asymmetrical information in economic markets, one concerning the asymmetrical power in political life. It would hold that whenever the playing field for disputes is tilted—where some individuals have more power than others (in other words, *always*)—fairness cannot be expected to win out over arrangements that benefit the powerful. Such is certainly the case with globalization. There is no cause to doubt Stiglitz's good intentions and genuine concern for the poor, and there is ample reason to appreciate his contributions as a critic of neoliberal extremism. But those who are working to fundamentally alter the balance of power between the world's dominant nations and those at the periphery, between the elite and the impoverished, and between corporations and working people can be forgiven if they base their more thorough-going visions of change on something other than the yet-to-surface enlightened self-interest of those who would save capitalism from itself.

TOWARD A REAL ALTERNATIVE

Slates of proposals for near-term reform are important, if for no other reason than that they defy the idea that "there is no alternative" to the current system or that opposing neoliberalism is like protesting the rising sun. Yet Stiglitz's vision, for all its good points, ultimately depends upon the beneficence and foresight of our current ruling elites to create change. The real issue in promoting a different type of world order, a globalization from below that rejects both political imperialism and economic neoliberalism, is not just coming up with fresh ideas. It is linking those ideas with concrete efforts to change the power relationships that determine who sets the rules for the global economy. Proposals for new rules must be coupled with campaigns to dismantle the old order, to take apart the institutions that have allowed an elite few to rule for so long, and to create space for more democratic alternatives to emerge. Such organizing requires real political savvy, and that is what Stiglitz lacks. Fortunately, many others are already creating this new globalization.

Even as Thomas Friedman celebrates the birth of a world that is flat, straightjacketed, and homogeneous, a different globalism has emerged from underneath his wireless, turbocharged radar. Dissident communities and nations are working to bring to life a world that is rich in diversity and in democratic self-determination. It is to their efforts that we now turn.

PART THREE

A Democratic Globalization

8

POWERING THE ALTERNATIVE

For residents of the United States, perpetually trained to think of our country as number one in the world, the annual rankings on the UN Human Development Index can come as a bit of a shock. Unlike other rankings of national development, the index—known as the HDI—goes beyond measuring raw economic output. Instead, it considers the health of a country's residents and what educational resources they have available to them. Adding these measures to more traditional standards of purchasing power, it gives a snapshot of the quality of life in different countries, a wider view of development than gross domestic product (GDP) alone. In doing so, it suggests that there might be something wrong with the ways we most commonly think about success in the global economy.

The United States has the largest economy in the world, but it ranked only number ten on the HDI in 2005.[1] The average person in Sweden earned about 30 percent less income than the average American, as measured by per capita GDP, yet Sweden ranked four places higher on the index. The reason is simple: Its citizens were much healthier, and more of its young people were enrolled in school. The United States also consistently falls behind nations like Australia and Iceland. If you're born in one of these countries, you can expect to earn slightly less income than if you are from the United States, but you can also expect to live a full three years longer.

The HDI reveals other surprises as well. On the 2005 index, South Africa, still struggling with the legacy of apartheid and the persistence of economic inequalities under subsequent neoliberalism, ranks sixty-eight places lower than it would if it were ranked by economic strength alone. Oil-rich Middle Eastern countries such as the United Arab Emirates, Qatar, and Oman, whose investments in public education have been lacking, also rank far lower than they would otherwise. Cuba ranks forty places higher than if it were ranked on income alone. Economic wealth, it seems, is not the whole of the development story.

The HDI is published each year as part of the broader Human Development Report, which is produced by a small and often-controversial office situated within the United Nations. While never framed as a radical enterprise, the office has propagated a brand of development thinking that contrasts with the dominant viewpoint of the Washington Consensus. For more than a decade and a half, it has worked to place the actual quality of life of the world's poor in the center of international dialogue, generating considerable attention and acclaim. The office would have never existed except for a determined and iconoclastic Pakistani economist named Mahbub ul Haq.

Changing the Measure of Success

Born in 1934, in the Punjab region of what was then British India, Mahbub ul Haq witnessed the violent partition of India and Pakistan when he was a young man—his own family narrowly escaping harm by fleeing into Pakistan in 1947.[2] The experience left a permanent mark, making him a lifelong foe of sectarianism. As a student at Cambridge University in the 1950s, Haq was part of a circle of economics students that included future Nobel Laureate Amartya Sen. There, at King's College, the outwardly shy Haq earned a reputation for being a fearless debater. When the undergrads had tea with visiting American professor Milton

Friedman, it was Haq who held up the students' end of the argument, stepping forward to defend the Keynesian welfare state against Friedman's neoliberal assault.[3] In the following decades, Haq, like Joseph Stiglitz, would spend his professional life largely among economic technocrats. He was always confined by the structures he chose to work within—among them Robert McNamara's World Bank in the 1970s, the Pakistani government during the Zia dictatorship in the 1980s, and the United Nations Development Program (UNDP) in the 1990s. Yet Haq was skilled at carving out spaces for dissident thought within mainstream organizations.

The greatest impact of Haq's dissent has been in helping to dethrone the "economic growth school" of development. For decades following World War II, gross national product ruled as the single standard by which economists judged a nation's progress. GNP is a measure, originally designed for wartime use, that tracks the total value of goods and services produced in a country. In the 1980s, economists began to focus on gross domestic product (GDP), which is akin to GNP, except that it does not credit a country with the economic output of its companies doing business abroad. More similar than they are different, both measures encourage us to think about development solely in terms of the size of the economy.

Well before the alternative framework of human development was established, observers had commented on the serious shortcomings of GNP and GDP measures. Perhaps most eloquent was Robert F. Kennedy. On the campaign trial in 1968, shortly before his death, Kennedy issued a challenge to policymakers encouraging them to think about progress in new ways. "Too much and too long," he said,

> we seem to have surrendered community excellence and community values in the mere accumulation of material things. Our gross national product, if we should judge America by that—counts air pollution and cigarette advertising, and ambulances to clear our highways of carnage. It counts special locks for our doors and jails for those who break them. It counts the destruction of our redwoods and the loss of our natural wonder in chaotic sprawl. It counts napalm and the cost of a nuclear

warhead, and armored cars for police who fight riots in our streets. It counts Whitman's rifle and Speck's knife, and the television programs which glorify violence in order to sell toys to our children.

Yet the gross national product does not allow for the health of our children, the quality of their education, or the joy of their play. It does not include the beauty of our poetry or the strength of our marriages; the intelligence of our public debate or the integrity of our public officials. It measures neither our wit nor our courage; neither our wisdom nor our learning; neither our compassion nor our devotion to our country; it measures everything, in short, except that which makes life worthwhile.[4]

Forty years later, few U.S. leaders have recognized the profundity of RFK's challenge. But even as Kennedy was speaking, Haq and other economists in the global South were working to challenge development models obsessed solely with economic growth. By the 1980s, Haq's efforts had crystallized into the paradigm of human development, which he worked tirelessly to promote for the rest of his life. This perspective argued that "while growth in national production . . . is absolutely necessary to meet all essential human objectives, what is important is to study how this growth translates—or fails to translate—into human development in various societies"; that is, how it translates into the actual welfare of a country's citizens.[5]

After becoming a special advisor to the UNDP in 1989, Haq convinced the organization to open an office that would promote this perspective, and the Human Development Reports were born. "The purpose of development," stated the first report, released in 1990, "is to offer people more options. One of their options is access to income—not as an end in itself but as a means to acquiring human well-being. But there are other options as well, including long life, knowledge, political freedom, personal security, community participation and guaranteed human rights."[6]

The concept of human development would have a substantial impact on the economic debate in the next decade, uniting a wide range of forces dissatisfied with traditional measures of economic growth. Still, the reports might have easily been ignored, suffering the fate of countless technical publications that never receive public attention.

Haq's strategy for avoiding such a fate arose out of a debate in the 1980s with his colleagues, including Amartya Sen. Haq argued for the creation of a Human Development *Index*—a single ranking that could go head-to-head with GNP. Others disagreed with the idea. As Sen would write years later, "At first I had expressed to Mahbub ... considerable skepticism about trying to focus on a crude index of this kind, attempting to catch in one simple number a complex reality about human development and deprivation."[7] After all, the Human Development Reports would contain a much broader set of tables and data—information covering a wide range of social and economic issues that affected peoples' lives. Sen thought the attention should be on this data and that the reports' authors should try to break the single-measure mind-set of GNP.

Haq shared the goal of challenging this mind-set, but he believed in fighting fire with fire, even if the HDI would be only very rough measure. "This crudeness had not escaped Mahbub at all," according to Sen. "But after some initial hesitation, Mahbub persuaded himself that the dominance of GNP (an overused and oversold index that he wanted to supplant) would not be broken by any set of tables."

"We need a measure," Haq argued to Sen, "of the same level of vulgarity as GNP—just one number—but a measure that is not as blind to social aspects of human lives as GNP is."[8] Such a measure would give policymakers and public interest advocates a better option than falling back on GNP when they needed a summary statistic. And only when the stranglehold of traditional growth measures had been broken would other data be considered seriously.

Sen ultimately helped devise the HDI, and Haq's public-relations device proved ingenious. Upon its launch in 1990, the Human Development Report captured the imagination of the international press. "It was rare for a U.N. report to be noticed at all," noted London School of Economics professor Meghnad Desai, "but unique for it to be covered by virtually every newspaper round the world."[9] Much of the initial media coverage focused on the HDI's direct challenge to GDP, but subsequent stories dug deeper into the information the reports presented.

The annual Human Development Reports go far beyond the single HDI, showing the impact of inequality, racial and gender disparities, and a host of other social and political considerations. They have frequently outlined policies designed to address these disparities. The annual editions have revealed some startling realities: Nearly three-fifths of the 4.5 billion people living in developing countries lack adequate sewers, a quarter reside in woefully substandard housing, and a fifth have no access to modern health services.[10] If measured as separate countries using basic indicators of social well-being, the African American population of the United States would fall thirty places behind the country's white population in a global ranking, as of 1993.[11]

The 1995 report, examining "Gender and Human Development," found that 70 percent of the 1.3 billion people living in absolute poverty were women.[12] The 2003 report showed that fifty-four countries—including some of the neoliberal "poster children" of the decade—were poorer at the end of the booming 1990s than at the start of the decade, even in GDP terms.[13] The finding prompted UNDP administrator Mark Malloch Brown to call for a "guerrilla assault" on the Washington Consensus.[14]

Haq died of pneumonia in 1998, but the office of the Human Development Reports continues to produce incisive data about the global economy. Haq's human development model has become an accepted strain of development economics that stands in sharp contrast to neoliberalism. Haq observed shortly before his death that the reports often enraged local elites who had been complicit in implementing Washington Consensus policies or had otherwise ignored the needs of the majority in their countries. Not a single year had passed, Haq noted, "without some government demanding the stoppage of these reports."[15] He also charged that "despite their professions to the contrary, the World Bank and the IMF are still fully committed to the defense of traditional economic growth."[16] Nevertheless, advocates of human development have influenced initiatives such as the UN's Millennium Development Goals, and they have inspired a plethora of new efforts to move beyond economic growth and rethink the goals of development.

Between Afterthoughts and Manifestos

Mahbub ul Haq and the Human Development Reports are significant not because they embody the pursuit of democratic globalization. They represent only one of many attempts to set out a worldview with different values and priorities than those of neoliberalism or empire. In fact, the Human Development Reports are more notable for having been produced within the mainstream confines of the United Nations and for effectively attracting media attention than for being unusually visionary or far-reaching. But the reports provide an excellent entry into the question of alternatives because they do two things that are essential to the emergence of any globalization from below: they demonstrate that policies other than those favored by neoliberalism have long been available, and they demand a change in the way that our societies define progress.

Where democratic globalization must go further is in insisting that we alter the relationships of power that govern the international system—changing *who* chooses the policies and *who* determines whether they have succeeded. The first part of this book focused on the rise of imperial globalization under George W. Bush, examining how this starkly militaristic worldview represented a break from earlier strategies of corporate rule. The second part discussed how the debate about trade and development has unfolded in this context, reviewing the dramatically altered fates of the World Bank, the IMF, and the WTO. The U.S. shift to imperial globalization and the decline of the international financial institutions have produced a new landscape for battles over the shape of globalization.

Today, strains on the U.S. empire and the discrediting of neoliberal ideology create exciting spaces for new ideas to emerge. Yet the situation provides no guarantees that a fairer or more equitable global order will solidify. The final part of this book highlights efforts already underway to alter the structures of power that allow corporate CEOs and Washington elites to impose their visions of how to rule. And it shows how a reinvigorated global movement may again seize the spotlight in the coming years.

I have always found it remarkable how consistently global elites deny that viable alternatives to the current global order exist, even as the debate about how to rule the world rapidly changes. Imperial globalists contend that without U.S. military strength decisively projected abroad, the forces of evil will sweep the globe. Meanwhile, corporate globalists persist in their belief that in the post–Cold War world, we have no choice but to embrace the continual advance of the "free" market.

Neither idea is credible. The disastrous war in Iraq has nullified the neocons' argument that preemptive war can create security. Meanwhile, mainstream pundits who proclaim neoliberalism to be inevitable and irreplaceable, even as it falls into ever-deeper disrepute, are either ignorant or disingenuous. Today, there exist scores of books, hundreds of reports, and thousands of summary articles and presentations that offer new directions for the global order—plus innumerable initiatives at local, national, and international levels to create political and economic systems that uphold human rights and defend the environment. To ignore these requires significant acts of failed reporting or ideological blindness.

In truth, a lack of viable ideas is hardly the problem for those who reject corporate and imperial models of globalization. Whether they are part of boisterous national uprisings or quiet, persistent community efforts to fuel a democratic globalization, members of grassroots networks are now engaged in a debate about the proper balance of vision, program, political strategy, and tactics needed to move forward.

Having witnessed and participated in this debate for many years, I believe that a key challenge is to avoid two common pitfalls. The first one is the tendency to approach alternatives as an afterthought, and the second one is the urge to fashion manifestos. Both inclinations have been easy to spot in the years since the Seattle protests. At many teach-ins and workshops it is common to hear speakers spend an hour detailing the terrors of the militarist agenda but then provide few answers to the question of what should be done to confront these forces. Likewise, many books spend chapter after chapter making lengthy critiques of corporate globalization, only to skim over the question of building truly democratic political and economic systems in just a few closing pages. They treat the topic as an afterthought, behaving as if criticism alone were sufficient to propel action.

On the other side are those individuals who prepare extensive manifestos for change, detailing their personal visions for a better world. Some works, like Joseph Stiglitz's *Making Globalization Work*, are founded on the premise that the best ideas will inevitably prevail in the "marketplace of ideas." They seem largely oblivious to the political battles over ideas and interests that are already being waged. Other works present more radical visions, yet they, too, can be disconnected from reality. These may delve into excessively abstract or obscure debates, or they might implicitly seek to impose consensus on diverse, multipronged, international movements challenging U.S. hegemony and corporate power.

In mid-2000, when globalization protests raged at international summits, journalist Naomi Klein attended a conference at the Riverside Church in New York City titled "Re-Imagining Politics and Society."[17] Event organizers stressed the uniqueness of the conference, emphasizing how discussions among the one thousand delegates would overcome the global justice movement's lack of vision. These progressives did not contend—as did conservative pundits—that the movement had no alternatives to offer. But they did believe that demonstrators were insufficiently cohesive. Their conference, they argued, would remedy this, "[giving] birth to a unified movement for holistic social, economic and political change."

Over the course of the event, Klein developed a contrary impression. "As I slipped in and out of lecture rooms, soaking up vision galore from Arianna Huffington, Michael Lerner, David Korten and Cornel West," she wrote. "I was struck by the futility of this entire well-meaning exercise." Her response to the situation cut to the heart of the issue:

> When critics say that the protesters lack vision, what they are really saying is that they lack an overarching revolutionary philosophy—like Marxism, democratic socialism, deep ecology or social anarchy—on which they all agree. That is absolutely true, and for this we should be extraordinarily thankful. At the moment, the anticorporate street activists

are ringed by would-be leaders, anxious for the opportunity to enlist them as foot soldiers for their particular cause. At one end there is Michael Lerner and his conference at the Riverside Church, waiting to welcome all that inchoate energy in Seattle and Washington inside the framework of his "Politics of Meaning." At the other, there is John Zerzan in Eugene, Oregon, who isn't interested in Lerner's call for "healing" but sees the rioting and property destruction as the first step toward the collapse of industrialization and a return to "anarcho-primitivism"—a pre-agrarian hunter-gatherer utopia. In between there are dozens of other visionaries, from the disciples of Murray Bookchin and his theory of social ecology, to certain sectarian Marxists who are convinced the revolution starts tomorrow, to devotees of Kalle Lasn, editor of *Adbusters*, and his watered-down version of revolution through "culture-jamming." And then there is the unimaginative pragmatism coming from some union leaders who, before Seattle, were ready to tack social clauses onto existing trade agreements and call it a day.

It is to this young movement's credit that it has as yet fended off all of these agendas and has rejected everyone's generously donated manifesto, holding out for an acceptably democratic, representative process to take its resistance to the next stage.[18]

Such a critique should not provide cover for anti-intellectualism or for a refusal to ground ourselves in political traditions that contain rich insights for today's challenges. But it does offer the important warning against those personalities who would see themselves as the sole solution to the question of vision.

Part of what was fueling public confusion about alternatives was specific to the political moment when globalization protests captured the attention of the mainstream media. During this period, around the turn of the millennium, global justice organizing was being covered only in contexts where participants were providing a voice of opposition—at the summit meetings of institutions like the WTO, the World Bank, and the IMF. These events became flash points of resistance for a reason, one rooted in the very structure of the movements creating a democratic globalization. For a time, the summit meetings were remarkably effective at drawing together a tremendously diverse body of global citizen activists.

The forces combating neoliberalism show so much diversity that some observers refer to them collectively as a "movement of movements." In one of the first meetings of its kind in recent decades, the Zapatistas of southern Mexico hosted an *encuentro* in the jungles of Chiapas in 1996—a meeting they called the First International Encounter for Humanity and Against Neoliberalism. The range of representatives that met was astounding, with some five thousand people from more than forty countries attending. A follow-up meeting in Geneva in 1998, which resulted in the formation of a network of autonomous organizations called Peoples' Global Action, included groups as diverse as the indigenous Maori of New Zealand, the Gandhian State Farmers' Association of Karnataka, India, and the Canadian Postal Workers' Union.

The breadth of activity in subsequent years has been just as amazing. Localized embodiments of the global justice movement include strikes by unions in South Korea, fights against water privatization in Bolivia and South Africa, the mass mobilization of civil society in Argentina following the country's 2001 economic collapse, heartfelt opposition to development of hydroelectric dams in rural India, farm occupations by the landless workers' movement in Brazil, African efforts to secure access to low-cost generic AIDS drugs, and demonstrations in Central America against CAFTA and the FTAA. Although many participants in these efforts see themselves as part of a wider struggle, such far-flung groups rarely appear in the same place at the same time.

In this context, the meetings of the financial institutions promoting corporate globalization served as critical rallying points for the transnational coalitions of activists. Perhaps nowhere was this clearer than in Seattle. There, opposition to the WTO brought together U.S. students waging campaigns against sweatshop labor, farmers from the global South decrying agribusiness dominance, European food safety advocates concerned about the spread of genetically modified foods, and indigenous rights activists defending cultural diversity. In an often-noted juxtaposition, union members concerned with how the WTO undermined workers' rights marched with environmentalists wearing turtle costumes to highlight how the organization threatened protections for endangered species. A sign worn by one protester, reading, "Teamsters and Turtles, United At Last," has become a famous marker of this unity. So frequently is it cited that one can easily forget that for decades the unionists and environmentalists of the Pacific Northwest often butted heads, with employers framing demands to protect the natural world as mandates that would eliminate jobs. The WTO allowed these parties to come together in opposition to a common enemy and work to resolve long-standing disagreements.

Having little idea what they were witnessing, reporters without a background in globalization battles heard only a cacophonous din. Blinded by the diversity of the demonstrations, they failed to see these incredible gatherings for what they were: places where representatives of an expansive global movement came together to assert a common identity and common cause.

Although they were extraordinary events, the summit protests also had limitations. At one point, a protest announcement condemning trade ministers vowed, "Wherever they go, we shall be there!" In response, Naomi Klein famously asked, "Is this really what we want—a movement of meeting-stalkers, following the trade bureaucrats as if they were the Grateful Dead?"[19] For those who saw the summit protests as ends in themselves, rather than the means for building a larger movement, undue preoccupation with the itinerary of trade and finance officials began to draw attention away from longer-term grassroots campaigns. This prompted self-criticism on the part of some protesters. The wider political moment in which this discussion took place, however, did not last long. The globalization scene began to shift early in the Bush years, with the attacks of 9/11 playing an important role in the change.

Just as abruptly as the major news outlets had announced the arrival of a "new" global movement after the Seattle protests, challenges to the Washington Consensus again became virtually invisible to reporters after 9/11. This only partially reflected what was happening on the ground. In the months following the attacks, some protests—notably a major mobilization against World Bank and IMF meetings in Washington, D.C.—were canceled as the world rose to express sympathy for the victims. However, the Bush administration's reckless response wiped out global good will and ultimately widened the scope of protests.

As strategies to impose elite visions of globalization continued, global justice protests throughout the world resumed. Many people, particularly in the global South, combined outrage at U.S. militarism with a repudiation of neoliberal policies. When Bush traveled abroad, he was met with large protests, many of which raised economic issues as well as antiwar concerns. Yet media outlets mostly reported these demonstrations as incoherent anti-American riots—if they covered them at all. Beltway pundits rushed to declare the global justice movement dead. Leading the pack was Edward Gresser of the Progressive Policy Institute, the think tank of the pro–"free trade" Democratic Leadership Council, who pronounced the movement "destined for irrelevance" in a realigned world.[20]

Millions of people had reason to protest. These activists were about to redraw the political map of Latin America, preside over the collapse of neoliberalism's legitimacy, lead a worldwide rebellion against preemptive war, and push issues of economic justice to ever more prominent places in the global development debate. Their efforts for a democratic globalization, they would assert, were very much alive.

THE VIEW FROM PORTO ALEGRE

As it turned out, a very visible manifestation of the next stage of global justice movement would come from a modest city of 1.5 million people deep in the south of Brazil, a place whose name has become synonymous with the pursuit of a more just and democratic global order. Today, mention of Porto Alegre should be sufficient to forever put to rest the knee-jerk contention that there is no alternative to dominant visions of globalization.

Proud residents of Porto Alegre will tell you that their city is "the last bastion of socialism and rock 'n' roll." Stalls covered with black Iron Maiden T-shirts line the public markets, and the municipality long served as a stronghold of the *Partido dos Trabalhadores* (PT), the Brazilian

Workers Party. The city itself became a model for democratic governance when it adopted a system of participatory budgeting in 1989. In this process, assemblies of thousands of local residents play a direct role in allocating a portion of the municipal budget—something that has resulted in greater attention to the needs of often-neglected neighborhoods. The model has since been replicated in more than two hundred cities worldwide.[21]

This claim to fame notwithstanding, Porto Alegre is now better known around the globe as the original home of the World Social Forum. In early 2001, after the Seattle protests but before the terrorist attacks on the Twin Towers, thousands of people first converged on the city to discuss the challenges presented by the likes of Bush, Enron, and the IMF. First conceived by the French-based Association for the Taxation of Financial Transactions for the Aid of Citizens (ATTAC) and the Brazilian Workers Party as a grassroots counterpoint to the World Economic Forum in Davos, Switzerland, the social forum has provided a space for global justice groups to come together on their own terms, present a positive vision, and reassert an identity as a unified international movement.

Even as progressives within the United States have turned to resisting Bush administration policies of preemptive war and its reactionary assaults on constitutional rights, social services, and environmental protections, international movements have not waited for regime change in the United States to respond to the decline of the Washington Consensus. Massive crowds have joined Americans in rallying against the war in Iraq. At the same time, local communities have waged battles to reverse privatization of public utilities, and transnational campaigns have fought for reforms like debt relief. In some countries, they have successfully overthrown neoliberal governments, elected leaders who oppose the Washington Consensus, and pressed those officials to enact social policies that serve working people.

Reflecting this sustained torrent of global activity, the World Social Forum has grown and matured. Whereas the first global forum hosted 12,000 participants, subsequent events have grown larger and larger, drawing crowds of up to 150,000 people.[22] In addition to returning to Porto Alegre three times since the initial 2001 summit, the event has convened in Mumbai, India, and Nairobi, Kenya, taking place almost annually. The forum is now organized by a committee of representatives from prominent civil society groups throughout the world. Beyond the unified global meetings, dozens of similar forums have been held at the regional level. The social forum process has attracted personalities ranging from wandering counterculturalists to powerful heads of state. Its influence on Davos, where elites are now photographed pondering problems of poverty and AIDS, has been undeniable.

When I traveled to Porto Alegre for the 2005 forum, the late-January summer was unrelenting. "Maybe if I were younger," a veteran activist commented to me, "I could deal with the heat." Yet throngs of Brazilians wandered the sweltering expanse of tented workshop areas sporting bare chests, Bermuda shorts, or skirts, enthusiastically heading off to discussions on creating a fairer global order as if they were embarking on a trip to the beach. Despite the heat, crowds packed seemingly innumerable workshops. During any given session in the five-day forum, dozens of speakers led panels taking place simultaneously in tents and warehouse spaces spread over a nearly three-mile expanse along the banks of Porto Alegre's Guaíba River.

These spaces have served as physical embodiments of the proposals for a democratic globalization. At World Social Forum, community leaders, nonprofit representatives, scholars, organizers, and progressive lawmakers have presented, debated, and refined ideas that collectively represent a set of policies for the global economy as comprehensive as any wonky campaign office could ever hope to devise.

Groups meeting in tents designated for discussion of energy and the environment have strategized about ways to break our dependence on the oil economy. They have proposed investment in mass public transportation, high mileage standards for cars, and shifting government subsidies for hydrocarbon exploitation to alternative energy. Other environmentalists have worked to promote an international carbon tax to penalize polluters—something undoubtedly in the public interest, especially given mounting evidence about the perils of global warming. All of these are perfectly viable public policies, but they have been vehemently opposed by the oil industry.

In other tents, family farmers and food safety advocates from throughout the world have gathered to promote models for redistributive land reform. Even the international financial institutions acknowledge that land reform would be beneficial for the poor, but it has been pushed off the political map by national elites and agribusiness conglomerates. Other advocates explained how current government subsidies for exports and for pesticides boost large-scale "mono-cropping" over organic agriculture; in response, they argued for a shift in public funds to support sustainable farming. Indigenous communities further asserted their right to self-determination, particularly with regard to maintaining traditional systems of land ownership and food production.

Tents holding discussions on the need to curb corporate power have advanced a slate of innovative proposals. These include public financing of elections to end what U.S. Senator Russ Feingold has called "a system of legalized bribery and legalized extortion."[23] They include laws that allow victims of corporate abuses in the developing world to sue in U.S. or European courts. They include detailed proposals for strengthening antitrust law to break up business monopolies—among them the massive media empires that do much to set the limits of public debate. And they feature strategies from research centers like the Program on Corporations, Law, and Democracy, which advocate revoking U.S. court rulings that grant corporations the status of "fictitious persons," lending these businesses the same constitutional rights as individuals without holding them to the same standards of legal accountability.[24]

Walking past workshop tents in Porto Alegre to the warehouse spaces along the river, one could find public interest groups making strong arguments for firm corporate disclosure laws. These would help anti-sweatshop advocates to determine the origins of products and would allow concerned community members to track the use of environmental toxins. Meanwhile, discussions about intellectual property have detailed the need to reject corporate patents on seeds and other forms of life—and have supported developing countries' right to produce lifesaving generic drugs in defiance of the pharmaceutical industry. Finally, progressive lawmakers have defended the prerogative of countries to take precautionary stances in controlling genetically modified organisms and other commodities with uncertain public health or environmental impacts. These stances are currently threatened by WTO mandates.

Other advocates at the World Social Forum have extended the challenge to GDP championed by the Human Development Reports. They have insisted that corporations be made to adopt "full cost accounting," a system that makes them liable for the true costs of their enterprises. Currently, damage done to the environment and to public health constitutes what in economics are known as "externalities." Corporations rarely have to pay for the cleanup of pollution or for the health care costs of those affected by their actions, especially if this pollution takes place in the global South. Therefore, this damage never becomes part of the economic equation for CEOs. But in affected societies, everyone eventually must pay. Full cost accounting would "internalize" those impacts and make corporations directly responsible for despoiling the public commons or endangering the well-being of local residents.[25] In the case of products like petroleum, which is greatly underpriced, given the damage it does, changing our systems of accounting could prompt a more thoroughgoing reconsideration of how we organize our societies.

ATTAC, one of the organizations that founded the World Social Forum, has set up tents promoting campaigning for the Tobin tax. First proposed by Nobel Prize–winning economist James Tobin in the 1970s, the initiative would impose a low-percentage tax on the hundreds of billions of dollars worth of international financial transactions that take place each day. This would provide a disincentive for short-term gambling on currencies, and it would encourage longer-term and more productive investment. Moreover, even a minuscule levy could create an annual fund of more than $100 billion, which could be used to stop the spread of disease and alleviate global poverty.[26]

Tents in Porto Alegre devoted to feminist discussions highlighted that women are often most affected by the harmful impacts of neoliberal economic restructuring. Activists have demanded that women's groups in local communities be given a strong voice in the direction of development aid, that agricultural reforms assert women's rights to hold land title, and that international agencies respect reproductive rights. Groups like the Women's International Coalition for Economic Justice have also stressed that UN-backed summits and other international efforts to advance women's rights must not be subordinated to multilateral trade agreements.[27]

Warehouse workspaces hosting labor organizations have offered myriad methods for protecting workers' rights and ending sweatshop conditions. Over seventy cities and localities in the United States have passed "living wage" laws since the early 1990s. These go beyond paltry minimum wage requirements and mandate that businesses pay employees at least enough to keep their families out of poverty. In Porto Alegre, U.S. advocates discussed how to spread these campaigns. Meanwhile, representatives from the estimated 180 worker-run factories that formed after capital fled Argentina's collapsing economy in 2001 spoke about their experiences in self-management.[28] A cross-section of Europeans, South Asians, and Latin Americans discussed other systems of employee ownership of corporations, as well as governance structures that would give workers and communities a say in the direction of the economic firms that affect them most.

Finally, workshops organized by representatives from the fair trade movement profiled endeavors to build direct ties between producers in the global South and Northern consumers. The fair trade model aims to eliminate exploitative middlemen, ensure that workers get a living wage for their labor, and give local collectives a greater say in determining the conditions under which international economic exchanges take place. Like organic food, fair trade remains a niche market, and it cannot substitute for wider structural changes in global economy. But it provides both a living alternative to exploitative trade and a hopeful model for future change.

Even this wide range of activity hardly constitutes an exhaustive survey. Contrary to individual manifestos that presume that a lack of ideas is the problem for progressives, the advocates at Porto Alegre have presented an agenda for change rooted in local struggles and campaigns that have long been underway. Excellent volumes such as *Alternatives to Economic Globalization*, a book compiled by the San Francisco–based International Forum on Globalization, and *Globalization from Below*, a book by veteran labor analysts Jeremy Brecher, Tim Costello, and Brendan Smith, have profiled other aspects of this agenda.[29] The Human Development Reports first devised by Mahbub ul Haq have given UN backing to many of these same initiatives. A number of progressive proposals have even been introduced as legislation in the U.S. Congress in such measures as the Global Sustainable Development Resolution and Jesse Jackson Jr.'s HOPE for Africa Act.[30] Needless to say, the elite beneficiaries of neoliberalism, still steadfast in their contention that no alternatives exist, would prefer that the public not take notice of any of these developments.

MANY YESES

As I ducked in and out of the tents of the 2005 forum in Porto Alegre, the debate about how to balance vision, program, and strategy was everywhere around me. During a discussion of the relevance of *Don Quixote* for social movements today—an event subtitled "Utopia and Politics"—Nobel Laureate in Literature José Saramago and famed Uruguayan author Eduardo Galeano held a vigorous exchange. With listeners clogging the aisles of a large auditorium, Galeano celebrated the paradoxes of a world in which a novel cherished for centuries would begin its life in prison, "because Cervantes was in debt, as are we in Latin America." He defended the utopian impulse as a force for change, citing Che Guevara's statement in his last letter to his parents: "Once again I feel under my heels the ribs of Rocinante," Quixote's horse.

Saramago would have none of it. "I consider the concept of utopia worse than useless," he argued. "What has transformed the world is not utopia, but need." He added, "The only time and place where our work can have impact—where we can see it and evaluate it—is tomorrow. . . . Let's not wait for utopia."

The ethos of the forum would seem to favor Galeano's view. The World Social Forum's charter indicates that it is not a deliberative body; it does not take official positions on behalf of the assembly. Yet Saramago's defense of short-term demands received a standing ovation. And reflecting this sentiment, a group of nineteen high-profile participants, including both of the writers, released a statement at the end of the week dubbed "The Porto Alegre Manifesto." Among its planks, the twelve-point platform called for cancellation of debts, a Tobin tax, local control of the food supply, and the democratization of international financial institutions. "We're confident that the great majority of the people of the forum will agree with this proposal," Ignacio Ramonet, editor of *Le Monde Diplomatique*, told reporters.[31]

The manifesto became the subject of a lively argument at the forum. Ramonet was right that the content of his manifesto would prove agreeable to a great majority of the forum's participants. At the same time, his group of luminaries pointed to a real problem. Although some of the groups that make up the global justice movement, especially within labor and nongovernmental organizations, maintain more traditional leadership structures, the movement as a whole claims no formal leaders. In the absence of official spokespeople, well-known writers or intellectuals are often called upon to represent the movement in public forums, becoming de facto figureheads. But as with Michael Lerner, Arianna Huffington, and John Zerzan in the United States, their personal philosophies can be controversial.

In Porto Alegre, critics immediately charged that the celebrities' document contravened the democratic and "horizontal" character of World Social Forum. Some signers, like Brazilian organizer Chico Whitaker, took pains to emphasize that the proposal was merely one of many to emerge. In contrast, others, such as Ramonet, made clear that they considered an explicit unifying platform essential for the forum to move forward as a political force.

Yet even as disagreement over the declaration raged, a different vision of the purpose of the social forum was taking shape. This did not involve nailing down a set of numbered priorities. Rather, it suggested that cultivating networks between people and formulating vision are not nearly so distinct as some might imagine. I encountered this vision while wandering through forum grounds and talking with participants about how their interactions had affected them.

Food stands and souvenir vendors lined the river and snaked through the workshop spaces in Porto Alegre, and the presence of the Youth Camp in the middle of the forum enhanced the fairlike atmosphere. This expansive tent city-within-a-city housed thirty-five thousand young people. There, passersby could see jugglers and drilling corps of drummers, late-night bonfires and the graffiti-covered Casa de Hip Hop. This carnival aspect of the event has been understandably maligned by those looking to dismiss the forum. But these open spaces also provided room for participants to wander and to meet. The impact they had on those actually working to build new structures of political and economic life could be profound.

Strolling through the forum could produce rewarding surprises. Stanford professor and free software guru Lawrence Lessig wrote on his blog of walking through the Youth Camp with Minister of Culture Gilberto Gil, a Brazilian music icon who had been appointed to government by the progressive administration of Lula da Silva. Gil was alternately accosted by young protesters demanding free radio (Gil relished the debate) and asked to perform songs from his pop opus (the whole crowd sang along). "Here's a Minister of the government, face to face with supporters and opponents," Lessig wrote. "There is no 'free speech zone.' No guns, no men in black uniform, no panic, and plenty of press. Just imagine."[32]

"Walking between sessions with an Italian senator, talking over ideas for our environmental campaigns—that's what I got out of the forum," one friend told me.

Another colleague, Zeynep Toufe of the Institute for Public Accuracy, told of how, "tired, hot, severely underslept," she stumbled into an afternoon panel on land rights and the "untouchable castes" of India.[33] She was unexpectedly blown away by the testimony of homelessness and dispossession she heard. "It's really the difference between 'knowing' something in the abstract and sitting there, looking at a human being and feeling in your heart that this is the ugly truth of this world. Of course I knew the *dalits* were discriminated against. Still, I felt crushed by the weight of just listening to [the speakers] explain how they were thought of as the 'polluted people,' how they were always denied land so that they would be forced to be semi-slaves to the landlords and the dominant castes." The session "was so un-cynical that I didn't know what to feel," Toufe reported. When the tent full of people burst into songs or chants, she stated, "It was one of the most sincere, the least contrived instances I have ever encountered of people shouting slogans. . . . I tried to explain what a privilege it felt like to be in their presence."

At a reception hosted by Grassroots Global Justice, a delegation of representatives from community-based initiatives around the United States, participants told me their interactions with other local leaders from a wide range of countries had been "inspiring," even "transformative." When Linda Sippio, a leader at the Miami Workers Center, visited a once-idle farm near Porto Alegre that had been taken over by the Brazilian Landless Workers' Movement, she saw links to her own people's struggle to hold ground in their gentrifying Florida neighborhoods. "We're meeting Brazilian groups that are organizing like we are, and we're showing our support," she said. "That helps us both build power."[34]

From this experience of the World Social Forum, two lessons about democratic globalization emerge. The first is that, unlike neoliberalism, a globalization from below does not take the form of a one-size-fits-all prescription for the global economy. Rather than promoting a single model for social reorganization, participants in the global justice movement defend diversity. Adopting a slogan of the Mexican Zapatistas, they envision "a world in which many worlds fit."

The vision of democracy promoted by the global justice movement goes beyond voting in periodic elections. It is a living, participatory democracy that seeks to increase popular control of political and economic life in the face of powerful corporations, unaccountable global financial institutions, and Washington militarism. This idea of democracy is reflected in many of the structures of the movement, which tend to emphasize grassroots participation and cooperative decision-making. Rather than operating as a single body, forces opposed to neoliberalism have undertaken what the RAND Corporation, a think tank closely aligned with the U.S. military, has dubbed "the war of the swarm." The movement, a RAND report stated, operates with no "central leadership or command structure; it is multi-headed, impossible to decapitate."[35] The report noted that this swarm is difficult for many governments and corporations to handle.

With regard to alternative policies, the model of participatory democracy produces, in the words of another slogan, "One No, Many Yeses." It generates a strong challenge to structures of neoliberalism and empire but allows for a wider sense of what might replace them. This does not mean that there cannot be efforts to build consensus around particular priorities or, as Ramonet endeavored, to codify a set of widely accepted demands that might be pursued in the short term. It does mean, however, that many questions of long-term vision will be the subjects of ongoing debate.

One particularly vigorous disagreement within the movement concerns whether combating corporate globalization should mean taking a turn toward local economies. For their part, a group of influential scholars and advocates gathered under the International Forum on Globalization promote "new rules and structures that consciously favor the local and follow the principle of subsidiarity—that is, whatever decisions and activities can be undertaken locally should be."[36] Under this model, communities would rely on local production as much as possible and turn to trade as a last resort rather than a first option.

Opposing this view, progressives such as *Left Business Observer* editor Doug Henwood are skeptical of any moves toward provincialism, and they criticize the romanticization of past periods of economic life. For example, Henwood takes IFG member and author David Korten to task for invoking a Golden Age when "rich and poor alike . . . shared a sense of national and community interest."[37] Henwood argues that such a notion overlooks the often brutal exploitation present in local and national economies of the past. He instead sides with *Empire* authors Michael Hardt and Antonio Negri, who would keep transnational systems of production intact but direct them toward more egalitarian ends than does private capital.

Henwood asserts, "*Empire* uses a lyric from Ani DiFranco as one of its epigraphs: 'Every tool is a weapon if you hold it right.' They could have also used a line from Patti Smith: 'We created it. Let's take it over.'"[38]

While there is real tension between these two positions, they might not be completely at odds. In the end there may be a need for a synthesis that recognizes the wastefulness of the oil-dependent global economy and the importance of local decision-making, but that is willing to harness some beneficial aspects of modern international production to serve the common good. Moreover, while the opposing camps are far apart on some questions of long-term goals, they agree on the pressing need to build stronger movements and to continue pushing to end the Washington Consensus. Their debate about localization is only one of many unresolved issues. Authors Jeremy Brecher and Tim Costello outline some of the other contentious questions among global justice advocates:

> Should the lifestyle of the industrialized countries be maintained, or does it need to be transformed in order to allow development in poor countries without destroying the global environment? Should enterprises be owned and controlled by private individuals, by their workers, by communities, by states, or by some combination of these? What combination of market, state, and direct cooperation should organize economic life?[39]

Standing against neoliberalism and empire does not require a single answer to these questions. Nor do diverse movements need to settle on a single stance, applicable across all economic sectors, to start creating new models of democratic economics that respect both human rights and the environment.

Indeed, if the first lesson from the World Social Forum is that democratic globalization will not come as a single, all-encompassing model, the second lesson is that formulating alternatives is intimately related to the process of building citizens movements. It is through creating ties between local campaigns, concerns, and demands that residents of different countries and communities understand their efforts as part of a united cause. They see a larger whole coming together from the disparate parts. The alternative proposals that emerge from their discussions are not conceived by technocrats and advanced as new entries into the "marketplace of ideas." Nor are they put forth with the expectation that those in power will be persuaded by the logic and fairness inherent in these ideas to enact them. Rather, the proposals are linked to specific political histories, to past battles and current conflicts taking place throughout the world.

A globalization from below learns from the mistakes and successes of movements for change. It draws lessons from the difficulties they encounter and from the opportunities they seize. And it constructs its vision for the next stage of democratic politics out of this ongoing dialogue. As we emerge from the Bush era, a time when fending off Republican assaults seemed like an all-encompassing challenge, the process of reconnecting to the energy and vision of international movements confronting neoliberalism will be particularly important for progressives in the United States. Few things, ultimately, offer more hope for powering a move to the offensive.

JUST SAYING NO, OR FIRST DO NO HARM

I believe that the ideas, experiences, and proposals of Porto Alegre provide a trove of information for those who want to construct a new agenda for the global economy. Instead of trying to invent a new set of alternatives, all of us thinking about the direction of globalization after neoliberalism should immerse ourselves in these proposals and debates. At the same time, as long as democratic movements do not have the power to overrule political and economic elites, I would also make the case for just saying "no"—for first insisting that those now in power stop doing harm.

When Wall Street neoliberals and Washington militarists ask, "What is the alternative?" they base the question on faulty assumptions. Their question serves to naturalize very radical agendas of empire and corporate rule, suggesting that these are normal and acceptable states of affairs. They are not. In a situation where power is grossly imbalanced, where crimes are being perpetuated in the name of democracy, and where ever larger sections of public life are being handed over to the market, saying "no" to these radical agendas can be a perfectly worthy task in itself.

In an important respect, the alternative to invading Iraq is not invading Iraq. The alternative to CAFTA is no CAFTA. In 1992 when the secret Defense Planning Guidance document drafted by Paul Wolfowitz, Scooter Libby, and Dick Cheney was leaked to the *New York Times*, elected officials, foreign allies, and the public at large reacted with outrage, arguing that its vision of preventive war and unilateral dominance were far too reckless and arrogant to serve as public policy. Yet these positions are now on record as tenets of the National Security Strategy of the United States. Likewise, in the 1960s, when neoliberalism was but a theory debated in academia and in conservative think tanks, it represented the fanatical frontier of economic thought. It was regarded as a set of ideas wholly unsuited for mainstream political debate, much less actual implementation. That it is now the leading doctrine of the IMF, the World Bank, and the U.S. Treasury represents an impressive ideological victory for the far right. But it does not make these ideas any less extreme.

By bullying its way into an elective war, the Bush administration made clear that imperial globalization is based on aggressive interventions on the global scene. The neocons' invasion of Iraq has cost thousands of American lives, taken the lives of hundreds of thousands of Iraqi civilians, produced some two million refugees, and squandered hundreds of billions of dollars in public funds. It has generated heightened regional tensions, greater instability, and more terrorism. Given the disastrous history of U.S. interventions—not just in Iraq, but also, to mention some particularly ignoble examples of the past sixty years, in Vietnam, Indonesia, Chile, Guatemala, El Salvador, Iran, the Dominican Republic, and Nicaragua—calling for a moratorium on such military actions, official and covert, is a first step in stemming the damage of imperial globalization.

Although the mechanisms of Clinton-model corporate globalization are subtler, this agenda, too, has relied on forceful maneuvering to come into existence. Neoliberalism involves aggressively opening markets, clearing the way for an unprecedented level of speculative capital transfer, and dictating the restructuring of local economies. None of these things occur naturally, and they deserve opposition. A moratorium on harmful "free trade" deals and on further expansion of the WTO, especially into areas beyond the traditional realm of trade, is vital as an immediate demand.

Another step is insisting upon a reversal of neoliberal structural adjustment policies. We have seen that Washington Consensus policies have failed miserably—even when measured by neoliberalism's preferred standard of GDP growth. If we go beyond GDP and account for the true costs of these policies, including the depletion of natural resources and the heightening of inequality, they have fared even worse. Not only have documents like the UN Human Development Reports made a case for a "guerrilla assault" on neoliberal mandates, but other more socially and environmentally conscious measures of development have also found that structural adjustment policies have led to negative results. The Genuine Progress Indicator (GPI), created by the Berkeley-based organization Redefining Progress, tracks factors such as environmental impact, level of income equality, and availability of leisure time in its assessment of human well-being. Until around 1980, GPI and GDP rose together in most countries. But since then, in the neoliberal era, GPI has fallen steeply.[40] Real human progress has been set back by the Washington Consensus far more than dismal GDP growth alone would suggest.

Simply refusing each of the mandates of the Washington Consensus—or at least rejecting the idea that they should be imposed on the world as a one-size-fits-all uniform for development—would allow for a substantial restructuring of globalization politics. The true utopians in the global economy are people who embraced the market fundamentalist fantasy that unchecked capital would serve the common good.

Refuting this idea can be fairly straightforward. Neoliberalism forces countries to open themselves fully to speculative capital flows. An alternative would be to allow countries to make intelligent use of capital controls. Neoliberalism prescribes the elimination of tariffs and other protections for local enterprises. An alternative would be to allow poorer countries to keep these intact, reviving what is known in trade agreements as "special and differential treatment." This model would give developing countries more flexibility in choosing to nurture infant industries and to protect agricultural commodities that are important to traditional cultures and to the security of their food supply. Neoliberal-ism prescribes tight monetary policy focused on controlling inflation, which is a primary concern of Wall Street investors. An alternative would be to allow governments to implement monetary policy designed to maximize employment, which is a pressing concern of most people on Earth who don't work on Wall Street.

When the Washington Consensus demands the privatization of pub-lic industry and the division of the commons into private property, an alternative is to keep these things in the hands of the public, defending the provision of public goods as a way of ensuring economic human rights—including guaranteed public access to water, electricity, and health care. If it calls for cuts in social services, an alternative is to reject the cuts, maintaining or bolstering these services and instead pushing for a redistributive tax system that makes the wealthy pay their fair share. When Washington mandates a more "flexible" labor market—one with-out unions or worker protections—an alternative is to defend living wages, collective bargaining, and the right to associate. And when IMF bailouts for wealthy investors create a situation in which, to paraphrase author Eduardo Galeano, "risk is socialized while profit is privatized," an alternative is simply to end these bailouts, making speculators bear the cost of their gambles.

The demand to reverse neoliberal structural adjustment policies pro-poses a fundamentally different relationship between wealthy nations and the global South than currently exists. It would grant countries the freedom to determine their own economic policies, priorities for gov-ernment spending, and rules for controlling foreign investment. Instead of imposing a single hegemonic model on the entire world, this new re-lationship would allow for broader diversity and experimentation in in-ternational development. Although this policy reversal would not by itself ensure human rights or protect the environment, it would consti-tute an important strategic gain. It alone would likely bring change of great enough magnitude to make the politics of the global economy look virtually unrecognizable to those who have grown accustomed to Washington-dictated neoliberalism.

THE OTHER MULTILATERALISM

Supporting the right of states to choose their own development policy raises a difficult question for advocates of democratic globalization: Does a quintessentially internationalist movement want to rely on the nation-state for change? At the World Social Forum, this challenge was highlighted by the appearance of two powerful presidents, representatives of the wave of progressive leaders that has taken power in Latin America in recent years.

On the first day of the 2005 forum, Brazilian President Lula da Silva addressed a stadium full of people. Clad in a white jacket, the stocky, bearded president—a former metalworker and union leader whom many viewed as a leftist icon when he took office in 2003—proclaimed, "I am a political militant," and declared, "I belong here." While loyalists from the Brazilian Workers' Party roared, a small but energetic section of protesters booed. Lula would have the record of his administration critically scrutinized by a variety of panels throughout the week. A more enthusiastic reception was given to Venezuelan President Hugo Chávez, who addressed the same packed stadium on the last day of forum workshops. Wearing a bright red button-down shirt over a red Che Guevara silkscreen, Chávez declared that the World Social Forum was one of "the most important political events taking place each year in the world today." He invoked his "Bolivarian revolution," and he labeled the 2002 coup attempt against him "Made in the USA."

The presence of Lula and Chávez forced a discussion of the issue of state power at the forum. The globalization movement has always had a troubled relationship with the state. On the one hand, some arguing against the power of unaccountable financial institutions have uncritically held up the principle of state sovereignty, contending that elected governments should be able to decide for themselves what economic policies to pursue. This stance is problematic for those campaigning in countries ruled by right-wing elites. On the other hand, the anarchist suspicion of any engagement with the state precludes some real challenges to neoliberalism—accomplishments such as Venezuela's redistributionist social programs and Argentina's decision to cancel a large portion of its private debt in defiance of the IMF.

Thus far the social forum's charter, which at least formally prohibits the participation of political parties, has held firm. Those who cheered Chávez's social democratic reforms cited active participation at the local level as the most positive part of the government's transformation. And even those inclined to defend Lula said that pressure is needed to focus the attention of elected officials on the needs of Brazil's poor majority. During each of these presidential addresses, dozens of panels outside strategized about how to generate this pressure—and how to apply it to all governments, no matter how friendly.

This perspective is a healthy one. Many analysts have warned against overreliance on the state as a venue for progressive hopes. They remind us that a focus on sovereignty can play into the hands of right-wing nationalists like Pat Buchanan. They caution that even without the IMF to clear its path, private capital is adept at pitting one state against another. And they observe that local elites have been instrumental in implementing neoliberalism and can hardly be relied upon to act in the interests of working people. Author Doug Henwood offers the further caveat against "fond memories of the pre-1980 protectionist regimes": "By the late 1960s, for example, growth slowed in Latin America as [the then-popular economic strategy of] import-substitution reached its limits. Domestic firms were inefficient, and average incomes were too low to sustain much of a consumer market. Labor agitation was met with repression."[41] We should not pine for a return to that situation.

In addition, some progressives have feared that if autonomous unregulated states are pitted against one another, the United States will continue to dominate. Recall that this concern spurred British journalist George Monbiot to declare, "The only thing worse than a world with the wrong international trade rules is a world with no trade rules at all."[42] Arguing for the need for multilateral controls on individual states, he called for the transformation of the WTO into "a Fair Trade Organization, whose purpose is to restrain the rich while emancipating the poor."[43]

Such a preference for reforming multilateral bodies rather than bolstering the power of states also has problems, however. Those who envision a "Fair Trade Organization" have little power at present to impose an egalitarian set of global rules. In trying to rebuild institutions like the WTO and the IMF, reformers will have to confront the same powerful corporate and U.S. interests that made the bodies what they are today. The experiences of initiatives such as SAPRI—the review of structural adjustment policies that the World Bank disowned as soon as it began to criticize the status quo—suggest that they will encounter entrenched resistance.

In contrast, those hoping to free countries from the Washington Consensus need not hold a naïve expectation that states will pursue an ideal set of policies on their own. A shift toward greater diversity and experimentation in the global economy will increase the power of social movements at the national level to pressure their leaders—something that has recently proved to be much more effective than reforming the Bretton Woods organizations. In his strategy for "deglobalization," Walden Bello argues for "a more fluid, less structured, more pluralistic world," contending that,

> today's need is for the deconcentration and decentralization of institutional power and the creation of a pluralistic system of institutions interacting with one another, guided by broad, flexible agreements and understandings.
>
> It was under such a pluralistic system of global governance, where hegemonic power was far from institutionalized in a set of powerful multilateral organizations, that a number of Latin American and Asian countries were able to achieve a modicum of industrial development between 1950 and 1970. It was under such a pluralistic system under a GATT that was limited in its power, flexible, and more sympathetic to the developing countries that the East and Southeast Asian countries were able to industrialize through activist state policies that departed significantly from the free-market biases enshrined in today's system.
>
> Of course, economic relations among countries prior to the attempt to institutionalize one global free market system beginning in the early 1980s were not ideal. But they did underline the fact that the alternative

to an economic Pax Romana built around the World Bank/IMF/WTO system is not a Hobbesian state of nature, the war of each against all. . . .

In other words, what developing countries and international civil society should aim at is not to reform the WTO and the Bretton Woods system but, through a combination of passive and active measures, to radically reduce their powers and to turn them into just another set of actors coexisting with and being checked by other international organizations, agreements, and regional groupings.[44]

Within this more open structure, advocates of a democratic globalization will need to express their internationalism in many ways—through solidarity actions, cross-border campaigns against multinational corporations, and grassroots initiatives for trade and cultural exchange. They can also support what some have called "the other multilateralism." As the WTO and other Bretton Woods systems arose under strategies of corporate globalization, they displaced other multilateral structures. They demanded, for example, that new trade deals trump preexisting multilateral environmental agreements. A democratic globalization should revive these alternative forms of multilateralism. It should include a critical defense of the Kyoto Protocol and other UN conventions on the environment, as well as advocacy of expanded agreements.[45] Likewise, under imperial globalization, the United States has worked more actively than ever to block or revoke mechanisms of international law. Measures that deserve popular defense include arms control treaties, conventions against torture, and the International Criminal Court.

As citizens work to strip power from the Bretton Woods institutions, both Bello and the International Forum on Globalization promote pursuing global rules to protect labor rights and the environment through the revival of UN subsidiaries such as the International Labor Organization, the World Health Organization, the Food and Agriculture Organization, and the UNDP.[46] Before the United States and other elite governments intentionally undermined it by creating the WTO, the UN Conference on Trade and Development advocated preferential treatment for poor countries that could counteract the inequalities of the global system and facilitate the transfer of technology to the global South.[47]

While imperfect, these institutions have very different histories than the IMF, the World Bank, and the WTO, and they could be reformed under very different terms. Even as democratic movements build power at the local level and demand national reforms, they can push for revived versions of these institutions to enforce international labor conventions, to oversee debt relief, to restructure the global currency reserve system, to mediate trade disputes, and to distribute subsidized funds for human development.

Those who reject corporate and imperial models of globalization have a wealth of ideas at their disposal, a healthy internal debate to refine their strategies, and a vibrant, growing international network of citizens that see their efforts as part of an interconnected whole. They also have very powerful enemies. Fortunately, as we enter the post-Bush era, the international community has voiced a firm rejection of unilateralism and preemptive war. Likewise, ever-larger swaths of the globe view neoliberalism as a failed and discredited ideology. This is creating exciting opportunities for citizens to bring a democratic globalization into existence. More exciting still is that many people are already engaged in this process and, as we will see in the next chapter, they are winning.

9

THE POLITICS OF PERSISTENCE

If the November 1999 Battle of Seattle represented a famous moment of protest, it also served as a striking instance of official denial. Even as protesters dressed as butterflies paraded through the streets, tear gas hung like mist throughout the city's downtown, and major trade officials were left to sulk inside their hotel rooms, WTO Director General Mike Moore insisted that all was well. Before assembled news reporters he dismissed the impact of the protests: "Negotiating groups are in full swing," he declared. "This conference will be a success."[1]

The conference was not a success. The opening session was canceled due to the demonstrations, and the overall WTO talks collapsed just days later, with negotiators from the global South echoing outside critics' arguments about the lack of transparency in the meetings.[2] But if Moore's disregard was remarkable given the intensity of those protests, it was not unusual in a more general sense. Being dismissed as ineffectual is a fact of life for organizers and public interest campaigners of all sorts. Anti-union employers and boycotted shop-owners will steadfastly deny that organized dissent has any impact at all on their operations—right up until they finally give in to protesters' demands. An old maxim in social

237

movements states: "First they ignore you, then they laugh at you, then they fight you, then you win." If this holds true, testimonials to the impotence of opposition will begin somewhere in stage two and continue until victory.

And so it has been with the emergence of a democratic globalization. Efforts to declare global justice activism dead started well before 9/11, commencing the very moment when resistance to economic neoliberalism could no longer be ignored. Before the Seattle Ministerial Conference ended, Thomas Friedman swiftly labeled demonstrators "a Noah's ark of flat-earth advocates,"[3] and many who had never acknowledged a global justice movement before then rushed to designate those same protests as the movement's retirement party. Marshall Wittmann of the right-leaning Hudson Institute asserted in early 2001: "Seattle was the high-water mark of the anti-globalization movement. Since then, it's been relegated largely to the fringe."[4] By the time centrist Democratic Leadership Council supporter Edward Gresser declared globalization activism "destined for irrelevance" after 9/11, this type of dismissal had become a well-worn trope.[5]

At the same time, opponents of neoliberalism and empire have received a strange sort of homage from their elite opponents. *Newsweek* noted in 1999, "One of the most important lessons of Seattle is that there are now two visions of globalization on offer, one led by commerce, one by social activism."[6] Since then global elites and officials at the international financial institutions have scrambled to respond to bad public relations generated by protests and to establish themselves as heartfelt advocates for the world's poor. The World Bank eliminated the use of the phrase "structural adjustment" and has tried to focus media attention on its ostensibly noble antipoverty initiatives. Meanwhile, the World Economic Forum became obsessed with showing that it cared. The *Washington Post* noted of the 2002 event, "The titles of workshops read like headlines from *The Nation*: 'Understanding Global Anger,' 'Bridging the Digital Divide,' and 'The Politics of Apology.'"[7] According to observer Doug Henwood, Bill Gates himself argued: "It's a healthy thing there are demonstrators in the streets. We need a discussion about whether the rich world is giving back what it should in the developing world. I think there is a legitimate question whether we are."[8]

Changing the Globalization Agenda

If we understand the creation of a democratic globalization, not as a matter of brainstorming new ideas for reforms, but rather as a process rooted in ongoing efforts to empower working people and grassroots organizations, it is critical to recognize the impact these efforts have already made. Although the White House has shifted its strategy from corporate to imperial globalization, citizens' organizing around trade and development issues has continued. And it has had important results.

Joseph Stiglitz described most clearly the remarkable shift in elite discussion that has taken place since global justice protests first captured the media spotlight:

> I have been going to the annual meetings at Davos for many years and had always heard globalization spoken of with great enthusiasm. What was fascinating about the 2004 meeting was the speed at which views had shifted. More of the participants were questioning whether globalization really was bringing the promised benefits—at least to many in the poorer countries. They had been chastised by the economic instability that marked the end of the twentieth century, and they worried about whether developing countries could cope with the consequences. This change is emblematic of the massive change in thinking about globalization that has taken place in the last five years all around the world. In the 1990s, the discussion at Davos had been about the virtues of opening international markets. By the early years of the millennium, it centered on poverty reduction, human rights, and the need for fairer trade arrangements.[9]

Of course, much of the shift at Davos was just talk. But the wider political changes go far beyond rhetoric. As we have seen, the legitimacy of neoliberalism as a whole has evaporated. Its most steadfast proponents have had to back away from several once-cherished tenets. As Stiglitz has noted, "Even the IMF now agrees that capital market liberalization has contributed neither to growth nor to stability."[10]

The evidence that Edward Gresser used to illustrate the global justice movement's irrelevance in late 2001 now stands as an indictment of his shortsightedness. "Activists could claim some successes," he wrote, "notably a four-year interruption in 'fast-track' legislative procedures and a two-year hiatus in full-scale WTO negotiations after Seattle. But the success of the Doha Summit and House passage of 'Trade Promotion Authority' make these seem temporary. . . ."[11]

In fact, it was the "free trade" boosters' successes that proved to be ephemeral. While the Bush administration, shamelessly exploiting the post-9/11 moment to advance its trade agenda, was able to make progress both in Doha and with fast-track authority, both victories were fleeting. WTO talks have since been notoriously rocky, and as of late 2007, Bush's fast-track negotiating authority has again expired. The new generation of Democrats that won control of Congress in November 2006 with promises to oppose unfair trade deals shows little eagerness to renew it. Gresser further argued that the AFL-CIO's willingness to stand behind White House foreign policy in the immediate aftermath of 9/11 represented a permanent fracturing of the American left. Yet today the AFL-CIO and other major union coalitions have announced their opposition of the Iraq War, have organized against the Bush agenda in economic policy, and are actively contributing to coalitions against corporate globalization.

Over the past several years, grassroots activity has translated into concrete change. Even some critics of the global justice movement have noted that activists have scored a number of significant policy victories. In a September 2000 editorial titled "Angry and Effective," the *Economist* reported:

> [I]t would be a big mistake to dismiss this global militant tendency as nothing more than a public nuisance, with little potential to change things. It already has changed things—and not just the cocktail schedule for the upcoming meetings. Protests . . . succeeded in scuttling the

OECD's planned Multilateral Agreement on Investment in 1998; then came the greater victory in Seattle, where the hoped-for launch of global trade talks was aborted. . . . The activists have also raised the profile of "backlash" issues—notably, labour and environmental conditions in trade, and debt relief for the poorest countries. This has dramatically increased the influence of mainstream NGOs, such as the World Wide Fund for Nature and Oxfam. Such groups have traditionally had some say (albeit less than they would have wished) in policymaking. Assaulted by unruly protesters, firms and governments are suddenly eager to do business with the respectable face of dissent.[12]

Various combinations of "respectable" negotiators and "unruly" dissidents have forced shifts on a wide range of issues. Beyond political and human rights advances that organizers in the developing world have made in their own countries, activists working across borders have realized a series of international gains. After the major demonstrations against the IMF and the World Bank in April 2000, Congress passed legislation mandating that the United States oppose any loans issued from those institutions that would impose user fees for basic health care and education. As Robert Weissman pointed out in a September 2002 article in the *Washington Post*, this move ultimately helped 1.5 million more Tanzanian children to start school.[13]

Public criticism has forced a measure of accountability and transparency among trade negotiators who prefer to do their business behind closed doors. Although disclosure has still been far from adequate, pressure from groups that protested in Quebec City in April 2001 eventually resulted in the public release of plans for a Free Trade Area of the Americas. Continued public protest helped to sink the FTAA altogether in subsequent years.

Movement pressure has also influenced intellectual property disputes. Jeremy Brecher, Tim Costello, and Brendan Smith, authors of *Globalization from Below*, describe a key incident that occurred in 2000. "When South Africa tried to pass a law allowing it to ignore drug patents in health emergencies, the Clinton administration lobbied hard against it," taking steps to initiate trade sanctions.[14] Appalled, the Philadelphia chapter of the advocacy group AIDS Coalition to Unleash Power (ACT UP) quickly responded and turned this policy decision into a liability for the Clinton-Gore White House. As the *New York Times* reported, the group moved to

> take up South Africa's cause and start heckling Vice President Al Gore, who was in the midst of his primary campaign for the presidency. The banners saying that Mr. Gore was letting Africans die to please American pharmaceutical companies left his campaign chagrined. After media and campaign staff looked into the matter, the administration did an about face.[15]

The following year, widespread public outrage and publicity generated by NGO campaigners compelled multinational pharmaceutical companies to drop intellectual property lawsuits against African governments seeking to provide affordable, generic AIDS drugs for their citizens. This victory served as a crucial step in combating the continent-wide public health crisis.

Food activists have also made progress. Journalist Naomi Klein noted, "The movement against genetically engineered and modified foods has leapt from one policy victory to the next, first getting many GM foods removed from the shelves of British supermarkets, then getting labeling laws passed in Europe, then making enormous strides with the Montreal Protocol on Biosafety."[16]

Campaigns that target individual corporations and demand changes in business practices have also been effective. Shortly after the turn of the millennium, campus and community activists joined with the Coalition of Immokalee Workers, a union of migrant farmworkers, to take on Taco Bell. These migrant workers are historically among the most exploited and powerless populations in the United States. Yet after publicizing their cause for four years and organizing a widespread consumer boycott, their coalition won. In 2005, the company agreed to nearly double the wages it paid to farmworkers picking tomatoes for Taco Bell, and it formed a joint committee with the union to investigate and punish future violations of workers' rights.[17]

Finally, student antisweatshop protesters on college campuses in the United States have won a series of victories to improve the conditions faced by those who make college apparel. The students first motivated companies to come together with unions and human rights groups to form the Fair Labor Association, an organization created to monitor working standards at factories. When that organization showed that it lacked teeth, civil society groups backed out, and United Students Against Sweatshops created a much stronger body, the Workers Rights Consortium (WRC). With tactics ranging from consensus-building petitions to militant sit-ins, the student activists have persuaded administrators at more than 140 colleges to make their schools take part in the WRC. Additionally, they have assisted workers organizing in the United States and abroad and have pressured universities to build direct ties with factories that have exemplary labor rights records.

"They won the verbal and policy battle," said Gary Hufbauer, a "pro-globalization" economist at the Institute for International Economics, speaking of the groups that have organized major globalization protests. "They did shift policy. Are they happy that they shifted it enough? No, they're not ever going to be totally happy, because they're always pushing."[18]

THE MAKING OF A "MAJOR ISSUE"

Of all the areas in which global justice advocates have influenced corporate and governmental decision-making, none stands out so clearly as the issue of debt. Activists led by the Jubilee debt coalition have waged a more than decade-long campaign to convince world leaders to cancel the huge debts that stunt development in the global South.[19] Debt campaigners have been prominent members of the coalitions that organized the major protests outside the meetings of the WTO, the IMF, the World Bank, and the G8, and they have rallied grassroots support across Africa, Europe, the United States, and beyond. With their efforts, they have moved the issue from the fringes of international debate to the center of global discussion, pressed beyond symbolic moves toward reform, and ultimately scored a policy victory that opened real possibilities for human development.

The stifling debts of the global South have long been recognized as an important factor perpetuating poverty and inequality. The origin of the debt crisis dates back to the 1970s. At that time, booming oil prices flooded Northern banks with deposits from oil-rich countries in the Middle East. Desperate to find investment opportunities for these resources, the banks poured loans into the "emerging markets" of the developing world—a move cheered by the World Bank. In some cases, banks loaned money to corrupt and undemocratic regimes in the global South, knowing that even if the funds were unlikely to ever benefit the country's people, the governments would have little ability to default on loan repayments.

The people, in time, would have to pay. When interest rates spiked in the late 1970s and early '80s, and prices for crops like coffee and cotton fell, poor countries were caught in a trap. Even though their debt payments to the North were clearly unsustainable, they had no way to declare bankruptcy. Thus, they had little choice but to go along when the World Bank and the IMF stepped in. These institutions agreed to give the developing countries new loans to pay off their old ones. But they made the countries submit to brutal structural adjustment programs in return, which often resulted in slashed social services. It was a bizarre solution in terms of helping the poor, yet it nicely served the interests of neoliberals and Northern lenders. In the end, the IMF and the World Bank deepened the crisis. The external debt of developing countries totaled $609 billion in 1980. By 2001, it had ballooned to $2.4 trillion.[20] Because interest rates had reached usurious levels, many countries had paid off their original loans many times over yet still owed large sums.

Those of us in advanced industrial nations are led to believe that our governments donate generously to help developing countries address crippling poverty, hunger, disease, and deprivation. In fact, debt service—or loan repayments—to the North constitutes what advocates call "foreign aid in reverse." Poor countries send $1.30 in debt payments for every dollar they receive in aid.[21] In 1997, the charity Comic Relief raised $200 million in donations for the impoverished. Yet it took only one week for Africa to pay back that amount in debt service.[22] Even while millions of men, women, and children die of preventable diseases, African countries spend four times more on debt service than on health care for their people.[23]

Despite the magnitude of the crisis, debt cancellation was far from the mainstream political agenda in the early 1990s. A discussion about the issue raged in the global South, but it had very little traction in wealthy nations. "There was almost zero awareness" of the debt issue in the United States at the time, according to Neil Watkins, National Coordinator of Jubilee USA.[24] When a small group of social movement activists, along with government leaders from the developing world, tried to gain a hearing for the issue at the 1995 UN Copenhagen Social Summit, the United States impeded discussion. Activists were told simply, "debt will not be a major issue."[25] President Bill Clinton and British Prime Minister John Major ultimately avoided attending the summit altogether.

Not long after, however, the grassroots work on the issue began to bear fruit. The formation of the Jubilee network in 1997 united a broad spectrum of religious, labor, and nongovernmental organizations into a joint international campaign. In May 1998, Jubilee helped mobilize 50,000 supporters to protest at the G7 summit in Birmingham, England.* The protests returned in full force at the following year's summit in Cologne, Germany, where another 50,000 people formed a human chain through the city's streets to dramatize the "chains of debt."

During the same period, concerned members of religious congregations, in particular, witnessed some gratifying developments. The efforts of Roman Catholics drew notice when, in 1996, the Catholic Bishops of Africa began publicly denouncing debt payments made "at the expense of providing basic healthcare, education, and other social services to the poor in our countries."[26] Bishops from Latin America came forward with similar statements. They were soon joined by Pope John Paul II, who began pointing to debt relief as "a precondition for

---

*The G7 includes Canada, the United Kingdom, France, Germany, Italy, Japan, and the United States. Russia is also included in some meetings, creating the G8, but it is not directly involved in debt discussions.

the poorest countries to make progress in their fight against poverty." Demanding immediate action, he asserted, "it is the poor who pay the cost of indecision and delay."[27]

Other religious bodies throughout the world came forward to endorse the Jubilee campaign. In the United States alone, these included the Episcopal Church, the Evangelical Lutheran Church of America, the Mennonite Church, the Union of American Hebrew Congregations, the Presbyterian Church, and interfaith groups like the Inter-Religious Task Force on Central America, Church World Service, and the Ecumenical Program on Central America and the Caribbean.

By that time, policymakers and pundits could no longer afford to ignore the call for debt cancellation. But some went on the attack. After the demonstrations in Birmingham, Andreas Whittam Smith, a columnist with the London *Independent*, echoed much of elite opinion by calling the Jubilee campaign's goals "laudable" but criticizing its political strategy as "badly conceived." He defended the laborious negotiations on debt taking place at the World Bank and the IMF, and he charged that the Jubilee coalition's political action would "be ineffectual . . . if not counter-productive."[28]

"If you make a campaign out of it," Smith chastised, or "use extreme language . . . the very people you want to influence, the ministers and officials of the rich democracies, stop listening to you."[29]

Do They Stop Listening?

In fact, as grassroots efforts to highlight the issue grew, the G7 responded at each stage by grudgingly creating and then expanding limited proposals for debt relief. In 1996, the countries controlling the IMF and the World Bank introduced their first Heavily Indebted Poor Countries (HIPC) plan, designed to offer forty-two of the world's most indebted poor nations some relief after six probationary years.

Unfortunately, actual cancellation of multilateral debt involved high levels of "conditionality." HIPC required poor countries to implement IMF-advised structural adjustment programs, which often resulted in cuts to health care and social service spending. Moreover, as HIPC progressed, it soon became clear that debt relief was coming far too slowly to have any substantial effect.

In 1999, with pressure mounting, the IMF instituted HIPC-2. This plan accelerated the pace of relief, but it kept debt cancellation contingent upon structural adjustment. Moreover, the amounts of debt it canceled still left poor countries with unmanageable burdens. By the end of 2000, twenty-two countries had received some relief from the HIPC initiatives, yet the program had canceled on average only one-third of each country's debt—hardly an adequate solution to the crisis. Economist Jeffrey Sachs responded in disgust, "It is perfectly possible, and indeed is currently the case, for a country or region to have a 'sustainable' debt" under IMF/ World Bank definitions "while millions of its people are dying of hunger or disease."[30] Throughout the developing world, huge debts persisted despite the fact that many countries had paid back their original loans several times over. As the American Friends Service Committee noted, Nigeria had paid more than $16 billion on an original $5 billion in loans, yet found itself owing $32 billion on that same debt.[31]

In September 1999, President Clinton responded to intensive lobbying by announcing that the United States would cancel 100 percent of the bilateral debts owed it by the heavily indebted nations. Two months later, the United Kingdom put forward a similar plan for bilateral debt cancellation; other creditor nations, such as Germany, France, and Japan, soon followed suit. The governments' actions marked a critical milestone. However, these bilateral actions did not eliminate the debt crisis among low-income developing countries. Whereas the total cost of this U.S. bilateral debt relief was estimated at $330 million, total debt owed by poor countries to multilateral creditor institutions, such as the IMF and the World Bank, was estimated to be in the hundreds of billions of dollars.

HIPC, despite its many limitations, did have an important impact. Because the program provided some debt relief, it created a track record for what cancellation could accomplish. Critics had regularly charged (and some continue to believe) that money from debt cancellation would be mismanaged and would not be used to reduce poverty. In fact, HIPC demonstrated that cancellation, while not a magical solution to social problems, could be a most effective form of foreign aid, allowing developing countries to retain and make use of their own resources. By 2004, HIPC had advanced some measure of relief to twenty-seven countries. A 2004 report from the World Bank showed that together these countries had nearly doubled their total spending on poverty reduction—including education, health care, and clean water—in the period from 1999 to 2004.[32]

The Jubilee campaign built from these successes and continued its outspoken advocacy. It called for its members to flock to Seattle to protest the WTO in late 1999. The night before the trade ministerial meeting was to start, thirty thousand people braved the drizzly Northwestern weather to form a human chain around the WTO's exhibition center. Jubilee organizers described the scene: "The human chain was vividly decorated with placards and signs reading 'Break the Chains of Debt' and 'People, Not Profits,' amidst union banners, flags from Mexico and people wearing 'Drop the Debt' t-shirts. . . . [S]upporters also carried torches and defied the rain by chanting: 'We're here! We're wet! Cancel the debt!'"[33]

When Congresswoman Maxine Waters addressed the Seattle demonstrators, she praised the Jubilee efforts: "Jubilee 2000 has created a defining moment in world politics. I work in a world where politicians make deals on behalf of special interests groups. Jubilee 2000 came into this world with moral authority and caused many politicians to change their ways and support debt relief for the poorest of the world's poor countries."[34]

Indeed, as development ministers and World Bank staffers scurried to get image makeovers in the post-Seattle moment, debt relief was one of the issues they prioritized in their efforts to quell public criticism. The topic quickly moved to the fore of development discussion, and over the next few years, negotiators from G7 countries proposed a number of more thoroughgoing plans for cancellation.

Calls for debt relief became increasingly mainstream. In perhaps the most visible example of the issue's popularity, U.S. Treasury Secretary Paul O'Neill made a highly publicized tour of debt-stricken African nations in May 2002 with Bono, the rock star turned humanitarian. Beyond O'Neill, a notable bloc of conservatives, led by economist Allan

Meltzer, also defended the economic soundness of debt cancellation. They argued that a scaled-back World Bank should extract itself from the hopeless cycle of debt reloaning and refinancing and that the institution should not try to sustain itself with debt payments. Whereas the corporate globalists of the Clinton administration had been concerned with preserving World Bank funding, Meltzer's position was influential among the imperial globalists of the Bush administration.

A final turn in U.S. policy came in the aftermath of the invasion of Iraq, when the Bush administration appealed to creditor nations to forgive Iraq's estimated $120 billion debt. Longtime advocates of debt cancellation unexpectedly heard their arguments adopted by the president. In December 2003, as George W. Bush was sending former Secretary of State James Baker on a special mission to lobby allies to cancel Iraq's debt, the president argued that such debt endangered the country's "long-term prospects for political health and economic prosperity" and that the world must not allow large payments to "unjustly burden a struggling nation at its moment of hope and promise."[35] By logical extension, the administration's stance on Iraq's debt put the United States on the record in favor of debt relief for a wide range of struggling countries.

With even the U.S. government on board, the moral legitimacy of debt cancellation had been almost universally acknowledged. What remained was for policy to catch up. G7 finance ministers limped toward an agreement at a series of meetings in 2004. Then, in early 2005, in the wake of the tsunami disaster in Asia, the wealthy countries issued a statement agreeing in principle to "as much as 100 percent multilateral debt relief" for the forty-two HIPC nations.[36] Their stance in support of full cancellation marked another milestone for the global justice movement. A major debt deal would come soon after.

WHERE'S THE JUBILEE?

In the summer of 2005, the persistence of campaigners in the global South and their international supporters paid off. George W. Bush stood with Tony Blair at the White House and echoed arguments that not long ago had only come from the mouths of fringe activists. He declared,

"[H]ighly indebted developing countries that are on the path to reform should not be burdened by mountains of debt."[37] Blair added, "In a situation where literally thousands of children die from preventable diseases every day, it's our duty to act."[38] Shortly thereafter, at a July 2005 meeting in Gleneagles, Scotland, G7 leaders approved a plan granting 100 percent multilateral debt relief for eighteen impoverished countries.

Author and activist Rebecca Solnit described the long road to this landmark achievement:

> In '98, I had gone to Birmingham to hang out with Reclaim the Streets (RTS), the raucous, wildly creative British movement that shifted the tone and tactics of direct action in many parts of the world and demonstrated early the power of the Internet for creating simultaneous demonstrations in many countries. At the same moment, Jubilee . . . formed a vast human chain around the G8 and much of central Birmingham. RTS condemned the G8's very existence; Jubilee 2000 asked it for something specific. At the time, I have to admit, the Jubilee group made little impression on me, and their "Cancel the Debt" message seemed hopeful but remote.
>
> Remote then, it has arrived now, as both a transnational awareness of the causes and costs of the loans forced on poor nations and as the recent debt cancellations. . . . [E]arly champions of debt relief took up . . . a complex, unglamorous idea and stuck with it for so long—long enough to matter, long enough to change the world. For debt relief exemplifies the often murky issues of much contemporary activism. Everyone agrees that children shouldn't be murdered, but it's hard to show people how arcane and intricate international financial rules can become the swords upon which small bodies are impaled. Zambia has already announced that cancellation of its debt will immediately translate into anti-retrovirals for some of its 100,000 AIDS sufferers (which exemplifies, as well, how debt translates into death; think of all those people who have not been getting medication).[39]

Interestingly, progressives were divided in their response to the debt deal. Many misinterpreted the victory as a smoke-and-mirrors trick. Of course, seeing Bush and Blair tout their good deeds on behalf of the world's poor, acting as if they were responding to an innate instinct for benevolence rather than a decade of dogged campaigning, was enough to make any opponent of empire and corporate globalization suspicious. So perhaps it is not surprising that while some on the left applauded the agreement, many others focused on asking, "What's the catch?" Some critics went so far as to charge that the agreement actually did more harm than good by attaching harmful strings to debt relief.

Ultimately, they were wrong. The debt deal, while far from perfect, was a genuine advance. Some large European aid groups, and even progressive stalwarts like John Pilger, complained that to finance the debt deal, the United States would shift some funding away from World Bank "aid" programs. Countries would lose in aid what they would gain in debt service relief, the argument went. However, this was a misreading of the compromise that was brokered to push through the debt deal. Although some funds would indeed be redirected, the United States and other lenders agreed to make more money available for World Bank "aid" to meet demands for a net increase in funding. For Pilger and the charities, that should have been viewed as a victory—albeit a qualified one. For those of us who don't look upon the defunding of the World Bank as such a bad thing, the question that remains is, why were the European advocates so set on protecting the Bank's revenues in the first place?

Other progressives who attacked the debt deal pointed out that even in announcing the cancellation, G7 finance ministers explicitly reaffirmed a neoliberal economic paradigm. In their statement, the G7 leaders declared that "boost[ing] private sector development" and "eliminat[ing] impediments to private investment, both domestic and foreign" remained central to their model for development.[40] With regard to debt relief, they stated that "good governance, accountability and transparency" would be required for countries to receive cancellation. Historically, such terms have been code words for the imposition of structural adjustment on poor nations. According to G7 ministers, a country practicing "good governance" is one that wholeheartedly embraces the Washington Consensus.

Their criticism was partly valid, but they also misunderstood the nature of the agreement. Although the rhetoric of the G7 statement seemed disturbing, such posturing comes as standard fare in official foreign policy declarations. In reality, the G7 deal did not create new conditions for cancellation; it merely kept in place the neoliberal economic conditions required by the existing HIPC framework. Under the new agreement, eighteen countries would receive full debt cancellation from the IMF and the World Bank, and nine other countries may be granted similar relief at a later date. The eighteen chosen countries were those that had reached "completion point" under HIPC, meaning that they had already complied with the onerous economic mandates. Since the G7 deal kept this "conditionality" in place, new countries wishing to be included in future cancellation would still have to endure structural adjustment. Obviously, this was a problem.

That said, it was clearly better for poor countries that had already suffered HIPC conditions to receive full cancellation, rather than inadequate, partial relief. Full, 100 percent cancellation had been one of the foundational demands of the debt relief movement—and had long been resisted by wealthy nations. By affirming the legitimacy of this long-denied demand, the G7 agreement set a historic precedent. This breakthrough marked a shift of approximately one billion dollars a year in resources back to poor nations.

In early 2007, Imani Countess, National Coordinator of the American Friends Service Committee Africa Program, noted that the impact of the debt cancellation secured in 2005 has been profound:

In Ghana, the money saved is being used for basic infrastructure, including rural feeder roads, as well as increased expenditure on education and health care.

In Burundi, elimination of school fees in 2005 allowed an additional 300,000 children to enroll.

In Zambia, since March 31, 2006, free basic health care has been provided for all [along with] a pledge to recruit 800 medical personnel and slightly over 4,000 teachers.

In Cameroon, [the government made] a pledge to recruit some 30 thousand new teachers by the year 2015 and to construct some one thousand health facilities within the next six years.[41]

Furthering the impact of the G7 deal, the Chinese government subsequently eliminated bilateral debts owed by thirty-one African countries, a cancellation worth a total of $1.27 billion.[42]

MORE TO BE DONE

Limited victories are problematic only if we see them as ends—if they encourage subsequent complacency instead of underlining people's power to achieve greater progress. Perhaps more important than what had been gained with the July 2005 debt agreement, the deal put advocates in the Jubilee movement in an excellent place to advance further demands.

Two especially pressing concerns that now must be addressed are finding a way to include more poor countries in the deal without making them submit to onerous economic conditions, and canceling illegitimate debts amassed by the dictators of the past. The current G7 agreement, while undoubtedly a key advance, includes only a fraction of the poor countries that need relief. For others to qualify they must spend years submitting to HIPC's long list of neoliberal economic mandates. The fact that countries pursuing other strategies for development must forgo needed assistance is offensive.

Advocates of debt relief are now highlighting the plight of indebted poor countries like Haiti, Nigeria, and the Philippines, which were not included in the HIPC program because of the specific formulas used by the World Bank to determine eligibility. In addition, some "middle-income" countries, such as Brazil and Mexico, have large populations living in desperate poverty yet are too prosperous to qualify for debt cancellation under the HIPC guidelines. These countries require a new process that would allow them to spend their resources on poverty reduction and human development rather than debt service and that would eschew neoliberal "conditionality."

The Gleneagles deal has allowed activists to leverage the G7 precedent to expand the list of institutions canceling their debts. An important victory on this front came in November 2006, when the Inter-American Development Bank, an often-overlooked multilateral creditor, agreed to a deal canceling the debts of five of the poorest countries in the Americas. If properly implemented, this agreement will eliminate obligations of up to $768 million for Bolivia, $365 million for Guyana, $1.1 billion for Honduras, $808 million for Nicaragua, and $468 million for Haiti.[43]

Past victories are also paving the way for more radical tactics. Many advocates in the international Jubilee campaign contend that poor countries still excluded should proactively renounce unjust debts rather than wait for overdue "forgiveness." The stance in favor of renunciation is doubly valid in cases of "odious" debt. Wealthy nations are still collecting payments from countries whose bills were run up by dictators that have since been deposed. Money lent to military governments was often used to line the pockets of corrupt officials or, worse yet, to purchase American and European-made arms, which were then deployed to repress democratic movements. Although odious debt, as such, was not included in the 2005 deal, the agreement contributed to the momentum that had been building around the issue at least since the Bush administration campaigned to have Iraq's odious, Saddam Hussein–era debts forgiven. George W. Bush's contention that the future of a people "should not be mortgaged to the enormous burden of debt incurred to enrich" a despot was absolutely correct.[44] Of course, countries should not have to be invaded by the United States before the White House sees the logic of eliminating unjust obligations. Washington has yet to propose the elimination of debts accrued by tyrants like Pinochet in Chile and Suharto in Indonesia, whom the United States supported when they were in power.

Taking Stock of Victory

Debt activists had been ignored, derided, attacked, and then finally won. For those who doubt the ability of social movements to effect real change, the movement in support of debt relief provides a case study that cannot be easily ignored.

For those advocating democratic globalization, it offers other lessons as well. An alternate version of the old maxim about the stages of political struggle is often attributed to philosopher Arthur Schopenhauer.[45] It states: "All truth passes through three stages: In the first, it is ridiculed. In the second, it is violently opposed. In the third, it is regarded as self-evident." Although the actual origins of this quote are unclear, the brilliance of this version is in highlighting how, once an idea is embraced, newfound converts rush to erase the history of controversy that came before. This rendering of the adage does not offer the tidy, emotionally satisfying ending of "then you win."

All the policy victories of the global justice movement—from anti-sweatshop monitoring, to reversals on generic AIDS drugs, to Starbucks agreeing to make fair trade coffee an option at its stores—are only steps toward more substantive change. We should not consider these shifts as satisfactory or struggle less fervently for broader change because of them. We need not become Frappuccino loyalists simply because the union-busting Starbucks corporation has become slightly less objectionable than before. But failing to acknowledge these reforms as points that power would not otherwise have conceded would, by extension, overlook a rich history of hard-fought wins. New Deal social programs, civil rights legislation, and environmental protections were all based on compromises with more thoroughgoing popular demands. And yet they represent some of the most significant gains of the past century.

The 2005 debt deal represented a measurable improvement over the previous state of affairs and put advocates in a much better position to organize for greater gains. That, in short, is a fine definition of a victory. In a world of challenges and setbacks, where the obstacles confronting progressive movements are enormous, it is all too easy to wallow in despair. If for no other reason, those promoting democratic globalization should take care to claim our wins—and to celebrate them—while continuing with the work of always pushing.

At the same time, the victories we claim need not always be slight. At rare moments, change comes in dramatic swoops. Such is the situation now in Latin America, where grassroots movements are proving that a wide-ranging assault against neoliberalism and empire can very quickly create a new political reality.

10

Latin America in Revolt

In January 2006, on a hill outside of La Paz, Bolivia, a traditional cere-
mony marked both a major shift in the country's politics and a milestone for a region in revolt against neoliberalism and imperial
globalization. At Tiwanaku, a site of pre-Incan ruins significant to the
country's indigenous populations, leaders of the Aymara people handed
a silver and gold staff to Evo Morales, barefoot and dressed in a red tu-
nic. It was the first time in five hundred years that this ritual transfer of
leadership had been performed in Bolivia, and it came the day before
Morales was officially inaugurated as his country's president.

It is difficult to overstate the symbolic significance of Evo Morales's rise
to power. In Latin America, the chasm between the wealthy and the destitute is the most extreme in the world. Presidents, especially in the era of
neoliberalism, have invariably come from the fortunate side of the divide—the side whose young people make shopping trips to Miami and
train in U.S. universities. One of Morales's immediate predecessors, multimillionaire Gonzalo Sanchez de Lozada, was widely known as "el
gringo" because he was raised in the United States and speaks accented
Spanish. Within Bolivia, inequality is further entrenched by almost

apartheid-like discrimination against indigenous people, whose communities are among the most desperately poor in the Americas.

In this context, Morales's life story is especially remarkable. He was born in an Aymara community, one of only three of his mother's seven children to survive their first years. As a young man he herded llamas in the Bolivian *altiplano* with his father, sometimes making long trips to agricultural markets. "We walked for days behind the llamas," Morales related to a biographer. "I always remember the huge buses that roared down the highways, full of people who threw orange and banana peels out the windows. I gathered up those peels to eat them."[1]

In the 1980s, when Morales was in his twenties, drought on the high mountain plains compelled him to move to the tropical Chapare region, where he found work in the coca fields. He eventually became a leader in the coca growers' union. Coca has deep traditional significance for indigenous people of the Andes—the natural plant leaves are used to make tea and are almost impossible to abuse in their natural form. Even the U.S. Embassy in La Paz has recommended it to tourists as a remedy for altitude sickness. However, because coca can also be refined into cocaine, Bolivia's farmers became targets of U.S.-sponsored drug eradication efforts. Morales was beaten by government soldiers and repeatedly jailed for his union activism but eventually became an internationally renowned champion of labor and indigenous rights. He was instrumental in building Bolivia's coca growers' union into one of the most prominent social movements in his country and helped to form the Movement Toward Socialism (MAS) political party.

Although few could have predicted it in the 1980s, the movements he worked to organize would ultimately propel Morales into office. From 2003 to 2005, massive demonstrations rocked Bolivia, with crowds railing against IMF-imposed tax hikes and the privatization of the country's national gas resources. Protesters fought off police repression, blockaded roads, and ultimately forced the resignation of two presidents. As the candidate for the MAS, Morales campaigned to replace the ousted elites on a platform attacking neoliberalism, highlighting the plight of the poor, and vowing to defend *Pachamama*, or "Mother Earth." His campaign motorcade proudly waved the *wipala*, the multicolored checkered flag that is a symbol of native pride and resistance. When election day arrived on December 18, 2005, people packed the polls. Morales won by a landslide, giving Bolivia its first indigenous president in its two-century history as a nation.

Upon taking office, Morales cut his own presidential salary by more than half, condemning corruption and the "pillaging of the country" by past politicians. "This is a government of the social movements," Morales subsequently declared. Joking about the far-fetched nature of such an administration, he added, "Many people still can't accept, can't understand that an indigenous *campesino* is president. . . . I can't understand it either!"[2]

For those with a stake in perpetuating corporate power and U.S. dominance in Latin America, Morales's victory was part of an alarming pattern. Since the turn of the millennium, boisterous popular movements throughout Latin America have overthrown neoliberal governments and demanded genuine democracy. They have created a new generation of leaders that looks very different from the region's typical rulers, and they have fought to hold these officials accountable. When Morales took office in early 2006, his administration joined left-of-center governments in Venezuela, Argentina, Brazil, Uruguay, and Chile. Within a year, newly elected progressives in Ecuador and Nicaragua furthered the push away from the Washington Consensus. The set of economic policies that held sway in the region for over twenty years is on its way out. A new approach to human development is starting to take its place.

During his campaign, Morales stated, "We're not just anti-neoliberal, we're anti-imperialist in our blood."[3] A very sizable portion of Latin America's population would be inclined to agree. More than 500 million people reside in the region, and nearly two-thirds of them now live under governments elected on a mandate to break with "free trade" economics, declare independence from Washington, and pursue a more democratic globalization. Had an opponent of neoliberalism won the Mexican presidential election in the summer of 2006 (a progressive candidate lost by just one-half of 1 percent of the vote), each of Latin America's major economies—and a full 80 percent of its people—would have been encompassed in the progressive shift.

Mainstream media outlets in the United States have often framed the sea change to the south as a rising tide of anti-Americanism. *Foreign Affairs* and the *Economist* have issued ominous warnings about the dangers of the new "populism." These portrayals of the recent changes are perhaps unsurprising given deep-rooted notions of Latin America as Washington's rightful sphere of influence. The Monroe Doctrine long claimed the region as the imperial backyard of the United States. And during the Cold War, Latin America served both as a laboratory for neoliberalism, home of Milton Friedman's experiments in market fundamentalism, and as a training site for many neoconservatives—figures like Elliott Abrams and John Negroponte helped manage the Reagan-era dirty wars in El Salvador and Nicaragua, only to find warm welcome in government once again when Bush, Cheney, and Rumsfeld rose to power.[4]

If, like these officials, we think of U.S. national interest in Latin America as requiring obedience, the region's search for new social and economic policies is indeed cause for alarm. These need not be considered frightening developments, however. The White House has long proclaimed that promoting democracy and reducing poverty are key foreign policy goals. Latin America's new leaders and reinvigorated social movements are now putting these ideas to the test. They are rejecting the legacy of Washington interventionism that propped up dictatorships in their region in the 1970s and 1980s; they are raising the standards for democratic participation in public life; and they are condemning the vision of the corporate globalization that has failed the impoverished majority of their population since then. Those of us who believe that the true national interest of the United States should be helping to expand citizen participation and fight poverty should applaud efforts to make the White House take seriously its own noble rhetoric.

Latin America is rapidly becoming a model for the rest of the world. Yet the process of transformation is not without challenges. The extent to which the recently elected governments in Latin America have broken with Washington Consensus policies varies by country, and leaders have often failed to live up to the high hopes of social movements. In grappling with significant challenges, the region has illustrated that forging a globalization from below is not a matter of following a fixed ideology. Rather, it is a living process that continues to unfold in unexpected ways.

But whatever the complexities of change, Latin America is sending a clear message to other developing nations seeking to free themselves from the grip of market fundamentalism, a message summed up by Argentinean President Néstor Kirchner in April 2005: "There is life after the IMF," Kirchner reported on a trip to Munich, "and it is a very good life."[5]

UPRISING IN ARGENTINA

For much of the world, the Asian financial crisis, which hit in 1997, was a watershed event that revealed the bankruptcy of Washington Consensus policies. In Latin America, the collapse of Argentina's economy served as a second critical event. Argentina's economic woes had been brewing for several years by the late 1990s. The country's globalized economy was hit hard by the skyrocketing interest rates in international markets, and its government was deprived of cash by the privatization of the social security system. In late 2001, it became clear that it would be unable to pay its debts. Foreign investors and local elites grabbed what they could and ran. In a panicked frenzy, they whisked $140 billion dollars out of the country, leaving the economy in shambles and condemning the rest of the population to live amid the wreckage.[6]

In response, a popular uprising took shape that toppled a series of presidents in just two weeks in December 2001. Millions took to the streets of Buenos Aires, outraged at the failures of the neoliberal government and the avarice of the country's wealthiest. They were united by the rallying cry "*Que se vayan todos*"—"Out with them all." Members of the once-prosperous middle class who lost access to their savings rallied angrily outside shuttered banks and joined with blue-collar workers in demanding accountability. The radical *piqueteros*, a movement of the unemployed active since the 1990s, deployed their well-honed tactic of erecting road blockades. But they also helped launch cooperative efforts to run bakeries, kitchens, schools, construction teams, and libraries.

Some newly jobless factory workers, many with bosses who fled the country with all the assets they could get their hands on, decided to go back to work. Under the call "Occupy, Resist, Produce!" they reopened as many as 180 factories, resuming production by themselves and functioning as democratically self-managing cooperatives.[7] They borrowed the slogan from the Brazilian Landless Workers' Movement (MST), which has organized an estimated 1.5 million members in rural Brazil to reclaim unused land for communal good. Since 1980 the MST has redistributed 7 million hectares of idle land—an area larger than the state of Ohio—and their example was a powerful one for the urban workers facing closed factories.[8]

Argentinean social movements not only voiced a heartfelt critique of the neoliberal system that had led their economy to ruin but organized to create a community-based alternative. Journalist Benjamin Dangl described the reaction to the crisis: "Out of the wreckage, people attempted to construct a new world. Citizens countered poverty, homelessness, and unemployment with barter systems and alternative currency. Neighbors organized assemblies and provided food to the neediest in their communities. . . . The economic depression pushed neighbors in Argentina together, unified social movements and created a space for further mobilizations and progressive electoral victories."[9]

Argentina's electoral politics stabilized with the election of left-leaning Néstor Kirchner as president in May 2003. Kirchner promptly set an important example for the region by breaking with the IMF and playing hardball with international creditors. As it had in East Asia, the IMF had responded to the 2001 crisis by demanding more belt-tightening in the form of fiscal austerity and high interest rates, policies that limit access to social services and drive up unemployment. Kirchner's government refused to go along. Appalled by the punitive demands, it threatened to default on its payments to the IMF. Such a stand was previously unheard of for middle-income countries, which feared the IMF's power over their access to credit. But the gambit worked. The Fund was terrified that if Argentina defaulted, other countries would follow its lead. So the institution backed down. Argentina was able to renegotiate more than $100 billion in foreign debt, forcing private creditors to bear a share of the economic crisis and accept 30 cents on the dollar for their outstanding claims.[10] The renegotiation went a long way toward alleviating Argentina's debt burdens and paved the way for a strong economic recovery based on policies despised by the IMF. The institution could only look on with chagrin, with the rest of the developing world taking notice of its diminished standing.

LEFT TURNS IN BRAZIL AND VENEZUELA

Even as Argentina commenced its reconstruction, events in Brazil furthered the leftward shift in Latin America. In October 2002 Luiz Inácio Lula da Silva, candidate of the *Partido dos Trabalhadores* (PT)—the Brazilian Workers' Party—emerged victorious in the country's national elections. Like Evo Morales, Lula, as da Silva is almost universally known, was born in poverty. Raised in a destitute section of northeastern Brazil, he was cared for by a struggling single mother who earned only a nominal living by washing clothes.[11] In the late 1960s and early 1970s, severe drought pushed many northeasterners into the cities. Lula was one of them. In search of a job, he migrated to São Paulo, Brazil's industrial hub, and became a factory worker. Laboring under harsh conditions, he lost part of a finger in a machine accident in the factory. The exploitation he witnessed prompted him to help organize his co-workers into a union. He went on to become president of the Union of Metalworkers of São Bernardo do Campo in 1975.

Lula played a central role in the historic strikes that shook Brazil in the late 1970s. The first, in 1978, took place at a time when strikes were still illegal under the country's military regime, yet it involved over a half a million workers at its peak. Lula and other union leaders were jailed for their involvement.[12] In the following year, waves of strikes spread across the nation, mobilizing more than 3 million workers and breaking government-imposed wage controls. These public displays helped to dispel the crippling fear instilled by the authoritarian government. New democratic organizations sprang up, among them the *Central Única dos Trabalhadores* (CUT), which Lula helped create in 1983 and which would become the country's largest trade union federation.[13]

Lula also worked to establish the PT. In 1980 the PT brought a broad coalition of labor activists, advocates of indigenous rights, environmentalists, feminists, and proponents of liberation theology into a party devoted to giving the country's impoverished majority a voice in the political process.[14] By the end of the decade, the PT, drawing on strong networks of grassroots support, won municipal elections in some of the country's largest cities, including São Paulo and Porto Alegre. Lula first ran for president in 1989—during Brazil's first free public presidential election in three decades. At the time, the idea that a candidate from the PT could win a presidential election still seemed quixotic. Nevertheless, Lula came in a strong second, signaling the arrival of the PT as a potent organizational force at the national level. A dozen years and several attempts later, Lula bested neoliberal opponent José Serra and won the 2002 presidential elections in a landslide, garnering 61 percent in the decisive second round of voting.[15] Lula's campaign, which emphasized "the priority of the social" and vowed to ensure that "all Brazilians eat three times a day," was a conspicuous departure from politics as usual in the world's eighth largest economy.[16]

Although Lula has been unexpectedly conciliatory toward Washington in recent years, an issue I will examine in more detail, his Venezuelan counterpart, Hugo Chávez, has turned out to be an unusually sharp thorn in the side of the White House. Chávez's rise to power was not as deeply indebted to social movement organizations as many other new Latin American governments. However, the shift from neoliberalism in Venezuela also has popular roots. The beginnings of the political process that enabled Chávez's 1998 election trace back a decade earlier, to a revolt known as the *caracazo*—an idiomatic expression that translates roughly as "the Caracas Explosion." In February 1989, President Carlos Andrés Pérez pursued a set of IMF-prescribed reforms that dramatically increased the price of gasoline and public transportation for the Venezuelan people. The public was furious. Spontaneous protests erupted throughout the country, demonstrators blocked major roads, and even the police went on strike.[17] The panicked government responded by using wanton violence to quell dissent. Soldiers fired indiscriminately into crowds, killing as many as three thousand people.[18]

Public anger at the repression lingered long after the *caracazo*, permanently crippling both the Pérez administration and the system of elite two-party rule that had long defined Venezuelan politics. In 1992 Chávez led a group of young military officers who had supported the uprising in an attempted coup against the government, which was then run by a successor of Pérez. Their effort failed, and Chávez was sent to prison. But before being jailed, Chávez famously promised in a television appearance that the effort to revitalize the country's politics had only been stopped "*por ahora*," for the moment.[19] The government decided to release the popular Chávez after he served a short prison term. And when the former military officer returned to civilian life, the phrase "*por ahora*" became a galvanizing electoral slogan that carried him to victory in the polls in December 1998.

That Chávez's government would become one of the most ardently anti-imperialist in the hemisphere was not immediately clear. In part, this is because the nature of the "Bolivarian Revolution" was obscured early on by an attempted coup against Chávez and by a management-led strike in the oil industry that crippled Venezuela's economy in 2002 and 2003. In April 2002, the Chávez government, which had once again won office after a 1999 Constitution Convention required new elections, was ousted in a military coup led by the head of the Venezuelan Chamber of Commerce, Pedro Carmona. Falsely claiming that Chávez had resigned, Carmona stepped in, dissolved the country's Congress, and dismissed the Supreme Court.

In a virtually unprecedented reversal, popular uproar quickly restored Chávez to power—but not, however, before the IMF declared its support for Carmona's new dictatorship. It vowed in a public statement that it was "ready to assist the new administration in whatever manner they find suitable."[20] The White House, too, was all too welcoming of the coup attempt and was left to backpedal when allies noted its apparent lack of concern for democracy. The Bush administration was also supportive of organizations that led a sixty-four-day oil strike that took place later that year—an attempt to force Chávez from office by cutting off the flow of the country's most significant export.[21]

These efforts, like a subsequent recall attempt in 2004, failed, and Chávez, whatever his faults, has demonstrated that he has broad-based support in Venezuela's voting public. In the wake of such challenges, he has emerged as an ever-more-vocal opponent of U.S. imperial designs. He has taken the leading role in promoting unity among the progressive governments of the region and advocating for a new "Socialism for the 21st Century." Although he is often cast in the mold of Fidel Castro, many observers have noted that the redistributionist programs that are the hallmark of Venezuelan social policy under Chávez owe more to Franklin Delano Roosevelt's New Deal than to Cuba's state-run economy. Using proceeds from oil sales, the government has funded an ambitious literacy program, free public education through the university level, job training, an antihunger program that provides subsidized food for over a third of the country, and a broad system of free public health clinics. In addition, an extensive network of cooperatives and community councils fostered by the Chávez government has promoted democratic decision-making at the workplace and neighborhood levels.

From Montevideo to Managua

If the rise of left-leaning governments holding office in Argentina, Brazil, and Venezuela reflected a call for change in the economic powerhouses of South America, events in several of the region's smaller countries added to the popular mandate. In the Uruguayan presidential elections of October 2004, Tabaré Vazquez, a doctor and cancer specialist by profession, defeated candidates from both of the traditional political parties that together had governed the country for more than 170 years.[22] Vasquez's party, the Frente Amplio, is made up of a remarkable collection of socialists, center-left social democrats, and former guerrillas who opposed the right-wing military dictatorship that ruled Uruguay from 1972 to 1985. Vasquez rose to prominence in 1989 as mayor of Montevideo and furthered his national acclaim by leading a successful campaign against the privatization of Uruguay's state-owned oil company early in the millennium. However, the most important factor leading to his election was an economic crisis that hit Uruguay in 2002, during which GDP declined by 11 percent, one out of five people in the workforce found themselves unemployed, and rural poverty skyrocketed.[23] The crisis destroyed the legitimacy of the neoliberals then in power and opened the door for Vazquez. As president, Vazquez has disappointed many supporters by adopting relatively conservative economic policies. But he has undoubtedly shown more concern for inequality than past regimes. As his first official act as president, he announced a $100 million "Social Emergency Plan," with planks concerning food, health, jobs, and housing, designed to address the hardship created by the economic crisis.[24]

In addition to Evo Morales in Bolivia, progressive presidents subsequently won elections in Chile and Ecuador. In Chile, a coalition of Christian Democrats and Socialists, known as Concertación, has governed since the end of Augusto Pinochet's dictatorship in 1990. In early 2006, Chileans elected socialist Michelle Bachelet, a pediatrician and former government minister, as their new president. Bachelet, who defeated billionaire right-wing rival Sebastián Piñera, is the first woman to govern the country and only the third female directly elected a head of state in Latin American history. Her family was imprisoned and her father killed by the Pinochet regime in the 1970s. Concertación leaders have been moderate in the past, distancing themselves from more radical governments in the region, and the new government in many ways resembles a Latin American version of the United States' none-too-bold Democrats. Nevertheless, the win by Bachelet, who is a single mother, a religious agnostic, and a supporter of reproductive freedom, marked an exciting cultural shift for the predominately Catholic country.

In Ecuador, voters in November 2006 chose progressive economics professor Rafael Correa over a banana magnate who happened to be the wealthiest man in the country. The last elected president in Ecuador had been forced out of office by demonstrators furious that he had reneged on vows to combat the Washington Consensus. Correa speaks four languages, including Quechua, the primary language of Ecuador's indigenous peoples. He was finance minister for a time in 2005 under an interim government. Despite being the only member of the administration with an approval rating over 50 percent at the time, he resigned from that position amid a conflict with the World Bank, which opposed his drive to increase social spending.[25] In his inaugural address as president he described neoliberalism as "the perverse system that has destroyed our democracy, our economy and our society."[26] He has sought to follow Argentina's lead and renegotiate more than $10 billion in external debt, payments on which have amounted to twice what the country devotes to social needs like combating hunger, homelessness, and disease.[27] And to the pleasure of international debt relief campaigners, he has launched an audit to determine which portions of the debt might be considered odious, or illegitimate, under international law.

The election of former Sandinista *comandante* Daniel Ortega as president of Nicaragua in November 2006 pushed the leftward tide north into a Cold War hot spot. Few observers of the country's politics would doubt that Ortega is a deeply compromised political figure—he stands accused of sexually abusing an adolescent stepdaughter, and as a power broker in the Nicaraguan parliament, he negotiated a political pact with corrupt conservatives that allowed him to avoid prosecution. Nevertheless, he won election to the presidency on a platform criticizing the "savage capitalism" imposed on Nicaragua since 1990. His campaign proposals provide a modest opening for hope that a new administration might do a better job of addressing endemic poverty than past governments. Today Nicaragua ranks among the poorest nations in the hemisphere, along with Haiti and Bolivia. Also significant is the fact that Ortega prevailed despite overt suggestions from the White House that the Nicaraguan people would be punished for voting against U.S. preferences.[28] His win provided a signal that threats of retaliation may no longer be sufficient to keep Central American citizens from voting for leaders willing to buck Washington's economic program.

Declarations of Independence

These governmental shifts, along with electoral near misses in places like Mexico, Costa Rica, and Peru, constitute a remarkable trend. Accompanied by increased popular pressure for change throughout the region, they represent a dramatic shift in the tenor of Latin American public life. Already, this shift has had three notable impacts on the international level: diplomatic distance from the United States has increased, the influence of institutions like the IMF has dwindled, and alternative approaches to regional development have moved to the fore of public debate.

After 9/11, the imperial globalists of the Bush administration sought to manage Latin American affairs by rebranding major U.S. foreign policy concerns in the region—from drug trafficking to immigration—as part of the "war on terror." They believed that by extending their "with us or against us" mentality to hemispheric affairs, they could secure the obedience of countries that wanted to remain in good standing with the United States. They could then use these countries to isolate figures like Hugo Chávez. To their dismay, the Latin American governments, particularly those with left-of-center leaders, would have none of it. Not only did they refuse to view regional issues through the lens of terrorism—instead keeping the challenges of poverty and inequality as key priorities—but they almost universally condemned the White House's war in Iraq. Large majorities across the region opposed the invasion, and a BBC poll showed that 85 percent of Brazilians and 80 percent of Mexicans disapproved of Bush's handling of the war.[29] Lula da Silva issued an official lament at the onset of the invasion, declaring that it was being conducted without UN authorization. Even Chile, normally the most tepid of Latin America's left-leaning governments, steadfastly opposed the U.S. military action in the UN Security Council in 2003.[30]

Such dissident behavior has been evident in other multilateral bodies as well. Never in recent memory has the United States failed to have its preferred candidate selected as head of the Organization of American States (OAS). Yet in May 2005, despite the White House's increasingly desperate diplomatic maneuvers, delegates to the body passed over Washington's pick in favor of a candidate for OAS secretary general backed by Venezuela, Brazil, and Argentina. Likewise, at the WTO, Brazil was an instrumental force behind the formation of the G20+, the group of developing countries that stood up to U.S. and European demands at the failed 2003 Ministerial Conference in Cancún.

Opening a new chapter in the struggle for human rights, governments in Argentina and Uruguay have supported the repeal of amnesty laws protecting military officers and have helped open a large number of legal cases against criminals from past dictatorships. Critics of the infamous U.S. Army School of the Americas (SOA) at Fort Benning, Georgia, have recognized the opportunity. The SOA was responsible for training numerous death squad members during the "dirty wars" of the 1970s and '80s. Opponents of the program have found new governments sympathetic to their campaign to close down the school. Venezuela, Argentina, Uruguay, and Bolivia agreed to stop sending troops for exchanges at Fort Benning, and Chile is also reevaluating its cooperation.[31] In a related move, Rafael Correa challenged the U.S. drive to project military power through a global network of bases by vowing not to renew the lease for an American air base in the city of Manta that expires in 2009.[32] The base is the largest U.S. military installation on the Pacific coast of South America and has been used as a center for counternarcotics and counterinsurgency operations, with U.S. pilots often showing little regard for Ecuador's right to control its own air space. "Ecuador is a sovereign nation, we do not need any foreign troops in our country," said Foreign Relations Minister Maria Fernanda Espinosa.[33]

Perhaps most significantly, new leaders in Brazil, Venezuela, and Argentina ended the Bush administration's hopes of securing a hemisphere-wide Free Trade Area of the Americas (FTAA). At the November 2003 FTAA summit in Miami, Hugo Chávez's government declared the trade deal a "colonial project that seeks to impose itself over the constitution of every sovereign nation."[34] At a subsequent summit in Monterrey, Mexico, President Bush was left to squirm as Lula, Chávez, and Kirchner blasted neoliberalism's track record. Referring to the FTAA, Argentina's Kirchner warned that a "[trade] pact that does nothing to resolve deep imbalances will do nothing but deepen injustice and the breakdown of our economies."[35] With the major economies of the region standing in opposition, the agreement faded into obscurity, unfinished and unsigned.

BUCKING THE IMF

While the White House has seen many once-subservient countries hold it at arms length, institutions like the IMF and the World Bank have had to endure being virtually kicked out the door. Argentina standing up to the IMF was like an underdog knocking down the schoolyard bully. The aura of invincibility surrounding the Fund vanished, and the institution will likely never again inspire the same grudging awe. Subsequently, a number of governments have moved to free themselves altogether of direct oversight from the institution by paying off their outstanding IMF loans early. Argentina and Brazil inaugurated the trend by announcing in December 2005 that they would pay off $9.8 billion and $15.5 billion respectively.[36] The IMF, which benefits from the interest payments on long-term loans and derives much of its power by negotiating ongoing agreements with recipient countries, was nonplussed. Kirchner triumphantly proclaimed that throwing off the chains of IMF debt constituted a move toward "political sovereignty and economic independence."[37]

Since then, the new Latin American governments have been one-upping each other in their acts of defiance. Bolivia was freed of its outstanding debt to the IMF by the summer 2005 debt relief agreement at the G7. Upon taking office in 2006, Evo Morales announced that he would let the country's standing loan agreement with the IMF expire.[38] In May 2007, he further declared that Bolivia would withdraw from a World Bank arbitration center that handles investment disputes. Nicaragua has similarly rejected the authority of the center.[39] Rafael Correa topped them by flat out ejecting the World Bank's representative to Ecuador. He declared the Bank officer a *persona non grata* in the country, insisting, "we will not stand for extortion by this international bureaucracy."[40] Finally, in the late spring, Hugo Chávez announced that Venezuela would withdraw from membership in the IMF and the World Bank altogether, a move unprecedented in the era of corporate globalization.

Interestingly, within the domestic political debates of Argentina and Brazil, many people were critical of the decision to repay IMF loans.

Social movement activists argued that the debts, some of which had been accumulated by past military governments, were unjust and should be renounced outright. In Argentina, critics contended that the IMF should have to pay for a crisis it was largely responsible for creating. Instead, billions of dollars that could have been used for needed social programs were sent back into the Fund's coffers. As the Darío Santillán Popular Front, a *piquetero* organization, pointed out, the move amounted to a full debt repayment, rather than a renunciation. "Despite the progressive rhetoric, the debt is paid off with the hunger of the people," the group said in a statement cited by the Inter Press Service.[41]

The activists may have had a solid argument. But even the moderate act of repayment has had a palpable affect. The IMF has lost almost all influence in the region, with lending plummeting to a paltry $50 million, less than 1 percent of its global loan portfolio. As recently as 2005, Latin America accounted for 80 percent of the Fund's outstanding loans.[42] Moreover, cutting ties with the IMF is not just a regional phenomenon. Russia, Thailand, Indonesia, and the Philippines, among others, have also pursued strategies of early debt repayment, sapping the institution of both clout and cash flow from interest payments.

The willingness of oil-rich Venezuela to provide Southern neighbors with financing they might otherwise have needed to beg from Washington is a significant factor in their ability to break with the IMF and the World Bank. Venezuela has offered billions of dollars in support to countries including Argentina, Bolivia, and Ecuador, and this source of backup funds makes the governments of Latin America considerably less susceptible than in the past to threats of capital flight. It dramatically reduces Washington's ability to starve dissident leaders of financial resources, which was once a central means of provoking "regime change" when governments grew disobedient.

Latin American leaders have moved to formalize their source of alternative funding by establishing a "Bank of the South."[43] The purpose of the institution, which finance ministers officially launched in December 2007, is to provide development loans at below market rates without neoliberal strings attached. Two of the region's largest economies—Venezuela and Argentina—have each committed 10 percent of their national reserves to the institution, or $1.4 billion and $350 million, respectively. A pending contribution from Brazil, which has currency reserves valued at $110.5 billion, will at least double the capital available to the Bank.[44]

One insider at the neoliberal Inter-American Development Bank told the *Financial Times* that the Bank of the South represented the largest threat to his institution in decades. "With the money of Venezuela and political will of Argentina and Brazil, this is a bank that could have lots of money and a different political approach," he explained. "No one will say this publicly but we don't like it."[45] Making things worse for the Washington-based financial institutions, Asian countries that were burned by the region's financial crisis have engaged in a similar process of pooling national reserves to eliminate any need to turn to the IMF.[46]

A REGIONAL BLOC?

Latin America has a history of internal disputes thwarting dreams of regional unity. Quarrels persist today, but efforts to bring Latin American countries into a unified bloc now seem much more plausible. One relevant initiative is Mercosur, the *Mercado Común del Sur*, or Southern Common Market. Mercosur was envisioned in 1991 as a regional market that could rival formations like the European Union. It aims to reduce or eliminate tariffs, allow goods and services to flow freely between member states, and increase coordination of economic policy in the region.[47] Mercosur's member nations—including Argentina, Brazil, Paraguay, Uruguay, Bolivia, Chile, Colombia, Ecuador, and Peru—have a total population of more than 250 million people and a combined GDP of $1.1 trillion.[48] Recently, Venezuela has made a bid to enter Mercosur, which would further expand the initiative's scope.

Although many progressives support the goal of regional integration and believe that a unified Latin American bloc would strengthen the region's hand vis-à-vis the United States and the European Union, they are concerned that Mercosur adopts neoliberal "free-market" rhetoric and policy preferences in its approach to integration.[49] They argue that market development should not be the sole basis of any plan for regional unity, but rather, such unity should also be based on commitments to meeting social needs, addressing poverty, and ensuring self-determination. Hugo Chávez, for one, promised in January of 2007, that should his country enter the trading bloc, he would "decontaminate it of neoliberalism."[50]

In addition to his proposals for renovating Mercosur, Chávez presented plans in 2001 for an alternative to the FTAA, called the Bolivarian Alternative for the Americas (ALBA). Cuba and Venezuela officially signed on to ALBA in December 2004 and were joined by Bolivia in 2006 and Nicaragua in 2007. The agreement remains in an embryonic state, and its details are not yet clear. Currently, ALBA involves programs such as "Operation Miracle," through which the Venezuelan government has paid for Cuban doctors to perform cataract surgeries, restoring vision to thousands of blind Latin Americans.[51]

In another ALBA-based exchange, Venezuela earmarked some $130 million for development programs in Bolivia in 2006. Cuba and Venezuela also agreed to buy all of Bolivia's soybeans, a crop that lacked a buyer after the United States signed a bilateral pact with Colombia.[52] Cuba and Venezuela also signed a series of cooperative agreements in early 2007 valued at more than $1.8 billion, including an initiative for the refinement of Cuban ferronickel to make stainless steel in Venezuela.[53] Ultimately, ALBA envisions a much wider network of joint social programs and cooperative political stances. As part of his vision for Latin America, Chávez has also proposed a joint oil company, PetroAmerica, which would help to safeguard regional energy flows and allow countries to negotiate collectively with the United States.[54]

Such efforts to increase economic cooperation are part of a wider international trend toward escalating South-South trade. As the WTO has faltered, the United States is not the only country that has shifted its policy toward bilateral trade deals. Regional powers such as China and India have sought out new trading partners, and Latin America has responded. China has invested more than $50 billion in the region in recent years and has brokered some four hundred investment and trade deals.[55] The trend is likely to escalate. As the United States reckons with its bloated trade deficit and sinking dollar, it will not be able to buy as many goods from abroad as in the past, diminishing the centrality of the North American market. And as the relative economic importance of the United States wanes, its leverage in Latin America will continue to plummet.

HAVE THE POOR BENEFITED?

Beltway pundits have long predicted that breaking with their preferred economic policies would lead to ruin. In a much-discussed article in *Foreign Affairs*, former Mexican foreign minister Jorge Castañeda distinguished between a "reformed," responsible left in Brazil, Uruguay, and Chile and an irresponsible, "populist" left in Argentina, Venezuela, and Bolivia. Whereas the former represents a moderate left that the White House could engage, he argued that the latter camp would destroy their own countries. "As in the past," he asserted, "its rule will lead to inflation, greater poverty and inequality, and confrontation with Washington."[56]

To the chagrin of Castañeda and IMF economists alike, the evidence suggests that the countries that have butted heads with the U.S. Treasury have reaped substantial economic rewards. In the past five years, Argentina's economy has enjoyed a remarkably robust recovery, with annual economic growth averaging an extraordinary 8.6 percent. As economist Mark Weisbrot reported, "Argentina had to fight the Fund every inch of the way to adopt the polices that enabled [this] economic recovery, among them a stable and competitive exchange rate, relatively low interest rates and a tax on exported goods. . . . Instead, the IMF advocated a number of politically unpalatable and economically dubious policies including raising utility rates, running bigger budget surpluses and paying more money to foreign creditors."[57] Fortunately, Argentina has been willing to brawl with the Fund, and an estimated 9 million people have been able to emerge out of poverty as a result.[58]

Venezuela has enjoyed similar success. After taking office, Chávez halted the trend toward privatization that would have sold off the state's social security system.[59] He also increased state control of oil resources. Venezuela has possessed a state-owned oil company since the 1970s, yet it was producing little money for the public good. Following the end of the destructive oil strike in 2003, Chávez renationalized the industry, and largess from the state oil company has since fueled a renaissance in social investment. In a related move, the government dramatically raised the royalty rates that energy companies like Chevron, BP, and ExxonMobil pay for doing business in Venezuela.[60] Although the international business press predicted mass capital flight, the corporations have put up with the changes and continue to operate profitably, even as the Venezuelan people gain much greater benefit.

Chávez's decidedly un-neoliberal economic policy has created the most robust growth in the hemisphere, with the country's GDP surging over 17 percent in 2004 and at approximately 9 percent in 2005.[61] Growth continued in 2006 at the rate of 10.3 percent.[62] Revealing the politicized nature of its supposedly objective economic analysis, the IMF has consistently underprojected growth in Argentina and Venezuela, making it more difficult for these countries to attract investors. "For three consecutive years now they've gotten it wrong with Venezuela," minister of finance Rodrigo Cabezas explained. "It seems like their prognoses have a kind of political commitment in order to discredit the success of the Venezuelan economy in the last few years."[63]

That Venezuela is Latin America's leading oil exporter is a central fact in the country's recent transformation. High oil prices—which produced $25 billion in profits for the Venezuelan government in 2004, and even more subsequently—have given Chávez abundant funds and political leeway to carry out his policies.[64] Of course, high export prices do not necessarily translate into widespread social benefit. Previous oil booms did nothing to boost the incomes of the poor or decrease inequality. In contrast, social spending under Chávez has tripled, with generous funding coming from both the government and the state oil company. The country's poverty rate has fallen by a third, and unemployment has been cut nearly in half.[65] Moreover, a report from the Washington-based Center for Economic and Policy Research has noted that "the private sector is still a larger share of the economy than it was before President Chávez took office."[66]

Of course, the Venezuelan model is not without its shortcomings. Although the government has vowed to combat the culture of corruption that has pervaded Venezuelan politics for decades, problems with widespread corruption persist. Chávez has pursued warm relations with reactionary governments, including that of Iran, acting on the flawed logic that Washington's enemies should be his friends. And a number of state initiatives have drawn fire from environmentalists, including a joint venture between the Venezuelan state energy company, ChevronTexaco, and Phillips Petroleum that risked doing irreparable damage to the ecosystem of the Orinoco river basin.

Most significantly, the centrality of Venezuela's president as a charismatic leader of reform raises concerns about whether the country's transformation can survive beyond Chávez. Having no lack of self-regard, Chávez regularly portrays himself as a key historical actor and has often worked to consolidate his personal power. For example, Chávez pushed to remove term limits, which would have paved the way for him to remain in office after his second six-year term expires in 2012. This move was narrowly defeated in a public referendum in December 2007.

Bart Jones, Associated Press correspondent for Venezuela and author of a 2007 biography of Chávez, titled *Hugo!,* has maintained that the most striking aspect of the Bolivarian revolution is "its inordinate dependence on Chávez, its one-man show aspect. If he were to leave the scene, there's a feeling the whole revolution would unravel tomorrow."[67] Progressive *Miami Herald* contributor Fred Rosen has echoed concerns about the strength of civil society in Venezuela. "Since [Chávez] took office in 1999, his government has actively encouraged the formation of grassroots social movements, many of which now play important roles in local politics and provide personnel for national campaigns," Rosen contended. However, he observed, "Most of these groups are fiercely loyal to Chávez, rather than to any particular political party or program."[68]

Not only does this situation have obvious potential for abuse, but it also puts the gains of the Chávez years in jeopardy, creating a real possibility for retrenchment if the president's supporters and mobilized local communities prove unable to continue the Bolivarian experiment without him.

Servicing Debt versus Serving the People

While Argentina and Venezuela have thrived by rejecting neoliberal policies, other countries have largely adhered to Washington Consensus mandates. Uruguay and Brazil have not strayed far from market orthodoxy, making debt repayment the focus of their economic programs. President Tabaré Vazquez of Uruguay has drawn significant fire for his centrist economic management. But the results that have likely been most disappointing are those of Brazil.

Early on, Lula pursued a "pragmatic" economic policy designed to reassure foreign investors and avoid precipitous capital flight—a genuine concern for any country wishing to avoid the economic collapse that Argentina had already experienced. Over time, his government's economic course has become virtually indistinguishable from the policy direction the *Partido dos Trabalhadores* (PT) once criticized harshly. Lula has opted to follow IMF prescriptions and continue making payments on Brazil's huge foreign debt, estimated in 2002 at $230 billion, or approximately one-third of the country's GDP.[69] For twenty years, the PT had campaigned against paying the debt, arguing that it took too much money from social programs and productive economic investment. The president's current position is far removed from even the most moderate of his party's past denunciations.

Lula's administration has been more aggressive in pursuing some neoliberal measures than even the IMF has demanded. IMF dictates call on the Brazilian government to maintain a primary budget surplus of 3.75 percent of the country's GDP.[70] Meanwhile, Lula has voluntarily elected to maintain an even greater primary surplus, upward of 4.25 percent, leaving money for only modest increases in government spending on social programs.[71] Several of these programs—such as Fome Zero, the government's flagship antihunger initiative—have been stunted by lackluster implementation and administration.

Early on, promises of strong economic growth were used to justify the government's cautious approach. However, growth during Lula's first term averaged only 2.6 percent.[72] This places Brazil, alongside Haiti and El Salvador, among the hemisphere's slowest growing economies. It has caused even some centrist economists to criticize the government's pre-occupation with controlling inflation with high interest rates, a policy that leads to high unemployment.

Brazil was influential in sinking the FTAA, and it was a leader of the G20+ at the WTO. Nonetheless, it subsequently showed itself willing to bully smaller countries to go along with trade negotiations that might benefit Brazilian agribusiness. Interest in increasing Brazil's agribusiness exports has also caused friction between Lula's government and the once-friendly Landless Workers' Movement, which has criticized the slow pace of land reform under the PT. In a final discouraging develop-ment, several important PT officials have been implicated in corruption scandals in recent years. These scandals have marred the party's reputa-tion of holding itself to a higher ethical standard than its competitors. As a result, the PT is now positioned unfavorably within a context of politics-as-usual, rife with patronage and bribery.

Despite the country's lackluster economic performance and charges of corruption within his government, Lula has remained personally pop-ular. He easily won reelection to a second term in October 2006. Many leftists, including prominent sociologist Emir Sader, ultimately sup-ported Lula in the second round of voting over opponent Geraldo Alck-min, who favored fully privatizing Petrobras, the state oil company, among other extreme neoliberal stances.[73] Lula has responded to critics by arguing that his government has accomplished far more with its so-cial programs than the regimes of past decades. In a promising sign, he announced an 8.6 percent increase in the minimum wage as one of the opening acts of his second term.[74] At the same time, Lula continues to express pride in his administration's economic policy, an indication that he is not likely to significantly revise his conservative approach.

RECLAIMING RESOURCES

In Bolivia, where a highly mobilized citizenry has repeatedly ousted un-popular governments, the balance of political muscle between the street and state makes it unlikely that Evo Morales could adopt Lula's "prag-matic" concessions to neoliberalism, even if he wanted to. Instead, the country has been engaged in an exciting process of reclaiming resources for the public good.

Long before Morales took office, social movements were already reversing neoliberalism at the community level. One particularly notable showdown took place in Cochabamba, a city of five hundred thousand. In early 2000, Cochabamba exploded in outrage after the sale of the once-public water supply to the San Francisco-based Bechtel Corporation. Water promptly went from being a subsidized public good to a commodity sold at prices that the majority of the population could not afford. In response, a far-reaching coalition including rural *campesinos*, students, and urban workers came together. Public resentment boiled over and culminated in a general strike that shut down the city for three days. Thousands rallied under a bright red banner reading *"El Agua es Nuestra, Carajo!"*—The Water is Ours, Dammit![75]

After months of road blockades and clashes with police, massive public opposition made it clear to Bechtel that it could not continue its profit-gouging endeavor. The corporation decided to save face and left the country in April 2000, opting for international arbitration against the Bolivian government for lost profits. The water supply again became public, managed by a cooperative whose board includes union members and antiprivatization community leaders. Although the initiative has encountered a fair number of difficulties and has struggled with water shortage problems familiar in the region, it has upheld the idea that economic human rights can be guaranteed even in one of the poorest countries in the hemisphere. Moreover, the victory has been replicated in other communities and other countries, including Uruguay, where citizens passed a referendum against water privatization in 2004, and in the community of El Alto, Bolivia, where residents expelled the French water company Suez in 2005.[76]

In the December 2005 Bolivian presidential elections, social movements supported Evo Morales as the best option in the electoral contest. His 54 percent victory in a contentious multiparty race represented a huge mandate. (His last elected predecessor took office after having won just over 22 percent of the vote in a similarly crowded field.) However, the allegiance of highly mobilized community organizations to the state remains limited. Many leaders contend that they are willing to uproot another government if it stands in the way of social reorganization centered on participatory civil society. As political analyst Helena Argirakis told *Los Tiempos*, Cochabamba's daily newspaper, "The [54 percent] isn't a blank check, it's a loan." Her colleague Fernando García added, "The social movements' support of Morales will always be conditional."

After taking office in January 2006, Morales shocked the international business press by actually delivering on his campaign promises and initiating the nationalization of Bolivia's oil and gas assets. The process culminated at the end of the year, when the government signed agreements with foreign energy companies giving it majority control over oil and gas extraction and directing over half the profits toward the public good. In late November 2006, Morales's party went further by passing an ambitious land reform bill that seeks to right a historic injustice by breaking up some of the enormous estates left over from colonial times and redistributing as many as 20 million hectares to *campesinos* who work the land.[77]

Morales's announcement of the oil and gas nationalization provided an excellent illustration of how large segments of the U.S. and British press have adopted roles as watchdogs for corporate globalization. Since Bolivia's energy exports go to Brazil and Argentina rather than the United States, and since the nationalization was never likely to significantly affect the price of natural gas on international markets, the direct impact on the United States was minimal. Yet in the weeks after Morales took action, U.S. citizens were treated to a wealth of hysterical commentary.

As Condoleezza Rice criticized South American "demagoguery" and industry groups warned that Morales was "embarking on a dangerous path," the editorial pages charged to advance the front.[78] The *Economist* warned from London that "Bolivia may be moving backwards" and "its people are likely to grow even poorer."[79] Editors at the *Los Angeles Times* declared: "Morales put his head in an oven this week and turned on the natural gas. There are only two likely outcomes: an explosion that ends his political career—or a slow suffocation for his people."[80] New York's *Newsday* also worked up a rabid editorial assault. There, columnist James Pinkerton derided Bolivia as "a country that is nationalizing, or, if you prefer, stealing, foreign-owned assets."[81] The paper's editorial page then grouped Bolivia with Cuba and Venezuela in an "Axis of Idiocy" and asserted that "nationalization of major industries has proved to be a road to economic ruin in an era of globalization."[82]

Despite the general trend, there were some levelheaded voices in the media. These exceptions helped to debunk many of the Evo-bashers' doomsday scenarios. Usually a defender of "free trade" policies, the *New York Times* ran an op-ed titled, "All Smoke, No Fire in Bolivia."[83] It noted that foreign energy companies will not be kicked out of Bolivia under Morales's framework, but merely will have to cooperate with the state on less lucrative terms than before. "The companies will still profit under the new rules," commentator William Powers wrote; "they won't see the huge profits they enjoyed under lax Bolivian control and the global rally in commodities prices, but they will make money."[84] Even the stodgy *Financial Times*, while generally suspicious of Morales, conceded "there is nothing intrinsically wrong in trying to maximize royalties and taxes" from the use of a country's natural resources.[85]

In predicting economic disaster for a renationalized Bolivian energy sector, the editorials turned a blind eye to the two-decade disaster of neoliberalism in the country. When Morales took office, 64 percent of the population lived in poverty, with a majority of people scraping by on less than $2 per day.[86] A March 2006 report by the Center for Economic and Policy Research showed that according to the IMF's own data, real per-capita gross domestic product (GDP) in Bolivia after complying with the Washington Consensus was lower than it was twenty-seven years earlier.[87]

Not all economists think that Morales's wager was a bad one. After meeting with Morales, Joseph Stiglitz, the Nobel Prize–winning economist and former chief economist at the World Bank, argued that Bolivia "felt all the pains [of structural adjustment] but has experienced no gains—it's clear that it must have a change in its economic model."[88] Stiglitz also contended that the previous sale of Bolivian hydrocarbons to private interests was illegal, since it was never approved by the country's Congress. "When a person was robbed of a painting and then it is given back to him," Stiglitz contended, "we don't call it re-nationalization, but return of a property that was his to begin with."[89]

For all their professed concern about democratic reform, critics have consistently missed past abuses of democracy and ignored the fact that Morales was elected in a landslide on a platform vowing nationalization. In the time since the Bolivian government began demanding greater concessions from energy companies, it has increased its revenue by 7 percent of GDP.[90] This windfall makes possible a huge increase in funding for social programs that can benefit Bolivia's majority, including the work of a new water ministry charged with providing clean water for public use.

Characterizing the past management of Bolivia's natural wealth as an epic boondoggle, Morales has noted that 2006 was the first year since 1960 that the resource-rich country ended the year with a budget surplus.[91] In September 2007, the *New York Times* conceded, "[T]he results of . . . the nationalization of the petroleum industry last year has surprised even skeptics. . . . In a touch of irony, the urban upper classes, many of whose members remain explicitly critical of Mr. Morales, are benefiting from the newfound stability and economic vibrancy."[92] While politics in Bolivia remain highly contentious, and the country continues to struggle with entrenched socioeconomic injustices, these recent changes have provided cause for hope, something that has been in scarce supply over recent decades.

The Democratic Challenge

As Latin America grows increasingly independent, Washington buzzes with talk about how the region has been "lost." However, the White House's attempts to respond to the regional revolt have often made things worse for itself. The Bush administration learned the hard way that intervening in foreign elections and condemning progressive candidates could backfire. In the eyes of Latin American voters fed up with having economic policy dictated from the North, such attacks became signs of credibility. This was the case in Bolivia in 2002, when U.S.

attacks on Evo Morales helped him gain the stature that would ultimately propel him to the presidency. Since then, with the exception of elections in Cold War hot spots like Nicaragua and El Salvador, Washington has usually opted to keep quiet as voters head to the polls.

A second Bush administration strategy, à la Jorge Castañeda, was to try to separate "good" Latin American leftists from "bad" ones. Bush repeatedly courted governments he thought he could pull away from a Chávez-led regional bloc. Unfortunately for him, Latin America's leaders did not fall for the ploy. Despite their political differences, Kirchner and Lula have repeatedly expressed support for Chávez. In May 2006, when the U.S. press attacked Bolivia and Venezuela, even Michelle Bachelet, one of the "responsible," centrist progressives favored by Washington, stood up to critics. "I would not want us to return to the Cold War era where we demonize one country or another," she said. "What we have witnessed in these countries is that they are looking for governments and leaders that will work to eradicate poverty and eliminate inequality."[93] Such displays of unity have severely hampered Northern attempts to isolate figures like Chávez and Morales.

The White House's diplomatic strategies failed in large part because Washington has been unable to understand the true nature of the Latin American shift. The search for alternatives in the region is not motivated by the personal whims of Hugo Chávez, as the White House would have it. It is rooted in a rejection of past models of U.S. interventionism and economic rule from afar. The need to recognize the profound failure of past U.S. policy is a challenge not only for Bush but also for the politicians who would replace him, Democrat or Republican. The Democrats have consistently claimed the Bush administration has failed to pay enough attention to Latin America. In his 2004 campaign, John Kerry asserted that Bush's Latin America policy was marked by "neglect, failure to adequately support democratic institutions, and inept diplomacy."[94] Since then, various Democrats have repeated the charge, using the language of "neglect" whenever Latin America comes up.

Yet this observation does not suffice as a position on hemispheric affairs. Democrats who propose a return to Clinton-era policy that values "free markets" above all else have missed a key lesson. They may vow to pay more attention to Latin America, but there's no guarantee that such attention will be a good thing. Given their past relations with the United States, Latin Americans are all too aware that there are worse things than neglect. Clinton, after all, was the president who ushered NAFTA through a Democratic-controlled Congress and envisioned spreading the trade deal throughout the hemisphere with the FTAA. The 1990s were supposed to be years of globalizing prosperity. Yet the IMF reported in 2001 that "nearly 36 percent of the population in Latin America and the Caribbean lives below the poverty line—the same proportion as a decade ago."[95]

Latin American governments are well aware of the numbers. They are under pressure from the region's angry and enlivened citizenry to forge a more independent and egalitarian path to development than what the United States is offering. This is a sign of healthy democracy. And it should not be considered a foreign policy failure that the United States must adapt to it by rejecting both Bush's Cold War–minded approach to hemispheric affairs and the flawed corporate globalization still favored by members of both major parties.

Witnessing a region in revolt, the United States now has a choice: It can become an ever-more-despised adversary of citizens throughout the region. Or it can redefine its national interests, acknowledge that the rigid economic program once forced into place by the IMF, the World Bank, and the U.S. Treasury does not fit all countries, and cheer a re- markable era of democratic renewal in the Americas.

Conclusion:
The Coming Battle

In many respects, people fostering a democratic globalization today share much in common with movements against the colonialists and robber barons of old. There are aspects of the struggle for political and economic democracy that remain constant for decades or even centuries. But there are other ways in which the political moment can change rapidly, presenting new challenges and demanding new analysis.

It is very difficult to understand the politics of the global economy in the past ten years without appreciating the divide between corporate and imperial approaches to globalization. No doubt, the two strategies overlap in important ways. Both envision a capitalist global economy where unrestrained markets govern large swaths of public life. Both are fundamentally undemocratic, willing to use coercive means to benefit the few. Because of these similarities, many have regarded corporate and imperial globalization as two faces of the same beast.

But while there are continuities between the agendas of the world's political and economic rulers, there are also critical ruptures. In the end, the two-headed beast may be the wrong metaphor. The interests in the global economy may be more like a pack of dogs, whose members prowl together but also split away, scuffle, or fight one another for alpha status.

To put it another way, when envisioning the world's rulers, it rarely helps to imagine a cabal of generals, presidents, and "economic hit men" hidden in some underground war room deep beneath the White House. It is much more illuminating to remember the bickering elites at Davos.

Too often, those of us who oppose corporate dominance and military aggression are adept at seeing divisions among progressives but overlook those that afflict our adversaries. This is a problem, because looking at political and economic power brokers as a seamless, unified bloc obscures some important trends. It hides instances in which states do not march in lockstep with the corporations they regularly advocate for, moments when they instead work to expand their reach or their national power in ways that might be bad for short-term business profits. It prevents us from recognizing the conflicts between heavily state-dependent industries—like energy companies and arms manufacturers—and more internationalist branches of the corporate world—such as finance capital and consumer megabrands like Disney and Coca-Cola. And it makes it hard to see how different political leaders develop distinct loyalties and allegiances.

We live in exciting and tumultuous times. Certainly, there is bad news. The global economy presents some daunting realities: Both corporate and imperial models of globalization have failed to create real peace or prosperity for the majority of people on the planet. They chain citizens of the developing world into a system of sweatshop exploitation, inequality, and imperial subservience. Meanwhile, Americans suffer under domestic neoliberalism as trickle-down economics reign. We watch CEOs grow fantastically wealthy while real wages for most people stagnate. We see the public's belief in democracy being exploited by leaders who prize power and control over liberty and self-determination. And we watch White House policies create a world that is ever more dangerous and insecure.

The good news is that these failures are fueling a drive for a better international order; they have propelled the rise of a democratic globalization. The system of neoliberalism that has dominated for twenty-five years is losing its grip on international economics. Local communities, national governments, and international social movements are all seeking out more equitable ways to manage work, investment, and trade. Moreover, the hubris of the imperial globalists has sparked a widespread revolt against the neocons' vision of U.S. dominance, a rejection of the idea that democracy can be imposed through military assault.

The rival interests of corporate globalizers, neocon nationalists, and grassroots democrats have set the stage for a coming battle over the global economy. There is no guarantee that this battle will produce a change for the better. It is possible that despite neoliberalism's decline, multinational businesses will consolidate their power. It is also possible that U.S. empire will reassert itself or that rival states will attempt to enforce their own brands of self-interested nationalism.

Tensions in the international system increase the risk of major conflicts. An overextended U.S. military, unable to retain its power, may try to hold on with violence rather than quietly recede. In a global economy marked by heightened competition among nations, economic powers that find themselves stalled may strike out to control resources. Large-scale problems like global warming may generate further instability. For a democratic alternative to win out in this context, people throughout the world will need to maintain determined efforts to combat militarism, to hold governments accountable to the public, and to curtail the influence of multinational corporations.

The shift from corporate to imperial globalization has important implications for these efforts, affecting questions of analysis, tactics, and focus. Therefore, understanding this shift is critical. It might be possible to say that Iraq was both a war for corporate benefit and a war launched over the opposition of Wall Street. But surely this deserves explanation. One can rightly note that the United States has used the World Bank to impose its preferred economic policies, but one must also be able to explain why, then, the White House has abandoned the institution at some critical moments. As recently as the 1999 Seattle protests, many people saw the WTO as an imposing international body that would displace the nation-state. The FTAA, which threatened to expand NAFTA throughout the hemisphere, hovered menacingly over discussion of the international order. Pundits celebrated the seemingly unstoppable advance of "free trade." And the IMF had the power to set economic policy in countries across the globe. All that has swiftly changed. A worthwhile framework for globalization politics must be able to account for these changes, to highlight the possibilities that now exist because of them, and to prepare us for what is likely to come next.

Distinctions and Differences

In March 1999, President Clinton toured several Latin American countries, surveying areas devastated by Hurricane Mitch and meeting with governmental delegations to promote his vision of globalized trade and shared prosperity. In each country, he received a warm welcome. When Clinton spoke before the National Assembly of El Salvador, members of the leftist FMLN party, former guerrilla leaders who had become elected representatives, responded with a standing ovation.

Given that the United States had worked diligently throughout the 1980s to destroy the rebel movement, sending millions of dollars each year to support El Salvador's right-wing government and its paramilitary death squads, this was an astonishing sight. Yet, in spite of the United States' long interventionist history, Bill Clinton himself enjoyed great popularity in Latin America. He had a way of charming would-be critics. Gabriel García Márquez shared dinner with Clinton, listened to the president spontaneously recite a long passage from *The Sound and the Fury* from memory, and subsequently wrote an admiring profile.[1]

Just a few years later, the world's Nobel Laureates were busy turning acid pens against the White House. The Bush administration succeeded in shocking the international community with its aggressive militarism, its belief in unitary executive power, its use of torture, and its good-versus-evil understanding of global affairs. Acting out visions of global dominance, the neocons inflamed a world of resentment and spawned multiplying challenges to American power. U.S. troops were embattled. Discourteous politicians hovered at every podium. President Bush's state visits attracted massive protests, and puppet versions of the president were burned in effigy on the streets.

Faced with the glaringly different receptions of the two presidents, mainstream commentators provided a simple explanation. Clinton believed in multilateralism; Bush was a unilateralist. The former's approach united the world; the latter's divided it. It was a fair observation—but also a limited one. If the analysis stops there, and becomes a vindication of Clinton's foreign policy, it is problematic for a host of reasons. For one, it overlooks that Clinton's multilateralism was always selective. His administration worked through institutions like the IMF and the World Bank because it could dominate them. Even in the strategy of corporate globalization, America's economic interests and the interests of its own multinational enterprises came first.

However, the differences in the worldviews of the two presidents are indeed significant. Understood within the context of the debate over how to rule the world, they reflect a divide bigger than two individuals— a rift that has reshaped discussion of the global economy. Walden Bello noted in December 2006, "During globalization's heyday, we were told that state policies no longer mattered and that corporations would soon dwarf states." This idea was consistently overhyped. States still mattered a great deal, and this became increasingly evident under George W. Bush. Bello explains:

> Fifteen years ago, we were told to expect the emergence of a transnational capitalist elite that would manage the world economy. Indeed, globalization became the "grand strategy" of the Clinton administration, which envisioned the U.S. elite being the *primus inter pares*—first among equals—of a global coalition leading the way to the new, benign world order. Today, this project lies in shambles. During the reign of George W. Bush, the nationalist faction has overwhelmed the transnational faction of the economic elite. These nationalism-inflected states are now competing sharply with one another, seeking to beggar one another's economies.[2]

Some analysts have proposed that the political rivalries that came to the fore in the Bush years may be the culmination of a longer trend. Political scientist Corey Robin observed, "We may also be seeing, and I suggest this only tentatively, the slow decomposition of America's ruling class." Unity among business and political power brokers, Robin posits, may have peaked with the Wise Men of the Vietnam era. Since then, the world of *Forbes* and that of the *Weekly Standard* have sharply diverged. Robin describes the split:

> On the one hand, we have a younger generation of corporate magnates who, though ruthless in their efforts to secure benefits from the state, have none of the respect or passion for government that their older counterparts had. . . . So long as the state provides them with what they need and does not interfere unduly with their operations, they leave it to the apparatchiks. As one Silicon Valley executive said to Thomas Friedman, when asked how often he talks about Iraq, Russia, or foreign wars, "Not more than once a year. We don't even care about Washington. Money is extracted by Silicon Valley and then wasted by Washington. I want to talk about people who create wealth and jobs. I don't want to talk about unhealthy and unproductive people. If I don't care about the wealth destroyers in my own country, why should I care about the wealth destroyers in another country?"
>
> On the other hand, we have a new class of political elites who have little contact with the business community, whose primary experiences outside of government have been in either academia, journalism, think tanks, or some other part of the culture industry. . . . Their endgame, if they have one, is an apocalyptic confrontation between good and evil, civilization and barbarism—categories of pagan conflict diametrically opposed to the world-without-borders vision of America's free-trading, globalizing elite.[3]

The boldest accounts of this rupture among the powerful suggest that it has the power to tear apart the Republican Party. There, pragmatic business leaders—especially those not associated with the oil or arms industries—have always sat uncomfortably amid conservative evangelicals and foreign policy radicals. Ample evidence exists of discontent amongst isolationist and realist Republicans, like Lawrence Eagleburger, the secretary of state in the first Bush administration, who stated in April 2003 that he would favor impeaching George W. Bush if the president invaded Syria.[4] In a front-page story titled, "GOP Is Losing Grip on Core Business Vote," the *Wall Street Journal* reported in October 2007 that the party could be facing a brand crisis as "[s]ome business leaders are drifting away from the party because of the war in Iraq, the growing federal debt and a conservative social agenda they don't share."[5]

A more moderate account would predict less cataclysmic changes but would nevertheless identify growing wariness on the part of the business class as a significant constraint on imperial ambitions. Canadian author and historian James Laxer has noted that, historically, the willingness of the rich to pay for empire has often had its limits. He explains:

> No empire can be sustained for long without a ruling class that is prepared to bear its burden. The Roman Empire ultimately collapsed because of an upperclass tax revolt. Similarly, when the French aristocrats refused to pay, their state faltered, and they went to the guillotine during the French Revolution. The British upper classes, on the other hand, were willing to pay the price and, after the happy ending at Waterloo in 1815, they enjoyed a century of low taxation and cheap empire. Do the American upper classes, with their pronounced taste for immediate gratification, have the stomach for a protracted struggle in the Middle East, to say nothing of a possible confrontation with China?[6]

Signs point to no. Early on in the Iraq invasion, *Business Week* authors observed with worry: "The game the Americans are playing has some of the highest stakes going. What they are attempting is nothing less than the biggest carve-out of a new U.S. sphere of influence since the United States became involved in the Middle East 50 years ago. The result could be a commitment of decades that exposes America to the threat of countless wars and dangers."[7] The prospect of such dangers produced political fallout. By late in his second term, President Bush's approval ratings had reached historic lows, with support for him eroding even among some deeply loyal sectors of conservatives. Politicians across the political spectrum have been willing to repudiate Bush. The question is, what would they hold up as an alternative?

A Battle for the Democratic Party

One of the most important reasons to discuss different visions for the global economy is to be able to combat efforts to revive corporate globalization. In recent years, many have declared Bush the worst president in the history of the United States. The threat of George W. Bush, however, is now mitigated by his tremendous unpopularity. The image of Bill Clinton, lauded by laureates, touring America's imperial backyard to standing ovations illustrates a more insidious danger. While Democratic candidates for president routinely slam the Bush administration, attacking its unilateralism and military adventurism, some still voice the pieties of "free trade" multilateralism. A number of these candidates would simply like to return to an earlier strategy of corporate globalization.

Recall that in his notorious April 2000 article in the *New Republic*, Joseph Stiglitz argued, "Economic policy is today perhaps the most important part of America's interaction with the rest of the world. And yet the culture of international economic policy in the world's most powerful democracy is not democratic."[8] During the Bush years, economic policy received far less attention in political discussion than in the Clinton years; the use of military force took center stage. However, the trade and development debate went on, and it continues to affect fundamental questions of global poverty, inequality, and opportunity. Under a new Democratic administration—or under a Republican administration that demotes the neocons in favor of the more traditional, realist foreign policy establishment—it is likely that economic policy will again become the most important part of America's interaction with the world. And it is likely that it will remain profoundly undemocratic.

The debate over economic policy is particularly electric right now within the Democratic Party. As we have seen, Clinton worked hard to bring Democrats within the "free trade" fold. During his tenure the centrist, corporate-oriented Democratic Leadership Council held considerable influence. However, since then, critics of corporate globalization within the party have grown increasingly vocal. The election of some thirty-five "fair trade" Democrats in the November 2006 election—candidates critical of neoliberal trade deals—has helped to shift the balance in a populist direction. If a new Democratic administration takes the White House, it remains to be seen which side of the party it will favor.

A group of more conservative Democrats, led by influential former treasury secretary and Wall Street banker Robert Rubin, is working hard to make sure leading presidential candidates pledge their loyalty to corporate globalization. On April 5, 2006, the Brookings Institution, a moderate, Democratic-leaning think tank in Washington, announced the launch of the Hamilton Project. The mission of the project, its founders state, is to "advance an economic strategy to restore America's promise of opportunity, prosperity and growth—and inject new policy options from leading thinkers across the country into the national economic debate."[9] These "new policy options" are largely a rehash of policies pushed during the Clinton administration. In the words of critic James K. Galbraith, the "purpose of the Hamilton Project, it seems clear, is to propose just enough creative social advances—such as wage insurance, better teacher pay and healthcare reform—so as to divert discussion from the bedrock commitments to free trade and a balanced budget."[10]

The project, largely funded by Rubin and his backers, has a $2 million operating budget.[11] These funds will be deployed with a focus on solidifying these "bedrock commitments" throughout Democratic campaign offices—or, in the words of the *New York Times*, on "pushing Democratic presidential candidates away from populist economic positions."[12] Barack Obama, for one, spoke at the project's launch event in Washington, D.C., lauding the "innovative, thoughtful policy-makers" and calling the initiative "the sort of breath of fresh air that I think this town needs."[13] Hillary Clinton, who has long been close to Rubin, has echoed his ideas in speeches.

Efforts by the likes of Rubin to entrench more conservative economics within the Democratic Party coincides with a wider drive to keep neoliberalism alive on the international scene. Although the ideology has lost its stranglehold on the global economy, Washington economists and local elites in the developing world still champion neoliberal policies. Washington Consensus prescriptions remain widespread, limiting the prospects for more equitable development in many countries. And proponents of these policies are working to get negotiations at the WTO back on track. While neoliberalism has suffered some major setbacks, it will only remain in decline if it continues to face vigilant resistance.

Debates over international trade and development policy can often seem distant to most people. Yet the battle within the Democratic Party shows that these issues matter a great deal to Americans as well as citizens overseas. Under neoliberalism, the international economy has been managed for the benefit of a very narrow slice of the population. It has placed the U.S. Treasury and the IMF in positions as economic overseers on a global plantation. This type of domination goes against the values of all those who decry sweatshop economics abroad. And it also has costs at home. The interests of Wall Street are not the same as our national interests or the interests of working people. As successive administrations in Washington have enforced a type of market fundamentalism in foreign affairs, they have pursued a parallel set of policies domestically. Since the days of Ronald Reagan, Americans, too, have been locked into the trickle-down economics of the "golden straightjacket," which, as we have seen, has been a lot more golden for billionaire families like Thomas Friedman's than it has for typical citizens. For some, like those left behind after Hurricane Katrina—when a stripped-down government did little to help those in New Orleans who could not afford to evacuate themselves—the results have been tragic.

Sadly, neoliberal economics are not the exclusive purview of Republicans. They are embodied in the "fiscal constraint" and "free market" provisos of the Hamilton Project. The financial community lauds these measures, even as the policies strike against some of the core constituencies of the Democratic Party. The majority of Americans have reason to cry foul and to work to bring home the drive for a democratic globalization. Citizen demands for good jobs, for full employment, and for investment in the public good go hand in hand with the call for fair trade and economic human rights throughout the world.

Bringing Down an Empire

Some analysts have painted Bush's militarism as a logical next step for corporate globalization. The United States invaded Iraq, this theory holds, because, with the neoliberal system in crisis, the state and its corporate sponsors could no longer achieve their goals through multilateral means. I do not believe that this was the case. I argue that the Iraq War was indeed a war of choice, pursued out of radical nationalist aims rather than the prerogatives of near-term profit. There is a real question, however, about whether America, having started down an imperial path and faced with undermined multilateral institutions, can simply go back to Clinton-style business as usual.

Never in the modern era was there so explicit a defense of U.S. imperialism as in the aftermath of 9/11. "People are now coming out of the closet on the word 'empire,'" the conservative columnist Charles Krauthammer told the *New York Times* in early 2002.[14] In an article for the *Weekly Standard* titled "The Case for American Empire," *Wall Street Journal* editor Max Boot argued against Pat Buchanan's belief that the United States should be a "republic, not an empire."

"This analysis is exactly backward," Boot asserted. "[T]he Sept. 11 attack was a result of insufficient American involvement and ambition; the solution is to be more expansive in our goals and more assertive in their implementation." He added, "Afghanistan and other troubled lands today cry out for the sort of enlightened foreign administration once provided by self-confident Englishmen in jodhpurs and pith helmets."[15] Joining the chorus, journalist Robert Kaplan contended, "There's a positive side to empire. It's in some ways the most benign form of order."[16]

Today, the catastrophic failure of the Iraq War has cooled celebration of America's imperial prowess. By Bush's second term, prominent neocons had left their government posts and returned to private life. It is highly doubtful that any new administration could get away with proclaiming the same unfettered confidence in U.S. ability to reshape the world in its image through preemptive invasion. And yet, many neoconservative tenets linger. The 2002 National Security Strategy remains on record as a statement of official policy, and Bush's successors may change it less than we might expect.

In the 1970s, a "Vietnam Syndrome" tempered interventionist tendencies on the part of America's political elite. The country had been chastened by a disastrous war in Southeast Asia, and the public was in no mood to tolerate new military adventures. Although some have predicted a similar "Iraq Syndrome," *New York Times* columnist David Brooks argued against this idea in early 2007:

> Today, Americans are disillusioned with the war in Iraq, and many around the world predict that an exhausted America will turn inward again. Some see a nation in permanent decline and an end to American hegemony. . . .
>
> Forget about it. Americans are having a debate about how to proceed in Iraq, but we are not having a strategic debate about retracting American power and influence. . . . No major American leader doubts that America must remain, as Dean Acheson put it, the locomotive of the world. . . .
>
> When you look further into the future, you see that the next president's big efforts will not be about retrenchment, but about expansion. They'll be about expanding the U.S. military, expanding the diplomatic corps, asking for more shared sacrifice, creating new interagency bureaus that will give America more nation-building capacity.
>
> In short, the U.S. has taken its share of blows over the past few years, but the isolationist dog is not barking. The hegemon will change. The hegemon will do more negotiating. But the hegemon will live.[17]

As a prominent conservative and supporter of the Iraq War, Brooks's view is in part wishful thinking. But he does make an important point. The neocons were unique in envisioning a post–Cold War order in which the United States would be unapologetically, preemptively, and unilaterally interventionist. But they were not alone in their faith that America must remain an unchallenged military power. The use or threat of force has always been a part of U.S. foreign policy. While a majority of leading politicians may now focus on exercising the nation's "soft power," none are lobbying to limit Pentagon spending, much less to dismantle the "baseworld" of sprawling American military encampments overseas.

Moreover, while the brashest defenders of empire have been quieted, the more genteel ones are taken seriously. Some, like British historian

Niall Ferguson, receive warm welcome in political circles by warning against the dangers of a new international era in which power would be more equally distributed. He predicts a chaotic future if America cedes its superpower status: "Critics of U.S. global dominance should pause and consider the alternative. If the United States retreats from its hegemonic role, who would supplant it? Not Europe, not China, not the Muslim world—and certainly not the United Nations. Unfortunately, the alternative to a single superpower is not a multilateral utopia, but the anarchic nightmare of a new Dark Age.[18]"

Although Ferguson counsels that America can afford to formalize its empire, we have good reason to reject the costs.[19] These costs are paid in lives—the lives of thousands of U.S. soldiers lost in the quagmires of Iraq and Afghanistan, as well as many, many more civilians killed in these occupations. The costs are financial: As of May 2007, Congress had appropriated $610 billion for wars in Iraq and Afghanistan—more than it would have cost to provide more than 30 million children with health insurance for a decade or to build more than 4 million public housing units.[20] The costs are moral, as empire undermines the spread of true democracy in the world. And we pay the costs in heightened fear and insecurity, as America's imperial stance brews hatred and resentment throughout the world, increasing the likelihood of future terrorist attacks.

The costs may also include some of the things Americans hold dearest about their country. There is an active debate among historians and political analysts about whether we can maintain an imperial foreign policy and still remain a democracy. James Laxer argues:

> Just as the British Empire attenuated British democracy by sustaining aristocratic power long into the age of democracy, the American empire is threatening to American democracy. The appointment of Attorney General Alberto Gonzales, who provided the legal foundations for Abu Ghraib and Guantánamo Bay, shows how empire strikes back at the vitals of America itself. The potent interests—military, corporate, political—that gain their sway as a consequence of empire can easily become the enemies of democracy at home, and, as many have argued,

the flouting of international law through the use of pre-emptive strikes will eventually lead to circumventions of domestic law and authority. The struggle for democracy and the rule of law takes place not only in failed states but in the imperial states themselves.[21]

As we enter the post-Bush era, we need more than an "Iraq Syndrome" to temporarily hold war-planners in check. We need to engage in a deeper reflection on the price the country pays for its empire and to initiate a process of redefining America's role in the world.

RETURN OF THE PROTESTS

The battle among corporate globalization, imperial globalization, and democratic globalization embodies some of the most important issues of our times. At its most basic level, it involves a debate about what type of world we want to live in. If Americans cannot stop the aggression of imperial globalization, our country will be alone and embattled in the world, and we will be forced to bear the heavy costs of empire. If we are unable to check the power of multinational corporations and their advocates in the international financial institutions, we will be made to live in an oligarchy. If we are content with neither rule by military might nor rule by the rich, then we must demand a democratic alternative.

Fortunately, efforts to propel this demand need not start from scratch. As we have seen, there is a vibrant international network of citizens' movements, drawing on deep histories of resistance, that has risen against neoliberalism and insisted that another world is possible.

In recent times, especially in the United States, it has been common for people to ask, "Where have all the protests gone?" Recall that after 9/11, critics charged that the "antiglobalization" movement would cease to exist. They were wrong. But the character of the movement, and media coverage of it, did indeed change. Protests in the United States and Europe against institutions like the WTO and the World Bank faded after 2001 for several reasons. For one, the international financial institutions took to holding their meetings in locales that flatly outlawed protest (such as Singapore), were too remote to be accessible to demonstrations (such as a resort in the Canadian Rockies), or both (Doha, Qatar). For another, the imperial globalists' shift away from the international financial institutions as central mechanisms of U.S. foreign policy complicated the dynamics of focusing antineoliberal protests on the meetings of these bodies.

Most importantly, social movements focused on the urgent task of opposing war in Iraq. In November 2002, activists at the European Social Forum issued the first call for a February 15, 2003, day of action against the impending U.S.-led invasion. The resulting demonstrations drew more than 10 million people in over five hundred cities, constituting the largest coordinated global day of action in history. At least 1 million people showed up for the largest-ever march in London, 2 million rallied in Spain, 500,000 in Berlin, and 200,000 in Damascus, Syria.[22] Another 2 million demonstrated in Rome, and over 150,000 turned out in Melbourne, Australia. Hundreds of thousands marched in New York and San Francisco.

Protests failed to stop the war in Iraq. However, it is possible that international outrage stopped the administration from fulfilling neoconservative desires to follow up on the invasion with assaults on Syria and Iran. In the wake of the February 15 protests, the New York Times famously labeled "world public opinion" as the second of "two superpowers on the planet."[23] In several countries, most notably Spain, forces standing in opposition to the invasion and occupation of Iraq significantly altered the balance of power within their governments. Due to strong expressions of dissent, the war in Iraq was framed as a fiercely disputed affair. The taint of controversy limited the swell of support that any U.S. president can expect to receive when commanding troops overseas, and it set the stage for the later scandals that would plague the Bush administration. The relentless scrutiny and criticism by the peace movement of the faulty case for invasion would ultimately gain mainstream traction and leave Bush flailing to defend his prewar lies.

While the shift in focus away from corporate globalization was notable, there were also important links between movements challenging war and those combating neoliberalism. That the call for the February 15, 2003, protests came out of the European Social Forum—a venue of the globalization movement—was not incidental. Although the media regularly covered major protests, especially in the global South, simply as anti-Bush or anti-American, outraged citizens often voiced sophisticated critiques of both military and economy policy. When Bush traveled abroad, his state visits frequently drew huge crowds of protesters, many of whom regarded IMF dictates and White House militarism as equally odious.

Since the invasion of Iraq, popular mobilizations expressly highlighting economic issues have also reemerged. Protests dogged the WTO, whether at its meetings in Cancún in 2003—where as many as twenty thousand demonstrating students, farmers, and community organizers were stunned when South Korean farmer Lee Kyung Hae committed ritual suicide in protest of neoliberal trade talks—or Hong Kong in 2005—where an especially repressive police force arrested one thousand demonstrators.[24] Protests followed FTAA negotiations from Miami in 2003, where police clouded the South Florida air with tear gas, to Mar Del Plata, Argentina, in 2005, where soccer legend Diego Maradona led tens of thousands in a boisterous march and where talks for the trade deal were officially scrapped.

In numbers that far exceeded the Seattle protests of 1999, more than 225,000 marched in Edinburgh, Scotland, on July 2, 2005 in a massive call to G8 leaders to "make poverty history" and provide debt cancellation for poorer countries.[25] Thousands more engaged in direct action during the G8 summit, creating street blockades and surrounding the hotels of delegates. Two years later, when the G8 met in Germany in the summer of 2007, 80,000 rallied in the streets of Rostock in the largest demonstration ever to take place in that city.[26]

Perhaps most significantly, the mainstream media has failed to take notice that resistance to neoliberalism in developing nations has only escalated, pulling the center of the movement for a democratic globalization to the South. World Social Forums in Porto Alegre, Mumbai, and Nairobi have attracted as many as 150,000 people. The IMF has grown ever more despised in Africa and Asia. And to someone in Buenos Aires, Cochabamba, Quito, or Mexico City, the question "Where have the protests gone?" would seem truly bizarre.

In the United States, this world of activity can often seem far away. Much of the energy from the surge in citizen activism opposing the onset of the Iraq War was later channeled into opposing Bush's reelection. The 2004 campaigns featured the largest protest ever held outside an American political convention, at the Republican National Convention in New York City. Nevertheless, Bush's electoral victory dealt a harsh blow. By the president's second term, the war had grown deeply unpopular, turning Bush into a lame duck well before the end of his tenure in office—yet many who worked hard to oppose him were left feeling demoralized.

At the same time, efforts to further a democratic globalization have persevered even in the United States, and continued activism will only grow more important in coming years. Global justice protests involved not a single constituency, but rather a dense network of movements. Often with little notice or fanfare, many of these movements have made significant strides in the recent past. Debt activists celebrated a major victory, organic and local food advocates achieved mainstream visibility, living wage campaigns proliferated, antisweatshop efforts won a variety of workplace gains, immigrant rights activists charged onto the national stage, and fair trade cooperatives flourished. The environmentalists, labor unionists, indigenous rights activists, and community organizers who together seized the global spotlight in Seattle and forced trade bureaucrats and corporate lobbyists onto the defensive have not gone away. They can unite again.

For people throughout the world working for change, the post-Bush era presents revitalizing opportunities. By themselves, the backlash against neocon militarism and the undermining of neoliberalism's legitimacy do not ensure a more positive future. But rarely are there moments so open to those who would reject both elite approaches to globalization and create an international order more just, more equitable, and more inclusive. It is now up to concerned citizens to act—to turn international discontent into a call for global economic democracy.

There is a divide among international elites over how to rule the world. But ultimately the internal disputes between the presidents and CEOs at Davos will not be the engines of transformation. The powerful will abandon their strategies of control only when it grows too costly for them to do otherwise. It is the concerted efforts of people coming together in local communities and in movements spanning borders that will raise the costs. Empire becomes unsustainable—it becomes bad business—when the people of the world resist. And democracy triumphs over privilege and exploitation when we make it a practice that is too alive for money to contain.

Acknowledgments

I am very grateful to all of the friends, family members, housemates, and colleagues who provided me support and encouragement in undertaking this project. I give my heartfelt thanks to all of you.

I also wish to give special thanks to the following people. My fellow New York City–based writers Joseph Huff-Hannon, Kendra Hurley, Erica Pearson, John Kearney, and Kate Levin provided invaluable suggestions throughout the writing process, helping me to shape the original proposal for this book and to greatly improve early drafts of many chapters. Rebecca Tuhus-Dubrow and Dania Rajendra read every page of the manuscript and were extraordinarily generous in providing thoughtful comments and edits, often on short notice.

Nichole Shippen and Andrew Greenberg took time from their own work to read the manuscript and provided much-appreciated critical feedback. Adam Hefty, Stephanie Greenwood, Aaron Jorgensen-Briggs, Benjamin Dangl, and Nadia Martinez also provided expert insights on important sections of the book and helped to challenge my thinking on the issues raised. Bill Hartung, Frida Berrigan, Jeremy Brecher, Anthony Arnove, and friends at Foreign Policy In Focus—including John Feffer, Laura Carlsen, Erik Leaver, and Emily Schwartz Greco—helped with collegial advice and assistance at many points. Additionally, I am grateful to

Josh Kamensky for his kind help in editing many articles that provided raw material for this book.

Since we first met, my agent, Anna Ghosh, has shown steadfast confidence in my writing, and I am indebted to her for her skilled efforts on my behalf. I also thank Carl Bromley and the team at Nation Books for their belief in the importance of this project and their work in making the book a reality.

The research assistants that have worked with me over the past five years—Kate Griffiths, Jason Rowe, and Sean Nortz—each contributed to this project in innumerable ways, helping me to form the core arguments of the book, aiding in the production of many related articles, digging up hundreds of hard-to-find quotes and statistics, and providing meticulous documentation for the facts cited. I am very thankful for their diligence, drive, and intelligence.

I thank my mom, Joan, and my brothers, Francis and Paul, for continually supporting me in my writing and my activism.

Finally, my partner Rosslyn Wuchinich believed in this project from start to finish, helped to shape my thinking on many key issues, challenged me to make my ideas clear and relevant, and kept me going through the most difficult parts of the writing process. I dedicate this book to her.

NOTES

A note on Internet sources: While I made frequent use of the LexisNexis Academic database for access to full text archives of news articles, I have tried to include URLs linking to any resources that are freely available online. However, because of the transitory nature of the Internet, some links may no longer be valid. The most recent date that I accessed the link is noted.

INTRODUCTION

1. Laurie Garrett, e-mail correspondence, as forwarded to the listserv of the Institute for Psychohistory by Adam Davis, "Swiss View," February 6, 2003, archived at lists.topica.com/lists/psychohistory/read/message.html?sort=d&mid=1711891071 &start=4389 (accessed March 26, 2007). For news analysis of the leaked e-mail, and confirmation by Garrett of the authenticity of the document, see Shaun Waterman, "Analysis: Click-forward Morality," *United Press International*, March 3, 2003, available online through LexisNexis Academic.

2. Pope John Paul II, "Homily of John Paul II," speech in José Martí Plaza, Havana, January 25, 1998, at www.vatican.va/holy_father/john_paul_ii/travels/documents/hf_jp-ii_hom_25011998_lahavana_en.html (accessed February 28, 2007).

3. Greg Grandin, *Empire's Workshop* (New York: Metropolitan Books, 2006), pp. 163–175.

4. Ibid., p. 171.

5. Milton Friedman, "Free Markets and the Generals," *Newsweek*, January 25, 1982, available online through LexisNexis Academic.

6. James Cypher, "Is Chile a Neoliberal Success?" *Dollars & Sense*, September/October 2004, www.dollarsandsense.org/archives/2004/0904cypher.html (accessed April 25, 2007).

7. Mark Weisbrot, "The Mirage of Progress," *American Prospect*, January 1, 2002, www.prospect.org/print/V13/1/weisbrot-m.html (accessed February 28, 2007). See also Mark Weisbrot, Robert Naiman, and Joyce Kim, "The Emperor Has No Growth: Declining Economic Growth Rates in the Era of Globalization," Center for Economic and Policy Research, November 27, 2000, www.cepr.net/publications/econ_growth_2000_11_27.htm (accessed March 13, 2007).

8. United Nations Development Program, *Human Development Report 2003*, hdr.undp.org/reports/global/2003 (accessed February 28, 2007). See also Larry Elliott, "The Lost Decade" *Guardian*, July 9, 2003, www.commondreams.org/headlines03/0709-05.htm (accessed February 28, 2007).

9. Elliott, "The Lost Decade."

10. Alan B. Cibils, Mark Weisbrot, and Debayani Kar, "Argentina Since Default: The IMF and the Depression," Center for Economic and Policy Research, September 3, 2002, www.cepr.net/publications/argentina_2002_09_03.htm (accessed March 23, 2007).

11. President Bill Clinton, address to trade ministers, "Market Access for Poorest Nations," Four Seasons Hotel, Seattle, Washington, December 1, 1999, www.us-mission.ch/press1999/122clin.html (accessed February 28, 2007).

12. As quoted in Nicola Bullard, "Another One Bites the Dust: Collateral Damage in the Battle for the Bank," Focus on the Global South, June 10, 2003, www.focusweb.org/content/view/195/27/ (accessed February 28, 2007). See also Lawrence Summers, "Personal View: The Troubling Aspects of IMF Reform," *Financial Times*, March 23, 2000, available online through LexisNexis Academic.

13. Walden Bello, "Washington's Political Transition Threatens Bretton Woods Twins," Focus on the Global South, January 2001, www.focusweb.org/publications/2001/Washington's%20Political%20Transition%20Threatens%20Bretton%20Woods%20Twins.htm (accessed February 28, 2007).

14. "Bush Sticks with Iraqi Contract Ban," *Associated Press*, December 11, 2003, www.msnbc.msn.com/id/3676000/ (accessed February 28, 2007).

15. Paul Blustein, "Anxiety Over Trade Rift Grows," *Washington Post*, March 23, 2003, available online through LexisNexis Academic.

16. Project for the New American Century, "Statement of Principles," June 3, 1997, www.newamericancentury.org/statementofprinciples.htm (accessed March 13, 2007).

17. Elizabeth Becker, "WTO Fears Bush Go-It-Alone Role," *New York Times*, March 15, 2003, available online through Trade Observatory, www.tdeobservatory.org/headlines.cfm?refID=18094 (accessed February 28, 2007).

18. As quoted in Duncan Green, "Not Yet at the Crematorium," *Guardian*, July 26, 2006, business.guardian.co.uk/story/0,,1830101,00.html (accessed February 28, 2007).

19. Sebastian Mallaby, "Why Globalization Has Stalled," *Washington Post*, April 24, 2006, available online through LexisNexis Academic.

20. Jonah Goldberg, "Takin' It to the Streets," *National Review*, April 17, 2000, www.nationalreview.com/comment/comment041700c.html (accessed February 28, 2007).

CHAPTER 1

1. Del Jones, "How MBAs Might Reshape the White House: Degrees Make This Administration All About Business," *USA Today*, January 19, 2001, available online through LexisNexis Academic.

2. Ibid.

3. "GMAC President to Comment on the New CEO of the United States," *Business Wire*, January 19, 2001, available online through LexisNexis Academic.

4. Del Jones, "Execs Give Cheney Good Grades," *USA Today*, July 25, 2000, available online through LexisNexis Academic.

5. Paul Krugman, "Succeeding in Business," *New York Times*, July 7, 2002, www.commondreams.org/views02/0707-03.htm (accessed July 27, 2007). See also George Lardner Jr. and Lois Romano, "Bush Name Helps Fuel Oil Dealings," *Washington Post*, July 30, 1999, www.washingtonpost.com/wp-srv/politics/campans/wh2000/stories/bush073099.htm (accessed July 27, 2007).

6. Daniel Gross, "The Cheney Curse," *Slate*, October 14, 2003, slate.msn.com/id/2089811/ (accessed March 23, 2007).

7. Jason E. Putman, as quoted in Mike France and Stephanie Anderson Forest, "What Cheney Did at Halliburton," *Business Week*, October 26, 2004, www.businessweek.com/bwdaily/dnflash/oct2004/nf20041026_2453_db038.htm (accessed March 23, 2007).

8. Allan Sloan, "Halliburton Pays Dearly but Finally Escapes Cheney's Asbestos Mess," *Washington Post*, January 11, 2005, www.washingtonpost.com/wp-dyn/articles/A64535-2005Jan10.html (accessed March 23, 2007).

9. Carl Hulse and David Firestone, "On the Hill: Budget Business as Usual," *New York Times*, March 23, 2003. As cited in Frances Fox Piven, *The War at Home* (New York: New Press, 2004), p. 41.

10. Alexandra Navarro Clifton, "Iraq War Bill Includes Millions for Trade Conference in Miami," *Palm Beach Post*, November 4, 2003, available online through LexisNexis Academic.

11. Naomi Klein, "Baghdad Year Zero," *Harper's Magazine*, September 2004, www.harpers.org/BaghdadYearZero.html (accessed March 26, 2007).

12. Antonia Juhasz, *The Bush Agenda: Invading the World One Economy at a Time* (New York: HarperCollins, 2006).

13. "Let's All Go to the Yard Sale," *Economist*, September 27, 2003, available online through LexisNexis Academic.

14. See Juhasz, *The Bush Agenda*, p. 248.

15. Piven, *The War at Home*, p. 13.

16. Ibid., p. 11.

17. Ibid., p. 11.

18. Robert Jensen, "Stupid White Movie," *CounterPunch*, July 5, 2004, www.counterpunch.org/jensen07052004.html (accessed March 23, 2007).

19. "Karachi Blasts Target Food Outlets," *CNN.com*, September 8, 2005, www.cnn.com/2005/WORLD/asiapcf/09/08/pakistan.blast/ (accessed March 23, 2007).

20. Declan Walsh, "Six Die in KFC Restaurant During Riots," *Guardian*, June 1, 2005, www.guardian.co.uk/pakistan/Story/0,2763,1496267,00.html (accessed March 23, 2007).

21. Laurie Garrett, e-mail correspondence, as forwarded to the listserv of the Institute for Psychohistory by Adam Davis, "Swiss View," February 6, 2003, archived at lists.topica.com/lists/psychohistory/read/message.html?sort=d&mid=1711891071&start=4389 (accessed March 26, 2007).

22. David Watkins, "Hearts and Mice," *South China Morning Post*, October 4, 2004, available online through LexisNexis Academic.

23. Jim Lobe, "Iraq War Is Bad for Business," Foreign Policy in Focus, December 31, 2004, www.fpif.org/fpiftxt/532 (accessed March 23, 2007).

24. Paul Maidment, "Is Brand America in Trouble?" *Forbes*, September 21, 2005, www.forbes.com/home/columnists/2005/09/21/us-branding-politics-cx_pm_0921brandamerica.html (accessed March 23, 2007).

25. Kevin Allison, "World Turning Its Back on Brand America," *Financial Times*, August 1, 2005, www.ft.com/cms/s/77868922-0228-11da-9481-00000e2511c8.html (accessed March 23, 2007).

26. Karen Krebsbach, "Business Gets on Diplomacy's Fast Track," *U.S. Banker*, August 2005, available online through LexisNexis Academic.

27. Greg Gatlin, "Mass Execs.: Iraqi War Hurting," October 20, 2004, *Boston Herald* available online through LexisNexis Academic.

28. Business for Diplomatic Action, "Who We Are: Overview," www.businessfordiplomaticaction.org/who/BDAOverview.pdf (accessed March 26, 2007).

29. Keith Reinhard, as quoted in Allison, "World Turning Its Back on Brand America."

30. James Cox, "Financially Ailing Companies Point to Iraq War," *USA TODAY*, June 14, 2004, www.usatoday.com/money/companies/2004-06-14-iraq_x.htm (accessed March 26, 2007).

31. Ibid.

32. Amy Yee, "US Tourism 'Losing Billions Because of Image,'" *Financial Times*, May 8, 2005, www.ft.com/cms/s/9d3b32bc-bfe8-11d9-b376-00000e2511c8.html (accessed March 26, 2007).

33. Rachel L. Swarns, "U.S. Is Urged to Step Up Plan to Attract More Visitors," *New York Times*, January 31, 2007, available online through LexisNexis Academic.

34. "Survey Shows U.S. Standing Around World at New Low," Associated Press, March 6, 2007, www.iht.com/articles/ap/2007/03/06/america/NA-GEN-US-Image.php (accessed March 27, 2007).

35. Frida Berrigan, personal interview, January 26, 2007.

36. William D. Hartung, "Soldiers versus Contractors: Emerging Budgetary Reality?" World Policy Institute, February 10, 2006, www.worldpolicy.org/projects/arms/reports/soldiers.html (accessed March 30, 2007).

37. Ibid.

38. Jonathan Karp, Andy Pasztor, and Greg Jaffe, "Pentagon Weighs Personnel Cuts to Pay for Weapons," *Wall Street Journal*, December 5, 2005, as quoted in Hartung, "Soldiers versus Contractors."

39. Dean Baker and Mark Weisbrot, "The Economic Costs of a War in Iraq: The Negative Scenario," Center for Economic and Policy Research, December 9, 2002, www.cepr.net/publications/econ_war_2002_12.htm (accessed March 26, 2007).

40. Michael Klare, "More Blood, Less Oil," *TomDispatch*, September 20, 2005, www.tomdispatch.com/index.mhtml?pid=22859 (accessed March 26, 2007).

41. "TomDispatch Interview: Juan Cole on Withdrawal from Iraq," *TomDispatch*, October 18, 2005, www.tomdispatch.com/index.mhtml?pid=29333 (accessed March 26, 2007).

42. Dana Bash, "What Would War with Iraq Cost?" *CNN.com*, January 2, 2003, www.cnn.com/2003/ALLPOLITICS/01/01/sproject.irq.war.cost/ (accessed March 27, 2007).

43. James Pinkerton, "It Ain't Beanbag," New America Foundation, December 9, 2002, www.newamerica.net/publications/articles/2002/it_aint_beanbag (accessed March 27, 2007).

44. Phyllis Bennis and Erik Leaver, "The Iraq Quagmire: The Mounting Costs of War and the Case for Bringing Home the Troops," Foreign Policy in Focus, August 31, 2005, www.ips-dc.org/iraq/quagmire/ (accessed March 27, 2007).

45. Joseph Stiglitz and Linda Bilmes, "The Economic Costs of the Iraq War," National Bureau of Economic Research, February 2006, www2.gsb.columbia.edu/faculty/jstiglitz/download/2006_Cost_of_War_in_Iraq_NBER.pdf (accessed March 27, 2007).

46. Thomas Friedman, *The Lexus and the Olive Tree* (New York: Anchor Books, 2000), p. 464.

47. John Cavanagh and Jerry Mander, eds., *Alternatives to Economic Globalization* (San Francisco: Berrett-Koehler, 2004), p. 8.

48. Arundhati Roy, "Confronting Empire," speech at the World Social Forum, Porto Alegre, Brazil, January 27, 2003, available online through *ZNet*, www.zmag.org/content/showarticle.cfm?ItemID=2919 (accessed March 26, 2007).

CHAPTER 2

1. Irving Kristol as quoted in Corey Robin, "Endgame: Conservatives After the Cold War," *Boston Review*, February/March 2004, bostonreview.net/BR29.1/robin.html (accessed March 13, 2007).

2. Ibid.

3. Robin, "Endgame."

4. David Brooks and Francis Fukuyama, as cited in Robin, "Endgame."

5. Michael Steinberger, "Neo-Economics," *American Prospect*, March 5, 2005, www.prospect.org/web/page.ww?section=root&name=ViewPrint&articleId=9207 (accessed March 13, 2007).

6. Project for a New American Century, "Statement of Principles," June 3, 1997, www.newamericancentury.org/statementofprinciples.htm (accessed March 13, 2007).

7. Kristol and Kagan, as cited in Steinberger, "Neo-Economics."

8. President George W. Bush, Second Inaugural Address, *New York Times*, January 20, 2005, www.nytimes.com/2005/01/20/politics/20BUSH-TEXT.html?ex=1174622400&en=aa7f7789efac2739&ei=5070 (accessed March 23, 2007).

9. Steinberger, "Neo-Economics."

10. E. J. Dionne Jr., "Visions in Need of a Little Realism," *Washington Post*, January 21, 2005, www.washingtonpost.com/wp-dyn/articles/A25277-2005Jan20.html (accessed March 19, 2007).

11. Robert Kagan, "The Money Trap," *New Republic*, April 7, 1997, www.carnegieendowment.org/publications/index.cfm?fa=view&id=279 (accessed March 23, 2007).

12. Ibid.

13. Ibid.

14. William Kristol and Robert Kagan, "Toward a Neo-Reaganite Foreign Policy," *Foreign Affairs*, July/August 1996, www.carnegieendowment.org/publications/index.cfm?fa=view&id=276 (accessed March 23, 2007).

15. Steinberger, "Neo-Economics."

16. President George W. Bush, Press Conference, December 20, 2006, The White House, www.whitehouse.gov/news/releases/2006/12/20061220-1.html (accessed March 26, 2007).

17. President George W. Bush, "Remarks by the President to Airline Employees," O'Hare International Airport, Chicago, Illinois, September 27, 2001, The White House, www.whitehouse.gov/news/releases/2001/09/20010927-1.html (accessed March 26, 2007).

18. David Brooks, as cited in Robin, "Endgame."

19. Robin, "Endgame."

20. President George W. Bush, as cited in David Armstrong, "Dick Cheney's Song of America," *Harper's Magazine*, October 2002, vol. 305, no. 1829, available online through EBSCOhost MasterFILE Select.

21. National Security Council, *The National Security Strategy of the United States of America*, September 17, 2002, as cited in Antonia Juhasz, *The Bush Agenda: Invading the World One Economy at a Time* (New York: HarperCollins, 2006), p. 44.

22. Peter Baker, "Bush to Restate Terror Strategy," *Washington Post*, March 16, 2006, www.washingtonpost.com/wp-dyn/content/article/2006/03/15/AR20060315 02297.html (accessed March 16, 2007).

23. Karen DeYoung and Mike Allen, "Bush Shifts Strategy from Deterrence to Dominance," *Washington Post*, September 21, 2002, www.washingtonpost.com/ac2/ wp-dyn/A43744-2002Sep20?language=printer (accessed March 16, 2007).

24. As cited in Armstrong, "Dick Cheney's Song of America."

25. Juhasz, *The Bush Agenda*, p. 42.

26. National Security Council, *The National Security Strategy of the United States of America*, September 17, 2002.

27. Project for a New American Century, "Statement of Principles."

28. Ray McGovern, as quoted by T. D. Allman, "The Curse of Dick Cheney," *Rolling Stone*, August 25, 2004, www.rollingstone.com/politics/story/_/id/645 0422?rnd=1126254738277&has-player=true (accessed March 13, 2007).

29. Brent Scowcroft, "Don't Attack Saddam," *Wall Street Journal*, August 15, 2002, www.opinionjournal.com/editorial/feature.html?id=110002133 (accessed March 13, 2007).

30. Patrick Buchanan, "Whose War?" *American Conservative*, March 24, 2003, www.amconmag.com/03_24_03/cover.html (accessed March 13, 2007).

31. William Kristol and Lawrence Kaplan, as cited in Robert Dreyfuss, "Just the Beginning," *American Prospect*, April 1, 2003, www.prospect.org/print/V14/4/ dreyfuss-r.html (March 23, 2007).

32. Laurie Garrett, e-mail correspondence, as forwarded to the listserv of the Institute for Psychohistory by Adam Davis, "Swiss View," February 6, 2003, archived at lists.topica.com/lists/psychohistory/read/message.html?sort=d&mid=1711891071 &start=4389 (accessed March 26, 2007).

33. Michael Ledeen, as cited in Robert Dreyfuss, "Just the Beginning."

34. Jonah Goldberg, "Baghdad Delenda Est., Part II," *National Review*, April 23, 2002, www.nationalreview.com/goldberg/goldberg042302.asp (accessed March 13, 2007).

35. David Rennie, "Saudi Arabia Is Kernel of Evil, Says US Brief," *Telegraph*, August 6, 2006, www.telegraph.co.uk/news/main.jhtml?xml=/news/2002/08/07/wsaud07.xml (accessed March 13, 2007).

36. Ibid.

37. Jim Lobe, "Veteran Neo-Con Advisor Moves on Iran," *Asia Times*, June 26, 2003, www.atimes.com/atimes/Middle_East/EF26Ak03.html (accessed October 8, 2007). See also International Relations Center, Right Web, "Profile: Michael Ledeen," last updated May 23, 2007, rightweb.irc-online.org/profile/1261 (accessed October 8, 2007).

38. Michael Ledeen, as cited in Jackson Lears, "Keeping It Real," *Nation*, June 12, 2006, www.thenation.com/doc/20060612/lears (accessed October 8, 2007). See also International Relations Center, Right Web, "Profile: Michael Ledeen," last updated May 23, 2007, rightweb.irc-online.org/profile/1261 (accessed October 8, 2007).

39. Jonah Goldberg, "Baghdad Delenda Est., Part II."

40. Daniel Pipes, "Iraq's Weapons and the Road to War," *New York Post*, June 3, 2003, www.danielpipes.org/article/1116 (accessed March 14, 2007).

41. Thomas L. Friedman, "Because We Could," *New York Times*, June 4, 2003, www.nytimes.com/2003/06/04/opinion/04FRIE.html (accessed March 13, 2007).

42. Department of Energy, "Country Analysis Briefs: Iraq," June 2006, www.eia.doe.gov/emeu/cabs/Iq/Oil.html (accessed March 23, 2007).

43. As cited in George Wright, "Wolfowitz: Iraq War Was About Oil," *Guardian*, June 4, 2003, www.truthout.org/docs_03/060503A.shtml (accessed March 14, 2007).

44. Robert Dreyfuss, "The Thirty-Year Itch," *Mother Jones*, March/April 2003, www.motherjones.com/news/feature/2003/03/ma_273_.html (accessed March 14, 2007).

45. Michael Klare, as quoted in Dreyfuss, "The Thirty-Year Itch."

46. President Jimmy Carter, State of the Union address, January 23, 1980, www.jimmycarterlibrary.org/documents/speeches/su80jec.phtml (accessed March 23, 2007), as cited in Juhasz, *The Bush Agenda*, p. 65, and in Dreyfuss, "The Thirty-Year Itch."

47. "Investigating Terror: Places—Saudi Arabia," *BBC News*, news.bbc.co.uk/hi/english/static/in_depth/world/2001/war_on_terror/investigation_on_terror/places_6.stm (accessed June 8, 2007).

48. Reuel Marc Gerecht, "Liberate Iraq," *Weekly Standard*, May 14, 2001, available online through LexisNexis Academic.

49. David Long and Ibrahim Oweiss, as quoted in Dreyfuss, "The Thirty-Year Itch."

50. Naomi Klein, "Baghdad Year Zero," *Harper's Magazine*, September 2004, www.harpers.org/BaghdadYearZero.html (accessed March 26, 2007).

51. "Bechtel Finishes US$2.3 Billion Iraq Job, Mourning 52 Dead," *Associated Press*, November 3, 2006, www.chinapost.com.tw/business/detail.asp?ID=94327&GRP=E (accessed March 14, 2007).

52. David R. Baker, "Bechtel Ends Iraq Rebuilding After a Rough 3 Years," *San Francisco Chronicle*, November 3, 2006, www.sfgate.com/cgi-bin/article.cgi?f=/c/a/2006/11/01/BECHTEL.TMP (accessed March 14, 2007).

CHAPTER 3

1. "Pacific Panopticon," *New Left Review*, July/August 2002, newleftreview.org/A2400 (accessed May 8, 2007).

2. Walden Bello, *Dilemmas of Domination* (New York: Metropolitan Books, 2005), p. 3.

3. See, for example, Suzy Hansen, "The Decline and Fall of the American Empire," *Salon*, December 2, 2002, dir.salon.com/story/books/int/2002/12/02/kupchan/index.html (accessed May 8, 2007); and Gore Vidal, *The Decline and Fall of the American Empire* (Maine: Common Courage Press, 2002).

4. Mark Weisbrot, "IMF and World Bank Face Declining Authority as Venezuela Announces Withdrawal," Center for Economic and Policy Research, May 1, 2007, www.cepr.net/index.php?option=com_content&task=view&id=1161&Itemid=45 (accessed May 8, 2007).

5. Alan Deutschman, "George Soros," *Salon*, March 27, 2001, archive.salon.com/people/bc/2001/03/27/soros/index.html (accessed June 8, 2007).

6. See Joseph Stiglitz, *Globalization and Its Discontents* (New York: W. W. Norton, 2002), pp. 40–41; and Walden Bello, *Dilemmas of Domination* (New York: Metropolitan Books, 2005), p. 164.

7. As cited in Bello, *Dilemmas of Domination*, p. 121; and Stiglitz, *Globalization and Its Discontents*, p. 97.

8. Stiglitz, *Globalization and Its Discontents*, p. 97.

9. Walden Bello, "Crisis of the Globalist Project and the New Economics of George W. Bush," *ZNet*, July 15, 2003, www.zmag.org/content/showarticle.cfm?ItemID=3920 (accessed May 8, 2007).

10. "Africa, Caribbean and Latin America Protest No Democracy in WTO," statement of the Ministers of Trade of Member States of the Organisation of African Unity/African Economic Community, as published by Third World Network, www.twnside.org.sg/title/deb5-cn.htm (accessed July 27, 2007).

11. Sir Shridath Ramphal, interviewed on "A Contentious Ending," *NewsHour with Jim Lehrer*, PBS, December 3, 1999, transcript available online at www.pbs.org/newshour/bb/international/july-dec99/sanger_12-3.html (accessed July 27, 2007).

12. Robert Brenner, *The Boom and the Bubble* (New York: Verso, 2002). Walden Bello notes that academics distinguish between the related terms "overproduction," "overaccumulation," and "overcapacity;" for our purposes, these will be used interchangeably.

13. Ibid., p. 8, Table 1.1, citing Organisation for Economic Co-operation and Development, *National Accounts, 1960–1997*, vol. 2 II, Detailed Tables, and *Flows and Stocks of Fixed Capital*, various issues; P. Armstrong, A. Glyn, and J. Harrison, *Capitalism Since 1945* (Oxford: Blackwell, 1991); and "Accumulation, Profits, State Spending: Data for Advanced Capitalist Countries, 1952–1983," Oxford Institute of Economics and Statistics, July 1986, updated version.

14. Brenner, *The Boom and the Bubble*, p. 47, Table 1.10, citing Organisation for Economic Co-operation and Development, *Historical Statistics, 1960–1995*, Paris, 1995, Tables 2.15, 3.1, 3.2: "Statistical Annex," *European Economy*, no. 71, 2000, Tables 11, 31, 32, and *Economic Outlook*, no. 67, 2001, Annex, Table 21; IMF, *World Economic Outlook*, Washington, D.C., May 2001, Database, Tables 1 and 4; Armstrong et al., *Capitalism Since 1945*.

15. See Bello, *Dilemmas of Domination*, p. 85. Bello provides excellent statistics on overproduction in many industries.

16. "Editorial: Could It Happen Again?" *Economist*, February 20, 1999, p. 15, as cited in Brenner, *The Boom and the Bubble*, p. 268; and Bello, *Dilemmas of Domination*, p. 85.

17. John Maynard Keynes, as quoted in Robert Pollin, "Is the Dollar Still Falling?" *CounterPunch*, October 6, 2005, www.counterpunch.org/pollin1006 2005.html (accessed May 10, 2007).

18. See Brenner, *The Boom and the Bubble*, p. 266.

19. Ibid., p. 282.

20. United States Bureau of Economic Analysis, "U.S. International Transactions: Fourth Quarter and Year 2006," March 14, 2007, www.bea.gov/newsreleases/international/transactions/transnewsrelease.htm; and Martin Crutsinger, "Bernanke Raps Economic Isolationism," Associated Press, May 1, 2007, *USA TODAY*, www.usatoday.com/money/economy/2007-05-01-1077322253_x.htm (accessed May 10, 2007).

21. Michael Steinberger, "Neo-Economics,"*American Prospect*, March 5, 2005, www.prospect.org/web/page.ww?section=root&name=ViewPrint&articleId=9207 (accessed March 13, 2007).

22. Stephen Roach, as quoted in Mark O'Byrne, "Commodities and Precious Metal Markets Weekly Analysis," *Safe Haven*, February 1, 2005, www.safehaven.com/article-2539.htm (accessed May 10, 2007). Also quoted in Steinberger, "Neo-Economics."

23. Jeffrey D. Sachs, "The Decline of America," *Project Syndicate*, March 2004, www.project-syndicate.org/commentary/sachs85 (accessed May 10, 2007).

24. Fred Kaplan, "2020 Vision," *Slate*, January 26, 2005, www.slate.com/id/2112697/ (accessed May 10, 2007).

25. Paul Kennedy, interview with Ezzat Ibrahim, "America Goes Too Far," *Al-Ahram Weekly*, 28 September–4 October 2006, Issue 814, weekly.ahram.org.eg/2006/814/intrvw.htm (accessed May 10, 2007).

26. Sydney J. Freedberg Jr., "Iraq Burden Shifts from Reserves to Regular Active Duty Troops," *National Journal*, February 16, 2005, posted at www.govexec.com/dailyfed/0207/021607nj1.htm (accessed May 10, 2007).

27. Barry McCaffrey, as quoted in Gordon Lubold, "Is US Army Bent to the Breaking Point?" *Christian Science Monitor*, April 4, 2007, www.csmonitor.com/2007/0404/p01s01-usmi.html (accessed May 17, 2007).

28. Robert Burns, "Study: Army Stretched to Breaking Point," Associated Press, January 24, 2006, www.sfgate.com/cgi-bin/article.cgi?f=/n/a/2006/01/24/national/w133017S88.DTL (accessed May 17, 2007).

29. William D. Hartung, "Bush Military Budget Highest Since WWII," *Common Dreams*, February 10, 2007, www.commondreams.org/views07/0210-26.htm (accessed May 10, 2007).

30. Chalmers Johnson, *Nemesis: The Last Days of the American Republic* (New York: Metropolitan Books, 2006), pp. 7–8.

31. Ibid., p. 138.

32. Ibid., p. 6.

33. James K. Galbraith, "The Unbearable Costs of Empire," *American Prospect*, November 18, 2002, www.prospect.org/cs/articles?article=the_unbearable_costs_of_empire (accessed May 10, 2007).

34. James K. Galbraith, "The Dollar Melts as Iraq Burns," *Guardian*, December 4, 2006, commentisfree.guardian.co.uk/james_k_galbraith/2006/12/the_dollar_melts_as_iraq_burns.html (accessed May 10, 2007).

35. Immanuel Wallerstein, "Geopolitical Cleavage of the 21st Century: What Future for the World?" lecture given at the COE International Conference, October 26, 2002, coe.asafas.kyoto-u.ac.jp/news/coe_sympo/Wallerstein2.htm (accessed May 8, 2007). See also Immanuel Wallerstein, *The Decline of American Power: The U.S. in a Chaotic World* (New York: W. W. Norton, 2003).

36. Immanuel Wallerstein, "The Eagle Has Crash Landed," *Foreign Policy*, July/August 2002, www.foreignpolicy.com/story/cms.php?story_id=2564.

37. Wallerstein, "Geopolitical Cleavage of the 21st Century."

38. "Imperial Overstretch?" *Economist*, June 29, 2002, available online through LexisNexis Academic.

39. John Cavanagh and Jerry Mander, eds., *Alternatives to Economic Globalization* (San Francisco: Berrett-Koehler, 2004), p. 10.

Chapter 4

1. James D. Wolfensohn, "Remarks at Promoting Dialogue: Global Challenges and Global Institutions," address at the annual meeting of the World Bank Group in Washington D.C., April 13, 2000, econ.worldbank.org/WBSITE/EXTERNAL/EXTDEC/EXTRESEARCH/EXTPROGRAMS/EXTTRADERESEARCH/0,,contentMDK:20035383~menuPK:64001880~pagePK:210083~piPK:152538~theSitePK:544849,00.html (accessed April 9, 2007).

2. Structural Adjustment Participatory Review International Network, "The Policy Roots of Economic Crisis and Poverty," first edition, April 2002, p. 1. Available online at www.saprin.org/SAPRI_Findings.pdf (accessed April 9, 2007).

3. Doug Hellinger, SAPRIN Secretariat, personal interview, October 10, 2002.

4. International Rivers Network, "Critics' Attempts at Constructive Dialogue Find World Bank Less Than Engaging," November 9, 2001, www.irn.org/programs/finance/pdf/011113.DGAP-IRN-release.PDF (accessed April 11, 2007).

5. As cited in SAPRIN Global Steering Committee, letter to James Wolfensohn, April 17, 2001.

6. SAPRIN, "The Policy Roots of Economic Crisis and Poverty," p. 2.

7. Ibid., p. 188.

8. Doug Hellinger, SAPRIN Secretariat, personal interview, October 10, 2002.

9. Structural Adjustment Participatory Review International Network, *Structural Adjustment: The SAPRI Report: The Policy Roots of Economic Crisis, Poverty and Inequality* (London: Zed Books, 2007). This is the book version of the report cited above.

10. SAPRIN, "The Policy Roots of Economic Crisis and Poverty," p. 173.

11. Ibid., p. 68.

12. Ibid., p. 125.

13. Ibid., p. 84.

14. Ibid., p. 158.

15. David Jonstad, "World Bank Policies a Fiasco," *Dagens Nyheter*, April 10, 2002, translated by Ann-Kathrin Schneider and John Y. Jones of SAPRIN.

16. Ibid.

17. SAPRIN Global Steering Committee, letter to James Wolfensohn, April 17, 2001.

18. Ibid.

19. Iván Cisneros, as quoted in Structural Adjustment Participatory Review International Network, "World Bank Stays Destructive Course Despite Contrary Findings of Joint Initiative," August 1, 2001.

20. World Bank, "Adjustment from Within: Lessons from the Structural Adjustment Participatory Review Initiative," July 2001, www.worldbank.org/research/sapri/WB_SAPRI_Report.pdf (accessed April 9, 2007).

21. Ibid., p. 15.

22. Lidy Nacpil, as quoted in SAPRIN, "World Bank Stays Destructive Course."

23. Doug Hellinger, SAPRIN Secretariat, personal interview, January 5, 2004.

24. Patrick McCully, as quoted in International Rivers Network, "Critics' Attempts at Constructive Dialogue Find World Bank Less Than Engaging," November 9, 2001, www.irn.org/programs/finance/pdf/011113.DGAP-IRN-release.PDF (accessed April 11, 2007).

25. Halifax Initiative, "Activists from 5 Countries Say Dialogue with the World Bank Has Been as Ineffective as Their Programs," November 16, 2001, www.halifax initiative.org/hi.php/general/240 (accessed October 8, 2002).

26. International Monetary Fund, "Poverty Reduction Strategy Papers (PRSP)," www.imf.org/external/np/prsp/prsp.asp. This Web site contains downloadable copies of PRSPs by country.

27. As quoted in Jubilee South, Focus on the Global South, AWEPON, and the Centro de Estudios Internacionales, "The World Bank and the PRSP: Flawed Thinking and Failing Experiences," November 16, 2001, www.focusweb.org/publica tions/2001/THE-WORLD-BANK-AND-THE-PRSP.html (accessed May 18, 2007).

28. Jubilee South et al., "The World Bank and the PRSP."

29. Independent Evaluation Office of the International Monetary Fund, "The IMF and Aid to Sub-Saharan Africa," 2007, p. vii, www.imf.org/external/np/ico/2007/ssang/pdf/report.pdf (accessed May 18, 2007).

30. Ibid., p. vii, as quoted in Soren Ambrose, "IMF Confidence Crisis," Foreign Policy in Focus, April 12, 2007, www.fpif.org/fpiftxt/4145 (accessed May 18, 2007).

31. World Bank Group, "Doing Business 2007: How to Reform—An Overview," September 6, 2006, www.doingbusiness.org/documents/DoingBusiness2007 _Overview.pdf (accessed April 11, 2007).

32. Senators Richard J. Durbin, Joseph R. Biden Jr., Byron L. Dorgan, Christopher Dodd, Paul S. Sarbanes, and Daniel K. Akaka, letter to Paul Wolfowitz, October 13, 2006, www.50years.org/cms/updates/story/342 (accessed April 11, 2007).

33. Shefali Sharma, as quoted in Elizabeth Becker, "WTO Fears Bush Go-It-Alone Role," New York Times, March 17, 2003, www.tradeobservatory.org/head lines.cfm?refID=18094 (accessed April 4, 2007).

34. Tom Barry, "U.S. Isn't 'Stingy,' It's Strategic," International Relations Center, January 7, 2005, www.irc-online.org/content/commentary/2005/0501aid.php (accessed April 4, 2007).

35. Raymond C. Offenheiser, press release for OXFAM America, "Needs of Poor, Not Politics, Should Drive Reform of US Foreign Aid," January 19, 2006, www.oxfamamerica.org/newsandpublications/press_releases/foreignaid (accessed April 4, 2007).

36. George Monbiot, "I'm with Wolfowitz," *Guardian*, April 5, 2005, www.guardian.co.uk/comment/story/0,3604,1452430,00.html (accessed April 4, 2007).

37. Adam Lerrick, "Forgive the World Bank but Don't Forget," American Enterprise Institute, February 6, 2006, www.aei.org/publications/filter.all,pubID.23836/pub_detail.asp (accessed April 4, 2007).

38. Adam Lerrick, "Why Is the World Bank Still Lending?" American Enterprise Institute, November 9, 2005, www.aei.org/publications/pubID.23440/pub_detail.asp (accessed April 4, 2007).

39. Report of the International Financial Institutions Advisory Commission, March 2000, www.house.gov/jec/imf/meltzer.htm (accessed April 9, 2007).

40. Jessica Einhorn, "Reforming the World Bank," *Foreign Affairs*, January/February 2006, as reprinted by the *New York Times*, www.nytimes.com/cfr/international/20060101facomment_v85n1_einhorn.hl (accessed April 4, 2007).

41. Lawrence Summers, as quoted in Lerrick, "Forgive the World Bank but Don't Forget."

42. Lawrence Summers, "The Troubling Aspects of IMF Reform," *Financial Times*, March 23, 2000, available online through LexisNexis Academic.

43. Sebastian Mallaby, "Saving the World Bank," *Foreign Affairs*, May/June 2005, www.foreignaffairs.org/20050501faessay84308/sebastian-mallaby/saving-the-world-bank.html (accessed April 11, 2007).

44. Sarah Anderson, "IMF: Reform, Downsize, or Abolish," Foreign Policy in Focus, September 2000, www.fpif.org/briefs/vol5/v5n32imf.html (accessed April 11, 2007).

45. Mark Weisbrot, "The IMF at 63—An Early Retirement?" Center for Economic and Policy Research, April 4, 2007, www.cepr.net/index.php?option=com_content&task=view&id=1108&Itemid=45 (accessed May 18, 2007).

46. Adam Lerrick, "What's Left for the IMF?" American Enterprise Institute, April 13, 2007, www.aei.org/publications/filter.all,pubID.25952/pub_detail.asp (accessed May 18, 2007).

47. Christopher Swann, "Chavez Exploits Oil to Lend in Latin America, Pushing IMF Aside," *Bloomberg*, February 28, 2007, www.bloomberg.com/apps/news?pid=20601086&sid=atN8OPWGA4nE&refer=news (accessed May 18, 2007); and Lerrick, "What's Left for the IMF?"

48. "IMF Faces Deficit, Doubts on Role as Brazil, Argentina Pay Debt," *Bloomberg*, February 2, 2006, www.cbonds.info/eng/news/index.phtml/params/id/332077 (accessed May 4, 2007).

49. David E. Sanger, "Wolfowitz Fight Has Subplot," *New York Times*, April 14, 2007, www.nytimes.com/2007/04/14/washington/14assess.html (accessed May 18, 2007).

50. Philippe Naughton, "Britain Splits with World Bank Hawks over Aid Conditions," *Times Online*, September 14, 2006, www.timesonline.co.uk/article/0,,3-2357572,00.html (accessed April 11, 2007). See also "UK Withholds World Bank Donation," *BBC News*, September 14, 2006, news.bbc.co.uk/2/hi/business/5344752.stm (accessed April 11, 2007).

51. Sebastian Mallaby, "Endgame at the World Bank," *Washington Post*, May 14, 2007, www.washingtonpost.com/wp-dyn/content/article/2007/05/13/AR2007051301122.html (accessed May 18, 2007).

52. Bradford Plumer, "Is Bob Zoellick the Next Paul Wolfowitz?" *New Republic*, June 8, 2007, www.tnr.com/user/nregi.mhtml?i=20070618&s=plumer061807 (accessed June 8, 2007).

CHAPTER 5

1. Isaac Rojas, interview with Nadia Martinez, June 26, 2003. See Mark Engler and Nadia Martinez, "True Gold of Our Future," *New Internationalist*, October 2003, www.democracyuprising.com/articles/2003/true_gold.php (accessed July 12, 2007).

2. Enrique Joseph, interview with Nadia Martinez, June 29, 2003. See Engler and Martinez, "True Gold of Our Future."

3. "Bush's Former Oil Firm Threatens Sea Turtles," Environmental News Network, April 10, 2001, www.forests.org/archive/samerica/bufooilf.htm (accessed June 14, 2007).

4. Isaac Rojas, interview with Nadia Martinez, June 26, 2003.

5. Enrique Joseph, interview with Nadia Martinez, June 29, 2003.

6. Isaac Rojas, interview with Nadia Martinez, June 26, 2003.

7. Ibid.

8. Jacob Scherr, as quoted in Sam Martin, "No Rigs Allowed," *OnEarth*, Fall 2002, vol. 4, no. 3, p. 46, available online through ProQuest.

9. Enrique Joseph, interview with Nadia Martinez, June 29, 2003.

10. President of the Republic of Costa Rica, Dr. Abel Pacheco, inaugural address, May 8th, 2002, www.guariadeosa.com/cr_president.htm (accessed June 14, 2007).

11. Enrique Joseph, interview with Nadia Martinez, June 29, 2003.

12. "Oil Company Drops Claim Against Costa Rica," Associated Press Worldstream, October 4, 2003, available online through LexisNexis Academic.

13. "Costa Rica Data Profile," World Bank World Development Indicators database, April 2007, devdata.worldbank.org/external/CPProfile.asp?PTYPE=CP&CCODE=CRI (accessed June 15, 2007).

14. Robert Collier and Glen Martin, "Canadian Firm Sues California Over MTBE," *San Francisco Chronicle*, June 18, 1999, www.sfgate.com/cgi-bin/

article.cgi?file=/chronicle/archive/1999/06/18/MN12059.DTL (accessed June 15, 2007).

15. Joseph Stiglitz, *Making Globalization Work* (New York: W. W. Norton, 2006), pp. 130–131.

16. Ibid., p. 197.

17. Lori Wallach, personal interview, March 11, 2004.

18. Jonathan Weisman, "U.S. Pushing for Trade Pact; Deal Would Expand NAFTA Through Central America," *Washington Post*, December 10, 2003, available online through LexisNexis Academic.

19. "New Guatemalan Law and Intellectual Property Provisions in DR-CAFTA Threaten Access to Affordable Medicines," *Médecins Sans Frontières*, March 11, 2005, www.msf.org/msfinternational/invoke.cfm?objectid=4304665C-E018-0C72 -09E4428F1E91FB09&component=toolkit.article&method=full_html (accessed June 16, 2007).

20. "Fact Sheet: U.S.–Central America Free Trade Agreement," The White House, Office of the Press Secretary, January 16, 2002, www.whitehouse.gov/news/ releases/2002/01/20020116-11.html (accessed June 16, 2007).

21. Bruce Stokes, "A Victory Yes, but for How Long?" *National Journal*, August 3, 2002, www.tradeobservatory.org/headlines.cfm?refID=17573 (accessed June 16, 2007).

22. John Fund, "Republican Rot," *Wall Street Journal*, February 9, 2004, www.opinionjournal.com/diary/?id=110004664 (accessed June 16, 2007). See also Judy Sarasohn, "Tauzin to Head Drug Trade Group," *Washington Post*, December 16, 2004, www.washingtonpost.com/wp-dyn/articles/A3504-2004Dec15.html (accessed June 16, 2007).

23. Matt Stearns, "4 for Free Trade Balk at CAFTA," *Kansas City Star*, June 30, 2005, p. C1.

24. "Bond: Water Resources Bill Long Overdue," from the Web site of Senator Kit Bond, May 16, 2007, bond.senate.gov/wrd7.cfm (accessed June 16, 2007). See also Richard S. Dunham, "The Doubtful Deals Driving CAFTA," *Business Week*, August 1, 2005, www.businessweek.com/magazine/content/05_31/c3945055_mz013.htm (accessed June 16, 2007).

25. "Dangerous CAFTA Liaisons," Public Citizen's Global Trade Watch, February 14, 2006, www.citizen.org/documents/CAFTA_Liaisons_Report.pdf (accessed June 16, 2007).

26. Todd Tucker, "New Year Sees Delay in CAFTA Implementation," International Relations Center, January 5, 2006, www.tradewatch.org/documents/0601 caftadelay%5B1%5D.pdf (accessed June 16, 2007).

27. "Statement by the Press Secretary," The White House, Office of the Press Secretary, Washington, D.C., September 14, 1993, as cited in Jeff Faux, *The Global Class War* (Hoboken, NJ: John Wiley & Sons, 2006), p. 33.

28. Faux, *The Global Class War*, p. 130.

29. Kate Bronfenbrenner, "The Effects of Plant Closings and the Threat of Plant Closings on Worker Rights to Organize," supplement to *Plant Closings and Worker Rights: A Report to the Council of Ministers by the Secretariat of the Commission for Labor Cooperation* (Chicago: Berman Press, 1993), p. 17, www.ilr.cornell.edu/library/downloads/keyWorkplaceDocuments/ReportonPlantClosing.pdf, as cited in Jeff Faux, *The Global Class War*, p. 131.

30. Faux, *The Global Class War*, p. 131.

31. Stiglitz, *Making Globalization Work*, p. 64.

32. John Lyons, "In Mexican Race, 'Wal-Mart' Voters May Hold the Key," *Wall Street Journal*, June 7, 2006, p. A1, available online through LexisNexis Academic.

33. Peter S. Goodman, "In Mexico, 'People Do Really Want to Stay'," *Washington Post*, January 7, 2007, www.washingtonpost.com/wp-dyn/content/article/2007/01/06/AR2007010601265_pf.html (accessed June 22, 2007).

34. Ana Corbacho and Gerd Schwartz, "Mexico: Experiences with Pro-Poor Expenditure Policies," IMF Working Paper, January 2002, www.imf.org/external/pubs/ft/wp/2002/wp0212.pdf (accessed June 22, 2007).

35. David Bacon, "Cananea and Han Young: Labor Resistance at the Border," Information Services Latin America, March 22, 1999, isla.igc.org/Features/Border/mex1.html (accessed June 21, 2007).

36. David Bacon, *The Children of NAFTA* (Berkeley: University of California Press, 2004), p. 181.

37. David Bacon, "Up for Grabs," *New Internationalist*, December 2004, www.newint.org/features/2004/12/01/mexico-labour-rights/ (accessed June 21, 2007).

38. Bacon, *The Children of NAFTA*, p. 201.

39. Ibid., p. 202.

40. Ibid., p. 204.

41. Ibid., p. 39.

42. "Fact Sheet: U.S.–Central America Free Trade Agreement."

43. Judith Sunderland, "From the Household to the Factory: Sex Discrimination in the Guatemalan Labor Force," Human Rights Watch, January 2002, hrw.org/reports/2002/guat/index.htm (accessed June 22, 2007).

44. Thea Lee, personal interview, December 18, 2003.

45. Public Citizen, "Election 2006: No to Staying the Course on Trade," November 17, 2006, www.citizen.org/documents/Election2006.pdf (accessed April 27, 2007).

46. Jane Bussey, "Democrats Won Big by Opposing Free-Trade Agreements," *Miami Herald*, November 20, 2006, www.miami.com/mld/miamiherald/16042179.htm (accessed November 2006).

47. Steven R. Weisman, "G.O.P. House Leaders Withdraw Vietnam Trade Bill," November 15, 2006, www.nytimes.com/2006/11/15/business/15trade.html (accessed April 27, 2007).

CHAPTER 6

1. United Nations Conference on Trade and Development (UNCTAD), "UNCTAD and WTO: A Common Goal in a Global Economy," press release, August 10, 1996, www.unctad.org/Templates/webflyer.asp?docid=3607&intItemID=2298&lang=1&print=1 (accessed June 15, 2007).

2. As quoted in Duncan Green, "Not Yet at the Crematorium," *Guardian*, July 26, 2006, business.guardian.co.uk/story/0,,1830101,00.html (accessed February 28, 2007).

3. See Richard Waddington, "Failed Cancun Talks Throw Up New Trade Power," Reuters, September 15, 2003, www.forbes.com/newswire/2003/09/15/rtr1081197.html (accessed June 22, 2007). See also, Soren Ambrose, "The WTO Stalemate," *Z Magazine*, November 2003, zmagsite.zmag.org/Nov2003/ambrose1103.html (accessed June 21, 2007).

4. Ralph Nader and Lori Wallach, "GATT, NAFTA, and the Subversion of the Democratic Process," in Jerry Mander and Edward Goldsmith, eds., *The Case Against the Global Economy* (San Francisco: Sierra Club Books, 1996), pp. 92–107. See also Michael Kranish, "Kantor Sees a Comfortable Win for GATT," *Boston Globe*, December 1, 1994, available online through LexisNexis Academic, as cited in Jeff Faux, *The Global Class War* (Hoboken, NJ: John Wiley & Sons, 2006), p. 160.

5. Emad Mekay, "Free Marketeers Have a Plan for Iraq," Inter Press Service, April 30, 2003, www.atimes.com/atimes/Middle_East/ED30Ak02.html (accessed June 29, 2007).

6. Russell Mokhiber and Robert Weissman, "Corporate Panhandling in Seattle," *Mother Jones*, October 28, 1999, www.motherjones.com/news/feature/1999/10/fotc8.html?welcome=true (accessed June 21, 2007).

7. Heather Stewart, "How Europe Cheats Africa," *Observer*, June 19, 2005, observer.guardian.co.uk/business/story/0,6903,1509560,00.html (accessed June 21, 2007).

8. Lee Kyung Hae, as cited in Laura Carlsen, "'The WTO Kills Farmers': In Memory of Lee Kyung Hae," International Relations Center, September 11, 2003, americas.irc-online.org/columns/amprog/2003/0309lee.html (accessed July 12, 2007).

9. Doug Henwood, "Collapse in Cancun," *Nation*, October 10, 2003, www.thenation.com/doc/20031027/henwood (accessed July 12, 2007). Henwood offers a contrary perspective on the issue, specifically with regard to South Korea and Lee Kyung Hae's death:

One of the [G20+] demands was that richer countries reduce their domestic farm subsidies and open up to [G20+] agricultural exports. At the same time, farmers in South Korea, a relatively rich country, were among the most vigorous of the protesters, with some activists praising the suicide of Lee Kyung-hae, who raised cattle on a small, snowy mountain plot. The only thing that kept the farm going was trade barriers; once Seoul opened up to Australian beef imports, the enterprise was doomed. Rice and other crops are grown on similarly difficult land; crops are expensive and often of low quality. Only vigorous protection makes such agriculture viable. But those are exactly the kinds of barriers the [G20+] want dismantled. . . . Which raises a question: What is progressive about using public resources to support farming on cold, snowy, mountainous land? Isn't the benefit of trade exactly to address something like this? South Korea isn't an impoverished country whose population is dominated by a peasantry that would be ruined by opening up to food imports—it makes cars and cell phones. Why shouldn't South Korea import food?

10. Walden Bello, *Dilemmas of Domination* (New York: Metropolitan Books, 2005), p. 161.

11. "Much Wind and Little Light," *Economist*, October 18, 2003, available online through LexisNexis Academic.

12. Alejandro Landes, "Venezuela Unfazed by Omission in U.S. Talks," *Miami Herald*, November 21, 2003, p. 28A.

13. Kieran Murray, "Bush Told U.S.-Imposed Policies Are 'Perverse,'" Reuters, January 13, 2004, www.commondreams.org/headlines04/0113-05.htm (accessed June 22, 2007).

14. Lisa J. Adams, "Bush Tries to Sell Americas Leaders on Free Trade, But Several Latin American Nations Not Buying," Associated Press, January 13, 2004, available online through LexisNexis Academic.

15. Sebastian Mallaby, "Why Globalization Has Stalled," *Washington Post*, April 24, 2006, www.washingtonpost.com/wp-dyn/content/article/2006/04/23/AR20060 42301016.html (accessed June 21, 2007).

16. "Talks Suspended. 'Today There Are Only Losers,'" WTO News, July 2006, www.wto.org/english/news_e/news06_e/mod06_summary_24july_e.htm (accessed June 22, 2007).

17. Brian Kenety, "Trade Restrictions Cost World's Poor 2.5 Billion Dollars Each Year," Inter Press Service, May 14, 2001, www.commondreams.org/head lines01/0514-01.htm (accessed June 22, 2007).

18. Kevin Watkins, Penny Fowler et al., "Rigged Rules and Double Standards," Oxfam report, April 2002, www.marketradefair.com/assets/english/report _english.pdf (accessed April 27, 2007).

19. Ibid., p. 7.

20. Walden Bello, "The Oxfam Debate: From Controversy to Common Strategy," Focus on the Global South, May 2002, www.focusweb.org/publications/2002/oxfam-debate-controversy-to-common-strategy.html (accessed April 27, 2007).

21. Belinda Coote, *The Trade Trap: Poverty and the Global Commodity Markets* (Oxford: Oxfam, 1992), pp. 1–16, as cited in Jessica Roach, *Agricultural Trade Liberalization: A Path Out of Poverty for the Rural Poor?* unpublished manuscript, April 2005.

22. Nancy Birdsall, Dani Rodrik, and Arvind Subramanian, "How to Help Poor Countries," *Foreign Affairs*, July/August 2005, www.foreignaffairs.org/20050701faessay84410/nancy-birdsall-dani-rodrik-arvind-subramanian/how-to-help-poor-countries.html (accessed April 27, 2007).

23. Mark Weisbrot, "World Bank's Claims on WTO Doha Round Clarified," Center for Economic and Policy Research, November 22, 2005, www.cepr.net/index.php?option=com_content&task=view&id=222&Itemid=77 (accessed June 29, 2007); and Mark Weisbrot, "Costs of WTO 'Development Round' Could Outweigh Benefits for Developing Countries," Center for Economic and Policy Research, December 15, 2005, www.cepr.net/index.php?option=com_content&task=view&id=201&Itemid=77 (accessed July 27, 2007). See also, Will Martin and Kym Anderson, "Agricultural Trade Reform and the Doha Development Agenda," World Bank Group, go.worldbank.org/PSIFOL9Q80 (accessed June 29, 2007).

24. Ibid.

25. Lori M. Wallach, "Indefinite Suspension of Doha Round WTO Expansion Negotiations Creates Opportunity to Rethink Current Global 'Trade' System," Public Citizen/Global Trade Watch, July 24, 2006, www.citizen.org/hot_issues/issue.cfm?ID=1413 (accessed April 27, 2007).

26. Celso Amorim, as quoted in Bernard Gordon, "Doha Aground," *Wall Street Journal*, July 26, 2006, Section A, Column 3, p. 14.

27. George Monbiot, "I Was Wrong About Trade," *Guardian*, June 24, 2003, www.guardian.co.uk/globalisation/story/0,7369,983684,00.html (accessed April 27, 2007).

28. Ibid.

29. Terrence McNally, interview with Joseph Stiglitz, "Globalization Has Increased the Wealth Gap," *AlterNet*, January 15, 2007, www.alternet.org/story/45833/ (accessed June 22, 2007).

30. Monbiot, "I Was Wrong About Trade."

Chapter 7

1. Alan Greenspan, speech at the Annual Dinner and Francis Boyer Lecture of the American Enterprise Institute for Public Policy Research, Washington, D.C., De-

cember 5, 1996, www.federalreserve.gov/boarddocs/speeches/1996/19961205.htm (accessed May 31, 2007).

2. Thomas Friedman, *The Lexus and the Olive Tree: Understanding Globalization* (New York: Anchor Books, 2000), p. 367.

3. Ibid., p. 9.

4. Ibid.

5. Ibid., p. 375.

6. Ibid., p. xxii.

7. Ibid.

8. Thomas Friedman, "Senseless in Seattle," *New York Times*, December 1, 1999, www.nytimes.com/library/opinion/friedman/120199frie.html (accessed May 31, 2007).

9. Thomas Friedman, *The World Is Flat*, first updated and expanded edition (New York: Farrar, Straus and Giroux, 2006), p. 230.

10. Thomas Friedman, as quoted in Oliver Burkeman, "'Some Things Are True Even If George Bush Believes Them,'" *Guardian*, August 5, 2003, politics.guardian.co.uk/iraq/story/0,12956,1012490,00.html (accessed May 31, 2007).

11. Thomas Friedman, "War of Ideas, Part 5," *New York Times*, January 22, 2004, www.nytimes.com/2004/01/22/opinion/22FRIE.html (accessed May 31, 2007).

12. Burkeman, "'Some Things Are True.'"

13. Thomas Friedman, "Time for Plan B," *New York Times*, August 4, 2006, available online through LexisNexis Academic.

14. Thomas Friedman, "The Chant Not Heard," *New York Times*, November 30, 2003, www.nytimes.com/gst/fullpage.html?res=9F05E2D7123AF933A05752C1A 9659C8B63.

15. "Thomas Friedman's Flexible Deadlines," Fairness and Accuracy In Reporting, May 16, 2006, www.fair.org/index.php?page=2884.

16. Friedman, "Time for Plan B."

17. Friedman, *The World Is Flat*, p. 554.

18. Ibid., p. 9.

19. Ibid., p. 10.

20. Ibid., p. 5.

21. Matt Taibbi, "Flathead: The Peculiar Genius of Thomas L. Friedman," *New York Press*, April 27, 2005, www.nypress.com/18/16/news&columns/taibbi.cfm (accessed May 31, 2007).

22. George Orwell, "Politics and the English Language," in *A Collection of Essays* (New York: Harcourt Brace Jovanovich, 1946), pp. 156–171.

23. Friedman, *The World Is Flat*, p. 7.

24. Taibbi, "Flathead."

25. "The Lessons of Seattle," *Business Week*, December 13, 1999, Number 3658, p. 212, available online through LexisNexis Academic.

26. Friedman, *The Lexus and the Olive Tree*, pp. 452–453.

27. Ibid., p. 160.

28. Ibid., p. 105.

29. Ibid., p. 106.

30. Thomas Friedman, "Senseless in Seattle II," *New York Times*, December 8, 1999, www.nytimes.com/library/opinion/friedman/120899frie.html (accessed June 1, 2007).

31. Thomas Friedman, *The World Is Flat* (New York: Farrar, Straus and Giroux, 2005), p. 248, as quoted in Robin Broad and John Cavanagh, "The Hijacking of the Development Debate: How Friedman and Sachs Got It Wrong," *World Policy Journal*, Summer 2006, p. 25, www.ifg.org/pdf/Broad%20Cavanagh.pdf (accessed June 1, 2007). Note: This citation refers to the first edition of *The World Is Flat*, not "Release 2.0," the first updated and expanded edition.

32. See David Sirota, "Caught on Tape: Tom Friedman's Truly Shocking Admission," *SirotaBlog*, July 24, 2006, davidsirota.com/index.php/2006/07/24/caught-on -tape-tom-friedmans-truly-shocking-admission/ (accessed June 1, 2007).

33. World Institute for Development Economics Research, "Pioneering Study Shows Richest Two Percent Own Half World Wealth," December 5, 2006, www.wider.unu.edu/research/2006-2007/2006-2007-1/wider-wdhw-launch-5-12 -2006/wider-wdhw-press-release-5-12-2006.pdf (accessed June 8, 2007).

34. United Nations Development Program, *Human Development Report 2003*, hdr.undp.org/reports/global/2003 (accessed February 28, 2007). See also Larry Elliott, "The Lost Decade," *Guardian*, July 9, 2003, www.commondreams.org/head lines03/0709-05.htm (accessed February 28, 2007).

35. Garrett M. Graff, "Thomas Friedman Is on Top of the World," *Washingtonian*, July 2006, www.washingtonian.com/articles/mediapolitics/1673.html (accessed June 1, 2007), as cited in David Sirota, "Billionaire Scion Tom Friedman," *DailyKos*, July 31, 2006, www.dailykos.com/story/2006/7/3121447/985 (accessed June 1, 2007).

36. Ibid.

37. Friedman, *The Lexus and the Olive Tree*, p. 26.

38. Roger Lowenstein, "The Inequality Conundrum," *New York Times Magazine*, June 10, 2007, select.nytimes.com/gst/abstract.html?res=FA0D1EF93A540C738 DDDAF0894DF404482 (accessed July 12, 2007).

39. Vandana Shiva, "The Polarised World Of Globalisation," *ZNet*, May 27, 2005, www.zmag.org/Sustainers/Content/2005-05/27shiva.cfm (accessed June 1, 2007).

40. Friedman, *The Lexus and the Olive Tree*, p. 373.

41. Ibid., p. 372.

42. Thomas Friedman, "A Race to the Top," *New York Times*, June 3, 2005, www.nytimes.com/2005/06/03/opinion/03friedman.html (accessed June 1, 2007).

43. Friedman, *The World Is Flat*, p. 354.

44. Friedman, *The Lexus and the Olive Tree*, p. 352.

45. Friedman, *The World Is Flat*, p. 426.

46. Ibid., p. 11.

47. Friedman, *The Lexus and the Olive Tree*, p. 342.

48. Friedman, *The World Is Flat*, p. 472.

49. Friedman, *The Lexus and the Olive Tree*, p. 335.

50. Jeremy Brecher, Tim Costello, and Brendan Smith, *Globalization from Below: The Power of Solidarity* (Cambridge: South End Press, 2000), p. 105.

51. Taibbi, "Flathead."

52. Joseph Stiglitz, "What I Learned at the World Economic Crisis," *New Republic*, April 17, 2000, p. 56, available online through LexisNexis Academic.

53. Jonathan Chait, "Shoeless Joe Stiglitz," *American Prospect*, July/August 1999, www.prospect.org/print/V10/45/chait-j.html (accessed April 16, 2007).

54. Ha-Joon Chang, *Joseph Stiglitz and the World Bank: The Rebel Within* (London: Anthem Press, 2001).

55. Joseph Stiglitz, "More Instruments and Broader Goals: Moving Toward the Post–Washington Consensus," address at the 1998 WIDER Annual Lecture, Helsinki, Finland, January 7, 1998, www.globalpolicy.org/socecon/bwi-wto/stig.htm (accessed April 16, 2007). Reprinted as Chapter 1 in Ha-Joon Chang, *Joseph Stiglitz and the World Bank: The Rebel Within*.

56. Ha-Joon Chang, "The Stiglitz Contribution," *Challenge*, March/April 2002, p. 86, available online through EBSCOhost Business Source Premier.

57. Doug Henwood, "Stiglitz and the Limits of 'Reform,'" *Nation*, September 27, 2000, www.thenation.com/docprem.mhtml?i=20001002&s=henwood (accessed April 16, 2007).

58. Ibid.

59. Robert Wade, "Showdown at the World Bank," *New Left Review*, January/February 2001, newleftreview.org/?view=2305 (accessed June 1, 2007).

60. Julia Llewellyn, "The Front Line: A Beautiful Mind at the Barricades," *Financial Times*, July 13, 2002, search.ft.com/ftArticle?queryText=Brockovich&id=020713000271 (accessed April 16, 2007).

61. Stiglitz, "What I Learned at the World Economic Crisis."

62. Joseph Stiglitz, *Globalization and Its Discontents* (New York: W. W. Norton, 2002), pp. ix–x.

63. Ha-Joon Chang, "The Stiglitz Contribution," p. 78.

64. Joseph Stiglitz, *Making Globalization Work* (New York: W. W. Norton, 2006), p. xiv.

65. Stiglitz, *Globalization and Its Discontents*, p. ix.

66. Ibid., p. 18.

67. Ibid., p. 73.

68. Ibid., p. xiii.

69. Ibid., p. 90.

70. Ibid., p. 91.

71. Ibid., p. 93.

72. Ibid., p. 18.

73. Benjamin M. Friedman, "Globalization: Stiglitz's Case," *New York Review of Books*, August 15, 2002, vol. 49, no. 13, www.nybooks.com/articles/15630 (accessed April 16, 2007).

74. Joseph Stiglitz and Andrew Charlton, *Fair Trade for All* (Oxford: Oxford University Press, 2005).

75. Stiglitz, *Making Globalization Work*, p. 4.

76. Ibid., p. 181.

77. Ibid., p. 101.

78. Ibid., p. 4.

79. Stiglitz, *Globalization and Its Discontents*, p. 208.

80. Ha-Joon Chang, "The Stiglitz Contribution," p. 91.

81. Stiglitz, *Globalization and Its Discontents*, p. 225.

82. Stiglitz, *Making Globalization Work*, p. 13.

CHAPTER 8

1. United Nations Development Program, *Human Development Report 2005*, hdr.undp.org/reports/global/2005/ (accessed July 19, 2007).

2. Tam Dalyell and Amartya Sen, "Obituary: Mahbub ul Haq," *Independent*, August 3, 1998, available online through LexisNexis Academic.

3. Ibid.

4. Senator Robert F. Kennedy, speech at the University of Kansas, March 18, 1968, available online through the John F. Kennedy Presidential Library and Museum, www.jfklibrary.org/Historical+Resources/Archives/Reference+Desk/Speeches/ RFK/RFKSpeech68Mar18UKansas.htm (accessed July 19, 2007).

5. United Nations Development Program, "Forward," *Human Development Report 1990*, p. iii, hdr.undp.org/reports/global/1990/en/ (accessed July 19, 2007).

6. Ibid.

7. Amartya Sen, "Special Contribution: Assessing Human Development," in United Nations Development Program, *Human Development Report 1999*, p. 23, hdr.undp.org/reports/global/1999/en/ (accessed July 19, 2007).

8. Ibid.

9. Meghnad Desai, "A New View of the Third World; Obituary; Mahbub ul Haq," *Guardian*, July 23, 1998, available online through LexisNexis Academic.

10. Barbara Crossette, "Kofi Annan's Astonishing Facts," *New York Times*, September 27, 1998, available online through LexisNexis Academic.

11. United Nations Development Program, press release, May 25, 1993, as reprinted in the *American Journal of Economics and Sociology*, October 1993, find articles.com/p/articles/mi_m0254/is_n4_v52/ai_14558042 (accessed July 20, 2007).

12. United Nations Development Program, *Human Development Report 1995*, hdr.undp.org/reports/global/1995/en/ (accessed July 19, 2007).

13. Larry Elliott, "The Lost Decade," *Guardian*, July 9, 2003, www.common dreams.org/headlines03/0709-05.htm (accessed February 28, 2007).

14. "UNDP Slams Washington Consensus; Lists 54 Countries Losing Ground," Associated Press, July 8, 2003, www.50years.org/cms/updates/story/26 (accessed July 19, 2007).

15. Mahbub ul Haq, *Reflections on Human Development* (Oxford: Oxford University Press, 1998), p. 229.

16. Ibid., p. 228.

17. Naomi Klein, "The Vision Thing," *Nation*, June 22, 2000, www.thenation.com/doc/20000710/klein (accessed July 19, 2007).

18. Ibid.

19. Ibid.

20. Edward Gresser, "Anti-Globalization Movement Grinds to a Halt," *Straits Times*, January 18, 2002, www.ppionline.org/ppi_ci.cfm?knlgAreaID=108&subse cID=206&contentID=250139 (accessed July 19, 2007).

21. Gianpaolo Baiocchi, "The Citizens of Porto Alegre," *Boston Review*, March/April 2006, bostonreview.net/BR31.2/baiocchi.html (accessed July 19, 2007).

22. "Background of the WSF Process," World Social Forum, August 30, 2006, www.forumsocialmundial.org.br/main.php?id_menu=2&cd_language=2 (accessed July 20, 2007).

23. Senator Feingold has made this accusation repeatedly, including in a speech at San Francisco's Commonwealth Club on March 12, 2001. A transcript is available online at www.commonwealthclub.org/archive/01/01-03mccain-feingold-speech.html (accessed July 19, 2007).

24. See John Cavanagh and Jerry Mander, eds., *Alternatives to Economic Globalization* (San Francisco: Berrett-Koehler, 2004), p. 277. See also the Web site of the Program on Corporations, Law, and Democracy, www.poclad.org/ (accessed July 19, 2007).

25. Cavanagh and Mander, eds., *Alternatives to Economic Globalization*, p. 191.

26. David Moberg, "On the Attac," *In These Times*, May 14, 2001, www.inthese times.com/article/1516/ (accessed July 19, 2007). For more information on the Tobin Tax, including a bibliography of relevant publications, see the Web site of the Tobin Tax Initiative, www.ceedweb.org/iirp/ (accessed July 20, 2007).

27. See Women's International Coalition for Economic Justice, "Critical Moments, Signs of Resistance and Evolving Strategies," Statement at the third World Social Forum, Porto Alegre, Brazil, January 2003, www.wicej.addr.com/portoale gre.html (accessed July 19, 2007).

28. Marie Trigona, "Recuperated Enterprises in Argentina: Reversing the Logic of Capitalism," International Relations Center, March 17, 2006, americas.irc -online.org/am/3158 (accessed July 19, 2007).

29. Cavanagh and Mander, eds., *Alternatives to Economic Globalization;* and Jeremy Brecher, Tim Costello, and Brendan Smith, *Globalization from Below: The Power of Solidarity* (Cambridge: South End Press, 2000).

30. House Resolution 479, submitted by Bernie Sanders on April 13, 2000, Global Sustainable Development Resolution, available online at thomas.loc.gov/cgi -bin/query/z?c106:h.res.479: (accessed July 20, 2007). As cited in Brecher, Costello, and Smith, *Globalization from Below,* p. 67. See also Jeremy Brecher and Brendan Smith, "The Global Sustainable Development Resolution," Foreign Policy in Focus, April 1999, www.fpif.org/briefs/vol4/v4n12gsdr.html (accessed July 20, 2007). For information on the HOPE for Africa Act, see Jesse Jackson Jr., "HOPE for Africa," *Nation,* February 25, 1999, www.thenation.com/doc/19990315/jackson (accessed July 20, 2007). For the full text of the bill, see thomas.loc.gov/cgi-bin/query/ z?c106:H.R.772: (accessed July 20, 2007).

31. Debra Anthony and José Antônio Silva, "The Consensus of Porto Alegre?" Inter Press Service, January 30, 2005, www.globalpolicy.org/ngos/advocacy/ conf/2005/0130wsfconsensus.htm (accessed July 19, 2007).

32. Lawrence Lessig, "Different Worlds," *Lessig 2.0,* January 28, 2005, lessig.org/blog/2005/01/different_worlds.html (accessed July 19, 2007).

33. Zeynep Toufe, "A Note from WSF 2005," *ZNet,* January 29, 2005, www.zmag.org/content/showarticle.cfm?ItemID=7132 (accessed July 19, 2007).

34. Linda Sippio, personal interview, January 29, 2005.

35. "The Non-Governmental Order," *Economist,* December 11, 1999, available online through LexisNexis Academic.

36. Cavanagh and Mander, eds., *Alternatives to Economic Globalization,* p. 83.

37. Doug Henwood, *After the New Economy* (New York: New Press, 2003), p. 164.

38. Ibid., p. 183.

39. Jeremy Brecher and Tim Costello, *Global Village or Global Pillage* (Boston: South End Press, 1994), p. 171.

40. See Cavanagh and Mander, eds., *Alternatives to Economic Globalization,* p. 205.

41. Henwood, *After the New Economy,* pp. 169–170.

42. Monbiot, "I Was Wrong About Trade."

43. Ibid.

44. Patrick Bond and Walden Bello, "After the IMF and Bank Are Gone," *Left Business Observer*, November 2002, www.leftbusinessobserver.com/PostBWI.html (accessed July 25, 2007). See also Walden Bello, *Deglobalization* (New York: Zed Books, 2002), and *Dilemmas of Domination* (New York: Metropolitan Books, 2005).

45. See Cavanagh and Mander, eds., *Alternatives to Economic Globalization*, pp. 139–140.

46. Ibid., p. 314.

47. Bello, *Dilemmas of Domination*, pp. 132–137.

CHAPTER 9

1. "Director-General's press statement," WTO News, November 30, 1999, www.wto.org/english/news_e/pres99_e/pr157_e.htm (accessed July 26, 2007).

2. "Africa, Caribbean and Latin America Protest No Democracy in WTO," statement of the Ministers of Trade of Member States of the Organisation of African Unity/African Economic Community, as published by Third World Network, www.twnside.org.sg/title/deb5-cn.htm (accessed July 27, 2007).

3. Thomas Friedman, "Senseless in Seattle," *New York Times*, December 1, 1999, www.nytimes.com/library/opinion/friedman/120199frie.html (accessed May 31, 2007).

4. Art Pine, "Fading Shouts—Anti-Globalization Movement," *Los Angeles Business Journal*, May 7, 2001, findarticles.com/p/artics/mi_m5072/is_19_23/ai_74654030 (accessed July 26, 2007).

5. Edward Gresser, "Anti-globalization Movement Grinds to a Halt," *Straits Times*, January 18, 2002, www.ppionline.org/ppi_ci.cfm?knlgAreaID=108&subsecID=206&contentID=250139 (accessed July 19, 2007).

6. Michael Elliott et al., "The New Radicals," *Newsweek*, December 13, 1999, p. 36, as cited in Jeremy Brecher, Tim Costello, and Brendan Smith, *Globalization from Below: The Power of Solidarity* (Cambridge: South End Press, 2000), p. 61.

7. Michael Powell and Ben White, "A Revolution in Reverse at Econ Forum," *Washington Post*, February 2, 2002, as cited in Doug Henwood, *After the New Economy* (New York: New Press, 2003), p. 177.

8. Henwood, *After the New Economy*, p. 178.

9. Joseph Stiglitz, *Making Globalization Work* (New York: W. W. Norton, 2006), pp. 5–6.

10. Joseph Stiglitz, "The Social Costs of Globalization," *Financial Times*, February 24, 2004, p. 19, available online through LexisNexis Academic.

11. Gresser, "Anti-Globalization Movement Grinds to a Halt."

12. "Angry and Effective," *Economist*, September 23, 2000, available online through LexisNexis Academic.

13. Robert Weissman, "The Enron of the Developing World," *Washington Post*, September 25, 2002, available online through LexisNexis Academic.

14. Brecher, Costello, and Smith, *Globalization from Below,* p. 29.

15. Donald G. McNeill Jr., "As Devastating Epidemics Increase, Nations Take on Drug Companies," *New York Times*, July 9, 2000, as cited in Brecher, Costello, and Smith, *Globalization from Below,* p. 29.

16. Naomi Klein, "The Vision Thing," *Nation*, June 22, 2000, www.thenation.com/doc/20000710/klein (accessed July 19, 2007).

17. See Antonia Juhasz, *The Bush Agenda: Invading the World One Economy at a Time* (New York: HarperCollins, 2006), pp. 332–334.

18. Warren Vieth, "Globalization Activists Go to Charm School," *Los Angeles Times*, September 24, 2002, www.commondreams.org/headlines02/0924-03.htm (accessed July 26, 2007).

19. For more information on the Jubilee debt coalition, see the Web sites of Jubilee South, www.jubileesouth.org/ and Jubilee USA, www.jubileeusa.org/.

20. John Cavanagh and Jerry Mander, eds., *Alternatives to Economic Globalization* (San Francisco: Berrett-Koehler, 2004), p. 57.

21. "A Silent War," Jubilee USA Network, www.jubileeusa.org/resources/debt -resources/beginners-guide-to-debt/a-silent-war.html (accessed July 26, 2007).

22. Ibid.

23. Cavanagh and Mander, eds., *Alternatives to Economic Globalization*, p. 57. See also Lydia Williams, policy advisor, Oxfam America, testimony before the U.S. House of Representatives Committee on Banking and Financial Services, on Highly Indebted Poor Countries (HIPC) Debt Relief, June 15, 1999, www.cid.har vard.edu/archive/hipc/lwilliams.html (accessed July 26, 2007).

24. Neil Watkins, National Coordinator of Jubilee USA, personal interview, March 24, 2005.

25. Ian Black, "World Leaders Shun UN's Social Summit," *Guardian*, March 6, 1995, available online through LexisNexis academic.

26. Association of Member Episcopal Conferences of Eastern Africa, "Message of the AMECEA Bishops from the 14th Plenary Assembly in Dar es Salaam, Tanzania: You Will Be My Witnesses (Acts 1:8)," July 26, 2002, available online through AME-CEA, www.amecea.org/message-14.htm (accessed May 3, 2007).

27. Pope John Paul II, "To the Group 'Jubilee 2000 Debt Campaign,'" speech in Vatican City, September 23, 1999, www.vatican.va/holy_father/john_paul_ii/ speeches/1999/september/documents/hf_jp-ii_mes_23091999_jubilee-2000-debt -campaign_en.html (accessed May 3, 2007).

28. Andreas Whittam Smith, "The Campaign for Third World Debt Relief Is Counter-Productive," *Independent*, May 19, 1998, available online through Lexis-Nexis academic.

29. Ibid.

30. Jeffrey Sachs, "Resolving the Debt Crisis of Low-Income Countries," Brookings Papers on Economic Activity, 2002, vol. 1, pp. 257–286, available online through Project MUSE, http://muse.jhu.edu/.

31. "Debt Talking Points for Activists," American Friends Service Committee, www.afsc.org/africa-debt/get-involved/debt-talking-points.htm (accessed July 26, 2007).

32. Staffs of the IMF and World Bank, "Heavily Indebted Poor Countries (HIPC) Initiative: Status of Implementation," August 20, 2004, www-wds.worldbank.org/external/default/WDSContentServer/WDSP/IB/2004/09/21/000160016_20040921094012/Rendered/PDF/298730GLB0orig.pdf (accessed May 3, 2007).

33. "30,000 Form Human Chain in a Peaceful Demonstration to Demand Debt Cancellation at WTO," Jubilee 2000 Coalition, www.jubileeresearch.org/jubilee2000/news/wto0212.html (accessed July 26, 2007).

34. Ibid.

35. President George W. Bush, "Statement on James A. Baker III," December 5, 2003, The White House, www.whitehouse.gov/news/releases/2003/12/20031205-3.html (accessed May 3, 2007).

36. As quoted in "After G-7, Britain Takes First Step Toward Debt Write-Off," International Herald Tribune, February 7, 2005, www.iht.com/articles/2005/02/06/business/g7.php (accessed May 3, 2007).

37. President George W. Bush, "President Welcomes British Prime Minister Blair to the White House," June 7, 2005, The White House, www.whitehouse.gov/news/releases/2005/06/20050607-2.html (accessed May 3, 2007).

38. Ibid.

39. Rebecca Solnit, "The Great Gray Whale" TomDispatch, July 25, 2005, www.tomdispatch.com/post/8260/rebecca_solnit_on_taking_the_measure_of_victory (accessed July 26, 2007).

40. George Monbiot, "A Truckload of Nonsense," Guardian, June 14, 2005, www.guardian.co.uk/comment/story/0,3604,1505816,00.html (accessed May 4, 2007).

41. Imani Countess, "Debt Cancellation: A National Priority," Common Dreams, January 30, 2007, www.commondreams.org/views07/0130-20.htm (accessed July 25, 2007).

42. Ibid.

43. Pablo Bachelet, "IDB OK's Massive Debt Relief Package for Five Nations," Miami Herald, www.miami.com/d/miamiherald/business/16042778.htm (accessed December 19, 2006).

44. President George W. Bush, "Statement on James A. Baker III."

45. Although this quote is often credited to Schopenhauer, the attribution cannot be verified. See Jeffrey Shallit, "They Never Said It," Skeptic, vol. 9, no. 3 (2002): 18, www.cs.uwaterloo.ca/~shallit/Letters/skeptic1.html (accessed July 25, 2007). In

a similar vein, Schopenhauer is known to have written, "To truth only a brief celebration of victory is allowed between the two long periods during which it is condemned as paradoxical, or disparaged as trivial." Mohandas Gandhi is frequently, but dubiously, credited with the version of the quote that states, "First they ignore you, then they laugh at you, then they fight you, then you win." This attribution also cannot be documented.

Chapter 10

1. Evo Morales, as quoted in Jubenal Quispe, "Evo Morales: Indigenous Power," *Yes Magazine*, Summer 2007, yesmagazine.org/article.asp?ID=1732 (accessed September 14, 2007). Original quotes in Spanish from Pablo Stefanoni and Hervé Do Alto, *La Revolución de Evo Morales: de la Coca al Palacio* (La Paz: CI Capital Intelectual, 2006).

2. Evo Morales, speech at Cooper Union, New York City, September 24, 2007.

3. Evo Morales, as quoted in Mark Weisbrot, "Latin America Shifts Left: It's the Economy," *AlterNet*, January 21, 2006, www.alternet.org/story/31056/ (accessed September 17, 2007).

4. See Greg Grandin, *Empire's Workshop* (New York: Metropolitan Books, 2006).

5. Néstor Kirchner, as quoted in Christopher Swann, "Hugo Chávez Exploits Oil Wealth to Push IMF Aside," *International Herald Tribune*, March 1, 2007, www.iht.com/articles/2007/03/01/business/imf.php (accessed June 30, 2007).

6. Notes from Nowhere, eds., *We Are Everywhere: The Irresistible Rise of Global Anti-Capitalism* (New York: Verso, 2003), p. 393.

7. See Marie Trigona, "Recuperated Enterprises in Argentina: Reversing the Logic of Capitalism," International Relations Center, March 17, 2006, americas.irc-online.org/am/3158 (accessed July 19, 2007); and Naomi Klein and Avi Lewis, "Argentina: Where Jobless Run Factories," *Nation*, July 30, 2007, www.thenation.com/doc/20070730/klein_lewis (accessed September 5, 2007).

8. Nadia Martinez, "Democracy Rising," *Yes Magazine*, Summer 2007, www.yesmagazine.org/article.asp?ID=1730 (accessed September 17, 2007).

9. Benjamin Dangl, *The Price of Fire* (Oakland: AK Press, 2007), pp. 83–84.

10. See Mark Weisbrot, "Latin America: The End of an Era," *Post-Autistic Economics Review*, No. 39, October 1, 2006, www.paecon.net/PAEReview/issue39/Weisbrot39.htm (accessed August 28, 2007).

11. "Fresh Hope for Brazil," *National Catholic Reporter*, January 24, 2003, findarticles.com/p/articles/mi_m1141/is_12_39/ai_97173600 (accessed August 28, 2007).

12. See Maria Helena Moreira Alves, "Building Democratic Socialism: The Partido Dos Trabalhadores in Brazil," *Monthly Review*, September 1990, findarticles.com/p/articles/mi_m1132/is_n4_v42/ai_9396661/pg_1 (accessed Sep-

tember 14, 2007); and Michael Lowy, "Without Fear of Being Happy: Lula, the Workers Party and Brazil," book review, *Monthly Review*, April 1992, findarticles.com/p/articles/mi_m1132/is_n11_v43/ai_12126917 (accessed September 14, 2007).

13. Mario Osava, "Brazil's New President: The Start of a New Dream," Inter Press Service, October 29, 2002, www.commondreams.org/headlines02/1029-09.htm (accessed August 28, 2007).

14. Emir Sader, "Taking Lula's Measure," *New Left Review*, May–June 2005, www.newleftreview.org/A2564 (accessed August 28, 2007).

15. Robert Lane Greene, "Real Politik," *New Republic*, October 29, 2002, www.tnr.com/doc.mhtml?i=express&s=greene102902 (accessed September 14, 2007).

16. Sader, "Taking Lula's Measure."

17. Saul Landau, "Buzz Words and Venezuela," *Progreso Weekly*, July 1, 2004, www.progresoweekly.com/index.php?progreso=Landau&otherweek=1088830800 (accessed September 14, 2007).

18. George Ciccariello-Maher, "The Legacy of Caracazo," *CounterPunch*, March 3–4, 2007, counterpunch.org/maher03032007.html (accessed August 28, 2007).

19. Becky Branford, "Analysis: Chavez at Eye of Storm," *BBC News*, August 13, 2004, news.bbc.co.uk/2/hi/americas/39668.stm (accessed August 28, 2007).

20. Mark Weisbrot, "IMF and World Bank Face Declining Authority as Venezuela Announces Withdrawal," McClatchy Tribune Information Services, May 1, 2007, www.cepr.net/dex.php?option=com_content&task=view&id=1161 (accessed August 28, 2007).

21. Sarah Anderson, Jeremy Orhan Simer, and Eva Golinger, "U.S. Role Turned Upside Down," *Yes Magazine*, Summer 2007, www.yesmagazine.org/article.asp ?ID=1738 (accessed September 14, 2007).

22. See Kevin Gray, "Uruguay Inaugurates First Leftist President," Associated Press, March 2, 2005, media.www.dailytexanonline.com/media/storage/paper410/news/2005/03/02/WorldNation/Uruguay.Inaugurates.First.Leftist.President -881974.shtml (accessed August 28, 2007).

23. Matthew Beagle, "Uruguay's Tabaré Vazquez: Pink Tide or Political Voice of the Center?" Council on Hemispheric Affairs, March 4, 2006, www.coha.org/NEW_PRESS_RELEASES/New_Press_Releases_2006/06.15_Urugua ys_Vazquez_Assessment.html (accessed September 14, 2007).

24. Larry Rohter, "Leftist Chief Is Installed in Uruguay and Gets Busy on Agenda," *New York Times*, March 2, 2005, available online through LexisNexis Academic.

25. Nadia Martinez, "Adios, World Bank!" *TomPaine.com*, May 09, 2007, www.tompaine.com/articles/2007/05/09/adios_world_bank.php (accessed September 17, 2007).

26. As quoted in Roger Burbach, "Ecuador: The Popular Rebellion Against the 'Partidocracia' and the Neo-Liberal State," paper for CENSA (Center for the Study of the Americas), globalalternatives.org/rebellion_against_the_partidocracia (accessed September 14, 2007).

27. Susana Chu Yep, "Ecuador in Figures," in Centro de Derechos Económicos y Sociales, *Upheaval in the Back Yard: Illegitimate Debts and Human Rights. The Case of Ecuador-Norway,* translated from the Spanish by Leslie Wirpsa, November 2002, www.cetim.ch/fr/documents/dette-CDES-ang.pdf (accessed September 21, 2007), p. 5.

28. See Mark Engler, "The Return of Daniel Ortega," *Nation,* November 7, 2006, www.thenation.com/doc/20061120/ortega (accessed September 28, 2007). See also Andrew O. Selsky, "Ortega Touts Evolution in Nicaragua Race," Associated Press, November 6, 2006, www.boston.com/news/world/latinamerica/articles/2006/11/06/ortega_touts_evolution_in_nicaragua_race/ (accessed October 8, 2007).

29. "Spring Break," *Economist,* May 1, 2007, www.economist.com/Printer Friendly.cfm?story_id=8780222 (accessed September 17, 2007).

30. Jorge G. Castañeda, "Latin America's Left Turn," *Foreign Affairs,* May/June 2006, www.foreignaffairs.org/20060501faessay85302-p40/jorge-g-castaneda/latin-america-s-left-turn.html (accessed September 17, 2007).

31. Anderson, Orhan Simer, and Golinger, "U.S. Role Turned Upside Down." See also "Morales Announces End of Bolivian Military Training at ex-US Army School of the Americas," press release, School of Americas Watch, October 10, 2007, www.commondreams.org/news2007/1010-04.htm (accessed October 17, 2007).

32. "U.S. Explores Alternatives for Ecuador Air Base," Reuters, September 13, 2007, www.reuters.com/article/politicsNews/idUSN1340626120070914 (accessed September 21, 2007).

33. Maria Fernanda Espinosa, as quoted in Roger Burbach, "Ecuador's President Takes Tough Stand," *Z Magazine,* April 2007, zmagsite.zmag.org/Apr2007/bur bach0407.html (accessed September 21, 2007).

34. Alejandro Landes, "Venezuela Unfazed by Omission in U.S. Talks," *Miami Herald,* November 21, 2003, p. 28A.

35. Tim Weiner, "Bush Meets Skepticism on Free Trade at Americas Conference," *New York Times,* January 14, 2004, available online through LexisNexis Academic.

36. "Morales to Shake Free of IMF Yoke," Inter Press Service, April 20, 2006, www.globalexchange.org/countries/americas/bolivia/3933.html (accessed September 5, 2007).

37. Raul Bassi, "Should Chavez Have Helped Kirchner Pay the IMD?" *Green Left Weekly,* February 15, 2006, www.greenleft.o.au/2006/656/7450 (accessed May 4, 2007).

38. "Morales to Shake Free of IMF Yoke," Inter Press Service.

39. Richard Lapper, "World Bank Crisis 'Grist to the Mill' of Chavistas," *Financial Times,* May 3, 2007, www.ft.com/cms/s/465656b4-f9a9-11db-9b6b-000b5df10621

,dwp_uuid=2114d450-df62-11da-afe4-0000779e2340.html (accessed September 17, 2007). See also Véronique Kiesel, interview with Eric Toussaint, "Bank of South Becoming Reality," Committee for the Abolition of Third World Debt, May 20, 2007, www.cadtm.org/article.php3?id_article=2656 (accessed August 28, 2007).

40. Rafael Correa, as quoted in Weisbrot, "IMF and World Bank Face Declining Authority."

41. Marcela Valente, "The Social Debt Will Have to Wait," Inter Press Service, December 16, 2005, ipsnews.net/news.asp?idnews=31463 (accessed May 4, 2007).

42. Swann, "Hugo Chavez Exploits Oil Wealth, Pushing IMF Aside."

43. See Kiesel, interview with Eric Toussaint, "Bank of South Becoming Reality."

44. Chris Carlson, "Brazil to Join Bank of the South," *Venezuelanalysis.com*, April 16, 2007, www.venezuelanalysis.com/news.php?newsno=2273 (accessed August 28, 2007).

45. Richard Lapper, "Washington Restive as Chávez Plans Pioneer Bank," *Financial Times*, March 23, 2007, www.ft.com/cms/s/0d2896b2-d8e4-11db-a759-000b5df10621.html (accessed September 17, 2007).

46. In May 2000, the finance ministers of thirteen Asian nations, including China, Japan, South Korea, Indonesia, and the Philippines gathered in Thailand to launch what became known as the Chiang Mai Initiative. Through this initiative, countries agree to hold one another's currencies, rather than U.S. dollars, in reserve. This strengthens the value of regional currencies and by extension improves the health of the economies as a whole. Eventually, the countries hope to establish a single regional reserve fund, putting their collective resources into a pool that any member nation could turn to in a time of economic crisis. With $79 billion already invested in Chiang Mai transactions by spring 2007, the collective resource will free Asian countries of the need to go begging to the IMF in the event of economic downturn. According to Fred Bergsten, director of the Institute for International Economics, "Chiang Mai is already starting to look like a shadow IMF and it may already be too late for the fund to stop this trend. . . . If Asia continues to break away, the IMF's role as a global body would be greatly weakened." Total Asian currency reserves are now approaching $2 trillion. See "Unified Currency Possible for East Asia," *China Daily*, April 10, 2007, news.xinhuanet.com/english/2007-04/10/content_5955327.htm (accessed August 28, 2007); Swann, "Chavez Exploits Oil Wealth, Pushing IMF Aside"; Christopher Swann and Arijit Ghosh, "IMF Role Under Threat as Asia Boosts Own Bailout Plan," *Bloomberg News*, September 19, 2006, www.bloomberg.com/apps/news?pid=20601080&sid=aoPmF4DXqxf4 (accessed September 17, 2007).

47. "Recent Trends in MERCOSUR," Inter-American Development Bank policy paper, 1995, www.iadb.org/int/intpub/nota/merco.htm (accessed September 17, 2007).

48. "Profile: Mercosur—Common Market of the South," *BBC News*, news.bbc.co.uk/2/hi/americas/5195834.stm (accessed August 16, 2007).

49. Jason Tockman, "Chávez, Morales Seek Transformation of MERCOSUR Trade Bloc," *ZNet*, January 21, 2007, www.zmag.org/content/showarticle.cfm ?ItemID=11906 (accessed August 16, 2007).

50. Ibid.

51. Tom Fawthrop, "Havana's Operation Miracle Helps Eye Patients See Light," *Scotsman*, November 26, 2005, news.scotsman.com/health.cfm?id=2305142005 (accessed August 16, 2007).

52. See Fiona Smith and Natalie Obiko, "Cuba, Bolivia, Venezuela Reject U.S. Trade," Associated Press, April 30, 2006, www.iht.com/articles/2006/04/30/amer ica/web.0430trade.php (accessed August 16, 2007).

53. Eduardo Dimas, "ALBA Advances," *Progreso Weekly*, February 15, 2007, www.progresoweekly.com/index.php?progreso=Eduardo_Dimas_ant2&other week=1171519200 (accessed August 16, 2007).

54. See Greg Grandin, "Latin America's New Consensus," *Nation*, May 1, 2006, www.thenation.com/docprint.mhtml?i=20060501&s=grandin (accessed September 17, 2007).

55. Ibid.

56. Castañeda, "Latin America's Left Turn."

57. Weisbrot, "Latin America Shifts Left."

58. Mark Weisbrot, "Argentina's Hold-Out Bondholders Try to Scare Ecuador, Not Very Effectively," *International Business Times*, July 24, 2007, www.cepr.net/in dex.php?option=com_content&task=view&id=1249&Itemid=45 (accessed September 17, 2007).

59. Landau, "Buzz Words and Venezuela."

60. Mark Weisbrot, "A New Assertiveness for Latin American Governments," *International Business Times*, June 11, 2007, www.cepr.net/index.php?option =com_content&task=view&id=1214&Itemid=45 (accessed September 17, 2007).

61. Steve Lendman, "Venezuela's Bolivarian Movement: Its Promise and Perils, Pt. I," Upside Down World, January 3, 2006, upsidedownworld.org/ main/content/view/161/35/ (accessed May 4, 2007).

62. See World Bank, "Medium-Term Outlook: Latin America and the Caribbean," 2007, go.worldbank.org/XZZWYUCK20 (accessed September 17, 2007).

63. Rodrigo Cabezas, as quoted in, "Just Say No: Vocal Rejection of Bank, Fund Increasing," The Bretton Woods Project, July 2, 2007, www.brettonwoodsproject.org/ art.shtml?x=554206 (accessed September 17, 2007).

64. Lendman, "Venezuela's Bolivarian Movement."

65. Mark Weisbrot and Luis Sandoval, "The Venezuelan Economy in the Chávez Years," report for Center for Economic and Policy Research, July 2007,

www.cepr.net/documents/publications/venezuela_2007_07.pdf (accessed September 17, 2007).

66. Ibid.

67. As quoted in Tim Padgett, "Chavez's Push for Permanence," *Time*, August 17, 2007, www.time.com/time/world/article/0,8599,1653937,00.html (accessed August 28, 2007).

68. Fred Rosen, "Sizing Up Hugo Chávez," *TomPaine.com*, January 25, 2006, www.tompaine.com/articles/2006/01/25/sizing_up_hugo_chvez.php (accessed August 28, 2007).

69. See USAID, "Brazil Overview," 2002, www.usaid.gov/pubs/cbj2002/lac/br/ (accessed September 17, 2007) and "Brazil Data Profile," World Bank World Development Indicators database, April 2007, devdata.worldbank.org/external/CPProfile.asp?PTYPE=CP&CCODE=bra (accessed September 17, 2007).

70. "IMF Approves US$30.4 Billion Stand-By Credit for Brazil," IMF press release, September 6, 2002, www.imf.org/external/np/sec/pr/2002/pr0240.htm (accessed September 17, 2007).

71. Fabrício Augusto de Oliveira and Paulo Nakatani, "The Brazilian Economy Under Lula: A Balance of Contradictions," *Monthly Review*, February 2007, www.monthlyreview.org/0207augusto.htm (accessed September 17, 2007).

72. Fabio Alves, "Brazil Posts 2.9% Growth in 2006, Region's Slowest," *Bloomberg News*, February 28, 2007, www.bloomberg.com/apps/news?pid=20601086&sid=akFP4ZfU9sws&refer=latin_america (accessed September 17, 2007).

73. Emir Sader, "Brazil: What Is at Stake in the Second Round," *MRZine*, June 10, 2006, mrzine.monthlyreview.org/sader061006.html (accessed September 17, 2007).

74. Martinez, "Democracy Rising."

75. Jim Shultz, "The Water Is Ours, Dammit!" in Notes from Nowhere, eds., *We Are Everywhere: The Irresistible Rise of Global Anti-Capitalism* (New York: Verso, 2003), p. 265.

76. Dangl, *The Price of Fire*, p. 70.

77. "Humble Beginnings for Evo Morales' Sweeping Land Reform in Bolivia," Associated Press, January 13, 2007, www.iht.com/articles/ap/2007/01/14/america/LA-FEA-GEN-Land-for-Bolivias-Poor.php (accessed September 5, 2007).

78. Javier Blas, Leslie Crawford, and Richard Lapper, "Watchdog Warns of 'Dangerous' Trend on Energy," *Financial Times*, May 4, 2006, available online through LexisNexis Academic.

79. "Bolivia's Nationalising President and His Anti-American Allies," *Economist*, May 6, 2006, available online through LexisNexis Academic.

80. "Unnatural Disaster," *Los Angeles Times*, May 6, 2006, available online through LexisNexis Academic.

81. James Pinkerton, "We'd Better Heed Our Own Backyard," May 4, 2006, available online through LexisNexis Academic.

82. "Oily Politics," *Newsday*, May 3, 2006, available online through LexisNexis Academic.

83. William Powers, "All Smoke, No Fire in Bolivia," *New York Times*, May 6, 2006, available online through LexisNexis Academic.

84. Ibid.

85. "Bolivia's Gas Gambit," *Financial Times*, May 3, 2006, available online through LexisNexis Academic.

86. Central Intelligence Agency World Factbook 2007, "Bolivia—Economy," 2004 estimate, www.cia.gov/library/publications/the-world-factbook/print/bl.html (accessed September 21, 2007).

87. Mark Weisbrot and Luis Sandoval, "Bolivia's Challenges," report for the Center for Economic and Policy Research, March 2006, www.cepr.net/index.php?option=com_content&task=view&id=56&Itemid=8, (accessed September 21, 2007).

88. Joseph Stiglitz, as quoted in Rosa Rojas, "Stiglitz: Those Who Must Be Compensated Are the Bolivians, Not the Companies," *Monthly Review*, May 20, 2006, mrzine.monthlyreview.org/rojas200506.html (accessed September 5, 2007).

89. Ibid.

90. Weisbrot, "A New Assertiveness for Latin American Governments."

91. Evo Morales, speech at Cooper Union, New York City, September 24, 2007.

92. Simon Romero, "A Radical Gives Bolivia Some Stability," *New York Times*, September 18, 2007, www.nytimes.com/2007/09/18/world/americas/18morales.html (accessed September 28, 2007).

93. See Weisbrot, "Latin America: The End of an Era."

94. John Kerry, as cited in Tom Barry, "Shallow and Formulaic," *Counterpunch*, July 29, 2004, www.counterpunch.org/barry07292004.html (accessed September 21, 2007).

95. Danny M. Leipziger, "The Unfinished Poverty Agenda: Why Latin America and the Caribbean Lag Behind," *Finance and Development*, March 2001, vol. 38, no. 1, www.imf.org/pubs/ft/fandd/2001/03/leipzige.htm (accessed September 5, 2007).

Conclusion

1. Gabriel García Márquez, "The Mysteries of Bill Clinton," *Salon*, February 1, 1999, www.salon.com/news/1999/02/cov_02news.html (accessed October 8, 2007).

2. Walden Bello, "Globalization in Retreat," Foreign Policy in Focus, December 27, 2006, www.fpif.org/fpiftxt/3826 (accessed October 1, 2007).

3. Corey Robin, "Endgame: Conservatives After the Cold War," *Boston Review*, February/March 2004, bostonreview.net/BR29.1/robin.html (accessed March 13, 2007).

4. Lawrence Eagleburger, as cited in Immanuel Wallerstein, "U.S. Weakness and the Struggle for Hegemony," *Monthly Review*, July/August 2003, www.monthly

review.org/0703wallerstein.htm (accessed October 1, 2007). See also Ben Russell, "The Iraq Conflict: US Warns Syria Not to Provide Haven for Wanted Iraqis," *Independent*, April 14, 2003, available online through LexisNexis Academic.

5. Jackie Calmes, "GOP Is Losing Grip on Core Business Vote," *Wall Street Journal*, Tuesday, October 2, 2007, p. A1.

6. James Laxer, "The Rising Fall of the American Empire," *The Walrus*, September 2005, www.walrusmagazine.com/print/2005.09-politics-the-rising-fall-of-the -american-empire/ (accessed October 1, 2007).

7. Paul Starobin, "The Next Oil Frontier," *Business Week*, May 27, 2002, www.businessweek.com/magazine/content/02_21/b3784008.htm (accessed October 1, 2007), as cited in William K. Tabb, "The Face of Empire," *Monthly Review*, November 2002, www.monthlyreview.org/1102tabb.htm (accessed October 1, 2007).

8. Joseph Stiglitz, "What I Learned at the World Economic Crisis," *New Republic*, April 17, 2000, p. 56, available online through LexisNexis Academic.

9. Brookings Institution, "Brookings Institution Launches the Hamilton Project," press release, April 5, 2006, www.brook.edu/comm/news/20060405_hamil ton.htm (accessed October 1, 2007).

10. James K. Galbraith, "What Kind of Economy?" *Nation*, March 5, 2007, www.thenation.com/doc/20070305/galbraith/ (accessed October 1, 2007).

11. Landon Thomas Jr., "Spotlight: A Wall Street Democrat with an Eye on Washington," *New York Times*, September 12, 2006, www.iht.com/articles/2006/ 09/08/business/wbspot09.php (accessed October 1, 2007).

12. Ibid.

13. William Greider, "Born-Again Rubinomics," *Nation*, July 13, 2006, www.thenation.com/doc/20060731/greider (accessed October 1, 2007). See also Brookings Institution, "Brookings Institution Launches the Hamilton Project."

14. Emily Eakin, "Ideas & Trends; All Roads Lead to D.C.," *New York Times*, March 31, 2002, query.nytimes.com/gst/fullpage.html?res=9806E7DF173AF932A05750C0 A9649C8B63&sec=&spon=&partner=permalink&exprod=permalink (accessed October 1, 2007).

15. Max Boot, "The Case for American Empire," *Weekly Standard*, October 15, 2001, www.weeklystandard.com/Utilities/printer_preview.asp?idArticle=318 (accessed October 1, 2007), as cited in Eakin, "Ideas & Trends."

16. Eakin, "Ideas & Trends."

17. David Brooks, "The Iraq Syndrome, R.I.P.," *New York Times*, February 1, 2007, select.nytimes.com/2007/02/01/opinion/01brooks.html (accessed October 1, 2007).

18. Niall Ferguson, "A World Without Power," *Foreign Policy*, July/August 2004, www.foreignpolicy.com/story/cms.php?story_id=2579 (accessed October 1, 2007).

19. Niall Ferguson, "Welcome to the New Imperialism," *Guardian*, October 31, 2001, www.guardian.co.uk/waronterror/story/0,,583902,00.html (accessed October 1, 2007).

20. See National Priorities Project, "The Cost of War," www.nationalpriorities.org/Cost-of-War/Cost-of-War-3.html (accessed October 1, 2007).

21. Laxer, "The Rising Fall of the American Empire."

22. See "Anti-war Protesters Hold Global Rallies," Associated Press, February 16, 2003, www.usatoday.com/news/world/iraq/2003-02-15-protests_x.htm (accessed October 8, 2007).

23. Patrick E. Tyler, "Threats and Responses: News Analysis; A New Power in the Streets," *New York Times*, February 17, 2003, query.nytimes.com/gst/fullpage.html?res=9902E0DC1E3AF934A25751C0A9659C8B63&sec=&spon=&partner=permalink&exprod=permalink (accessed October 8, 2007).

24. John Cavanagh and Robin Broad, "A Turning Point for World Trade?" *Baltimore Sun*, September 18, 2003, www.ifg.org/news/cancun/trnpnt.htm (accessed October 8, 2007). For Hong Kong, see Keith Bradsher, "Arrests of Trade Protesters Embroil Hong Kong with China and South Korea," *New York Times*, January 10, 2006, www.nytimes.com/2006/01/10/international/asia/10hong.ready.html (accessed October 8, 2007); and Deborah James, "The Meaning of Hong Kong WTO," Global Exchange, January 14, 2006, www.globalexchange.org/campaigns/wto/3688.html (accessed October 8, 2007).

25. See Make Poverty History, overview of Edinburgh 2005, www.makepovertyhistory.org/edinburgh/ (accessed October 8, 2007).

26. "146 German Police Officers Injured in Violent G8 Protests," Associated Press, June 3, 2007, www.cnn.com/2007/WORLD/europe/06/02/g-8.protest.ap/index.html (accessed October 8, 2007). See also "Riots Break Out at German Rally," *BBC News*, June 2, 2007, news.bbc.co.uk/2/hi/europe/6714429.stm (accessed October 8, 2007).

INDEX